VOLUME 608

NOVEMBER 2006

THE ANNALS

of The American Academy of Political
and Social Science

PHYLLIS KANISS, *Executive Editor*

Politics, Social Networks, and the History of Mass Communications Research: Rereading Personal Influence

Special Editor of this Volume

PETER SIMONSON

University of Colorado

SAGE Publications Ⓢ Thousand Oaks · London · New Delhi

The American Academy of Political and Social Science

3814 Walnut Street, Fels Institute of Government, University of Pennsylvania,
Philadelphia, PA 19104-6197; (215) 746-6500; (215) 573-3003 (fax); www.aapss.org

Editors, THE ANNALS
PHYLLIS KANISS, *Executive Editor*   RICHARD D. LAMBERT, *Editor Emeritus*
JULIE ODLAND, *Managing Editor*

Origin and Purpose. The Academy was organized December 14, 1889, to promote the progress of political and social science, especially through publications and meetings. The Academy does not take sides in controverted questions, but seeks to gather and present reliable information to assist the public in forming an intelligent and accurate judgment.

Meetings. The Academy occasionally holds a meeting in the spring extending over two days.

Publications. THE ANNALS of The American Academy of Political and Social Science is the bimonthly publication of the Academy. Each issue contains articles on some prominent social or political problem, written at the invitation of the editors. Also, monographs are published from time to time, numbers of which are distributed to pertinent professional organizations. These volumes constitute important reference works on the topics with which they deal, and they are extensively cited by authorities throughout the United States and abroad. The papers presented at the meetings of the Academy are included in THE ANNALS.

Membership. Each member of the Academy receives THE ANNALS and may attend the meetings of the Academy. Membership is open only to individuals. Annual dues: $84.00 for the regular paperbound edition (clothbound, $121.00). Members may also purchase single issues of THE ANNALS for $17.00 each (clothbound, $26.00). Student memberships are available for $53.00.

Subscriptions. THE ANNALS of The American Academy of Political and Social Science (ISSN 0002-7162) (J295) is published six times annually—in January, March, May, July, September, and November—by Sage Publications, 2455 Teller Road, Thousand Oaks, CA 91320. Telephone: (800) 818-SAGE (7243) and (805) 499-9774; Fax/Order line: (805) 499-0871; e-mail: journals@sagepub.com. Copyright © 2006 by The American Academy of Political and Social Science. Institutions may subscribe to THE ANNALS at the annual rate: $612.00 (clothbound, $692.00). Single issues of THE ANNALS may be obtained by individuals who are not members of the Academy for $34.00 each (clothbound, $47.00). Single issues of THE ANNALS have proven to be excellent supplementary texts for classroom use. Direct inquiries regarding adoptions to THE ANNALS c/o Sage Publications (address below). Periodicals postage paid at Thousand Oaks, California, and at additional mailing offices.

All correspondence concerning membership in the Academy, dues renewals, inquiries about membership status, and/or purchase of single issues of THE ANNALS should be sent to THE ANNALS c/o Sage Publications, 2455 Teller Road, Thousand Oaks, CA 91320.Telephone: (800) 818-SAGE (7243) and (805) 499-9774; Fax/Order line: (805) 499-0871; e-mail: journals@sagepub.com. *Please note that orders under $30 must be prepaid.* Sage affiliates in London and India will assist institutional subscribers abroad with regard to orders, claims, and inquiries for both subscriptions and single issues.

Printed on acid-free paper

THE ANNALS
1570 E. Colorado Blvd.
Pasadena, CA 91106

© 2006 by The American Academy of Political and Social Science

Editorial Office: 3814 Walnut Street, Fels Institute for Government, University of Pennsylvania,
Philadelphia, PA 19104-6197.
For information about membership* (individuals only) and subscriptions (institutions), address:
Sage Publications
2455 Teller Road
Thousand Oaks, CA 91320

For Sage Publications: Joseph Riser and Esmeralda Hernandez

From India and South Asia, write to:		From Europe, the Middle East, and Africa, write to:
SAGE PUBLICATIONS INDIA Pvt Ltd B-42 Panchsheel Enclave, P.O. Box 4109 New Delhi 110 017 INDIA		SAGE PUBLICATIONS LTD 1 Oliver's Yard, 55 City Road London EC1Y 1SP UNITED KINGDOM

*Please note that members of the Academy receive THE ANNALS with their membership.
International Standard Serial Number ISSN 0002-7162
International Standard Book Number 1-4129-5094-5 (Vol. 608, 2006 paper)
International Standard Book Number ISBN 1-4129-5093-7 (Vol. 608, 2006 cloth)
Manufactured in the United States of America. First printing, November 2006.

The articles appearing in *The Annals* are abstracted or indexed in Academic Abstracts, Academic Search, America: History and Life, Asia Pacific Database, Book Review Index,CABAbstracts Database, Central Asia: Abstracts &Index, Communication Abstracts, Corporate ResourceNET, Criminal Justice Abstracts, Current Citations Express, Current Contents: Social & Behavioral Sciences, Documentation in Public Administration, e-JEL, EconLit, Expanded Academic Index, Guide to Social Science & Religion in Periodical Literature, Health Business FullTEXT, HealthSTAR FullTEXT, Historical Abstracts, International Bibliography of the Social Sciences, International Political Science Abstracts, ISI Basic Social Sciences Index, Journal of Economic Literature on CD, LEXIS-NEXIS, MasterFILE FullTEXT, Middle East: Abstracts&Index, North Africa: Abstracts&Index, PAIS International, Periodical Abstracts, Political Science Abstracts, Psychological Abstracts, PsycINFO, Sage Public Administration Abstracts, Scopus, Social Science Source, Social Sciences Citation Index, Social Sciences Index Full Text, Social Services Abstracts, SocialWork Abstracts, Sociological Abstracts, Southeast Asia: Abstracts& Index, Standard Periodical Directory (SPD), TOPICsearch, Wilson OmniFileV, and Wilson Social Sciences Index/Abstracts, and are available on microfilm from ProQuest, Ann Arbor, Michigan.

THE ANNALS

OF THE AMERICAN ACADEMY OF POLITICAL AND SOCIAL SCIENCE

Volume 608   November 2006

IN THIS ISSUE:

Politics, Social Networks, and the History of Mass Communications Research: Rereading Personal Influence

Special Editor: PETER SIMONSON

FORTHCOMING

Race and Inequality in the U.S. Labor Market
Special Editor: GEORGE WILSON
Volume 609, January 2007

NAFTA and Beyond:
Alternative Disciplinary Perspectives in
the Study of Global Trade and Development
Special Editors: PATRICIA FERNÁNDEZ-KELLY
and JON SHEFNER
Volume 610, March 2007

Introduction

By
PETER SIMONSON

Robert K. Merton (1968, 36-37) once wrote that any classic text worth reading is worth rereading periodically, for "what is communicated by the printed page" changes as a result of changes in the readers and the worlds they inhabit. This volume takes that dictum seriously, revisiting a classic book on the fiftieth anniversary of its publication. Elihu Katz and Paul Lazarsfeld's *Personal Influence: The Part Played by People in the Flow of Mass Communications* came out in 1955 and quickly made an impact in the partially overlapping fields of communications, public opinion research, political science, and marketing. It became the canonical statement of the "two-step flow of communication"—the idea that mass media flow to "opinion leaders" and from them via face-to-face talk to others around them—but it was also a number of other things as well.

Harold Lasswell (1951, 295) believed the influential "are those who get the most of what there is to get." If that is true, *Personal Influence* is an influential text, for over the years it has gotten what there is to get for an academic book: attention, readers, citations, professional status, extensions, criticisms. Kurt and Gladys Lang trace its reception and diffusion in this volume, from its emergence at the institutional center of postwar American sociology, Columbia University, and the Bureau of Applied Social Research. The Bureau, as those who worked there called it, was a remarkable

Peter Simonson studies the history and social philosophy of mass communication. He teaches courses in rhetoric and social thought at the University of Colorado.

NOTE: I gratefully acknowledge former executive editor Robert W. Pearson for making publication of this volume possible. I had high hopes for the papers that would come out of the October 2005 conference at Columbia University, but the articles that follow surpassed what I could have imagined at the time. I want to thank Elihu Katz for agreeing to the project.

DOI: 10.1177/0002716206292527

site that has itself called forth a range of responses over the years. It allowed for a kind of large-scale, on-the-ground social research on mass media that had not been done before, and so generated data of an often impressive sort, produced by a blend of state-of-the-art methodologies and emerging sociological theories. At the same time, as critics of the Bureau have made clear from the beginning, there were costs to its work—political, institutional, intellectual, personal. This volume explores *Personal Influence* with both eyes open.

Even before *Personal Influence* came out in 1955, it had attracted a great deal of attention, at least within the local confines of the Bureau. It had begun in 1944 as a study of women's decision making in Decatur, Illinois, financed mostly by Macfadden Publications and their popular lowbrow women's magazine, *True Story*. C. Wright Mills, just hired as a research associate at the Bureau, was put in charge of the fifteen-person team that conducted the study in the summer of 1945; and as John Summers shows here, that project provided the occasion for the famous and consequential rift that opened between him and Paul Lazarsfeld. When Mills didn't finish a write-up to Lazarsfeld's liking, three successive graduate students were given a turn with the data before a fourth, Elihu Katz, put it all together in a manner that pleased the sometimes difficult Lazarsfeld. *Personal Influence* was an amalgam of several parts. One was the Decatur study (Part II of the book), produced through the labor of many at the Bureau. Another was a review of the literature and "convergence" of media and small-group research, preceded by an influential narrative about the course of mass communications research up to that point (Part I). This was Katz's work, and it arguably supplied the rhetorical force that helped make the book influential. In the liberal pluralist intellectual climate of the 1950s, the idea that mass media was refracted through small groups and opinion leaders was good news indeed, as Thelma McCormack reminds us in this volume. Others argued that the two-step flow only meant that mass media were the wholesalers, opinion leaders the retailers, and democratic publics were nowhere to be found, but those critics remained in a decided minority.

By the 1970s, the ground had shifted, and *Personal Influence* was attacked from several quarters. No critique was more influential than Todd Gitlin's (1978) "Media Sociology: The Dominant Paradigm." Written by a former leader of the student left while he was still a graduate student in sociology at Berkeley, Gitlin's long piece in the British journal *Theory and Society* skewered Lazarsfeld and his "administrative research" on the basis of both its epistemological and sociological inadequacies and its political complicities. It was a masterful and widely read essay, which had the effect of raising the status of *Personal Influence* even as it was attempting to destroy it. It is not uncommon to find people who learned of the importance of *Personal Influence* through Gitlin's critique of it (something especially true in cultural studies) and who were persuaded that Katz and Lazarsfeld's book represented "the dominant paradigm" in the study of mass media from World War II through the 1970s. One might question the extent to which the paradigm actually dominated thinking, but one cannot overstate the importance of Gitlin's attempt to carve out a left-democratic critical media sociology in the tradition of one of *Personal Influence*'s most eloquent early critics, C. Wright Mills.

Now more than twenty-five years old, Gitlin's is still the most significant reframing and critical rereading of *Personal Influence* since its publication.

The rereadings in this volume come at a different moment than Gitlin's did. Media and mass communication studies have been enriched by feminism, critical and cultural studies, the new historicism, and a range of other currents in the humanities and social sciences that find voice in these articles. Empirical research has progressed even as the media environment has transformed itself. The field is twenty-five years older, and its problems and problematics have shifted, as has its historical self-understanding. It seemed like a good opportunity to gather together authors from across generational, disciplinary, and national boundaries and ask them to reread the text from contemporary horizons, not unlike Katz's own recent edited collection of essays that consider proposed "canonic texts" in the field, as well as the reader of primary texts with commentary that John Durham Peters and I put together (Katz et al. 2003; Peters and Simonson 2004).

The opportunity came together at a conference held October 21, 2005, at Columbia University, where earlier versions of most of the following articles were given public hearing. Participants were called to reread *Personal Influence* from the perspective of their own interests and field of study. "We welcome papers that are critical, appreciative, or agnostic; that use the book as an opportunity to reflect upon mid-century contexts; that find possibilities never pursued or agendas pursued too much; that look to the text as an exemplar of old approaches best left behind or as filled with fruitful suggestions that might yield productive new research," went the charge. The conference was generously sponsored by Peter Bearman and Columbia's Institute for Social and Economic Research and Policy (ISERP) and by Michael Delli Carpini and the University of Pennsylvania's Annenberg School for Communication, both institutions that can lay claim to performing some of the functions of Lazarsfeld's Bureau, circa 1945 to 1955. Michael Delli Carpini was also kind enough to fund a companion documentary film, shot and produced by Jason Balas and Glenda Balas.

It is fortunate and fitting that this volume has found publication in this journal. *The Annals* has long devoted special issues to mass media, from a 1929 volume on radio to a 1996 number that included Elihu Katz's "And Deliver Us from Segmentation," his resonant and mildly apocalyptic worry about the multiplication of media channels in the narrowcast age. In 1935, the words "mass communication" first appeared in the *Annals*, reflecting the new world of radio broadcasting, motion pictures, print media, and competing propagandas of the day. In 1946, Robert K. Merton drafted but never completed a paper for an issue on organized social action, which later found its way into the joint-authored ur-text of Columbia mass communications research, Lazarsfeld and Merton's "Mass Communication, Popular Taste, and Organized Social Action" (1948).[1]

Though mass media are a longtime focus of *The Annals*, this may be the first time that an issue of the *Annals* has been devoted to rereading a classic text from the social sciences and using it for the purposes of what Lazarsfeld's colleague and Katz's teacher Merton called "history" and "systematics" of sociological theory.

For Merton, an authentic history of sociological theory would be a *sociological* history, which among other things would address "the interplay between theory and such matters as the social origins and statuses of its exponents, the changing social organization of sociology, the changes that diffusion brings to ideas, and their relations to the environing social and cultural structure" (Merton 1968, 35). This was a different enterprise than "systematics," or the building of substantive theory over time, but he suggested there were ways the two could productively overlap.

This collection aims for that productive overlap between investigating the past and finding our way in the present, and it is ordered in a way that moves progressively from the 1940s to the present and from history to "systematics." On the historical side, articles probe origins and statuses of the book's key people (Jews and Gentiles, women and men) and the social organization of research in which it grew up (the Office of Radio Research/Bureau of Applied Social Research in conjunction with Macfadden Publications). They trace the diffusion of the book's ideas and bring out dimensions of its social and cultural contexts, manifest and previously repressed. They also do things not mentioned in Merton's list, like attend to the individuals who played key roles in the book and the ways that personalities also played a part in the making of a classic text.

Beyond historically piecing together and pulling apart one key text in the history of mass communication theory, the articles here also extend, refute, or dialectically engage the substantive arguments and conceptualizations of *Personal Influence*. We might think of these as convergences of a sort, coming after the historical contexts and consequences of the book have been traced. Politics is a main topic, including in the case of Robert Hornik the special pre-politics that occurs between siblings in relation to illicit social practices. Authors use *Personal Influence* as a way to address citizenship and consumption in contemporary media environments. They put *Personal Influence* in conversation with contemporary research on social capital and media persuasion, and they extend the book's analytics by means of state-of-the-art research of a sort Lazarsfeld himself would have admired.

Since the authors of these essays were called to reread a *text*, I will offer a few preparatory comments about *Personal Influence* from a kind of history-of-the-book perspective, interweaving insights from some of the articles included here to give a sense of the origins and circuitous career of a research project that grew into a controversial classic. Those comments then lead me into a more formal introduction of this volume's contents in the last section of my Introduction.

Personal Influence: The Book and Its People

For a book at the center of the dominant paradigm, a lot of contingency went into the building of *Personal Influence*. Through much of the 1940s, Lazarsfeld's Bureau existed on shaky economic and institutional ground. As David Morrison recounts in this volume, just as planning for the Macfadden/*True Stories* study was picking up in the fall of 1944, Columbia was investigating the Bureau and raising serious questions about how it was operated. Lazarsfeld, the Austrian émigré whom his first wife called "so obviously Jewish," was running a show that worried the still WASP-ish university, both because the Bureau stood semi-autonomous from it and because Lazarsfeld was engaging in commercial research that seemed inappropriate and perhaps was exploiting student labor to do it. Lazarsfeld was a marginal man, cast in the role of outsider and Jew by both himself and others.[2]

Lazarsfeld was also an entrepreneur. In the 1940s, he kept his Bureau afloat by bringing in outside money to fund research that satisfied the funder and, ideally, had some sociological importance as well, so graduate students could make something of it academically. The model for this "applied research institute" was imported from Lazarsfeld's Vienna, and he re-created it more than once when he came to the States. (Louis Guttman would transplant the model back east and south in 1947, founding the Israel Institute of Applied Social Research, which Katz would later head.) While Max Horkheimer's Frankfurt *Institut* benefited from a private endowment and did not need to beat the capitalist streets, Lazarsfeld's had no such advantage. He had to fund his research, which required people, and he had to find a way to pay them or otherwise co-opt their labor. This brought out his entrepreneurial side, which from 1937 to 1945 issued in contracts, business, and research grants from, among others, the Rockefeller Foundation, the Office of War Information, CBS radio, the American Jewish Committee, Lucky Strike cigarettes' *Hit Parade* radio show, the *Saturday Evening Post*, Bloomingdale's Department Store, Kolynos Tooth Powder, and Golden Wedding Whiskey.[3]

During World War II, a lot of the people who worked at the Bureau were women, in part because so many of the men were called to duty elsewhere. Universities had record numbers of women in their ranks. Some who worked at the Bureau were graduate students, like Thelma McCormack, a contributor to this volume, who had graduated from the University of Wisconsin, where she had studied philosophy and economics after deciding that a journalism class was not interesting enough for her. She took a class with Mills there, whom she remembers as "very, very offensive." She went on to Columbia (1942-1944), where she studied with Robert Lynd and the rest, but she was none too pleased to find herself administering surveys door to door or helping Herta Herzog conduct focused interviews (Thelma McCormack, personal communication, October 22, 2005). She and others in her cohort might have been sympathetic to the idea that Lazarsfeld's Office of Radio Research exploited graduate students, women and men alike. Others who worked at the Bureau were paid staff members, and they were always overwhelmingly female. Many were college graduates, and they were trained to conduct the empirical research the Bureau needed in its studies. They administered surveys, conducted focused interviews, wrote out and sorted data cards, tabulated results, and summarized findings for Lazarsfeld, Merton, or another lead researcher. During the war, some helped with the Lazarsfeld-Stanton program analyzer—the primitive polygraph device that allowed test audiences to register likes and dislikes as they heard a radio morale show or watched a film to be shown to those entering the military or to the population at large. There was a status difference between graduate student women and staff women, some of whom would travel by train to Decatur in the summer of 1945.

Lazarsfeld had gotten a grant from Macfadden Publications and a second smaller one from CBS Radio. The former is acknowledged in the Preface to *Personal Influence*, but the latter is not, perhaps because Lazarsfeld simply inserted radio-related questions in the survey being administered in Decatur (see Katz and Lazarsfeld 1955/2005, 345-46).[4] CBS Research Director Frank Stanton was an old friend of Lazarsfeld's and funded other Bureau work as well, including Merton's study of Kate Smith's war bond drives (Merton 1946/2004).

Lazarsfeld, who was exceptionally good at tailoring his message to different audiences (Pooley, this volume), apparently made a pitch to Macfadden and its research director, Everett Smith (Morrison, this volume). It was probably based on the findings of the Sandusky *People's Choice* study (Lazarsfeld, Berelson, and Gaudet 1944), as Lazarsfeld described in the official history of the project that appeared in the Introduction to *Personal Influence* (Katz and Lazarsfeld 1955/2005, 3-4). The idea that opinion leaders were scattered throughout the social strata, were plugged into media, and influenced the people around them was one that would appeal to Macfadden, focused as it was on "the wage earning class," which, like today, was a less attractive market for advertisers. If Macfadden could say that readers of *True Story*, *Photoplay*, and other of its lower-brow publications influenced others about consumption, fashion, and moviegoing, then the company could say that there was a kind of multiplier effect that made its advertising dollar doubly effective.[5] In November 1944, Macfadden made a presentation to its salesmen, outlining the findings of the *The People's Choice* and announcing the upcoming *True Story* readership study ("Macfadden Readers" 1944).

On the social scientific side of things, the Macfadden money would finance the second of Lazarsfeld's U.S. community studies, both of which used the "panel method" of administering survey and follow-up questions to a group of people over time (see Lazarsfeld, Berelson, and Gaudet 1944, 1-8). In the Sandusky study that fed into *The People's Choice*, this method had allowed Lazarsfeld to chart the way people changed their minds over the course of a presidential election season and was the genesis of the opinion leader idea. He hired Bernard Berelson to do the preliminary work to select a city and establish a research plan. Berelson had taken his doctorate from the University of Chicago's Library School, an early site for communications research (see Wahl-Jorgensen 2004) and sharpened his research methodologies working with Harold Lasswell during the war. In 1944, Berelson did a preliminary study of *True Story* in Sandusky, facing head-on the problem of probable reluctance to admit readership of the magazine,[6] then did the statistical work that led to the selection of Decatur—chosen from a pool of cities of around sixty thousand population located in the Middle West "because that part of the country is least characterized by sectional peculiarities," *Personal Influence* told us (Katz and Lazarsfeld 1955/2005, 335), but probably also because it was presumed there would be plenty of *True Story* readers in the population. Decatur won out, the most average of the average. Over dinner and drinks in January of 1945, Lazarsfeld and Merton recruited Mills to be research associate at the Bureau and direct the study in Decatur that summer, and the three plotted big things together, in a manner that reveals a good deal about the era (see Summers, this volume).

In part because the University of Chicago has for so long been associated with community studies in the popular academic image, it is easy to forget that Columbia had its tradition as well. Robert Lynd, coauthor with his wife Helen of the classic *Middletown* studies (1929, 1937), had been hired at Columbia in 1931, and he in turn brought on Lazarsfeld, impressed among other things by the study Lazarsfeld had conducted of unemployment in the Austrian town of Marienthal. Lazarsfeld continued his community-based studies at Columbia, with Decatur sandwiched between two voting studies carried out in Sandusky and in Elmira, New York (Berelson, Lazarsfeld, and McPhee 1954). Merton in the 1940s carried out research for a massive unpublished study of three housing communities, for which he entertained for a time *Middletown*-type ambitions. More than the classic Chicago and Middletown studies, however, Lazarsfeld's community-based research generally abstracted itself from geographical and cultural particularities and tended to universalize their findings (cf. Katz, this volume).[7]

For the Decatur study, the Bureau team worked up a plan that would both satisfy its funding agencies and contribute to Lazarsfeld's research agenda, especially his interest in decision making, action (*Handlung*), and the influences that contributed to them. The manifest social scientific aim was "to make a start in mapping the flow of influence concerning several everyday matters in a middle-sized American city" (Katz and Lazarsfeld 1955/2005, 137). The route there led through "four arenas of everyday decisions": marketing (shopping for groceries and other small consumer goods), fashion, moviegoing, and public affairs. All were of direct interest to Macfadden, whose stable of magazines collectively addressed the topics through advertising and articles. (In 1940, Bernarr Macfadden had boasted to New York District Attorney Thomas E. Dewey, "Through my editorial page in *Liberty*, I believe that I have more influence politically on the masses than any one individual in the United States" [quoted in Ernst 1991, 127].) Public affairs also functioned to legitimize the study from an academic point of view and was no doubt the area of most substantive interest to Mills and the other Bureau researchers. Interviews would probe for a variety of information useful both to the Macfadden and CBS marketing departments as well as to the Bureau's attempt to map social influence, parse out the factors that contribute to decision making, and determine the social locations and characteristics of opinion leaders (for the questionnaire, see Katz and Lazarsfeld 1955/2005, Appendix B).

The Macfadden study was the biggest on a busy research docket at the Bureau, which in 1945 included two others with rather different political implications, one conducted for the American Jewish Committee and the other for a labor union. Both were tests of comic strips, that popular medium for the less literate, which the Bureau studied with little condescension, no small thing in that era. In addition to *True Stories*, Bureau researchers also conducted studies of

"There Are No Master Races" and "They Got the Blame"; comics aimed at combating prejudice; and "The Story of Labor," a cartoon strip that ran in the union periodical *United Automobile Worker*, which Bernard Berelson oversaw. A year later, Patricia Kendall would show three antiprejudice "Mr. Biggott" cartoons to 692 women in Decatur itself, another American Jewish Committee project (Kendall 1946; Kendall and Wolf 1949). Beyond commercial marketing studies, the Bureau spent a good deal of energy working for the cause of social tolerance.[8]

In June, though, just as Mills and his team of fifteen were readying to administer the first set of surveys, two items appeared side by side in an issue of the advertising and publishing trade journal *Printer's Ink* and indicated the focus that year. One was an article by Lazarsfeld (1945), "Who Influences Whom—It's the Same for Politics and Advertising." The other was a full-page ad trumpeting *True Story* magazine as a place to advertise. In the article, Lazarsfeld, prominently identified as Director, Bureau of Applied Social Research, was keeping himself in public view and spreading the news of Sandusky: opinion leaders have an important "activating effect" and thus "play a dominant role in the process by which people make up their minds." Opinion leaders are found within each social group, and within each group, there were *many* opinion leaders. ("One person in every five is an opinion leader," Lazarsfeld suggested.) As the title of his piece suggested, this was the same for politics as for advertising (cf. Schudson and Glickman, this volume). "It is only a slight exaggeration to say that propaganda often has a two-step flow," he wrote. Thanks to "a considerable grant to Columbia University's Bureau of Applied Social Research" made by Macfadden Publications, Lazarsfeld and company were in a position to study the question further, "especially to see how far the wage earners follow the advice of leaders who are in their own class" (pp. 35-36).

Just after the article came the Macfadden advertisement, "The Common Touch: It Makes New Millions Respond." Below the banner announcement was a half-page image of a George Caleb Bingham painting of social newspaper reading outside a post office: one younger white man reading out loud to four other white men gathered on a porch around him and an African American man and boy off the porch nearby below them. It represented exactly the kind of two-step flow of communication that Tocqueville, Tarde, and now Lazarsfeld had all lit upon, though from the other side of the gender aisle than the Decatur study. Below the image appeared the syllogism:

> THOMAS PAINE had it . . . and America's new colonial millions believed and fought for his ideals, made his "Rights of Man" a new nation's "Bill of Rights."
>
> TRUE STORY has it . . . and has kept its unchanging hold on new millions through 25 changing years.

And then, to fill in the reasoning: "Today more than ever before, the Wage Earner market has the money and the numbers to make any product great." The common touch had given *True Story* the confidence of its readers, which advertisers could not help but share. With *True Story*, "you not only get Wage Earner coverage, you also get *acceptance* and *buying action.*" Concluding this blended appeal to commerce and nationalism, the ad ended with the *True Story* logo and a rousing claim: "The common man, well informed, is the greatest force toward building the America we want."

As subscribers were receiving that issue of *Printer's Ink,* C. Wright Mills and his crew settled in at a downtown Decatur hotel and commenced their part of the multifront epistemological-cum-marketing campaign in June of 1945. Jeannette Green had trained the field staff in New York, having gained experience on an opinion leader–type research study in 1943 (Green 1943). As Summers (this volume) tells us, when the team got to town, they ran a series of advertisements announcing that the Bureau of Applied Social Research was in town and wanted to know how ordinary women made everyday decisions. Decatur women were also enlisted in the fieldwork. Interviewers were assigned districts in the town and instructed to call on every thirteenth house and interview any woman older than sixteen who was not domestic help. They were provided a scripted intro- duction: "How do you do. I am Mrs. _____ and I live on ____ Street. I am doing some interviewing for The Community Survey of Decatur. Would you be good enough to tell me how many women 16 years or over live in this house?" If the resident asked for further details, the interviewer was instructed to say it was "a study of people's opinions and buying habits . . . you know, something like the Gallop [*sic*] polls. It is being done under the guidance of Columbia University" (Community Survey of Decatur n.d.). By today's standards, the procedure wasn't exactly ready for the institutional review board, but such were the times.

As Susan Douglas (this volume) reminds us, the summer of 1945 was no ordi- nary time in the social history of women's decision making. The war had taken men of a certain age overseas, drawn record numbers of women into the work- place, and jumbled roles and decision making in the process. A lot of news was in the air that summer. Roosevelt had recently died in office, and the war had just ended when Mills and his team gave the first survey. In August, when follow-up interviews took place, the United States dropped atomic bombs on Hiroshima and Nagasaki. None of that historical particularity would make it into *Personal Influence*, whose "veneer of timelessness" as Douglas calls it is matched only by the universalism with which eight hundred women in Decatur are taken to stand in for "the people" and the parts they play in the flow of mass communications.

Before those things could happen, though, the Decatur study would have to actually be written up. Four women conducted the first of tabulations and analy- ses of the data, and wrote a series of memoranda. "Especially valuable were the many contributions of Helen Dinerman and Thelma Anderson," *Personal Influence* would acknowledge. "Leila A. Sussmann and Patricia L. Kendall con- tributed early analyses of the marketing and movie materials" (Katz and Lazarsfeld 1955/2005, xiii). Someone made a report for Macfadden, who in con- sultation with the Bureau put together a glossy booklet that communicated the findings to advertising audiences and emphasized the two-step marketing poten- tial of *True Story.* In the spring of 1946, *True Story* ran a series of ads in trade journals trumpeting the study: "750 Leading Ad Men said 'Rush the final report!' . . . after previewing these new research facts on how ideas get across to people." Ideas and influences work horizontally, they said. "Dr. Paul F. Lazarsfeld and Dr. C. Wright Mills have asked two million questions, piled up a fund of information on some 10,000 punch cards. Right now Hollerith machines are grinding out the first grist of facts."[9]

It would take a while before the "grist of facts" would see the light of day. Mills was supposed to be writing up the research, but his work was not to Lazarsfeld's liking, which set in motion a number of events that Summers chronicles in this volume. Lazarsfeld eventually fired Mills from the study, and then apparently passed parts or all of it off to a series of graduate students, who drafted sections of what became Part II of *Personal Influence*. Three men, David Gleicher, Peter Rossi, and Leo Srole, are singled out by name in the Preface; but others, including Jeanette Green, Leila Sussmann, Helen Schneider (1947), and Thelma Anderson (1950) also worked on the data.[10] Collectively, their work did not apparently satisfy Lazarsfeld, or he decided for other reasons to give it to someone else. That someone was Elihu Katz, who inherited the study and made it significant.

Smart, hardworking, and well educated, Katz was in a position to be successful when Lazarsfeld turned the project over to him, probably in 1953. Katz grew up in Flatbush, a middle-class, overwhelmingly Jewish neighborhood in Brooklyn, during the Great Depression and into the war years. He was bilingual and had read and heard the news voiced as conditions in Europe deteriorated. Like practically everyone else within broadcast range in the United States during the 1930s, Katz listened at home to President Roosevelt as he addressed the nation. Mass communication was part of his social experience, and two-step flows of conversation part of everyday life. He entered Columbia College in February of 1944 at the age of seventeen and wrote "Journalist" when asked about his career intention, an occupation he would keep in his sights for several years (Katz 1949).

After two semesters of college, he was drafted into the army and was sent to the Japanese Language and Area School at the University of Chicago where he spent a year learning a new tongue and editing its newspaper, *The Geisha Gazette*, unaware of course that C. Wright Mills was just then doing his thing downstate in Decatur. After several months spent as an interpreter in U.S.-occupied Japan after the war ended, Katz returned to Columbia in the fall of 1946, funded like many others in his cohort by the GI Bill, and with a year's credit under his belt for language and area experience in Japan. At the same time, Katz resumed his earlier Hebraic studies at the Jewish Theological Seminary, enrolled as a non-matriculated student studying literature, poetry, and Talmud alike. In his senior year at Columbia, after pursuing a broad liberal arts education, he took Lazarsfeld's two-class sequence in public opinion and communications, an earlier iteration of which Seymour Martin Lipset (1998, 258) called the worst class he took as a graduate student at Columbia, but which moved the once-aspiring journalist and advanced undergraduate Katz in 1947 and 1948. Attracted by the "Opinion and Communication field," as he called it in a short intellectual autobiography he wrote for Merton, Katz decided to pursue graduate study. That interest came through in an "Empirical Generalizations" exercise he handed in to Merton. Assuming that "isolated troops are more vulnerable to propaganda than large masses of troops," Katz asked, what it was "in the isolated units that makes for vulnerability to propaganda" and what it was among "large masses of troops that makes for greater resistance?" (Katz 1949). Working through the Decatur study and writing up *Personal Influence* would help him begin answering these questions.

Before Lazarsfeld offered him the Decatur study, though, Katz would finish a master's project with Leo Lowenthal, a mail study of letters received by "a daytime radio raconteur and practical philosopher in answer to his request to keep an accurate record of all of the happiest events of the month (February 1948) and at the end of the month to name and describe your happiest day," Katz (1949) wrote in the intellectual autobiography.

Katz had been drawn to Lazarsfeld's lecture courses as an undergraduate but had not yet been able to work with him as a graduate student. His career trajectory at that point was in conflict with the dominant paradigm of sociology at Columbia—one centered around the ideals and practices of *science* instead of social reform, philosophy, public service, or any of a number of other conceptions that brought some students into sociology and animated their intended work in the field (see Lipset 1998, 262-65). Lowenthal assigned Katz the job of summarizing the statistical data from studies of four Arabic countries for a report related to the Voice of America (VOA) and Lowenthal–funded Near East study in 1952 (Katz 1952), parts of which found their way into Daniel Lerner's *Passing of Traditional Society* (1958). It was probably after Lazarsfeld saw what a good job Katz did on that synthesis that he determined to draw in the talented graduate student on the Decatur study. As James Coleman and others have noted, Lazarsfeld always tried to persuade smart people he knew to work on projects in which he himself was interested. This was not a style for everyone, particularly when coupled with a propensity to see the person he put on the project as an "extension of himself," and being one who could not tolerate it if the work done did not line up with his own ideas (Coleman 1998, 280). Coleman called this Lazarsfeld's own "medium of personal influence" (p. 281), exercised with regard to the way problems were posed, researched, interpreted, and written up. Lazarsfeld was brilliant, his appetite for learning was huge, and he was willing to listen to graduate students "whenever he thought he could learn from them"— William McPhee, Allen Barton, and Elihu Katz among them (p. 283). Katz found a way to make it work.[11]

Soon after he finished his report for the Near East study, Katz was given another synthesizing assignment, this time for a large project overseen by Lazarsfeld for the New York State Television Commission, with additional funding perhaps from the Ford Foundation. It issued in a remarkable series of eleven reports including Katz's report, "The Part Played by People: A New Focus for the Study of Mass Media Effects" (1953).[12] This was the origin of the hugely influential Part I of *Personal Influence*, which established the dominant historical understanding of the development of mass communications research in the United States (Pooley 2006) and laid out the basic view of opinion leaders, two-step flows, and interpersonal influence that Lazarsfeld had been developing since Sandusky and *The People's Choice*. Part II would be the Decatur study, finally worked up, and based on data of perhaps questionable empirical validity.

The Television Implementation Committee report functioned as a first draft that Lazarsfeld circulated around, to David Riesman among others. This was customary practice for him—typically, he dictated papers into a machine; had his secretary type them up and mail them off to people he thought could help the project; and then waited for reactions, references, and relevant data (Lipset 1998, 267). After comments came back, Katz returned to work, and Part I emerged with the same title as the 1953 report. It laid out a vision of the field and Columbia's place in it and drew attention to the significance of opinion leaders and interpersonal communication in the broader flow of mass communications. A well-written Introduction capped production of the book in May 1955, recounting the studies to which this book was an answer and stating its own position forcefully and spaciously. By then, Katz had taken a job at the University of Chicago, and Lazarsfeld was spending a year at Stanford's new Center for Advanced Study. The book was published later that year by the Free Press, the second volume in a series edited by Lazarsfeld and Berelson and titled Foundations of Communications Research (the first volume was Berelson's book on content analysis). Reviews came out soon after, blending appreciation and criticism. Other readings followed, producing their own effects, uses, and gratifications. This volume continues in that interpretive tradition.

Rereadings Fifty Years Later: Contexts, Consequences, Convergences

One might divide the articles in this volume roughly into two groups, realizing there is bleed-over between them. The first might be called Contexts and Consequences and includes articles whose primary allegiance falls on the historical side of Merton's "history and systematics" ledger. The second might be called Convergences and includes articles that fall more toward the systematics side, broadly conceived. "Convergence" is what Katz called the linking he did of small-group and mass media research, with the hope of better understanding the overall flow of mass communications through interpersonal groupings and networks.[13] The convergences here are more varied in type, but the impulse to link literatures of different sorts is present throughout. Questions of politics and influence run steadily through the volume, and there is a thread of continuity from the first essay to the last, so it makes some sense to read them sequentially. I will here introduce them briefly and in order.

Collectively, the historical articles that appear in the first half of this volume have the effect of peeling back some of the universality of tone and argument in *Personal Influence*, where the featured characters are not eight hundred women in Decatur, Illinois, in the summer of 1945 but are rather "people" and the part they play in the flow of mass communications. The book is not just an argument, a collection of analyzed data, or the presentation of a paradigm. It is also a text, produced backstage by institutionally constrained individuals interacting with one another, in gendered, "religioned," and historically situated ways. John Summers tells us a fascinating story at the individual level, focusing on C. Wright Mills and his trajectory in relation to Lazarsfeld from Decatur through *Personal Influence* and beyond. He fills in a key episode in the history of American sociology and communications research, the riff between two of the giants in the field and the intellectual orientations they represented. Susan Douglas follows by peering back to the gendered contexts that were bracketed in *Personal Influence* but very much alive when Mills's team of interviewers were talking with the women of Decatur. She explores the study's "routinely contradictory attitudes toward women" and looks at some of the things going on with the women of Decatur that we do not learn from the text.

The next three articles together reveal a good deal about the institutional and intellectual contexts in which Lazarsfeld and then Katz worked at the Bureau for Applied Social Research. David Morrison gives us a compelling and finely grained picture of Lazarsfeld and the research organization out of which *Personal Influence* arose. He shows how the Decatur study came to be and brings us close to the man who most influenced production of *Personal Influence*: the scholar, entrepreneur, and marginal man Paul Lazarsfeld. Gertrude Robinson then brings Katz into the picture and ties him to the other great institute in residence on Morningside Heights in the 1940s, the Frankfurt Institut für Sozialforschung, through the person of Leo Lowenthal, Katz's master's adviser. Robinson's comparative analysis of the career paths and research of Lowenthal and Katz enriches and complicates some of the received wisdom about Columbia and Frankfurt, "critical" and "administrative" research (a line Sonia Livingstone picks up in her later article as well).

The next two articles provocatively place *Personal Influence* within grander scale narratives about Jewish history and modernity/postmodernity. John Durham Peters argues that *Personal Influence* represents one moment in the long tradition of Jewish involvement in and commentary upon communication. He brilliantly enriches the text with his reading and uncovers some of the meanings of "people" that resonate through its pages. Paddy Scannell follows with an addition to the big picture understanding, arguing that *Personal Influence* indexes the moment of transition from modernity to postmodernity—from production to consumption, work to leisure—and the development of a sociology of everyday life that matches it. Scannell situates the book against the social and intellectual history of the masses in the nineteenth and twentieth centuries and draws out gendered aspects of both the social processes and research done about them.

Jefferson Pooley returns us to the micro-historical by tracing the genesis and diffusion of the highly influential narrative of the history of mass communication research that appears in Part I of *Personal Influence*. Pooley shows how Lazarsfeld framed media research and its findings differently for different audiences in the 1940s and 1950s before settling into that of *Personal Influence* and shows how Edward Shils influenced the process along the way.

The next two articles, both composed by people who were among the original reading public for *Personal Influence*, continue in the vein of tracing the book's influences and trajectory into politics over time. Kurt and Gladys Lang trace the book's reception and uptake through reviews and citations and sketch some of the "inadvertent consequences" of its success. They argue that the book's downplaying of media influence discouraged sociologists from studying the phenomenon, cemented a paradigm that made it difficult to advance alternate views of the subject, and diverted researchers' attention from the power of mass media. Bureau alumna Thelma McCormack offers a complementary retrospective of *Personal Influence* that, like the Langs', comes from a privileged historical position. McCormack follows *Personal Influence* from its birth into the liberal intellectual framework of the 1950s through its rejection in the wake of the transformations wrought by Vietnam and rise of the New Left. Her thoughtful discussion of communications, polling, and election studies and their varying political economies shows some of the cosmopolitan and cross-disciplinary purview of many of those trained at Columbia in the 1940s and 1950s.

The series of articles that follows continues the emphasis on politics and moves into convergences of various sorts and resistance to them. Both Michael Schudson and Lawrence Glickman address questions of consumption and citizenship that were so central to the Decatur study and *Personal Influence*. Schudson picks up the apparent equivalence between politics and consumption in the book and Todd Gitlin's critique of it. Schudson dialectically maneuvers through critiques of consumption and questions the belief that political and consumer choices are fundamentally different. Glickman then gets at the issue from a complementary perspective by contrasting Lazarsfeld's analysis of decision making with that held by consumer activists in his era. While Lazarsfeld was always interested in the inputs that influenced a concrete political or consumer decision, activists like Florence Kelley attended instead to the "outputs" of choice—the social and moral aftermath of buying products or brands and the impact on distant laborers and others.

Lance Bennett and Jarol Manheim follow by arguing that the two-step flows that the Bureau charted in the 1940s and celebrated in the 1950s have been supplanted by a number of "one-step flows" in our own day. These are driven by a number of technological and social changes that effectively short-circuit peer group interaction that formerly mediated mass communicated messages. Their sophisticated engagement with the changes in thinking, political communication, and technology since *Personal Influence* both historicizes Katz and Lazarsfeld's findings and extends some of their aspirations by drawing upon a wide range of research about media and society to question the adequacy of an earlier paradigm.

Also touching upon new media, Sonia Livingstone follows with a discussion of *Personal Influence* within developments and debates in the field of audience studies. Using Katz's career as a narrative device, Livingstone parses out differences in the analytics and politics of classic critical and administrative research, then uses Katz's own stylistic convergences as a bridge to making a case for convergence between administrative and critical camps today (cf. Sterne 2005). Her turn at the end toward social research about new media has precedent in the experiences of Lazarsfeld himself, since he conducted radio research in Austria before 1932 and until the time it became an old technology itself, supplanted by television, which he also set out to study, in 1952.

The next article, written by Livingstone's colleagues Nick Couldry and Tim Markham, also has elements in common with Lazarsfeld's work, in that it is based on a research study funded by outside sources and aims to determine something about media and democratic society by looking toward ordinary people. Couldry and Markham put Katz and Lazarsfeld in conversation with Alain Touraine, Robert Putnam, and other theorists of contemporary society and compare *Personal Influence* to their own Public Connection project, which investigates media consumption, conversation, and involvement with public issues in contemporary Great Britain.

Charles Kadushin picks up where Couldry and Markham leave off, with the question of action. He argues that in the course of devising an accounting scheme to determine different influences on a decision, Lazarsfeld also articulated a radical theory of action—one that counted interpersonal influence as a key component of the process. Kadushin goes on to link *Personal Influence* to recent studies of social capital—"a study of social capitalists," he calls it—and discusses both its limits and comparative advantages over contemporary work.

Robert Hornik then brings things home by relating *Personal Influence* to another type of state-of-the-art social science, this one focused on media effects. Drawing on a data set of the type Lazarsfeld himself never got to analyze, Hornik offers what is perhaps the volume's most fitting tribute to the book—he tests its hypotheses in a particular case. Hornik deftly parses five hypotheses the book makes about how social context affects mass media exposure, then draws upon data from the evaluation of a national antidrug campaign to examine the effects of siblings on one another. Given Lazarsfeld's own scientific hopes and commitments to "social research as a continuing endeavor," he would no doubt be disappointed to hear how few studies Hornik found that followed up Lazarsfeld's hypotheses but pleased with the way Hornik was doing it now and fascinated by the possibilities of computer technologies as a way to ply his methodological trade.

In closing, let me say that *Personal Influence* turned out to be a more remarkable book historically than I had reason to know and to lead into contexts that reveal a great deal about midcentury life in a localized but influential place, the Bureau of Applied Social Research. It was a place that drew out many ambivalent—and some outright hostile—feelings, none of which was without reason. But Lazarsfeld and the Bureau through the time of *Personal Influence* have not, from where I sit, deserved the dismissal they have received since the 1970s from critical, cultural, and interpretive students of media and communication. Whatever its shortcomings, epistemological or political, Lazarsfeld's Office of Radio Research and the Bureau produced a series of remarkable pioneering texts through commercial or government sponsored administrative research: from Herta Herzog's "On Borrowed Experience," to *The People's Choice, Mass Persuasion*, and *Personal Influence*. (I leave aside the more complicated—or complicit—*Passing of Traditional Society*.) As a field and a society, we are in a different place than we were then, as we are in a different place than we were when Todd Gitlin forcefully brought the critiques to bear in 1978. Media are more developed, differentiated, converged, and collectively powerful than they were in 1945. They are more ubiquitous in everyday social life. They are more global. The two-step flows of Decatur women in 1945 are not the two-step flows of today, and cultural repertoires of personal influence have taken on new forms. These are not reasons to discard *Personal Influence* but rather reasons to take it seriously, as a guidepost and platform, as we work out our own problems. This volume attempts to do just that.

Notes

1. *The Annals* ran issues in 1929, 1935, and 1941 on radio; on communication and social action in 1947 (a volume edited by scholars of speech communication); and in that same year another volume on the motion picture industry. Katz's 1997 essay appeared in a volume on the media and politics edited by political communication scholar Kathleen Jamieson.

2. For portraits of Lazarsfeld and an introduction to writings on him, see the special issue on him in the *International Journal of Public Opinion Research* (IJPOR), vol. 13 (2001), and the harder to find but indispensable collection edited by Jacques Lautman and Bernard-Pierre Lécuyer, *Paul Lazarsfeld (1901-1976): La sociologie de Vienne à New York* (Paris: L'Harmattan, 1998), which includes a valuable long piece by Merton ("Working with Lazarsfeld"); excellent accounts of Lazarsfeld's Austrian years (see especially Christian Fleck's); and revealing remembrances by former Columbia graduate students Seymour Martin Lipset, James Coleman, David Sills, and Terry Nichols Clark among others. David Morrison's piece in this volume and others he has published (e.g., 1978, 1988, 1998) draw on extensive interviews Morrison conducted with Lazarsfeld in the summer of 1973. For excellent, sociologically grained historical accounts of Lazarsfeld's institutes, see Allen Barton (1982), along with his contribution to the *IJPOR* volume. See also the posthumous festschrift edited by Merton, Coleman, and Peter Rossi, *Qualitative and Quantitative Research: Papers in Honor of Paul F. Lazarsfeld* (1979). Lazarsfeld's own self-recollection is found in *The Intellectual Migration* (1969) edited by Donald Fleming and Lazarsfeld's son-in-law Bernard Bailyn, which also includes an autobiographical remembrance by Theodor Adorno that makes reference to Lazarsfeld. For an account of Lazarsfeld's early partnership with Merton, built on propaganda and communications research, see Simonson (2005).

3. For a good introduction to the Bureau of Applied Social Research (BASR), see Judith Barton's *Guide to the Bureau of Applied Social Research* (1984), which compiles titles of its reports, monographs, books, articles, master's essays, doctoral dissertations, audiovisual materials, and foreign publications, from which these titles are taken. See also the online finding aid for the BASR archives housed at the Rare Book and Manuscript Library, Columbia University: http://www.columbia.edu/cu/libraries/indiv/rare/guides/BASR.

4. The questionnaire also included at least one question of particular interest to Leo Lowenthal, the Frankfurt School émigré who was a research associate at the Bureau and wrote the classic "Biographies in

Popular Magazines" (1944, reprinted in Peters and Simonson 2004): "Do you try to read fairly biographies of prominent people in magazines?" (Katz and Lazarsfeld 1955/2005, 62).

5. For the fascinating life story of Bernarr Macfadden, brilliant and eccentric self-promoter, health freak, and publisher (Ernst 1991), see http://www.bernarrmacfadden.com.

6. See BASR File B-0218, Rare Book and Manuscript Library, Columbia University, New York.

7. For an alternative "community study approach to radio research" (supplemented by "the life-history narrative approach"), see John Rowland's 1947 sociology dissertation at the University of Pittsburgh, based on research he conducted in Columbus, Ohio, and elsewhere in the late 1930s and early 1940s.

8. In 1944, for instance, Bureau researchers undertook what they called a " 'dragnet' on the literature on the general problem of the 'Anglo-Saxons' and the 'foreigners' in American life," broken down into literature on the existence of antiminority prejudice, studies of environmental causes of such prejudice, and "studies of the content of the media of communication and the anti-minority prejudice," the last of which was their primary concern (BASR 1944; see also Berelson and Salter 1946; Lazarsfeld 1947).

9. The ads were designed by the Walter M. Swertfager advertising agency and ran in *Advertising Age* (March 18 and May 6, 1946), *Drug Trade News* (March 25 and May 20, 1946), *Food Field Reporter* (April 1 and 29, 1946), and *Automotive News* (April 8 and May 6, 1946). Copies of the ads, which include visuals of flowcharts of influence and Bureau staff members busy at work, are found in BASR File B-0218, Box 9, Rare Book and Manuscript Library, Columbia University, New York. Two different glossy reports are also housed in the archives, one in Box 9 and the other, Proofs for Published Report, in Box 10.

10. Memos and drafts from Rossi, Srole, Schneider, Green, and Sussmann, mostly from 1947, are found in BASR File B-0240, Memos (in the Sphinx Business Paper box) and Decatur Assessment Memo, Box 10, BASR Archives, Rare Book and Manuscript Library, Columbia University.

11. For discussions of Katz's work over the course of his career, see Livingstone (1997) and Curran and Liebes (1998), as well as Livingstone (this volume).

12. Other reports included "New Strategies for Research on the Mass Media" (William McPhee), "Children and Television: A Review of Socially Prevalent Concerns" (Joseph Klapper), "Collection and Analysis of Prevailing Criticisms of Television Programming" (Charles Siepmann), "Television as an Instrument of Political Communication" (Robert Leigh), "New York State Television Commission: A Case Study of the Use of Research by a Public Commission" (Harvey Levin), "Television and Organized Groups" (Jeanette Sayre Smith), "Television Research: An Annotated Bibliography" (Rolf Meyersohn), "A Study of Commissions of Inquiry" (Thomas Francis), and "Report from Implementation Committee to the Citizen's Group on Television Regarding Plans for a Television Development Center" (Paul Lazarsfeld).

13. It was something he had learned from Merton, as he made explicit in the Preface to his dissertation a year later: "The tactics which I have tried to employ in these essays on theoretical 'convergences' represent, in large measure, my attempt to follow the example set by Robert K. Merton. I hope this is a successful imitation" (Katz 1956, ii).

References

Anderson, Thelma. 1950. Communications research: Movie-going. Unpublished report, Bureau of Applied Social Research. BASR File B-0240, Rare Book and Manuscript Library, Columbia University, New York.

Barton, Allen. 1982. Paul Lazarsfeld and the invention of the university institute for applied social research. In *Organizing for social research*, ed. B. Holzner and J. Nehnevajsa, 17-83. Cambridge, MA: Schenkman.

Barton, Judith, S., ed. 1984. *Guide to the Bureau of Applied Social Research*. New York: Clearwater.

Berelson, Bernard, Paul F. Lazarsfeld, and William N. McPhee. 1954. *Voting: A study of opinion formation in a presidential campaign*. Chicago: University of Chicago Press.

Berelson, Bernard, and Patricia Salter. 1946. Majority and minority Americans: An analysis of magazine fiction. *Public Opinion Quarterly* 10:168-90.

Bureau of Applied Social Research (BASR). 1944. Summary of the literature on anti-minority prejudice. December 14. BASR File B-0215, Rare Book and Manuscript Library, Columbia University, New York.

Coleman, James S. 1998. Paul Lazarsfeld: The interaction of his relation to people and his relation to social science. In *Paul Lazarsfeld (1901-1976): La Sociologie de Vienne à New York*, ed. J. Lautman and B.-P. Lecuyer, 271-87. Paris: L'Harmattan.

Community Survey of Decatur: General instructions to interviewers. N.d. [1945]. BASR File B-0240, Miscellaneous Questionnaire Material, Rare Book and Manuscript Library, Columbia University, New York.

Curran, James, and Tamar Liebes. 1998. The intellectual legacy of Elihu Katz. In *Media, ritual and identity*, ed. T. Liebes and J. Curran. London: Routledge.

Ernst, Robert. 1991. *Weakness is a crime: The life of Bernarr Macfadden*. Syracuse, NY: Syracuse University Press.

Gitlin, Todd. 1978. Media sociology: The dominant paradigm. *Theory and Society* 5:205-53.

Green, Jeannete. 1943. The American community leader looks at the drugstore. BASR Report B-0151, Rare Book and Manuscript Library, Columbia University, New York.

Katz, Elihu. 1949. Untitled autobiographical reflection, and "Empirical generalizations" exercise for Sociology 213. Robert K. Merton, personal files.

―――. 1952. Communications behavior and political attitudes in four Arabic countries. BASR Report B-0370-18, Rare Book and Manuscript Library, Columbia University, New York.

―――. 1956. Interpersonal relations and mass communications: Studies in the flow of influence. PhD diss., Columbia University, New York.

―――. 1996. And deliver us from segmentation. *Annals of the American Academy of Political and Social Science* 546:22-33.

Katz, Elihu, and Paul F. Lazarsfeld. 1955/2005. *Personal influence: The part played by people in the flow of mass communications*. With a new Introduction by Elihu Katz. New Brunswick, NJ: Transaction. (Originally published by Free Press)

Katz, Elihu, John Durham Peters, Tamar Liebes, and Avril Orloff. 2003. *Canonic texts in media research. Are there any? Should there be? How about these?* Cambridge, UK: Polity.

Kendall, Patricia. 1946. The women meet Mr. Biggott. BASR Report B-0250-2, Rare Book and Manuscript Library, Columbia University, New York.

Kendall, Patricia, and Margery Wolf. 1949. The analysis of deviant cases in communications research. In *Communications research, 1948-1949*, ed. P. F. Lazarsfeld and F. Stanton, 152-79. New York: Duell Sloan.

Lasswell, Harold. 1951. *The political writings of Harold D. Lasswell*. New York: Free Press.

Lazarsfeld, Paul F. 1945. Who influences whom—It's the same for politics and advertising. *Printer's Ink* 211 (10): 32, 36.

―――. 1947. Some remarks on the role of mass media in so-called tolerance propaganda. *Journal of Social Issues* 3 (summer): 17-25.

―――. 1969. An episode in the history of social research. In *The intellectual migration*, ed. D. Fleming and B. Bailyn, 270-337. Cambridge, MA: Harvard University Press.

Lazarsfeld, Paul F., Bernard Berelson, and Hazel Gaudet. 1944. *The people's choice: How the voter makes up his mind in a presidential campaign*. New York: Duell, Sloan and Pearce.

Lazarsfeld, Paul F., and Robert K. Merton. 1948. Mass communication, popular taste, and organized social action. In *The communication of ideas*, ed. L. Bryson, 95-118. New York: Harper.

Lerner, Daniel. 1958. *The passing of traditional society: Modernizing the Middle East*. Glencoe, IL: Free Press.

Lipset, Seymour Martin. 1998. Paul F. Lazarsfeld: A great methodologist and teacher. In *Paul Lazarsfeld (1901-1976): La Sociologie de Vienne à New York*, ed. J. Lautman and B.-P. Lecuyer, 255-70. Paris: L'Harmattan.

Livingstone, Sonia. 1997. The Work of Elihu Katz: Conceptualizing media effects in context. In *The international handbook of media research*, ed. J. Corner, P. Schlesinger, and R. Silverstone. London: Routledge.

Lynd, Robert S., and Helen Merrell Lynd. 1929. *Middletown: A study in American culture*. New York: Harcourt, Brace.

―――. 1937. *Middletown in transition: A study in cultural conflicts*. New York: Harcourt, Brace.

"Macfadden Readers." 1944. *Tide*, November 15. BASR File B-0230, Rare Book and Manuscript Library, Columbia University, New York.

Merton, Robert K. 1946/2004. *Mass persuasion: The social psychology of a war bond drive*. Republished with an introduction by Peter Simonson. New York: Howard Fertig. (Orig. pub. New York: Harper)

Merton, Robert K. 1968. On the history and systematics of sociological research. In *Social theory and social structure*, 1-38. New York: Free Press.

Merton, Robert, James Coleman, and Peter Rossi, eds. 1979. *Qualitative and quantitative research: Papers in honor of Paul F. Lazarsfeld*. New York: Free Press.

Morrison, David. 1978. *Kultur* and culture: The case of Theodor W. Adorno and Paul F. Lazarsfeld. *Social Research* 45:331-55.

———. 1988. The transference of ideas: Paul Lazarsfeld and mass communication research. *Communication* 10:185-209.

———. 1998. *The search for method: Focus groups and the development of mass communication research*. Luton, UK: University of Luton Press.

Peters, John Durham, and Peter Simonson. 2004. *Mass communication and American social thought: Key texts, 1919-1968*. Lanham, MD: Rowman & Littlefield.

Pooley, Jefferson. 2006. An accident of memory: Edward Shils, Paul Lazarsfeld, and the history of American mass communication research. PhD diss., Columbia University, New York.

Rowland, John Howard. 1947. A sociological analysis of radio as a form of mass communication in American life. PhD diss., University of Pittsburgh, PA.

Schneider, Helen. 1947. Memo to Paul Lazarsfeld, personal influence vs. media influence. September 29. BASR File B-0240, Rare Book and Manuscript Library, Columbia University, New York.

Simonson, Peter. 2005. The serendipity of Merton's communications research. *International Journal of Public Opinion Research* 17 (1): 1-21.

Sterne, Jonathan. 2005. C. Wright Mills, the Bureau for Applied Social Research, and the meaning of critical scholarship. *Cultural Studies/Critical Methodologies* 5 (1): 65-94.

Wahl-Jorgensen, Karin. 2004. How not to found a field: New evidence on the origins of mass communication research. *Journal of Communication* 54 (3): 547-64.

This article narrates the prehistory and posthistory of
Personal Influence as an episode in the biographies of
Paul Lazarsfeld and C. Wright Mills. It begins in 1945,
when Lazarsfeld sent Mills to Decatur, Illinois, to undertake the fieldwork, and ends with Mills's death in 1962.

Keywords: C. Wright Mills; Paul Lazarsfeld; Robert
Merton; Columbia sociology; *Personal
Influence*; sociological imagination

Perpetual Revelations: C. Wright Mills and Paul Lazarsfeld

By
JOHN H. SUMMERS

The Decatur Study

The study was in full swing by June 1945.
C. Wright Mills, the field supervisor, was bark-
ing assignments to a staff of fifteen interviewers, assistants, and stenographers. Mills had
$20,000 to spend, and he did not plan to bring
any of it back to New York. He had installed
himself and his staff in the Hotel Orlando, in
downtown Decatur, Illinois.

A slew of advertisements in the newspapers
and on the radio announced the reason. The
Bureau of Applied Social Research, from
Columbia University, wanted to know how ordinary women made decisions in their everyday
lives. Decatur was happy to oblige. About eight
hundred volunteers, chosen from a cross-section
of the population, sat for thirty-minute interviews. Everybody answered three questions:

1. Has anybody recently solicited your opinion concerning international, national, or community
   affairs or news events?
2. Have you changed your opinion recently about
   any such events?
3. Do you know anybody who keeps up with the
   news, anybody you trust to help you decide your
   opinion?

*John H. Summers is a lecturer on social studies at
Harvard University. In 2006 he finished his doctorate
in American history from the University of Rochester.
His biography,* C. Wright Mills, American Rebel, *will
be published by Oxford University Press.*

DOI: 10.1177/0002716206292374

The three questions asked—in the same sequence and with varying follow-up questions—covered not only public affairs but also fashions, movies, and brands. The intention was straightforward. Who were the "opinion leaders" in Decatur? The first question yielded a list of self-declared opinion leaders. Here were people who claimed they had been consulted. Answers to the second question yielded another list. Here were people who had influenced the opinions of the women interviewed. The staff took down their names and addresses and went to find them for follow-up interviews.

Answers to question number three yielded a third list, a general list of esteemed people in Decatur. Mills sought out these people himself. He went to see the mayor, visited the bankers, the clergymen, the newspaper publisher, the businessmen big and small.

The Bureau's staff interviewed the eight hundred women in June, again in August, and again in December, each time asking about changes of mind in the interval. At each step, the women, the questions, the subjects, and the answers were broken down into indices of age, sex, income, and occupation and dutifully recorded onto checkbook-sized cards.

Complex in its design, ingenious in its procedures, laborious in its execution, the Decatur study excited a feeling of camaraderie that carried Mills and his staff through the arranging, recording, and coding of approximately 2,000 interviews, all in all. The staff ate dinners together in the Hotel Orlando and enjoyed drinks late into the evening. During the daylight, they took opportunities where they found them. As it happened, public opinion in Decatur appeared to be changing over a proposal to build a new section of U.S. highway 36. The staff interviewed 718 women about the proposal, and Mills published the results in a Sunday edition of the *Decatur Herald*. In eight dramatic days in August, the government dropped two atomic bombs, the Soviet Union entered the Pacific War, and Japan surrendered. Mills wrote and revised questions in a frantic effort to discern the flow of opinion about these events as well. At the end of the month, he reported his progress. "I worry a lot about the whole thing flopping because figures can go screwy, but sometimes it looks like a damn nice little study" (Mills 1945a).

Paul Lazarsfeld

The plan of the Decatur study originated with the founder and director of the Bureau of Applied Social Research, Paul Lazarsfeld. For an earlier book, *The People's Choice* (Lazarsfeld, Berelson, and Gaudet 1944/1948), Lazarsfeld and his collaborators had interviewed a cross-section of voters in Erie County, Ohio, every month for the six months that led up to the 1940 presidential election, and then once more after the election. Those interviews had suggested something Lazarsfeld found intriguing enough to pursue for years afterward. Those voters who had changed their political opinion over the course of the election attributed the change to casual conversations among family and friends—to face-to-face inter-actions, rather than to formal media. Upon this insight, Lazarsfeld mounted his "two-step flow of information" hypothesis. Step one: information came from the formal media. Step two: informal groups or individuals mediated the information for other groups or individuals. Perhaps the technologies of mass communication were not as powerful as the intellectuals believed.

Paul Lazarsfeld held a doctorate in applied mathematics from the University of Vienna, and he thought of himself as a psychologist. These two dimensions of his biography converged in the approach he made when he went to design his study of opinion leadership in Decatur. Select a sample of ordinary people. Ask a standard set of questions. Codify the answers. Classify the variables. Make the tables. Build an index structure from the tables. Now make the indexes talk to you. In a time before computers, the procedure could be maddeningly complex. But Lazarsfeld believed a well-designed study that employed the correct statistical procedure could pry insights from everyday psychology. If the idea sounded a little like psychoanalysis, that was not a coincidence. Back in Vienna, Lazarsfeld's mother had been trained in individual psychology by Alfred Adler.

The quantitative procedure often raised objections on the part of social theorists. That opinions could be represented by putting a standardized set of questions to a cross-section of a community, that they could be measured on scales of magnitude, and then converted into statistical summations—these assumptions were by no means evident, wrote Robert Merton, a young sociologist at Tulane University, in an essay published in 1940 in the *American Sociological Review* (Merton 1940). Merton's essay did not mention Lazarsfeld, but it challenged the synonym linking opinion and action as assumed by the style of research toward which Lazarsfeld was moving. There was another kind of resistance as well. Lazarsfeld's "empirical analysis of action" needed manifold resources, not only teams of interviewers, stenographers, and analysts, but offices, data-processing machines, travel and communication equipment, plus a large infusion of money to keep the whole operation going (Converse 1987, 272). To organize these tasks, in brief, a new kind of research institute needed to be hooked up to a money pump. Foundations, state agencies, and corporations would have to play a role: this Lazarsfeld had known from the beginning. The Vienna Institute, the first of several organizations he founded, had signed as its first client a major chocolate corporation in Germany.

In 1934, while Lazarsfeld visited the United States on a fellowship, the swift political turn in Austria made him a refugee. He had a stint with the National Youth Administration, and another one as director of a research institute at the University of Newark. Then he won a job as director of the Office of Radio Research at Princeton University. When its funder transferred the radio project to Columbia University in 1939, he found himself in New York. The sociology department at Columbia offered him a courtesy appointment, but not much more. Not many officials or professors wanted to be associated with a style of research that relied so heavily on commercial money.

But the success of *The People's Choice* and other such studies gained Lazarsfeld growing notice in the United States. During the early 1940s, the radio project analyzed propaganda for the Office of War Information, and began to draw more and more contract work from American corporations. Lazarsfeld renamed the project the Bureau of Applied Social Research. Most important, he hired an associate director, the newly converted Robert Merton, who had joined the Columbia sociology department in 1940. By 1944, Lazarsfeld was ready to try to go beyond *The People's Choice*. If certain people mediated information between media and its consumers, what psychological dynamics might the "two-step flow" hypothesis betray? In Macfadden Publications, the owner of *True Story* magazine, he found a client willing to entrust him with $20,000. Because most of the subscribers of *True Story* were women, Macfadden's sponsorship would limit the study accordingly. Nonetheless, Lazarsfeld could use the money to trace the actual flow of opinion in politics, fashion, movies, and marketing. He looked at each midwestern city with a population between fifty and eighty thousand. From the sample, he derived thirty-six statistical indicators. He made the number one hundred stand for "most typical." Decatur, Illinois, scored ninety-nine. All that remained was to find a field supervisor.

A Meeting of the Minds

One day in January 1945, Robert Merton surprised C. Wright Mills with a telephone call. Would he come up from Washington and pay a visit to the new Bureau of Applied Social Research?

So far as professional interests went, Merton and Mills had more in common with each other than either man shared with Lazarsfeld. For several years, they had engaged in a vigorous correspondence about the sociology of knowledge, crossing pens over matters technical, but agreeing wholeheartedly about the need to develop in the United States what had been a European preoccupation. Merton, having studied with Talcott Parsons, came to the field from reading Emile Durkheim. Mills, having studied with Chicago-trained sociologists at the University of Texas, came to it from John Dewey and George Mead. For the theoretical acuity of their early essays in this emerging field, Merton and Mills were widely considered two of the most promising young sociologists in the country.

There was another, more personal affinity. Unlike Lazarsfeld, who came from a politically prominent, highly educated family in Austria, Merton and Mills were on their own. Merton was born in Philadelphia to immigrant parents—his father worked as a carpenter and storekeeper—and attended Temple University on scholarship. After graduate school at Harvard, and after a brief tenure at Tulane University, he joined Columbia at the age of thirty-one, already considered a leader in the field (Merton 1994). Mills was born in Waco, Texas, into a middle-class home—his father was a traveling salesman—without a tradition of cultural aspiration. When he graduated from high school in Dallas, his father sent him to military school. He transferred to the University of Texas the next year. Like Merton, Mills proved himself in a state school, caught the attention of older men in graduate school, and looked upon the expanding field of sociology as a way up and out. Such were the expectations laid up around him; the sociology department at the University of Maryland gave him his first job in 1941 as associate professor, allowing him to leap over the assistant rank completely. And this was *before* he had finished his dissertation, a sociological history of pragmatism.

On a Friday night in January 1945, Lazarsfeld, Merton, and Mills, three men whose combined work would transform American sociology, met in Manhattan for seven hours. Everything about the evening gave off the scent of possibility. Over a big meal in an expensive restaurant, the conversation passed easily over the study, over the city of Decatur, over the moral problems involved in commercial research. Now and then, several handsome young women from Smith and Vassar (invited to the table by Lazarsfeld to seduce Mills into joining the team) spoke in sugary voices. After the women departed, Lazarsfeld set forth the terms. Mills was to have the title of research associate at the Bureau. He was to go to Decatur in the summer and direct the opinion study. He could publish under his own name. If all went well, he might expect to join the sociology faculty of Columbia University on a permanent basis. Mills reported the evening in a starry-eyed letter to his parents:

> After they had laid out the job and said: "Well that's it; we want you. Will you come?" I said (holding myself in with bursting joy at the whole idea: christ I'd go for food and shelter) anyway I kept the face immobile and just said: "for how much?" They wouldn't say, but replied: "You know what you're worth, name it." To which little charlie said very quietly, "I won't charge you that much, but I cdnt think of it in terms less than 4500." Immediately the guys said "Then your beginning salary will be 5000." To which the appropriate reply was "That is closer to what I'm worth." and everybody laughed and felt good. (Mills 1945b)

On January 26, 1945, having secured a leave of absence from Maryland, Mills wrote to Lazarsfeld to accept the offer. Each week that spring, he rode the train from Washington to Manhattan and spent one day at the Bureau, feeling his way around its cavernous offices on 59th and Amsterdam Avenue, getting to know his colleagues, paying visits to friends in the city. Meanwhile, a fight raged uptown. Those opposing the hiring of Mills at Columbia feared that Lazarsfeld and Merton were using him to drive the Bureau closer to the university and its plentiful resources. In this, they were correct. At the end of May, as Mills set out for Decatur, the Bureau signed its first formal agreement with the university.

The Progress of the Study

To detect the "opinion leaders," the analysis of the data needed to yield clues to three main problems. Could the actual flow of interpersonal influence in Decatur be isolated? Could "opinion leaders" be isolated as a social type? And could the influence be isolated in relation to the class structure of a community? Did the influence flow vertically, up and down class lines, or horizontally, within classes?

Lazarsfeld and his team had not had the chance to interview opinion leaders for *The People's Choice.* If there was a singular methodological imperative in the Decatur study, here it rested. To find and talk to the opinion leaders was to isolate the structure and the flow of decision all at once. To isolate the structure and the flow of decision in a typical community would make Macfadden's advertising department happy, no question. But the implications could not fail to strike up interest among scholars too. Inasmuch as the opinion leader could be isolated at the crossroads of structure and flow, it disclosed the how and the why of decision making. Nobody had attained quite this much insight into the psychology of everyday decisions. And no wonder. When Mills went to analyze the data, more than six thousand tables, holding as many as ten variables at once, spread before him in a river of numbers and symbols. His initial worry about "the whole thing flopping" tightened into acute anxiety.

Could the flow of influence be isolated? Answers to question two (have you recently changed your opinion?) should have yielded the relevant data. Here, the women in the cross-section attested that an opinion flowed from one person to another. Did their testimony mean that the first person could be called an opinion leader, and the second, an opinion follower? The actual answers seemed to require a third category, so that the "opinion leaders" could be said to have given advice; "opinion followers" could be said to have gotten advice; and a third, "opinion relayers," could be said to have given and gotten. But the design of the study had not anticipated the need for this third category.

[T]he data on politics yielded the best chain *of opinion leaders, the data on fashion yielded the best* flow *of opinion.*

Could "opinion leaders" be isolated as a social type? Answers to question one (has anybody recently solicited your opinion?) did give a list of self-elected opinion leaders; whether they could be believed was an open question. The bigger problem was that Mills's staff had not been able to track down all the people named in questions two and three. And when they did conduct follow-up interviews, they could not always confirm that the influence had transpired.

Could the direction of the influence be isolated in the class structure of the community? Answers to question three (Do you know anybody whom you trust to help you decide your opinion?) showed the chain of opinion leadership on politics to be stratified vertically; most of the named people belonged to the top class, with a steady graduation downward. But while the data on politics yielded the best *chain* of opinion leaders, the data on fashion yielded the best *flow* of opinion. Mills could not connect opinion leaders in the chain to the same kind of opinion transaction. There appeared to be no way to get them to coincide.

Lazarsfeld flew to Chicago now and then to meet him. There the two men talked about the progress of the study, discussed what they could accomplish with the data. Mills's ongoing success in other fields, plus Lazarsfeld's ongoing success in establishing the Bureau, plus the fertility of fresh data, all this, in combination, must have made it easy to hope for the best. At the end of December 1945, Mills finished the third and final round of interviewing in Decatur. Good news awaited him when he arrived back in New York. Columbia College wanted to keep him on the sociology faculty. In the spring, Lazarsfeld opened up a division of labor research in the Bureau. He hired Mills to run it. Inside of three months, Mills made contact with every major union in every major city in the United States and won a contract from the Office of Naval Research besides.

The deadline for the Decatur manuscript came and went.

Lazarsfeld paid regular visits to Mills's apartment in Greenwich Village in 1946. They made some progress. Mills produced approximately three hundred pages of text and put the interviews at the center of a widely noticed article, "The Middle-Classes in Middle-Sized Cities," published in the *American Sociological Review* (Mills 1946). Lazarsfeld, too, published a widely noticed article based on the interviews, "Audience Research in the Movie Field," which appeared in the *Annals of the American Academy of Political and Social Science*. Of the Decatur study, he boasted that it offered "probably the most detailed approach to the movie audience yet undertaken." Mills's article relied on data from question three (chain of local political elites) to present a picture of class awareness in Decatur's social structure. Lazarsfeld, in his article, asked how moviegoers decided, from the fantastic volume of information available in the mass media, which movies to see. "There are people, distributed all over the population" who mediated a "horizontal flow of influence" from person to person, Lazarsfeld wrote. "Actually, it is not too difficult to spot these opinion leaders" (Lazarsfeld 1947).

Mills went to Boston in December to present the dilemmas of the Decatur study to an audience of the American Association for the Advancement of Science. He gave a copy of his address to Lazarsfeld, and added two memoranda, in which he explained the "technical tragedy" of the thing. Soon after, he gave another talk about the study, this time at a seminar at Columbia. After he finished, Lazarsfeld rose and remarked, "So that's what you spent all my money on."

In the summer of 1947, the study was sixteen months overdue. Mills was living in a cabin in the Sierra Nevada Mountains. He wrote to Lazarsfeld to say that he had decided, once and for all, that the tables and equations and figures made no sense. He had the files with him right there in his cabin. He was going to set aside the tabulation machinery and he was going to write the goddamned book then and there. He promised to be back in New York in two months with a completed manuscript in hand.

Lazarsfeld fired him.

C. Wright Mills after the Study

For a brief time, Mills's career at Columbia looked like it might not survive the blow. Since he had been hired to teach in the college in December 1945, he had been enormously productive. He had a steady stream of material appearing in the magazines and periodicals; he performed contract research for the government; he expanded the labor division of the Bureau; and *From Max Weber*, the book of translations he published with Hans Gerth, was transforming American social science (Gerth and Mills 1946). In December 1946, Robert Merton warned an inquirer to stay away from his hotshot sociologist. "I can best summarize my opinion of Mills by saying that I regard him as the outstanding sociologist of his age in the country. The tenacity with which I hold this view is indicated by my hope that he will remain at Columbia. It is only fair to say that should be he offered an appointment by the New School, I, for one, shall recommend to Columbia that it do whatever it can to keep him within our Department" (Merton 1946). Three months after Lazarsfeld's action, Merton joined with the rest of the department in declining to support Mills's promotion, citing "deep disappointment over the Decatur episode" (Merton 1947b).

Mills tried to make amends. When the governor of Puerto Rico asked the Bureau for a study of immigration, he volunteered for the job and carried it out well. He made some headway toward a saving compromise as well. The Decatur manuscript would be divided into two parts, he reported in 1948. Lazarsfeld and two assistants would be responsible for writing one part, and he would be responsible for "theory unburdened by the silly figures." Given everything, he thought this made "a fine solution and [I] am very pleased with it" (Mills n.d.). In a second edition of *The People's Choice*, published in 1948, Lazarsfeld told readers the Decatur study "will soon appear" (Lazarsfeld 1944/1948, xxvi). Two years later, however, the project languished. "Paul is giving me a lot of trouble on [the] Decatur manuscript, and the guy who talks for one of us, to the other, has goofed off," Mills wrote. "God, will I ever get that crap off my desk? It is continually in my hair. I just hate to work on it" (Mills 1950a).

The Columbia sociology department had hired Merton with the idea that he might mediate such disputes between theorists and empiricists. But the complexities of *this* dispute defeated even his skills. "I've read every bit of correspondence that's passed between NY and Reno," he told Mills, "and I'm convinced that there's been a break in communication. Paul hasn't been able to put what he has to say in a letter, that I know. Perhaps you haven't either. I know I couldn't. Having started four or five letters to you, I gave up the thing up as an impossible job" (Merton 1947a).

History has not made the job a whole lot easier. Mills's manuscript seems not to have survived, so it is difficult to judge how Lazarsfeld and Katz, in publishing the Decatur study as *Personal Influence* (Katz and Lazarsfeld 1955), may have solved or ignored the technical dimensions of the dispute as it stood in 1950. It would be foolish for a historian untrained in quantitative research, working with limited evidence, to attempt to adjudicate. Many talented scholars struggled to make sense of the data before Lazarsfeld and Katz made a book of it (Barton 1982, 45-46).

The political dimension of the dispute set another trap. Certainly, it is possible to set Mills's views on public opinion against the conclusions in Lazarsfeld and Katz. This procedure might expect to find Lazarsfeld and Mills squaring off, the one bemoaning the omnipotence of the mass media, the other proving the sovereignty of the primary group. But Mills's views on this subject defy paraphrase. In an essay from 1950, for example, he used the Decatur interviews to make the same point made later in Lazarsfeld and Katz. "No view of American public life is realistic that assumes public opinion to be merely the puppet of the mass media. There are strong forces at work among the public that are independent of these media of communication, forces that can and do at times go directly against the opinions promulgated by them" (Mills 1950b).

How could two men, enjoined to study the resilience of personal communication, fail so miserably to communicate?

How could two men, enjoined to study the resilience of personal communication, fail so miserably to communicate? One thing is certain. The dispute that started during those first meetings in Chicago, which tangled and deepened in Greenwich Village in 1946, which stole into seminars in Boston and New York, did not end with the publication of *Personal Influence*. Mills did not get the Decatur material off his desk or out of his hair. He folded away the interviews into the book that made him famous outside professional sociology, *White Collar* (1951). Later, he made them the basis of "local society" chapter of the book that made him yet more famous outside sociology, *The Power Elite* (1956). Lazarsfeld thought Mills, in using the Decatur material for these books, was repaying his debts to the Bureau in scorn and contempt. In retrospect, the originating dinner in New York, that seven-hour marathon discussion in January 1945, was the best time they had together. For the dispute twisted into ugly personal shapes, produced volumes of emotion and ideas as each man pressed his claim aggressively, relentlessly.

Criticisms Fly

Mills lost little time striking back. In a stream of essays written as he made his exit from the Bureau (and indeed from collaborative work altogether), he criticized the kind of administrative research he had undertaken in Decatur. "IBM plus Reality plus Humanism = Sociology" (1954), the title of an essay published in the popular periodical, *Saturday Review*, more or less summed up the point. That he had Lazarsfeld in his sights nobody could question. Another of his essays was a rewrite of the address he had given in Boston in 1946; this time, it made Lazarsfeld's book *The People's Choice* the villain (1953). One can catch the tone of these essays shifting from extenuation, to criticism, then breaking into competitive action. "On Intellectual Craftsmanship," a primer on social research Mills composed in 1952, advocated sociology as a way of life, as a means of transcending the split between science and poetry. By the time Mills handed out his primer to his students at Columbia, *White Collar* had become a best seller. He wished for the book to be read as a set of "prose poems" (Mills 2000, 164.)

Lazarsfeld thought *White Collar* was "a very dumb book" (see Gordon 1962, 366). As Mills pursued his independent public, Lazarsfeld pursued *his* style of research at Columbia. What progress he made! Although the Bureau of Applied Social Research never received more than 10 percent of its funding from the university, Lazarsfeld won virtually every moral and intellectual battle he waged. The Bureau moved to 117th Street, near the campus, and employed approximately one hundred staff members. Even its critics knew it was the most important center of quantitative social research in the country. They knew it because Lazarsfeld was busily teaching a whole generation of sociology graduate students how to reproduce the methods featured in *The People's Choice* and *Personal Influence*. Either Lazarsfeld or Merton had held the title of "executive officer" of the Columbia graduate department since 1949. Either way, a strict professional ethos was set in place. Sociology at Columbia was not a way of life or a means of transcending science and poetry. It was a technical discipline. Lazarsfeld thought *White Collar* was "a very dumb book" because it mixed up the analytic and the impressionistic. Merton was more flexible and searching than Lazarsfeld in his vision of sociology, yet he too expected it to evolve into a science (Bernstein 1990, 8). When an assistant professor of sociology published a film review in the New York press, he was summoned to the office. Did he wish to continue teaching in the department? "Well, both Merton and I hope that this movie review you wrote is the last one; that it is not the kind of sociology you plan to practice," Lazarsfeld said, adding under his breath, "The last thing we need is another C. Wright Mills" (Etzioni 2003, 54).

Young intellectuals in every industrial society in the world did what Columbia's graduate students and assistant professors were not permitted to do, namely, discuss and debate Mills's books. By the end of the decade, translations appeared in Argentina, France, Germany, Italy, Japan, Mexico, Spain, and the Soviet Union. Lazarsfeld found that whenever he went to Europe to lecture, somebody in the audience asked him about the author of *The Power Elite*. Why didn't more sociologists write such interesting books? Asked this in Warsaw, Lazarsfeld exploded with a denunciation so caustic it embarrassed his hosts. Zygmunt Bauman witnessed the occasion: "Mills baiting was a favorite pastime among the most distinguished members of American academe: there were no expedients, however dishonest, which the ringleaders of the hue-and-cry would consider below their dignity and to which they would not stoop" (Bauman and Tester 2001, 27).

Mills did not exactly elevate the tone of the dispute. *The Sociological Imagination* (1959) renewed the criticisms he had laid away in his essays of the early 1950s, now elaborated into a sustained attack against the schools and sects of academic sociology. The profession, Mills charged, was in the grip of "grand theory" and "abstracted empiricism"; the first tendency he charged to Talcott Parsons, the second, to Lazarsfeld. "As practices, they may be understood as insuring that we do not learn too much about man and society—the first by formal and cloudy obscurantism, the second by formal and empty ingenuity" (Mills 1959, 75).

No single set of propositions or problems could be said to characterize Lazarsfeld's "abstracted empiricism," Mills said. Although Lazarsfeld had carried out a great number of studies of public opinion since the publication of *The People's Choice*, the results of these studies has added no new ideas to the field. Their real subject was the perfection of method and the production of sociologists as technicians. If Lazarsfeld managed to institutionalize his administrative style over the long haul, sociologists would become state functionaries, their capital-intensive projects dependent upon corporate monopolies to introduce their questions and problems, their mental life given over to measurement at the expense of thinking. "The details, no matter how numerous, do not convince us of anything worth having convictions about" (Mills 1959, 55).

These observations and criticisms Mills drew directly out of his experience in Decatur. A casual reader would not have known this, for although he made Lazarsfeld the central figure in the chapter, he did not mention *Personal Influence* by name. Surely he kept it at the front of his mind. After all, he criticized authors who added a "literature of the problem" section to empirical data. This practice, he said, allowed casual readers to assume that the data had been shaped by theory, even when the data had come first and the "literature of the problem" had been added at the end to emboss the known results. Then there was the passage where he said the trouble with Lazarsfeld's method was not only that it generated a great number of trivial truths. "If you have ever seriously studied, for a year or two, some thousand hour-long interviews, carefully coded and punched, you will have begun to see how very malleable the realm of 'fact' may really be" (Mills 1959, 72).

The Sociological Imagination, Political Influence, and Backlash

The Sociological Imagination envisioned a social inquiry ranged around shared ethical convictions, rather than around a special set of techniques or a science of concepts. For Mills, these convictions bespoke freedom and reason as paramount values in human affairs. What is most important to grasp, though, is that his interpretation of social inquiry did not forsake fact-consciousness; Mills called for "a much broader style of empiricism" (Mills 1959, 68). Nor did it necessarily entail any particular political position. Mills's list of forerunners and exemplars included John Kenneth Gailbraith, Johan Huizinga, Harold Lasswell, Robert Lynd, Karl Mannheim, Gunnar Myrdal, David Riesman, Joseph Schumpeter, George Simmel, Arnold Toynbee, Max Weber, and William H. Whyte. Nor was he alone in his distaste for Lazarsfeld's methodology. In *Fads and Foibles in Modern Sociology*, Pitiram Sorokin blamed Lazarsfeld for an "epidemic of quantophrenia," and earned for his effort a letter of commendation from Mills (Sorokin 1956, 21-30, 122-30). Of the Bureau's influence in sociology, Hans Speier said, "certain analytical methods were refined, but the substantive questions that were being asked became shallower. Interest in the structure of modern society faded along with the interest in the fate of man in that society. As the techniques of *interviewing* became increasingly standardized, the art of *conversation*, which also provides civilized access to the life of the mind, deteriorated" (Speier 1989, 14).

In Western freethinking, there has been a consistent tendency to charge concept mongering and fact grubbing as twin villains in the crime of unreality. There has been, moreover, a tendency to view methodology as a science of mental estrangement, another form of ascetic self-annihilation. "I mistrust all systematizers and avoid them," Nietzsche wrote. "The will to a system is a lack of integrity" (Nietzsche 1968, 25). In the United States, Mills's protest against "methodological inhibition" goes at least as far back as the nineteenth-century academies and their bids for ecclesiastical guardianship over social knowledge. "It is plain that there are two classes in our educated community: first, those who confine themselves to the facts in their consciousness; and second, those who superadd sundry propositions. The aim of a true teacher now would be to bring men back to a true trust in God and destroy before their eyes these idolatrous propositions: to teach the doctrine of the perpetual revelation" (Emerson 1957, 119). Substitute "sociological imagination" for God in Emerson's commandment and you have the leitmotif of Mills's dissent.

The stricter the technical establishment of mind, the more elaborate the bureaucracy; the greater the seduction of antipolitics, the better the chance for misuse and exploitation. A scholar named Christopher Simpson has produced some evidence that appears to warrant the syllogism in the matter at hand. Happily, Simpson's evidence patches in the gap between December 1950, the last month Mills mentioned the Decatur project in his correspondence, and the publication five years later of *Personal Influence* (Simpson 1994).

According to Simpson, the Bureau of Applied Social Research received as much as 75 percent of its funding in this period from military and government propaganda agencies. This revelation should amend the accounting sheet for the Bureau to include not only corporate money, but state money. Yet the bare fact of state patronage says little in itself about the dispute between Mills and Lazarsfeld. They agreed that the Bureau's empirical methodology could aid in the study of propaganda. (Mills himself had won one of the Bureau's largest government contracts, from the Office of Naval Research.) Mostly, they differed on the ethical responsibilities of the inquirer. Here the matter grows thick indeed. For as Simpson goes on to observe, the State Department put the Bureau's "personal influence" methods at the center of its "psychological warfare" operations campaigns in the Middle East and Philippines. Lazarsfeld wrote the questions himself (Simpson 1994, 4, 55-57, 73-74). Mills opposed the American attempt to prop up the decaying British and French empires, and said so in his books. Lazarsfeld did not oppose the attempt, or if he did oppose it, he did not say so publicly, which amounted to the same thing. If this difference seems to be a mere historical fact, consider what the American attempt managed to accomplish. In 1953, military intelligence toppled the democratically elected prime minister of Iran, Mohammad Mossadegh. The CIA controlled the "opinion leaders" in the Tehran press almost completely.

Here stands one of the biggest blunders in American foreign policy, an augury of "regime change" and a plague on our daily news. Yet it was Lazarsfeld, not Mills, who carried the day at the conference that preceded this book. A large and active audience, an excellent group of panelists, an entire day devoted to retrospection, the privilege of historical knowledge—yet the connection passed, unmentioned. What *was* the connection between "personal influence," psychological warfare, opinion management, and the Middle East?

Before Mills, these kinds of questions were taboo in academic sociology. For graduate students and assistant professors on the margins of the profession, *The Sociological Imagination* was a source of wonder and liberation. But the official organs and leading representatives of sociology angrily rejected the book and the author. Edward Shils, whose writings on the "primary-group" supplied a theoretical armature for *Personal Influence*, rapped Mills on the knuckles in a nasty pair of essays (Shils 1960, 1961). Lewis Coser reproached him in *Partisan Review* (1960). Seymour Martin Lipset and Neil Smelser issued a declaration of his nonexistence in the *British Journal of Sociology* (1961). In a speech in Stresa, Italy, Robert Merton referred to (but did not name) a "little book by C. Wright Mills" as one of the "violent attacks" strafing sociology (Merton 1973).

The only public response Paul Lazarsfeld made to the book showed up at the end of a forward to a monograph about college students. There he claimed (apparently without intending any irony) that Mills promoted "a kind of sophisticated commercialism" (Lazarsfeld 1960, ix). In truth, Lazarsfeld did not know what to make of *The Sociological Imagination*, and he could not avoid thinking about it either. In an interview, he disburdened himself of his feeling of agitated confusion. "I find what Mills writes, you see, just ridiculous. There is nothing in the world he can, as a research man, contribute to anything, by what he's writing about, power or whatever it is and how bad the world is and so on. Why does he mix it up? I mean, why doesn't he leave us alone?" (Lazarsfeld 1973, 149).

The International Sociological Association Fiasco and Mills's Death

And this was how the whole thing ended. In the spring of 1961, the International Sociological Association (ISA) was planning for its next World

Congress. This Congress was coming to Washington, D.C., which meant that a joint meeting was going to be held with the American Sociological Association (ASA). Lazarsfeld, as president of the ASA, was going to chair the keynote panel, which was going to feature two American speakers. Probably nothing unusual would have happened if he had answered his mail. For the chair of the ISA's program committee sent him several letters asking for candidates for the keynote panel. The chair did not receive an answer, and as there was already some confusion concerning jurisdiction over the joint session, he went ahead and found a speaker on his own. Mills accepted right away. Lazarsfeld was flabbergasted.

"I obviously don't want to bring such matters up with the International Organization," he wrote to Talcott Parsons. "This letter is addressed to you as the ranking permanent officer of the American Association. I am sure you will find a way to cope with the problem" (Lazarsfeld 1961). Parsons concurred that the invitation to Mills was "extremely unfortunate." He would make some inquiries. "If it seems clear that this invitation was issued without any real clearing from the Association, I shall write a strong letter of protest" (Parsons 1961a). Parsons raised "the problem" during a meeting of the ASA's Committee on Organization and Plans in New York. And he enlisted the aid of Seymour Martin Lipset. Lipset and Lazarsfeld met in London with the chair of the ISA's program committee. They exerted the academic equivalent of diplomatic pressure.

The letters exchanged on "the problem" conveyed no speculations as to *what* Mills might talk about, should the invitation stand. Nor did they betray any qualms in conspiring against the world's most widely read American sociologist at the world's most prominent sociology congress. So far as the letters showed, Lazarsfeld, Parsons, and Lipset were unanimous in their desire to deprive Mills of his right to speak. They wished only to do so "without embarrassment" to the ASA, as Lipset stipulated (Lipset 1961). This they achieved. The ISA rescinded the invitation.

Because the ISA explained its decision to Mills on a false pretext suggested by Lipset, there was a chance the stratagem could collapse. "If Mills should insist on coming, I do not know what we can do," Lipset wrote (Lipset 1961).

But by the middle of July 1961, with no sign of trouble in view, Parsons relaxed. "I gather that the whole thing is now worked out and it will be one of the senior American 'organization men' who will do it" (Parsons 1961b).

Mills died the next year of a heart attack at age forty-five. Lazarsfeld and Merton, the men who urged him to New York in 1945, declined an invitation to attend his campus memorial service. Lazarsfeld refused even to write his widow a note of sympathy. It was not that he overlooked these gestures. "I absolutely refused even after his death to have anything to do with him," he said. "That is to say, I never regretted whatever harm I might have done. You see, I had the absolutely opposite feeling. Not only did I not regret . . . but I made it an external point not to take the slightest notice of whether he was dead or not" (see Gordon 1962, 369).

At least Lazarsfeld did not indulge any facile talk about the tragedy of it all. Perhaps he knew that without a genuine possibility of success, there can be no tragedy. Perhaps someone had finally told him that back in college, and then again in graduate school, Mills had flunked his statistics exams.

Appendix
Additional Sources

Lazarsfeld, Paul F. 1968. An episode in the history of social research: A memoir. *Perspectives in American History* 2:270-337.

———. 1975. *Oral memoir of Paul F. Lazarsfeld*. New York: Oral History Collection, American Jewish Committee, New York Public Library.

McCaughey, Robert A. 2003. *Stand, Columbia: A history of Columbia University in the city of New York, 1754-2004*. New York. Columbia University Press.

Mills, C. Wright. 1945. What women think of the U.S. 36 plan. *Decatur Sunday Herald*, November 25.

———. 1946a. Consumption: Leaders, relayers, and followers. Box 4B385, C. Wright Mills Papers, University of Texas, Austin.

———. 1946b. The influence study: Some conceptions and procedures of research, an address by C. Wright Mills to the American Association for the Advancement of Science in Boston. December 29, 1946. Box 10, Bureau of Applied Social Research Papers, Rare Book and Manuscript Library, Columbia University, New York.

———. 1946c. A line-up of movie leaders. April. Box 9, Bureau of Applied Social Research Papers, Columbia University Rare Books and Manuscript Library, New York.

———. 1947a. Mills to Lazarsfeld, "Memorandum: The Labor Research Division," Jan. 28, 1947, Box 4B368, C. Wright Mills Papers, University of Texas, Austin.

———. 1947b. Mills to Lazarsfeld, Memorandum: "Opportunities for Research in the Navy, and Other Related Matters," Jan. 1947, Box 4B368, C. Wright Mills Papers, University of Texas, Austin.

Sills, David L. 1987. Paul F. Lazarsfeld, February 13, 1901—August 30, 1976. *Biographical Memoirs* 56:251-81.

References

Barton, Allen. 1982. Paul Lazarsfeld and the invention of the university institute for applied social research. In *Organizing for social research*, ed. Burkart Holzner and Jiri Nehnevajsa. Cambridge, MA: Schenkman Publishing.

Bauman, Zygmunt, and Keith Tester. 2001. *Conversations with Zygmunt Bauman*. Cambridge: Polity.

Bernstein, Richard J. 1990. *The restructuring of social and political theory*. Philadelphia: University of Pennsylvania Press.

Converse, Jean M. 1987. *Survey research in the United States: Roots and emergence 1890-1960*. Berkeley: University of California Press.

Coser, Lewis. 1960. The uses of sociology. *Partisan Review* 2 (winter): 166-73.

Emerson, Ralph Waldo. 1957. *Selections from Ralph Waldo Emerson: An organic anthology*. Edited by Stephen E. Whicher. Boston: Houghton Mifflin.

Etzioni, Amitai. 2003. *My brother's keeper: A memoir and a message*. Lanham, MD: Rowman & Littlefield.

Gerth, Hans, and C. Wright Mills, eds. 1946. *From Max Weber: Essays in sociology*. New York: Oxford University Press.

Gordon, Joan. 1962. *Interview with Paul Lazarsfeld*, Aug. 26, 1962. Oral History Research Office, Columbia University, New York.

Katz, Elihu, and Paul F. Lazarsfeld. 1955. *Personal influence: The part played by people in the flow of mass communication*. Glencoe, IL: Free Press.

Lazarsfeld, Paul F. 1947. Audience research in the movie field. *Annals of the American Academy of Political and Social Science* 254:160-68.

———. 1960. Forward. In *What college students think*, ed. Rose K. Goldsen, Morris Rosenberg, Robin M. Williams Jr., and Edward A. Suchman. Princeton, NJ: Van Nostrand.

———. 1961. Lazarsfeld, Paul, to Talcott Parsons, May 22, 1961, Talcott Parsons Papers, Harvard University, Cambridge, MA.

———. 1973. *The reminiscences of Paul Felix Lazarsfeld.* 1973. New York: Oral History Research Office, Columbia University.

Lazarsfeld, Paul F., Bernard Berelson, and Hazel Gaudet. 1944/1948. *The people's choice: How the voter makes up his mind in a presidential campaign.* New York. Columbia University Press.

Lipset, Seymour Martin. 1961. Lipset, Seymour Martin to Talcott Parsons, June 26, 1961, Talcott Parsons Papers, Harvard University, Cambridge, MA.

Lipset, Seymour Martin, and Neil Smelser. 1961. Change and controversy in recent American sociology. *British Journal of Sociology* 12:50-51.

Merton, Robert K. 1940. Fact and factitiousness in ethnic opinionaires. *American Sociological Review* 5:13-28.

———. 1946. Merton, Robert to Albert D. Saloman, December 6, 1946; in the author's possession.

———. 1947a. Merton, Robert to C. Wright Mills, August 1, 1947; in the author's possession.

———. 1947b. Merton, Robert to Theodore Abel, Nov. 19, 1947; in the author's possession.

———. 1973. *The sociology of science: Theoretical and empirical investigations.* Edited by Norman W. Storer. Chicago: University of Chicago Press.

———. 1994. A life of learning. Charles Homer Haskins Lecture, American Council of Learned Societies Occasional Paper no. 25. http://www.acls.org/op25.htm.

Mills, C. Wright. 1945a. Mills, C. Wright, to Hans Gerth, Aug. 23, 1945; in the author's possession.

———. 1945b. Mills, C. Wright, to parents, Jan. 1945; in the author's possession.

———. 1946. The middle-classes in middle-sized cities. *American Sociological Review* 11:520-29.

———. 1950a. Mills, C. Wright, to Hans Gerth, December 18, 1950; in the author's possession.

———. 1950b. Public opinion. Box 4B375, C. Wright Mills Papers, University of Texas, Austin.

———. 1951. *White collar.* New York: Oxford University Press.

———. 1952. On intellectual craftsmanship. Columbiana Room, Columbia University Archives, New York.

———. 1953. Two styles of research in current social studies. *Philosophy of Science* 20 (October): 266-75.

———. 1954. IBM plus reality plus humanism = sociology. *Saturday Review of Literature*, May 1, pp. 22-23, 54.

———. 1956. *The power elite.* New York: Oxford University Press.

———. 1959. *The sociological imagination.* New York: Oxford University Press.

———. 2000. *C. Wright Mills: Letters and autobiographical writings.* Edited by Kathyrn Mills with Pamela Mills. Berkeley: University of California Press.

———. n.d. Mills to Lewis Coser, undated letter, Box 1, "Correspondence, 1947-1948," in Lewis A. Coser Faculty Papers, John J. Burns Library, Boston College, Chestnut Hill, Newton, MA.

Nietzsche, Friedrich. 1968. *Twilight of the idols/the anti-christ.* Translated by R. J. Hollingdale. London: Penguin.

Parsons, Talcott. 1961a. Parsons, Talcott to Paul Lazarsfeld, June 5, 1961, Talcott Parsons Papers, Harvard University, Cambridge, MA.

———. 1961b. Parsons, Talcott to Seymour Martin Lipset, July 13, 1961, Talcott Parsons Papers, Harvard University, Cambridge, MA.

Shils, Edward. 1960. Imaginary sociology. *Encounter* 14 (June): 77-80.

———. 1961. Professor Mills on the calling of sociology. *World Politics* 13 (July): 606-21.

Simpson, Christopher. 1994. *Science of coercion: Communications research and psychological warfare, 1945-1960.* New York. Oxford University Press.

Sorokin, Pitirim A. 1956. *Fads and foibles in modern sociology and related sciences.* Chicago: H. Regnery.

Speier, Hans. 1989. *The truth in hell and other essays on politics and culture, 1935-1987.* New York: Oxford University Press.

Personal Influence and the Bracketing of Women's History

By
SUSAN J. DOUGLAS

This article reviews both what *Personal Influence* revealed about the two-step flow within women's interpersonal networks and what it failed to capture about women's experiences during the tumultuous changes in gender roles between 1945, when the data were collected, and 1955, when the study was published. One of the central contradictions of the Decatur Study is that it simultaneously disguises that it is women who are being studied here yet universalizes them as representative of the general population. But the article also argues that despite the blind spots and ahistoricity of *Personal Influence*, it was a crucial reminder that women, despite being individual targets of much media fare, were also embedded in social networks through which they influenced other women and were, in turn, influenced by them.

Keywords: women; women and World War II; opinion leaders; gregariousness; Herta Herzog, *Personal Influence*

On the original, aqua-colored cover of *Personal Influence*, the subtitle reads, "The part played by *people* in the flow of mass communications."[1] The first question just below this subheading asks, "How do *people* exercise choice?" (italics added). Except for the small sketches on the cover showing women doing what they do best—shopping and gabbing on the phone—we would have no idea that "the people" the subtitle refers to are, indeed, all women. Inside, we learn on page 4 that the study "begins with a cross-section of women and then proceeds to identify the persons who are influential for these sample members," yet

Susan J. Douglas is the Catherine Neafie Kellogg Professor of Communication Studies at the University of Michigan. She is author of The Mommy Myth: The Idealization of Motherhood and How It Undermines Women *(with Meredith Michaels, Free Press, 2004),* Listening In: Radio and the American Imagination *(Times Books, 1999),* Where the Girls Are: Growing Up Female with the Mass Media *(Times Books, 1994; Penguin, 1995), and* Inventing American Broadcasting, 1899-1922 *(Johns Hopkins, 1987).*

DOI: 10.1177/0002716206292458

by constantly using the words "people," "respondents" "influential persons" and "consumers" in the introduction to the book, the fact that the entire study is focused on women is often effaced. Indeed, by also using the pronoun "he," as in "the leader is a strategic element in the formation of group opinions; he is more aware of what the several members think; he mediates between them; and he represents something like the 'typical' group-mind" (p. 9), the authors further mask who is being studied here. And while African Americans lived in Decatur and had their own cafes where people gathered, the study is silent about race; given the times, we assume that the people in the study were all white.

And the Decatur Study remains utterly silent on *why* it focuses solely on women, especially when opinion leaders were assumed to be male. Indeed, in the introduction to the study itself in part II of the book, we learn that opinion leaders are "the Key Men of a work-gang, the Sparkplugs of a salesman rally, the Elder Statesmen who sit on park benches talking for the newspapers" (p. 137). Two paragraphs later, without missing a beat, we learn that eight hundred *women* formed the core of this study to learn who influences whom and how. Why was the leap, in gender and realms of influence, made? Of course, we learn that MacFadden Publications, producers of women's magazines like *True Story*, were interested in how the two-step flow might play a role in the lives of "the wage earning class" and whether only the elites were or could be opinion leaders. They were also interested in whether the two-step flow worked beyond the realm of politics and in the area of everyday consumer choice. So one implication here is that if you wanted to get at both nonelites and those who were the major targets of magazine advertisers, then women indeed were exactly who you needed to study; they mattered, possibly more so than men, despite their lower overall status in society.

At the same time, by referring to the respondents as people and even with the pronoun "he," the researchers also do something rare then or now—have women serve as surrogates for the entire population, standing in for people as a whole.[2] Thus, one of the central contradictions of the Decatur Study is that it simultaneously disguises that only women are being studied and universalizes them as representative of the general population. The study represses what was distinctive to women's experiences in the 1940s; stereotypes them by focusing on their interest in fashion, marketing, and movies; and yet elevates women as exemplars for everyone. Here we have a path-breaking study of women's reception of and relations to the mass media that underplays that very fact and, as a result, misses enormous opportunities.

It is this tension and the routinely contradictory attitudes toward women in this study and, indeed, in the Bureau of Applied Social Research (BASR) that I wish to explore in this article. I also want to itemize how, by failing to address the rather convulsive changes in women's history and experiences between the time of the study, 1945, and publication of the book, 1955, *Personal Influence* perpetuated the rather retrograde notion that women's experiences are somehow timeless. The study also quarantined discussion of the similarly dramatic changes in the mass media environment, and women's uses of these media, during this period. In the following pages I want to review both what *Personal Influence* revealed about the two-step flow within women's interpersonal networks and what it failed to capture that we so much wish we knew.

With the advantage of hindsight, and fifty years' worth of advances in our field, not a few of them centrally informed by feminism, it is easy to identify the shortcomings of *Personal Influence*. So it is also important to keep in mind what it did accomplish, and to note that the precedent it established—to explore women's consumer choices at that nexus between media and interpersonal influence—has been all too rarely replicated. And let us remember that *Personal Influence* came out during the height of the Frankfurt School–influenced "mass culture" debates of the 1950s in which the allegedly narcotized, media-entranced masses were frequently assumed to be female; *Personal Influence* directly contradicted this assumption. So in this article I will review what *Personal Influence* did find out about women and girls of different ages and classes that we would do well to remember today.

Given the sociological goals and methods of the study, *Personal Influence* presents itself as a snapshot of social networks, the two-step flow, and, thus, of limited media influence. There is an authority to the Decatur Study that comes from its veneer of timelessness: it does not seem to matter much that the data were collected in 1945 but not published until ten years later; we are to assume the findings would be the same whenever. Historical change is bracketed. Women, it would seem, are outside of history, a constant, unchanging category.

But the three-hundred-pound gorilla sitting in the room *is* history and, in particular, both women's history and media history. It is a fool's game to try to label any ten-year period as *the* most turbulent and fraught with change for women, but certainly, 1945 to 1955 would be right up there. (Indeed, given the war and its end, the G.I. Bill, the expansion of white-collar jobs, and the baby boom, this was also a time of major transformations for men as well.) From 1941 through 1945, American women were confronted, paradoxically, by a more intensive and yet constrained media environment. On one hand, in the movies, in magazines (although maybe not *True Story*), on the radio, and in newspapers, women were subject to one of the most concentrated, coordinated propaganda campaigns ever designed to get them to enter the workforce and to assume jobs previously held by men.[3] This campaign involved getting women to see their skills and capabilities quite differently, to see themselves as producers and citizens rather than as consumers, and, most important, to reimagine gender roles and boundaries in new and often reversed ways. On the other hand, the moratorium on advertising certain consumer goods and the restrictions on manufacturing these goods during the war meant that the commercial media environment surrounding women was more spare of consumer goods and their accompanying appeals than it had been or would be in a few years. In June 1945, women were carefully managing their food rations; in 1955, they were surrounded by an endless media parade of consumer goods just there for the buying. And millions were able to buy these goods because they were working for wages. And let us not forget that in 1945, so many men were still absent from Decatur, fighting in the war and serving the government in other capacities. By 1955, many were back home, so the social dynamic in Decatur had changed significantly between the time of the study and its publication.

Despite the roller-coaster changes in expectations about women's roles and the dramatically mixed messages women received from the media during this period, *Personal Influence* divided women into seemingly eternal "Life-Cycle Types": the transition from girlhood to womanhood (in which a girl's "major concern" is marriage), motherhood, and "older matronhood" (p. 223). In this biology-as-destiny schema, puberty, reproduction, and menopause provide handy, overarching categories. Nowhere does work outside the home, the war, and women's participation in both enter into the picture.

> *[N]owhere does the role or influence of being in the workforce (or the military) appear as a factor in a woman being—or not being—an opinion leader.*

Yet between 1941 and 1945, more than 6 million women responded to the government's campaign by entering the workforce, and 250,000 joined the armed forces. The vast majority of those who had taken up employment during the war wanted to keep their jobs. But beginning in 1945, another campaign began, the one to persuade women to return to their kitchens and to pre-1940 conceptions of gender roles and women's place. Women were the first to be laid off from industry jobs—in 1946 alone 4 million were fired—and were warned not to steal jobs from deserving returning veterans. By the late 1940s, popular psychologists were labeling women who would not comply as neurotic, castrating, and suffering from "penis envy."[4] Nonetheless, the percentage of women in the workforce continued to increase every year after the war; by 1955, nearly 36 percent of women were working outside the home, more than at any point in the nation's previous history.[5] Yet nowhere does the role or influence of being in the workforce (or the military) appear as a factor in a woman being—or not being—an opinion leader.

It is true that in 1945 Decatur was no San Diego, Baltimore, or Portland when it came to women working in war industries. But even in Illinois—skewed, of course, by Chicago—28.6 percent of the state's workforce was female by 1950. As a reading of the town's newspapers reveals, Decatur women worked in war industries, drove taxis, taught at the local university, and served in the military.

Articles and want ads from the *Decatur Herald* and the *Decatur Review* show that there were various industries in town, including steel companies, brass works, auto accessories production companies, the Crown-Cork Specialty Company that made cans and bottle tops, and the A.W. Cash Valve Manufacturing Company. The want ads for June to August 1945 (when C. Wright Mills and his mostly female research team were collecting their data), segregated by gender as most want ads were back then, show that women were both recruited for traditional women's jobs such as hairdresser, saleslady, waitress, stenographer, and maid (some of which specified "white" only), but also for light manufacturing jobs, telegraph operations at Western Union, and work at the Sangamon Ordnance Plant. The women's pages of the papers reported on Decatur women serving in the Red Cross overseas, getting master's degrees in mathematics, serving in the military, and presiding as the head psychologist at the local Family Service Agency. These papers suggest that many women's experiences in Decatur were often as varied and contradictory as women around the country during this time of enormous social flux.

Let us also note briefly the broader historical context that was shaping these women's lives and engagement with the media. World War II was grinding down to its grisly end in 1945. In January, Russian troops liberated Auschwitz and discovered five thousand starving survivors and thousands more dead. Churchill, Roosevelt, and Stalin met in Yalta; Roosevelt died in April with Truman assuming the presidency. In May, the Germans surrendered, and the bloody battle for Okinawa ended in June. The United Nations was formed. And of course, during the second wave of interviews in Decatur in August, atomic bombs fell on Hiroshima and Nagasaki. These were all major front-page stories in the national and local press that provide the context for these women's lives when they were interviewed.

To begin to identify those who served as opinion leaders, or what they called "general influentials," the researchers asked the women, "Do you know anyone around here who keeps up with the news and whom you can trust to let you know what is really going on?" "About half . . . were unable or unwilling to name anyone within their acquaintance whose competence and trustworthiness in public affairs they accepted to let them know 'what is really going on.' " Nonetheless, we learn that 40 percent of older women who did not finish high school and 64 percent of younger women who had finished high school indeed named such a person. Yet the researchers quickly concluded, "Many women are simply out of the public affairs market" (p. 140). While we do not know what "many" equals, this assertion is not completely sustained by the evidence offered. And while the Decatur newspapers are relatively silent on this issue, they did feature photographs of women voting and staffing the local polling places in June of 1945; one photograph featured the country court probation officer, a woman. A major public lecture in town on June 1 featured Geraldine Chappell, a military nurse who had been imprisoned by the Japanese for three years in Manila.[6]

Not surprisingly, two-thirds of the "general influentials" the women named were men: husbands, neighbors, fathers, friends. What is interesting is that one-third

are women, and when women influentials were named they were more likely to
be a neighbor or friend than a relative, suggesting that at least in some female circles outside the home, current affairs and politics were indeed being discussed.
Also tantalizing is that, when asked whether they discussed what they heard on
the radio or read in the newspapers with others before making up their minds,
about half said they did not, complicating the two-step flow theory (p. 143). In
addition to an exploration of public affairs decisions, the researchers focused on
three other areas of decision making: choices in the supermarket, fashion
choices, and movie choices. Interestingly, given the prevailing controversies
about child rearing, panics about "latchkey children," the ongoing terrors of polio
in 1945, and women's expertise in these areas, decision making about parenting
was not included. This was, of course, years before the personal became political.
And it was consumer choices, not women's knowledge or opinions, that
MacFadden cared about.

One of the most telling and insightful categories the researchers developed
was that of "gregariousness": the extent of a woman's contact with other people,
which was measured by the number of her friendships and her club-oriented
social activity. The authors found that "the higher a woman's status, the greater
the range of her social activity," but they also documented the relative social isolation of young women and young wives of lower status (pp. 223-31). So status
and gregariousness were linked, and both helped determine whether a woman
was an opinion leader.

The Decatur papers document why "gregariousness" was such an astute category to analyze. The *Herald* and the *Daily Review* were typical small-town papers
that specialized in local announcements of club activities and the social comings
and goings of some of its citizens, and thus we get a sense of the quite extraordinary proliferation of organizations to which girls and women belonged in 1945.
Of course there was a 4-H club, and the YWCA hosted meetings for the wives,
sisters, and sweethearts of servicemen. But there were all kinds of announcements for potluck dinners, picnics, recitals, and, because Milliken University was
in town, sorority activities as well. There was a group dedicated to music called
"Mothersingers" (all the officers were female), the American Legion Auxiliary
Club for Women, the National Catholic Council of Women, a Past Worthy
Matrons Club of the Eastern Star, the Women's Progressive Club, the White
Rose Club, the Decatur Women's Council, the Mt. Zion Junior Women's Club,
and so on and so forth. One wonders whether, in 1955, with the daily responsibilities of raising all those baby boomer children, women had the time to continue with this level of club participation. Certainly this is a quite different social
terrain from the one most women inhabit today and raises the question of how
researchers, if they were going to replicate aspects of this study, would capture
"gregariousness" in the early twenty-first century.

The *Decatur Herald* indicates that there were at least six movie theaters in
town, many of which showed double features, and during the time of the study
they were showing *Nevada* with Robert Mitchum, *Our Hearts Were Young and
Gay*, *Irish Eyes Are Smiling*, *Hangover Square* with Linda Darnell, and the

Abbott and Costello comedy *Here Come the Coeds*. The ads for these movies provide a glimpse of the complicated address to women: some promoted romantic fantasies while others hailed women as independent and strong. (Indeed, a regularly featured comic strip in the paper was *Flyin' Jenny*, about a woman military pilot.) A movie about Joseph Goebbles was titled *Enemy of Women*. The ad for *A Song to Remember* with Paul Muni and Merle Oberon had the teaser "I wore the trousers to remind men I was equal . . .". The next day the ad read, "She made her own rules of love! She made her own rules for living! What she set out to do . . . SHE DID!" How we wish we knew which of these films women urged each other to go see, and why.

Personal Influence, following in the footsteps of *The People's Choice*,[7] further documented the importance of the two-step flow. Given the techniques available at the time, the researchers had to rely on self-reports about the relative influence of the media versus the influence of friends and family on consumer choices. Here, the media emerge as not nearly as important as word of mouth when women made choices about marketing and movies. But the opinion leaders they turned to read more magazines, newspapers, and books and listened to the radio more often than did those they influenced, so the mass media remained an important resource as part of the nexus and diffusion of decision making. Indeed, as even the limited effects school acknowledged, the media had its greatest influence in shaping peoples' ideas about events and trends that were remote and about which people had little firsthand knowledge, which was the case with world affairs and fashion.

The study also found important class-based differences in zones of influence. While not quite stating it this way, *Personal Influence* found that in the realm of more private, personal, domestic decisions, influence among women tended to move laterally, within class/status groups; but that in the realm of public affairs, authority was more of a top-down affair, with high-status, gregarious women being the most sought out opinion leaders. So in those areas where female knowledge was privileged and deemed superior to men's, certain women in all SES groups could be opinion leaders to others in their group. But in an area of knowledge deemed to be the province of men, women whose education, class status, and spheres of influence made them, well, more like men could exert influence on those below them in status. In addition, certain of these women were deemed "cosmopolitans": people concerned with news and trends outside of their own community who consumed national media that originated elsewhere, like New York or Washington. Not surprisingly, it was these cosmopolitans who were the leaders in fashion and public affairs.

What is difficult to determine from this study is the role of the third-person effect in shaping some of the results. When asked about decisions to change from buying one product brand of, say, coffee, cereal, or soap flakes to another, the respondents reported that personal contacts had the most influence, magazine and newspaper advertising the least; and of those exposed to radio advertising, only 7.5 percent reported it to have affected their choices (pp. 176-77). More emphatically, women insisted overwhelmingly that newspapers and magazines played a minimal role in influencing their choice of movies to attend and, also, that magazines and newspapers were not effective in persuading them to change their hair or clothing styles (pp. 179-82). As the media historian Kathy Newman has recently shown, a backlash against advertising and the hypercommercialization of radio was brewing in the 1940s, and women were hardly oblivious to the massive propaganda campaigns on all levels at work during the war (including the one directed at them), so we do not know the extent to which the women of Decatur sought to distance themselves from these media machinations.[8] Nonetheless, the fashion leaders, not surprisingly, admitted to being influenced by the media; after all, fashion magazines and movies set themselves up as the arbiters of glamour and the latest styles, so it would be gauche not to be informed by them. Indeed, certain department store ads for women's clothing in the Decatur papers made a point of emphasizing "as seen in *Vogue*." It is in these interstices of the study that we begin to get glimmering clues of what we so want to know: which media, but more specifically, which movies, or ads, or radio shows grabbed these women, and which ones did not?

So, given what we do learn about informal networks and their influences, there is still so much more that we wish the Decatur Study had told us about these women. Not one of the public affairs questions in the survey is about women and work, changing gender roles, or child rearing, where women are expected to produce the future citizens of the nation and where there was much controversy during and after the war. We learn virtually nothing about these women's attitudes toward different media or their content. We do not know which ads or news events or movies stood out for the women who were opinion leaders and which ones did not. Not ever on the table here was what meanings women made of the media texts they attended to, and how one element of personal influence—seeing certain behaviors or attitudes in the movies, for example, and then passing those on to others—might have operated. What is missing is their voices.

Here is where one wishes for the keen sensibilities of Herta Herzog. In her work for the Office of Radio Research (ORR) on quiz shows and soap operas, Herzog pioneered what we might now call "uses and gratifications" and was keenly interested in how people projected themselves into media texts, measuring their knowledge, skills, and troubles against those on the air.[9] With Herzog, we got the dirt—accounts from listeners themselves about what radio programs meant to them. This is no limited effects hypothesis—her work assumed that women saw the media as available cultural materials, as offering behavioral resources and building blocks for them to use. She also appreciated that women liked to talk back to radio and to feel, at times, superior to the characters or quiz show contestants they listened to. She found listeners to be, by turns, active and passive ("semi-active," as she termed it), and to inhabit multiple, often conflicting subject positions as they listened. As I have noted elsewhere, Herzog was years ahead of her time in anticipating the poststructuralist appreciation of how the media hail people in contradictory ways and cultivate fragmented subjectivity.[10]

Herzog's brand of research remained dormant in the 1950s, but the study of women's often deeply contradictory relationship to the media, including "down market" fare like soap operas and romance novels, gained new life in the wake of the women's movement. Indeed, it was, in part, feminist reaction against the limited effects model, as embodied in *Personal Influence*, that gave rise to new pathbreaking work on gender and the media.

Feminist scholars took up this work because they recognized the absolute centrality of the mass media to women's sense of self, to their possibilities, and to sustaining prejudices that kept women as second-class citizens. The explosive changes in the mass media between 1945 and 1955, and their possible effects on women, also were not addressed in *Personal Influence*. By 1955, despite the fact that more women were working outside the home than ever before, the mass media hailed women as housewives, mothers, and consumers, not as producers or citizens. And let us not forget that in 1945 there was no TV; by 1955, 65 percent of American households had one. TV and magazines brought an explosive rise of advertising for consumer goods, much of it directed to women. In other words, how the mass media sought to hail, influence, and constitute women went through seismic and deliberate upheavals during this period. A major takeaway message from the study—"In regard to marketing, then, the impact of informal personal advice is greater than the impact of mass media advertising" (p. 178)— might indeed have been true about specific product choices. But what *Personal Influence* did not concern itself with was the broader impact of the discourses of advertising, or other media, on consumer culture and the ideology of gender roles. It was precisely because the Decatur Study remained silent on this broader issue and relied, probably too readily, on women's self-reports of being minimally or ineffectively influenced by the media, that feminist scholars challenged its findings and basic assumptions about the media's power.

Personal Influence *was a crucial reminder that women, despite being individual targets of much media fare, were also embedded in social networks through which they influenced other women and were, in turn, influenced by them.*

Despite the blind spots and ahistoricity of *Personal Influence*, the Decatur Study paid explicit attention to women's reception of media messages and to their influence on other women in areas where women traditionally made the major decisions—shopping, fashions, and movies—and an area where they did not, public affairs. Thus, *Personal Influence* pioneered the study of the flow of influence among women about products and information first laid before them in the mass media. One could claim that, with the exception of *The Feminine Mystique*, which implicitly argued against limited effects and for the media's powerful influence in promulgating sexist stereotypes of women, no comparable attention was again paid to women as audiences of the media until the early 1970s and the rise of feminist media studies scholarship. Thus, *Personal Influence* was a crucial reminder that women, despite being individual targets of much media fare, were also embedded in social networks through which they influenced other women and were, in turn, influenced by them. Too few studies today—exceptions such as Janice Radway's *Reading the Romance*[11] stand out—have picked up the lead of the Decatur Study to analyze how media representations become transmitted, prioritized, or dismissed among different networks of women and girls. Rereading the book reminds one how much still needs to be done here by scholars about the interactions between individual girls and women, their social networks, and the mass media.

Notes

1. All quotations are from the first edition, Elihu Katz and Paul F. Lazarsfeld, *Personal Influence: The Part Played by People in the Flow of Mass Communications* (Glencoe, IL: Free Press, 1955).

2. I am grateful to Pete Simonson for pointing this out.

3. Susan J. Douglas, *Where the Girls Are: Growing Up Female with the Mass Media* (New York: Times Books, 1994), pp. 45-46.

4. Ibid., 47.

5. Ibid., 55.

6. *The Decatur Daily*, June 1, 1945, p. 1.

7. Paul F. Lazarsfeld, Bernard Berelson, and Hazel Gaudet, *The People's Choice* (New York: Columbia University Press, 1948).

8. Kathy M. Newman, *Radio Active: Advertising and Consumer Activism, 1935-1947* (Berkeley: University of California Press, 2004).

9. See Herta Herzog's study of "Professor Quiz" in Paul F. Lazarsfeld, *Radio and the Printed Page* (New York: Duell, Sloan & Pierce, 1940).

10. For further discussion of Herzog's contributions to audience research, see Susan L. Douglas, *Listening In: Radio and the American Imagination* (Minneapolis: University of Minnesota Press, 2004).

11. Janice Radway, *Reading the Romance* (Chapel Hill: University of North Carolina Press, 1984).

The Influences Influencing *Personal Influence:* Scholarship and Entrepreneurship

By
DAVID E. MORRISON

The article examines how the study that resulted in *Personal Influence* came to be funded by *True Story* magazine. It does so by looking at Lazarsfeld's research career. Lazarsfeld is seen as an institutional innovator in higher education, having established in Vienna in 1925 the first social science research center of its kind in the world, and later the Bureau of Applied Social Research at Columbia University. The structural situation of the Bureau is examined in detail, showing how Lazarsfeld developed the role of entrepreneurial scholar to finance its operations. The article examines Lazarsfeld's psychological makeup, which meshed well with the world of business as well as the Bureau's need for commercial fund-raising. Having given the context of Lazarsfeld's operations, the final part of the article examines how the study was "sold" to *True Story* magazine.

Keywords: *Personal Influence*; Lazarsfeld; *True Story* magazine; Katz

In 1980, Peter Rossi titled his presidential address to the American Sociological Association "The Challenge and Opportunities of Applied Social Research." His opening lines read, "The stance of our profession toward applied work of all sorts in sociology has been one of considerable ambivalence" (Rossi 1980, 889). This is added to a few lines further on: "Indeed, some of our colleagues gloss over their applied work as if it were a vice best kept

David E. Morrison is a professor of communications research at the Institute of Communications Studies, University of Leeds, United Kingdom. He has held several university research appointments. He has also worked in market research, holding the position of director at Research International, where he was head of media. His research interests include audience research, news-gathering processes and news reporting, methodological development, and the history of communications research.

NOTE: The article owes much to Benjamin Peters, a doctorate candidate at Columbia University, both for his research in the Bureau archives on papers related to the financing of *Personal Influence* and for his insightful comments and interpretation of material.

DOI: 10.1177/0002716206292864

from public view." Getting into the body of his address and into his stride, Rossi comes to the defense of applied social research in face of the low esteem he perceives it is awarded by presenting the case of *Personal Influence:* "How many of us recall (or ever knew) that Lazarsfeld's seminal work on personal influence (Katz and Lazarsfeld 1955/2006) stemmed from very applied work financed by Macfadden Publications in an effort to obtain evidence that would convince would-be advertisers that placing ads in *True Story* magazine would reach opinion leaders?" (Rossi 1980, 894)

In a strict sense, Rossi should have referred to the seminal work of Katz and Lazarsfeld, but in the circumstances of pressing his point about applied social research then to focus on Lazarsfeld, the arch, and some might add villain,[1] extoller of applied social research, it is understandable.[2] The fact is, however, that if not for the efforts of Elihu Katz it is questionable whether the study would ever have seen the light of day. As it was, it took ten years from commission to publication. Allen Barton, one-time director of the Bureau of Applied Social Research, the institutional base of the study,[3] said,

> The fact that the book appeared ten years after the study was fielded is one of those Bureau stories—C. Wright Mills was supposed to produce a manuscript but instead took the salary and worked on *White Collar*.[4] Then a whole series of people tried to write up the study. Finally Elihu Katz came to the rescue, combining his review of small groups and network research, part I, with the analysis of the Decatur (site of the study) survey, part II. (Personal communication, February 9, 2006)[5]

To extend Barton's account, it would appear that part one of *Personal Influence* grew out of, or was intertwined with, both a report to the Ford Foundation written by Katz for Lazarsfeld and Katz's doctorate thesis.

The background here is that Lazarsfeld had been appointed in the summer of 1952 to become head of an Advisory Committee on Television, established by the Ford Foundation, which would take evidence and write reports to guide the Foundation in its planned entry into television research. The Committee was to report in the summer of 1953 (Morrison 2000). The Bureau had an "Implementation Committee" for which a series of reports were written on a range of topics, one being by Katz in 1953. This report, perhaps written directly for Lazarsfeld, was packaged off to the Foundation, but it was also to form not only part of Katz's doctorate but the basis for part one of *Personal Influence*. In referring to the report, his doctorate, and part one, Katz recounted, "My best guess is that Part One was written for PL and for my PhD dissertation—and I can't even say which came first (draft of thesis or idea of Part One). It became a Report—I'm guessing as fodder to show Ford how hard the Bureau was working on the project" (Katz, personal communication, April 6, 2006).

The above certainly has the ring of Lazarsfeld about it, of packaging and repackaging writing. Any piece of writing, report, research proposal, and so on could and would be made to serve more than one purpose should the opportunity or necessity occur. Thus, one can see with part one of *Personal Influence* that its formation is not straightforward, added to which, the study grows out of a complex machinery for research, making it difficult at times to trace lines of direction or influence at various points in the production process.

Research Organization

The acknowledgements to the 1955 edition of the book show just how many people worked on or assisted with the study, including Peter Rossi. As Katz points out in his foreword to the 2006 edition, "Work of this scale cannot be done alone" (Katz and Lazarsfeld 1955/2006, XVII). Indeed, it cannot. Nor can work of this nature be undertaken without an organizational structure capable of managing the various components necessary for the production of such knowledge.

It is the organization of knowledge, its institutionalization and funding, that the rest of the article will address. For while *Personal Influence* has rightfully come to occupy one of the intellectual peaks of mass communications research, its facilitation was a dependent of a development in the organization of knowledge, namely, the research bureau or center.

The development of research bureaus in the 1940s and 1950s represented a new organizational form of intellectual life more appropriate for large-scale empirical social research than the traditional structure of a teaching department. They involved a hierarchy of roles: organization along specialist functions, teamwork, fund-raising, financial research management, and training in research skills of junior members. Above all, such developments saw the creation of an absolutely new intellectual role: that of the managerial or entrepreneurial scholar not just capable of managing a research organization but also able to sell research.

Rossi has already been quoted as mentioning that *Personal Influence* was funded by *True Story* magazine. The nature of the association with Macfadden Publications, who owned *True Story* magazine, will be detailed later, but it is worth picking up here Rossi's point about applied social research lacking respectability in the eyes of sections of the academic community. If that was so at the time of Rossi's presidential address in 1980, how much more so was this in the early 1940s when *Personal Influence* was commissioned? Amusingly, and ironically, Bernard Berelson, in discussing the suspicion of many academics at Columbia toward Lazarsfeld, said, "I can still hear Wright Mills saying, 'Why, Paul Lazarsfeld works for *True Story* magazine' as if no self-respecting academic of any persuasion would do that." He then added, "Paul always felt, 'I don't understand what Wright is complaining about. These people are generous with the research funds, they allow me to raise questions . . . we have the opportunity to do the Decatur study' " (Berelson interview, July 12, 1973, New York).

The industry was generous in support of Lazarsfeld's research. Indeed, without such benefaction there would have been no Bureau of Applied Social Research to even contemplate undertaking the work for Macfadden Publications. Lazarsfeld was only too aware of this. In discussing the foreword that he wrote for *Culture for the Millions* (Jacobs 1959), where he attempts a conciliatory position between the culture critics and the industry apologists, he mentioned that he became "really interested in the mass culture debate" because of his "ambiva-lence." As he explained, "On the one hand I got money from the industry—every-thing depended on that—and on the other hand I was tied to a team—my union card as a socialist" (Lazarsfeld interview, June 15, 1973, New York). "Everything," by which he means his whole research operation and activities, did indeed depend on support from the media industry. His reference to his "union card as a socialist" is to his time among the Austro-Marxists of the Social Democratic Party in Vienna, but it is interesting, and will be raised later, that even in this exchange one can see how Lazarsfeld is capable of addressing different con-stituencies without apparent difficulty. There is no such thing for Lazarsfeld as the audience, but audiences, each one requiring to be spoken to differently. The same study delivered to different audiences would be made to tell a different story—the story that he wanted to interest them in, which by extension would be of advantage to him. This was a superb skill, or trait, in raising research monies in that one story could be delivered to a business audience and find favor with them, but when told a different way would find favor with an academic audience (see Pooley 2006).

Nevertheless, the skills he had of playing to his audience, or what in business terms might be called market segmentation to put it politely, could not offer com-plete protection, merely limit the fallout. As noted by Berelson, his very rela-tionship with the world of business brought challenge. His enmeshment with the media industry, at one point, made even those close to him question his commit-ment to academic life. Robert Lynd, for example, who had been Lazarsfeld's key supporter at Columbia, said to John Marshall of the Rockefeller Foundation responsible for overseeing the Rockefeller-funded Princeton Radio Research Project, of which Lazarsfeld was director, that Lazarsfeld must make his mind up whether he would prefer a research career within industry or the university research sector. Lynd had become concerned about the offers of research con-sultancy being made to Lazarsfeld. He wrote, "The acceptance of any consul-tancy such as outlined will make it necessary for Lazarsfeld to decide which of the two alternatives confronting him he is to take . . . Lazarsfeld has always said he preferred academic research but he must now decide" (Marshall's summary of conversation with Lynd, April 21, 1941, Rockefeller Archives). We will see later, however, that acting as a consultant for a media group brought him into direct contact with a senior research figure at Macfadden Publications, the "buyer" of the *Personal Influence* study.

In somewhat the same way that Lazarsfeld refused to be confined within a particular field by the acceptance of some disciplinary label (Boudon 1972, 418), his operating world was not confined to any particular sector—business, univer-sity, government. This brought problems. Although Lynd might have been a big supporter of Lazarsfeld, this did not stop him being suspicious of the operating practices of the Bureau. Patricia Kendall, Lazarsfeld's third wife, talking of her time as a graduate student at the Bureau, mentioned that she had a university fel-lowship that stipulated that she must not accept any payment from other organi-zations: "Lynd got quite excited. I was working at the Bureau in addition to having the university fellowship—so he was very much on the lookout, watching what the Bureau was doing." Evidently, Lynd "felt the Bureau was a trivial enterprise and discouraged people from working at the Bureau." According to Kendall, who actually worked on the *Personal Influence* project, the attitude of some faculty members toward the Bureau was mirrored at the student level.

> Well, as I say there was a schism between the students who were theoreticians and didn't want anything to do with the Bureau and those of us who were more empirical, and wanted to work on these kinds of studies even though we were doing the most menial kind of tasks. Some of us were very pleased to work there. I'm sure I started publishing much earlier than my classmates. I started to publish with Paul and Bob Merton. (Kendall interview, June 9, 1973, New York)

Be that as it may, some students felt exploited. According to Lewis Coser, Lazarsfeld always wanted his research organizations to be more than a place of work, namely, "collaborative *Gemeinschaften* rather than tightly organized bureaucratic machines" but he then observes that "those who worked in the organized chaos did not always find it the happy *Gemeinschaft* that Lazarsfeld dreamed of. Some graduate students complained that they were not really being trained by learning through doing but were in fact exploited drudges" (Coser 1984, 114, 115).

It is important to understand the training situation and work principles of the Bureau to fully understand the context surrounding and from within which the *Personal Influence* study emerged. After all, Katz was only a graduate student when he was co-opted onto the study.

Training, Commerce, and Opportunity

There is evidence, as recorded by Pratt in his report on the in-service training program of the Bureau, that although a dominant motive for joining the Bureau was to gain research experience, in practice the students were not "generally selected for learning potentials, but because of an already established skill that fits a given existing need" (Pratt 1954, 53). While he notes that training is one of the Bureau's goals, he points to the fact that "projects are not selected first and foremost for their training potential" and mentions "the sponsor assumes both qualified personnel and unitary policy objectives and agrees to the budget on this basis" (Pratt 1954, 53).

Given the commercial pressure to "perform," it is perhaps not surprising that most of the students' time was taken up with the mastery of routine research procedures, the most complex aspects being left to senior researchers. The depth of training given was questionable. Of the sample of trainees studied by Pratt, the majority spent between six and eight months at the "Bureau" but had worked on remarkably few jobs—33 percent had held one position, 30 percent two, and 30 percent three. No trainee had occupied more than five jobs. Even for those who had managed to extend the number of projects worked upon, it is doubtful that it involved much of an extension of their training, the skills required, or work given, being fairly similar for each job. The most frequently learned skills, or improved skills, were machine tabulation, table construction, search techniques, coding, and preliminary and revision report writing. The least frequently learned or improved skills were those involved in analysis, design, and the final drafting of reports (Pratt 1954, 96). Indeed, the principle of hiring as opposed to training is evinced very clearly in the fact that "at all levels improvement of skill was as frequent as first learning" (Pratt 1954, 98). In other words, the student was basically employed to fit the research goals, and these goals were not modified to accommodate the need of trainees. This is not to deny that valuable training took place; even where skills had already been acquired, the value of applying them in concrete practice by working on "real" as opposed to imaginary projects should not be underestimated. As Kendall recalled,

> Some of us disapproved, no not disapproved, felt reluctant about some of the studies that were taken on. The first study I did on my own was Sloan's Liniment (an embrocation). I felt it was a pity . . . it was good experience for me. It was a very trivial study. It gave me experience and brought in a small amount of money to the Bureau. (Kendall interview)

Business as Usual

The position of the graduate student at the Bureau is an interesting one. As stated, Katz was only a graduate student when he began work on *Personal Influence*, and in effect rescued it, for which Lazarsfeld was so grateful that he did not exercise the director's "right" of first name authorship. It might seem amazing, certainly it would be now, that a graduate student could become responsible for one of the major texts in the history of mass communications research, but it says much for the opportunity structures available at the Bureau that a graduate student could accede to the role of coauthoring *Personal Influence*.

While accepting that a constellation of factors came together to make the study somewhat unusual, not least the situation with Mills, and the extended period from commission to publication—ten years—the fact is that *Personal Influence* should not be viewed much differently, or at least not so in terms of operating logic, from other market research contracts worked on at the Bureau. True, it was much larger in terms of size, complexity, and conceptual sophistication, and substantive interest than the type of commercial or applied projects that made up many of the studies of the type mentioned by Kendall, but its coming into being is framed by the same approach to the organization and support of research that characterized the Bureau and Lazarsfeld's managerial style.

Organizational and Managerial Style

In the interview with Berelson, the whole question of the attacks on Lazarsfeld for his type of work was raised. He said,

It wasn't a political criticism, and in many ways it wasn't even—I think it is fair to say—
a scientific or academic criticism. It was a little of that . . . that it wasn't theoretical
enough, it was all dirty empiricism, fact grubbing and so on. It was a little unfair, but a
large part of it was sort of personal on a grand scale.

The personal nature of the criticism, according to Berelson, stemmed from the
fact that the "academics didn't really trust him." Asked to explain, he said: "Well,
you know how it is with academics—he was too pushy, he was foreign, he was too
bright . . . and he was too tied up with the business and commercial world." Not
only that, "he was supporting this personal institute of his which attracted all sorts
of bright young people around Columbia, and this was a source of resentment."
These "bright young people" of course included Elihu Katz. It was, however, his
commercial activity that raised real resentment in some quarters, and alarm in
others: Berelson continued, "With commercial contracts he was always wheeling
as he was doing it—as indeed he was—with a kind of sleight of hand. You know
the joke around the Bureau was that you paid the deficit of the last study with the
grant from the next study, and that's how people lived around there" (Berelson
interview).

It might seem amazing, certainly it
would be now, that a graduate student
could become responsible for one of
the major texts in the history of mass
communications research.

The paying the deficit of a study by the money of a new study was not a joke
in the manner suggested by Berelson. It was a fact. One might even raise the fact
to the level of a habit, or if one wished to dignify the practice consider it part and
parcel of Lazarsfeld's management strategy. It was certainly something that he
had engaged in to survive bankruptcy in the running of the Österreichische
Wirtschaftspsychologische Forschungsstelle[6] that he established in Vienna in
1925. His first wife, Maria Jahoda,[7] commenting on the Forschungsstelle, said,
"Paul was a messy administrator. He paid for an old study with the money from
a new study and of course the books didn't add up" (Jahoda interview, September
26, 1973, Sussex, UK).

This continuation of practices between Vienna and New York may have been
familiar to Lazarsfeld, but it was not so for Columbia University, nor approved.

In what must be an understatement of historic proportion, Lazarsfeld recalled, "In the first year or two at Columbia all the contracts were made by me on my personal account and then salaries were paid that way as well. It was a most unlikely situation and I think if the Bureau of Internal Revenue would ever have looked at it, I might have been in great trouble" (Lazarsfeld interview, June 2, 1973, New York).

Forced Behavior and Inescapable Practices

The practice of Lazarsfeld acting as personal banker may have gone on as late as 1945, but no matter. On October 25, 1944, the Cheatham Committee, under the chairmanship of Elliot Cheatham, professor of law, was set up at Columbia by the University Council for Research in the Social Sciences to examine the running and operation of the Bureau. This coincided with the beginning of the Decatur study, preparations for which were made in the autumn of 1944, with fieldwork beginning in the spring of 1945. Thus, Lazarsfeld was not only defending the Bureau to the University, but at the same time engaging in one of the Bureau's most major works, supported by industry funds that had, ironically, raised questions about the Bureau's operations in the first place. The Committee declared that the Bureau had been acting illegally in accepting research accounts, in that "neither the Bureau nor the Department of Sociology is a legal entity" (Cheatham Committee Report 1945: Report 1:5).

The rationale of the Committee was to attempt to formalize and regulate the position of the Bureau with the University. But what one sees in the exchange between Lazarsfeld and the Committee is how the Bureau, representing a new organizational structure within higher education, sat uneasily with the existing structures of teaching and research, and also, how operational rationale and ideology differed, making it difficult for the Bureau to legitimate itself to the university. The fact is, however, the refusal of the university to accept full responsibility for the Bureau, or accept greater responsibility for it than had hitherto been the case, pushed the Bureau into the very practices that were worrying to the university. The situation is well captured by a former member of the staff recounting, in an unpublished article, her days at the Bureau.

> There was a continued pressure to keep academic. We all looked down our noses at our bread and butter. Lazarsfeld would say, "make something out of this." We tried to pull our market research into an academic context. The University questioned the commercialization of the Bureau, yet forced us into it. (Brown n.d., Bureau files, p. 7)

The university did question "the commercialization of the Bureau," or more accurately questioned the very rationale of its operations. Although Lynd had reservations about the Bureau, as chairman of the Sociology Department he offered a strident defense of the Bureau to the Cheatham Committee. He used the opportunity to round on a sociology that "in the past . . . has stressed overmuch theory and generalization without data," and then squared up behind the Bureau, stating, "If sociologists are to use empirical data they simply have to go out and dig them up. And that is precisely what the Bureau is doing" (Lynd, letter to Cheatham Committee, January 31, 1945, Bureau files). The charge, however, was not that it was digging empirical data, but the manner in which the excavation was financed. The charge was that some of the digging was done by exploitation of student labor.

Coser has already been noted as saying that some of the students felt exploited, but Katz apparently did not. Referring to his contemporaries, students and junior staff, he related,

> I don't remember any of these had feelings of being exploited; most were grad students on way to dissertations, and felt easier than working outside the Bureau, say for Merton. Some of course were despondent about how long it took to finish, and some never finished. The career researchers—mostly women—may have felt exploited. We were paid, but I don't know how much. (Personal communications, March 15, 2006)

Lazarsfeld, in his defense against the charge of exploiting students, reversed the charge. His position was that if it were not for the money that his market research activity provided, many of the students would not be in a financial position to complete their studies.

No Relief

In examining Lazarsfeld's correspondence with the Cheatham Committee, the picture gained is that of a research director wearied by the sheer difficulty of running a research organization that is dependent on outside income for its survival. The charge of wheeling and dealing that has been noted might reasonably be translated as creative entrepreneurial activity. Whichever way, and we will see this shortly in Lazarsfeld's response to Cheatham, what cannot be denied is that raising research money demanded effort of a tiresome degree. A good illustration of this, and insight into the entrepreneurial scholastic world of Lazarsfeld, is given by the manner in which he raised the $100,000 needed to finance his study of the 1940 presidential election, which resulted in his first major book, *The People's Choice* (Lazarsfeld, Berelson, and Gaudet 1944). It was possible for him to use $15,000 remaining from the Rockefeller Foundation grant for the study of radio (Princeton Radio Research Project). He then sold the first reprint rights of the study's results to *Life* magazine for $10,000 or $15,000. He also managed to raise another $10,000 from radio set manufacturers in payment for the placement of questions in the survey asking respondents about preferences for radio sets. This was still not enough to cover the costs of the study, however, which he then did by the selling of a question about refrigerator preferences.[8] Everett Rogers summed up the situation very neatly: "Through such nickel-and-diming, and illustration of his entrepreneurial skills par excellence, Lazarsfeld was able to put together the needed funding" (Rogers 1994, 287).

The sheer drive of Lazarsfeld in raising the necessary funds is impressive, but such activity has to be seen within the total context of the funding situation of the times. There were, for example, no governmental sources such as the National Science Foundation (created 1950); thus, Lazarsfeld had little option but to "sell" research in the manner that he did if his type of empirical research was to be undertaken. A large part of the success of the Bureau, the impact that it made on American academic life, stemmed from Lazarsfeld's very ability to win research income, and he was not too concerned about how he did it.

Although Lazarsfeld never really bothered to respond to his critics, one can see in the occasional exchange with the Cheatham Committee a shortening of temper that the situation that he faced was not understood or appreciated. Given the above example of how he funded the *People's Choice* study, it is not surprising that he waspishly wrote,

> It is obvious that I, as well as all my associates in the "Bureau," would much prefer to be free of all commercial entanglements. Nothing would make me happier than to be able to spend all of my time on actual research, without the necessity of worrying about public relations, negotiating for funds and the like. (Lazarsfeld letter to the Cheatham Committee, January 30, 1945, Lazarsfeld's files)

This is clearly the voice of a weary research director. But, as ever, it probably contains a bit of Lazarsfeld the politically adroit operator in that he wishes to paint a picture where if life does not get easier there is the risk that he will not, or cannot, continue. Such sotto voce threats were part of a strategy to have the Bureau converted into a regular part of the Sociology Department's activities and budget. Furthermore, he was in no mood to seek forgiveness for the employment and training of students at the Bureau:

> It should not be forgotten, however, that up to the beginning of the war the "Bureau" was one of the few places where students could get work that was somehow related to his field of study. A large number of cases could be traced where students could finish their studies only because they worked here. (Lazarsfeld letter to Cheatham Committee, February 27, 1945, Lazarsfeld's files)

This letter was more than likely in response to one that Cheatham had written to Lazarsfeld a few weeks earlier in which he expressed his fears that education of the students was not paramount when engaging them on research:

> in so far as students of the University have a part in the work of the Bureau, the time devoted to that work must be as valuable proportionately in their education as the rest of their university time. If that is not so, then any university bureau is misusing the students. (Cheatham letter to Lazarsfeld, February 1, 1945, Lazarsfeld's files)

"Misusing the students" is an overharsh description of the situation, or at least when seen in the operational context of the Bureau, but then, of course, it was the operational context that so worried Cheatham. Student training took place as part of the operational functioning of the Bureau and not as some separate discrete activity, and that operational functioning was projects paid for by commercial sponsors. Nevertheless, Charles Glock, recounting his time at the Bureau, 1946-1957,[9] states, "A premium was put on attendance at formal seminars and informal discussions with everyone—faculty, staff and students—to initiate such discussions of any topic that suited their methodological fancy and for which they could attract participants." After mentioning the difficulty of conveying the "excitement and zest for learning which prevailed among the students who held apprenticeships," he states, "the most important ingredient, as in other effective training organizations, was Lazarsfeld's lifelong practice of involving students deeply in the process of ongoing research." The upshot was that

> students became more nearly collaborators than research assistants on Bureau projects. Indeed, once they had learned the basics, they came to fill the role of project director with Lazarsfeld, Merton and other faculty and staff serving as consultants. In effect, each project became a collateral seminar focused on the project's effective development with faculty and students sharing responsibility for the outcome. As a result, students acquired a taste for research and a proficiency in doing research very early in their careers. (Glock 1979, 28-29)

Glock's account of the position of the student within the Bureau makes it that much easier to understand how Katz came to play such an important part in producing *Personal Influence*. It was clearly not unusual, and in line with Lazarsfeld's habit of handing over work to others in the expectation that they would, and could, complete tasks (Merton 1987, 553), for someone in Katz's position to not just be given opportunities, but expected to perform.

> In about '52 or '53, Lazarsfeld named me to try to help complete Decatur (site of the study) after fighting or despairing of Mills, Rossi, Gleicher, Srole, though each of these had substantial chunks of input (analysis and writing) included in the book. My job began as editing, writing one or two missing chapters (especially a key chapter summarizing evidence for 2-step flow), and then writing a Part 1 which argued that IF interpersonal influence were as relevant as Lazarsfeld studies were finding, then small group research (primary group, group dynamics etc.) ought to have something to say to mass communications research, even if the two seemed so far apart conceptually. (Katz, personal communication, March 15, 2006)

This conceptual connection of Katz was indeed crucial to the rescue of the study. However, Katz knew very little of the "influences" influencing the study in terms of background to the funding, stating, "I was a much-too-naïve grad student in those days." In other words, how the study was put together, how it was financed, was not part of his sphere of competence.

History and the Maneuvers of Establishment

It probably was the case, as Lazarsfeld informed Cheatham, that "nothing would make [him] happier" than to be rid of the necessity of constantly having to raise research monies and instead concentrate entirely on research as such. The brute fact was, however, that Lazarsfeld was running a *Betrieb*—a research enterprise, or business—and, whether he had wanted it or not, the unfolding of history, and at the biographical level Lazarsfeld's response to the circumstances of his situation, locked him from an early age into a course of action that would, at least for a major part of his career, make escape from that which he complained to Cheatham about, impossible. It is worthwhile to briefly support that statement, since in doing so it will at one and the same time illuminate the stage upon which *Personal Influence* can be seen as a scene in a much larger play. The opening scene of the unfolding of the play is Vienna between the wars.

Born in 1901, and graduating from the University of Vienna with a doctorate in applied mathematics in 1925, Lazarsfeld established the aforementioned first social science research institute of its kind in the world, the Österreiche Wirtschaftspsychologische Forschungsstelle.[10] The importance of the Forschungsstelle, independent of its innovation in the production of knowledge, is, as Lazarsfeld said: "This formula of this Viennese Forschungsstelle remained absolutely the same whatever I have done since" (Lazarsfeld interview, May 25, 1973, New York).

It is not possible to go into the detail of the structure and organization of the Forschungsstelle, or the historical circumstances of its founding,[11] but the basic idea was that money earned from market research studies would be used to fund social research. It never worked out that way since, as already noted, Lazarsfeld was a hopeless administrator. The Forschungsstelle was full of debt, and in constant danger of bankruptcy. Even so, he learned during this period how to talk with the business community, and how to sell research.

As a Jew in the most anti-Semitic university in Austria, it was impossible for Lazarsfeld to gain appointment at the university other than a lowly position at the Psychology Institut assisting Charlotte Bühler, the wife of the head of the Institut, Karl Bühler. His political ambition of holding a leading position within the Social Democratic Party was also blocked due to anti-Semitism within the party, or rather the fear of reaction to another leading figure being Jewish, since nearly all the leading figures were. What one witnesses in the establishment of the Forschungsstelle is creativity in marginality, but even if Lazarsfeld had been acceptable to the University it is difficulty to see, given that it was in dire financial straits within what was a poverty stricken country, where the money for expensive empirical work was to be found.[12]

The solution to the situation—blocked career, blocked political ambitions, and lack of money for expensive empirical research—was to create his own research organization funded by market research accounts and staffed by his socialist friends, many of whom were unemployed and pleased with the research training opportunity afforded by working on the projects and also for the money, no matter how little or irregular, that working at the Forschungsstelle gave. The parallels with the Bureau are obvious. Indeed, he faced similar "hostility" toward his commercial activity in Austria as he did in America. For example, Jahoda said of Charlotte Bühler, "it suited her to have Paul available at the University and do his dirty business not quite close to her" at the Forschungsstelle (Jahoda interview).

The Making of a Businessman

Never would Lazarsfeld lose his awareness of, and appreciation for, commercial money as a source for funding research that was learned during this period. As he said in talking about the establishment of the Forschungsstelle, "In order to do empirical studies you needed a machinery and you needed money" (Lazarsfeld interview, May 25, 1973). The Forschungsstelle was the organization, and the money came from the market research accounts—studies of beer, butter, chocolate milk, perfume, and radio among many others. His appreciation for money was, in effect, one of dependency: his style of work required money, substantial amounts, and the organization necessary for the conduct of his empirical work also required money, substantial amounts. Indeed, there can be no finer example of the entrepreneurial bureau director worrying about future sources of income than the discovery that at one point he made the staff of the Bureau learn Spanish. He explained,

> Look that was just a complete political misjudgment. I thought that. . . . This was during the War . . . I was sure somehow that the building of South America would be the main task . . . post war task of the United States. I didn't know that the main task would be to build up Germany and Japan. I didn't foresee the Cold War. You see if it hadn't been for the Cold War I still think that would have been very important. I was absolutely sure there lay the cultural international future of the United States. It was not a stupid exercise. I remember the lessons. I sat in on them. (Lazarsfeld interview, June 15, 1973)

The above is the language of a businessman looking for new markets to exploit, but what should not be overlooked is that Lazarsfeld was always attracted to areas that would allow for methodological development; thus, if South America was going to be opened as a source of research funds, Lazarsfeld would study whatever was considered required study, the subject matter was not important. As he once said in response to a discussion on the value of data banks, "Stouffer did more in the direction, but I never did. You see my interest was really always in the logic of survey work. I was never very interested in the results so a data bank had no attraction for me. I mean that is completely personal" (Lazarsfeld interview, June 2, 1973).

In talking with Berelson about Lazarsfeld's interest, or rather lack of interest, in communications research, he said, "Paul was more delighted in having a clever methodological table come out of the Holerith machine in those days . . . and whether it had major substantive importance was secondary to that." The opportunity for methodological engagement offered by communications research was noted by Berelson, but then added to by the observation,

> Funds were in the air. If he were what, twenty-five years younger, he might be doing it on population because population became an attractive subject in the sixties for funding. Mass communications just happened to have a vogue then, but it could have been another subject. (Berelson interview)

Lazarsfeld followed the money. "One of the reasons," according to Jeff Pooley, "that he withdrew from the media research field in the late 1940s was that the networks had by then moved nearly all their research in-house" (Pooley

2006, 269). Given what has been said, the reason for this is obvious: no funds, no research.

It was perhaps understandable that someone with Mills's critical approach to social order should look with contempt at scholarship dependent upon the financial support of a magazine such as *True Story*,[13] but for Lazarsfeld it represented the continuation of working habits begun in Vienna, and then honed in America, which allowed the development of empirical social research, especially survey research, and the institutional structures necessary for its furtherance. The institution building was, however, more than a story in the history of social research; it was the very means by which Lazarsfeld built a position for himself within American academic life.

Exile and Acceptance

Lazarsfeld did not arrive in the United States with any international reputation; nor did he arrive as a member of a school of thought that would have assisted employment and assimilation. He first came in 1933 courtesy of a Rockefeller Fellowship, which Karl Bühler had put him forward for by way of recompense of not being able to promote him amid the rising tide of radical anti-Semitism—his wife Charlotte was partly Jewish and he felt it dangerous to confront the University by offering up Lazarsfeld for promotion. The deteriorating political situation in Austria saw the Foundation extend his fellowship from one to two years, by which time, in 1935, returning to live in Austria made poor sense.

He may not have been part of a school of thought, but by 1935 the quantification wing of American sociology was already established and forging forward. In short, the opportunity structure was such that it favored his establishment, but only in the sense of proximity of ideas. In discussing Lazarsfeld's work in Austria, Jahoda observed, "You know Paul says he is a marginal character—he's right because he was really in his research style an American long before he went to America." She then added,

> But he had the advantage of the much more deep and broad intellectual education that one used to get on the continent. Researchers in America are trained in statistics and question asking and they go ahead and they are technicians—so he brought this extra, not just methodological technician thing with him to America. (Jahoda interview)

Thus, although at the intellectual level there was a fit between his work and his host culture, in a way that was not the case for most social scientists from the German-speaking world schooled in the veneration of theory (Neumann 1953, 17), he still had to be accepted into that world. Indeed, much about Lazarsfeld revolves around the issue of acceptance.

It was quite clear to Lazarsfeld, judging by his memoir, that he would have to build his own world, so to speak. He says, "I took it for granted that I would have to make some move similar to the creation of the Vienna Research Centre if I wanted to find a place for myself in the United States" (Lazarsfeld 1969, 301). There is no space to go into how he did that (see Morrison 1998), but a large part of that effort involved the attraction of research funds to build the Bureau at Columbia into one of the great powerhouses of American social research.

[After he moved to the United States, it] was quite clear to Lazarsfeld . . . that he would have to build his own world, so to speak.

It is easy to say that, from his experiences of running the Forschungsstelle in Vienna, he had learned how to talk to the business community and how to sell research, but there is more to such attributes than capability. In talking of the influences influencing *Personal Influence*, it is more than appropriate to stretch the story beyond the research context as such, of how the Bureau operated and so on, and into consideration of Lazarsfeld the person, for whom acceptance by corporate America was more than just a research strategy. Although somewhat of an overstatement, in selling research, he was selling himself, and not, as Mills would have it in working for *True Story* magazine, "selling out."

Personality and Acceptance as an Influence

John Marshall, who was well positioned to observe Lazarsfeld, after seeing fit to mention how fond he was of him, said, "at times he was a highly manipulative person. . . . He was after all—he was typical of a refugee—they felt they had to manipulate the people around them in any way they could to secure their position." Appeal to the structural position of the émigré is useful in placing Lazarsfeld's "wheeling and dealing" within a sociological framework, but there was more at work than that in his efforts at gaining a favorable position for himself. Marshall himself mentioned, "He was one of those people who was never completely sure of his mind. He had enormous energy, but I suspect that there was something in his psychological make-up that forces him to belittle himself . . . forces him to shrug off his own success" (Marshall interview, July 6, 1973, Connecticut).

The mysteries of the personality must remain just that, mysteries, but it is worth documenting some aspects of his psychological makeup that made for his entrepreneurial spirit, or rather his willingness to entertain the business world.

The question of Lazarsfeld's self-description as a marginal person was raised with Marshall, who said,

> He published something on that (in his Memoir). I thought this was exaggerated and I probably wrote Paul to that effect at the time. I think its truth would be in Paul believing it was so. I think it was not so, but if Paul believed it was so he would have acted as if it was true. (Marshall interview)

It is difficult to disentangle the objective and subjective aspect of marginality, but there is certainly sufficient in Lazarsfeld's life at the objective level to foster feelings of marginality. To begin with, the whole intellectual professional class to which he belonged in Vienna was devoid of purpose after the fall of the empire.[14] It was, as Jahoda expressed it, "a class alienated," but the feeling of marginality, of not truly belonging (*Entfremdung*), can be imagined from the fact of his blocked political career within the Social Democratic Party due to anti-Semitism, and similarly his blocked career at the University due to anti-Semitism. Jahoda, in discussing the block to his political career, said, "Paul was so obviously Jewish and he just didn't have a chance in the political party." She continued by saying, "he was always sensitive about his Jewishness" (Jahoda interview).

He was undoubtedly, at least in his early days in the United States, conscious of difference; that he looked and sounded the outsider. If that was so in the United States, it is difficult to say what he would have felt had he "escaped" to England, but the fact is he was aware of the difficulties he might face. In looking for a job, he said, "There was still a certain amount of genteel anti-Semitism. And my accent . . . as a matter of fact, I was less affected because of my foreignness—the accent saved my life." To anybody who knew Lazarsfeld, the idea that his Jewishness would not present itself as a most obvious and unmistakable feature is preposterous. How true this is, is difficult to say, but Lazarsfeld stated, "I think I could not have been appointed at Columbia at that time—not really—not if I had been an American Jew" (Lazarsfeld interview, June 2, 1973). The above statement, therefore, that "the accent saved my life" might be taken to refer to a foreign Jew being acceptable to the university more than a home-grown Jew, but if so it is a peculiar way of seeing anti-Semitism—he was still unmistakably Jewish.

Whatever the truth of the situation, acceptance was an emotional game that he needed to play, and to change Jewishness for foreignness meant that the latter still had to be negotiated. In a discussion concerning his relationship to Theodor Adorno, and the social nightmare that he was when it came to dealing with industry figures, Lazarsfeld said, "He wasn't aware of it like I was," referring to his foreign appearance: "I was aware that I sounded funny." Even with the passing of many years, he remembered a visit to the Lynds' household where the issue of his accent was raised: "I remember one day going to Robert Lynd's house and his boy said to his father, 'Why does this man talk so funny?'" Well, Adorno, he would have blamed Lynd and said, "Aren't you ashamed that. . . ." Lazarsfeld's tactic was one of accommodation, or, if not too strong a word, ingratiation:

You know for years I had a collection of jokes that I used in public about my accent because I know people are shocked, especially when I talked as some official representative at Columbia. The first minute I would make a joke that I didn't come with the Mayflower or something like that. Adorno would never have done that—it's your problem if you don't understand. (Lazarsfeld interview, June 2, 1973)

Personality and Approval

Without meaning to make any judgments, then, if Jahoda can say that Lazarsfeld was always very sensitive about his Jewishness, one can also say that he was sensitive, perhaps excessively so, about his foreignness, suggesting deeper factors were at work than mere smoothing of differences between himself and others. Indeed, at the same time as discussing his sensitivity toward his Jewishness, Jahoda commented, "He had the most idiotic, but persistent inferiority feeling." She considered that, in part, this formed part of the social basis of his friendship with Merton: "Paul's relationship with Merton was a strong one— you know all sorts of personal factors play a role. . . . There was the established Merton, and Stouffer was another friendship—leading Harvard people who would take him seriously" (Jahoda interview).

If the social base of the friendship is accepted, of how the friendship functioned at a level other than enjoyment of the other, one can now see how the making of jokes about not arriving on the Mayflower is not simply a technique of introduction, but an apology for one's presence, especially so in cases where he was acting as an "official representative at Columbia." It is a mark of insecurity. While he never lost his German accent, his foreignness probably fed a basic insecurity that the psychiatrist Siegfried Bernfeld possibly detected. Bernfeld had been a student of Freud, who, along with Erich Fromm and Wilhelm Reich, became recognized as Left Freudians. Bernfeld questioned Lazarsfeld as to why he wasted his time with measurement and statistics. His conclusion was that he did so "because of his basic fear of people" (see Morrison 1998, 16-18).

One does not have to subscribe to Bernfeld's theory[15] to accept that some kind of insecurity or inferiority feeling—call it whatever—created what Lazarsfeld called marginality, but translates in practice as a desire for acceptance: a desire that in its workings can never be complete, certainly not if Marshall's witness to Lazarsfeld's psychological makeup is accepted, that there was something that forced him "to belittle himself . . . forces him to shrug off his own success."

It's More than Just about the Money

Lazarsfeld has already been observed as recognizing the debt he owed to the media industry for providing much-needed research funds; as he said, "Everything depended on that." According to Berelson, "His unkind critics would feel he was a paid lackey of the capitalist media with *True Story* and CBS and some newspaper accounts." He added, "I didn't feel it ever troubled Paul. His socialist background was there, but his foreground was with American business and Paul was always delighted that he could phone up the President of Columbia Broadcasting System and get him on the phone" (Berelson interview).

To get the president of CBS (presumably Frank Stanton) on the phone, is the exact same point that Jahoda makes concerning the social basis to his friendship with Merton and Stouffer; the desire, indeed need, to be taken seriously by established figures. To have corporate America give recognition is, in his new-found home, acceptance indeed. The self-esteem he gained by association with business leaders is evidenced by the mention in his memoir of how, while working at the Retail Research Institute at the University of Pittsburgh on studies of "How Pittsburgh Women Decide Where to Buy Their Dresses" and "How Pittsburgh Drivers Choose Their Gasoline," "the first study once made me a house guest of local Pittsburgh tycoon, Edgar Kaufman, and the second brought me into repeated contact with Paul Mellon" (Lazarsfeld 1972, 255).

There is something noteworthy in the above mentioning of brushing shoulders with "tycoons," but this sense of the pleasure of recognition by the commercial estates is found elsewhere. He was, for example, invited by the Ford Foundation in 1952 to chair an Advisory Committee on Television. The whole project was stillborn (Morrison 2000). But in talking about the board that he presided over, he said, "We worked endlessly and this was a very distinguished group. After all, there were top people on this board. I was very proud. One day, out of the blue, it all ended" (Lazarsfeld interview, June 15, 1973).

By 1952, Lazarsfeld was a very important figure in the social sciences, indeed, world-renowned; thus it is strange, one would have thought, to talk about the board in the way that he does—top people, very proud to be the leader—as if he had no real right to be there. Such description reinforces Jahoda's analysis, and also Marshall's, about his uncertainty of the self.

At no point is one replacing structural explanations for Lazarsfeld's enmeshment with the world of commerce with psychological ones, merely showing how personality interacts with structure to assist process. There is no question that the overwhelming reason for enmeshment was the sheer necessity of obtaining funds for research. As late as 1959,[16] for example, in response to a study by UNESCO into social science research institutes, the Bureau showed itself to be funded totally by sponsored research and had no core funds to draw upon. To question 5c of the UNESCO survey, asking, "What percentage of the budget can be looked on as basic budget, on which the Institute can count for a longer period?" the response was,

> At the present time, there are no funds on which the Bureau can count that are free of the commitment to perform specific research for specific sponsors. The University contributes to the Bureau's work in student training. It advances funds for overhead costs and for publication, but these are reimbursed from the Bureau's operations. (UNESCO 1959)

Multiple Audiences, Multiple Realms

Berelson's account of Mills's dismissiveness of Lazarsfeld working for *True Story* magazine, "as though no self-respecting academic of any persuasion would do that," and Lazarsfeld's puzzlement over such sentiment, given that *True Story* paid for the study that produced *Personal Influence*, must be set firmly within the portrait of Lazarsfeld pictured above. It is the expression of a process of institutional activity begun years before in Vienna, and continued in the United States, facilitated by Lazarsfeld's own psychological makeup. This notwithstanding, to have a sponsor such as *True Story* magazine offer to fund the study must have been a welcome relief in light of the difficulty of patching together the funds for the *People's Choice* study.

The magazine was aimed at working-class women of poor formal education and dealt with personal "true stories" of women's problems, as well as running gossipy features on Hollywood and the movies. According to Charles Glock, the magazine was so downmarket that getting "*True Story* readers to identify themselves proved a problem in the first data collection operation." Evidently, "some readers were embarrassed to acknowledge readership"; hence "a procedure adopted to identify readers was to arrange for field workers to examine the 'garbage' of designated respondents to see if issues of *True Story* had been discarded" (personal communications, March 11, 2006).

It was possibly the case that the absence of mention of *True Story* magazine was so contrary to expectation that a "garbage search" was undertaken as a way of classifying what was read to understand the flow of information between people. Difficult to say, but it might be that Lazarsfeld especially wished for information on *True Story* readers to relay information of use to Macfadden Publications as part of how he sold the study. This is highly likely, as will be seen shortly by the manner in which the data were used to promote the magazine.

On page 3 of the introduction to *Personal Influence*, some mention is made of the background to the study. Although it is signed by both of the authors, the part written on the funding must have been penned by Lazarsfeld, since Katz was not around at the time of the study's inception, and, as already noted, claimed, as a "naïve grad student," not to know much about how the study came to be supported. Lazarsfeld notes, however, the findings from *The People's Choice*, undertaken with Berleson and Gaudet, related to decision making during the 1940 presidential election and the role of personal influence. Referring to personal influence he states, "For it develops that, in all walks of life, there are persons who are especially likely to lead to the crystallization of opinion in their fellows." He immediately follows this by saying, "This finding came to the attention of Mr. Everett R. Smith, research director of the Macfadden Publications, Inc." who "felt that it might have important implications for his firm, many of whose publications are aimed at reaching readers in the wage-earning class" (Katz and Lazarsfeld 1955/2006, 3). By "wage-earning class," Lazarsfeld is referring to that section of the population making up the readership of *True Story* magazine.

Following the Money

What is intriguing in the above is the statement, "this finding came to the attention of Mr. Everett R. Smith," as if by happenchance, or casual exposure to the results.

The People's Choice was primarily intended as an effects study, but when no, or little, direct media effects were discovered it was, in classic Lazarsfeld style, repackaged and "sold" as an election study. It is reasonable to assume that, since Lazarsfeld wished to follow up the work of the Bureau on two-step flow and personal influence, the findings from *The People's Choice* that so interested Mr. Everett R. Smith, and came to his "attention," did so by direct intervention of Lazarsfeld, and furthermore, that Lazarsfeld spelled out to him how they might have "important implications for his firm."

Given what has been said about Lazarsfeld's career, and how the institutionalization of knowledge through the creation of a research center or bureau depended on commercial money not just for development but also for survival, and how Lazarsfeld came to create the new role within higher learning of the managerial or entrepreneur scholar, it is doubtful that Lazarsfeld, in his constant search for research monies, would not have exploited his commercial network of contacts.

We can return here to the previously noted instance of Lynd's and Marshall's concern over Lazarsfeld's closeness to commercial research and the consultancies that he was being offered, to the point where they felt that he had to make a decision either to follow a university career, or pursue the riches offered by employment in a market research company. Lazarsfeld did not see it that way. Applied social research for him did not mean a clear separation between academia and commerce; indeed, his contacts made through consultancy and other work could be exploited, and in the case of the *Personal Influence* study it looks as if they very much were. Glock is very much of that view. Drawing on his memory of the times, he said, "As early as 1940 Lazarsfeld was a consultant to the Magazine Audience Group, a collaborative enterprise of the *Saturday Post, Colliers, Life,* and *Liberty* (a Macfadden publication) that was engaged in research on the audience to the four magazines. It was out of that consultantship, I feel sure, that PFL made his first contact with Macfadden" (personal communication, March 11, 2006). With such contact made, Lazarsfeld was in a good position to sell the idea of the *Personal Influence* study to Macfadden Publications, who were having trouble, according to Allen Barton, "getting big advertisers because their magazines had a relatively low-income audience." What Macfadden wanted was to show advertisers "that their audience was worth reaching" (personal communication, February 9, 2006).

The background to the "sell" ran like this: "*The People's Choice* published in 1944 had introduced the idea of 'opinion leaders' [see Lazarsfeld, Berelson, and Gaudet 1944, chap. V] and showed that opinion leaders existed (although in varying proportions) in all classes, including housewives [ibid., chap. V, Table III] and that opinion leaders were more likely to read magazines [ibid., chap. V, Table IV]." It was but a short step from here, but nevertheless clever of Lazarsfeld, as Barton informed, to "come up with the idea that low-income women who read movie and true-story magazines might 'multiply' the effect of advertising in those magazines and therefore more valuable advertising targets than their low income would imply." It is Barton's judgment that "that idea induced Macfadden to pay for the study" (personal communication, February 9, 2006). Barton is undoubtedly correct. The study was sold, if not as a piece of marketing, then as a study that would have very real marketing benefits.

Knowledge as Sale Value

One of the principal aspects to Lazarsfeld, as Pooley so admirably and clearly points out, was his willingness, and indeed ability, to deliver different stories to different audiences all from the same data, or, as Pooley puts it, "He was exceptionally skilled at kneading data into an audience pleasing shape." Put even more prosaically, "It was Lazarsfeld's singular talent—to borrow a media-industry cliché—to give the audience what it wants" (Pooley 2006, 180-82). If we translate this to Mr. Everett R. Smith of Macfadden Publications, we can read that Lazarsfeld knew what Smith would like to hear, and one can be assured that Lazarsfeld concentrated his story on just what he would want to hear in terms of what the proposed study could deliver, whether it actually could or not.

Applied social research for [Lazarsfeld]
did not mean a clear separation between
academia and commerce.

Having said that, it is unclear in going through the Bureau of Applied Social Research archives at Columbia University what precisely was promised to the sponsors. The search through more than one hundred boxes of poorly indexed material failed to find any contract between the Bureau and Macfadden. Even if one had, it would only document the formal agreement, and not capture the "sales talk" on which the agreement was made, but such a document of the legal arrangements would have at least formed an index of sorts of promises expressed in securing the account.

Nevertheless, what does exist in the various record boxes relating to the Bureau's activity is clear evidence, or at least sufficient evidence, to support Barton's statement about how the study was sold. The interesting boxes are Box 9-B0240 and Box 10-B0240. In Box 9 is a ten-page memo, "*True Story* magazine in Decatur" from Paul Lazarsfeld to Messrs Drake and Smith of Macfadden publishers dated May 8, 1946. In the memo, Lazarsfeld promises to send "in a few days" two parts of a three-part report, the first part of the report simply being the memo. Parts two and three are missing; they will no doubt have been sent. From the existing memo of Box 9,[17] energy is directed at showing how the Bureau determined readership and popularity—two key variables for a marketer—and some of the questions used in the interviews. It is very "markety" in concentrating only on the basic variables of potential sales. In Box 10, there is a memorandum to the above Mr. Drake, but this time from C. Wright Mills, which includes one page of clearly boring introduction and eight pages of graphs. Each of the graphs ranks the impact of five different magazines upon different readership groups (self-selected opinion leaders, active advice seekers, and so on). The magazines include *Ladies Home Journal, Life, Colliers, Good Housekeeping*, and *True Story*. The performance of the magazines is ranked, with *True Story* doing very well on a variety of dimensions. The impression gained is that the material delivered has been for the purpose of impressing the marketing specialists at Macfadden that the Bureau is making progress, indeed, that the Bureau is giving value for money in line with promises made. It is reasonable to conclude that, in short, these incidental memos demonstrate something of the brisk marketing and salesmanship that took place on a regular basis between the Bureau and Macfadden.

The most intriguing find is forty-eight pages of "Proofs for Published Report" found in Box 10, from the same year as the above. Unfortunately, who authored these proofs or what they are is not entirely clear, but most certainly appear to have been written for advertising purposes. They were found buried at the back of the box, folded in half behind thick folders of miscellaneous tabulation sheets. The proofs are stunning in their willingness to unabashedly promote *True Story* magazine. The proofs begin, for example, with the statement that "a social research grant by *True Story*" ("Columbia's 17 month study") involved "over 40,000 man hours" "to get, sift and analyze the word of mouth findings"; it then states that "on the average, nearly 3/4 of all changes in opinion involve word of mouth." These well-illustrated findings, akin to something like today's PowerPoint presentations, are accompanied by visuals featuring a set of pyramids showing that people influence each other in their same class, or purchasing market: one demonstrates that end of a trickle-down society, where high-brow tastes influence middle- and lower-class tastes; another shows that by far the largest market sector in contemporary America is the middle class (the middle swath of a three-swath pyramid) comprised predominantly by wage earners, namely, the readership profile of *True Story* magazine.

One can ignore the rather nonanalytic use of class references in the above, which seems par for the course with American popular discourse on stratification, but we can see that the results presented relate directly to the problems that *True Story* magazine was facing—a low-income readership unattractive to advertisers. The final two pages of the "proofs" are not so much the presentation of research findings, but an out-and-out sales pitch in the fight to sell advertising space. On page 47, one reads, "And *True Story* with its three kindred 'True Type' magazines reaches more word of mouth leaders in the big wage earner market than all the women's services, home services, and general monthly magazines put together." On page 48, the final page, one finds, "*True Story* magazine for nearly three decades, the favorite magazine of influence among wage earners. The Great New Middle Market of America."

What is noteworthy about these claims intended for prospective advertisers is the mention of "influence" and "word of mouth leaders." Yet it is highly unlikely that Lazarsfeld wrote any of the above statements. They look like the work of copywriters at Macfadden Publications. The complicated pyramids demonstrating *True Story*'s market position could have been produced by Lazarsfeld, but that is again highly unlikely. These proofs, one can feel sure, have originated within the sales and promotional orbit of Macfadden. One can feel equally sure, however, that Lazarsfeld was feeding Macfadden Publications material drawn from the study that was of use to their sales activity, that which he had promised would be produced when securing the sponsorship deal, and advising them of what the data meant in terms of the central questions posed by the sales situation of the magazine. That is the reason, it is reasonable to assume, why the proofs, produced by Macfadden, are to be found in Box 10-B0240 of the Bureau's archives. The proofs are in Box 10 because Lazarsfeld would, as likely as not, have "checked" the story told against the data given. The storyline, but not the story, since that depended on the actual data, would, however, have been created before the study went into the field at the time that Lazarsfeld sold the study to Macfadden Publications. In short, the findings from *The People's Choice*, the role of opinion leaders and personal influences in the communications process, did not simply "come to the attention of Mr. Everett R. Smith," but found their way there and were sold to Smith by Lazarsfeld as a way out of the advertising sales problem faced by the company.

Return to Funder

In some ways, it looks a good move on the part of Macfadden Publications to support the study of *Personal Influence*. It would appear that the results of the study were good news, even if late news. In the acknowledgements to the original edition of *Personal Influence,* one finds, presumably written by Lazarsfeld, the following: "To Everett R. Smith of Macfadden Publications, and Jeremiah Caplan of the Free Press, we owe thanks for a degree of patience considerably in excess of that which one has a right to expect even from sponsors, publishers and friends." The book was ten years in coming.

Whether Macfadden Publications got their money's worth is not the point of the story of the influences influencing *Personal Influence*. It looks as if they got data that they could use. The proofs of report are dated 1946, but Lazarsfeld sees fit in the introduction to *Personal Influence* of 1955 to almost apologize for its academic value as opposed to applied usefulness, noting "it seemed wise to point up its usefulness for the world of affairs," and then thanks the pollster, Elmo Roper, for being "kind enough to do this in a special preface" (Katz and Lazarsfeld 1955/2006, 7, footnote).

What the evidence shows, however, supports the position adopted by Rossi in his presidential address and quoted in the opening of the article, namely, that one of the most important works in the history of communications research came out of administrative research, the very area that has relatively low academic esteem.

Yet to understand fully the influences influencing *Personal Influence*, it is necessary to move beyond administrative research to a wider research setting that Lazarsfeld was instrumental in creating, namely, the development of a new form for the organization of knowledge, the research bureau. In terms of the production of knowledge, such institutions, at least in the case of the Bureau of Applied Social Research, had to depend for their existence on conducting applied work for a variety of "administrations." In the case of *Personal Influence*, it was a magazine publisher. The scholastic position of *Personal Influence* is established, but that position, as shown, was created out of a much wider set of influences than those that immediately came to bear on the Midwest town of Decatur, not least Lazarsfeld's own personal path to establishment.

Notes

1. See Wright Mills (1959), Stein (1964), and Vidich (1964).

2. Rossi had worked at the Bureau of Applied Social Research of Columbia University from which the study was based; in fact, he did some of the analysis work on *Personal Influence*.

3. The Bureau of Applied Social Research will be used throughout when referring to the research center that Lazarsfeld established at Columbia University. Before 1944, it was known as the Office of Radio Research.

4. See Horowitz (1983, 77-82).

5. Allen Barton wished to point out that he was not around when the *Personal Influence* study was set up. The above is based on what he has been told. Barton, however, has written on Lazarsfeld and the Bureau (Barton 2001) and is an authority on the history of the Bureau.

6. A literal translation would be the Austrian Economic and Psychological Research Centre.

7. The interview took place many years after the breakdown of the marriage and can be regarded as a good witness. Indeed, Jahoda even worked at the Bureau years later when Lazarsfeld had remarried.

8. See Converse (1987, 271) and Rogers (1994, 286), where he discusses Converse.

9. Charles Glock was at the Office of Radio Research on a Rockefeller Fellowship from August 1941 to January 1942. The fellowship was for a year but had to be cut short for Glock to enter military service. After the war, beginning in November 1946, Lazarsfeld hired him to serve, more or less, as a research apprentice and the Bureau's office manager. Glock continued his association with the Bureau until June 1957 except for a nine-month leave of absence taken in 1949 and 1950. He was named director in 1952, immediately after earning his Columbia PhD. Prior to this, he was managing director from 1950 to 1952 and executive director from 1948 to 1949.

10. Lazarsfeld misdates the Forschungsstelle, saying that it was established in 1927, and not 1925 which was the case, and therefore believed Howard Odum's Research Centre at the University of North Carolina to predate his (Lazarsfeld 1969, 758).

11. For full detail, see Morrison (1998, chaps. 1-2).

12. See Morrison (1998, chaps. 1-3) for a full account of the complexities of the intellectual and political situation facing Lazarsfeld in Vienna.

13. Sterne (2005) questions the presentation of Mills as a "radical," considering it a story Mills wished to present, of himself and to himself. He points out that the attacks that Mills makes on administrative research are, in terms of his own working life, mistaken—he was deeply enmeshed in many features of administrative research and recognized himself how much he owed to the operations of the Bureau.

14. An administrative structure constructed to rule 50 million people was reduced virtually overnight to ruling a mere 6 and a half million people, of which 2 and half million lived in Vienna (Bullock 1939, 68).

15. See Morrison (1998, 18-21) for an alternative and more plausible theory of attraction to statistics.

16. Lazarsfeld stepped down as director in 1950.

17. Jonathan Sterne, in discussing Box 9 and a presentation constructed by Macfadden, cleverly notes that the publisher uses vertical as well as horizontal influence and presents a very good discussion of disagreements between Mills and Lazarsfeld concerning class, ideology, and manipulation of opinion from above (Sterne 2005, 72-76).

References

Barton, Allen H. 2001. Paul Lazarsfeld as institutional inventor. *International Journal of Public Opinion Research* 13 (3): 245-69.

Boudon, Raymond. 1972. An introduction to Lazarsfeld"s philosophical papers. In *Qualitative analysis: Historical and critical essays*, ed. Paul F. Lazarsfeld. Boston: Allyn & Bacon.

Bullock, Malcolm. 1939. *Austria, 1918-38; a study in failure*. Microform. London: Macmillan.

Converse, Jean M. 1987. *Survey research in the United States: Roots and emergence, 1890-1960*. Berkeley: University of California Press.

Coser, Lewis A. 1984. *Refugee scholars in America: Their impact and their experience*. New Haven, CT: Yale University Press.

Glock, Charles Y. 1979. Organisational innovation for social science research training. In *Qualitative and quantitative social research: Papers in honour of Paul F Lazarsfeld*, ed. Robert K. Merton, James S. Coleman, and Peter H. Ross. New York: Free Press.

Horowitz, Irving Louis. 1983. *C. Wright Mills: An American utopian*. New York: Free Press.

Jacobs, N. 1959. *Culture for the millions: Mass media in modern society*. Boston: Beacon.

Katz, Elihu, and Paul F. Lazarsfeld. 1955/2006. *Personal influence: The part played by people in the flow of mass communication*. New Brunswick, NJ: Transaction Publishers.

Lazarsfeld, Paul F. 1969. An episode in the history of social research. In *The intellectual migration*, ed. D. Fleming and B. Bailyn. Cambridge, MA: Harvard University Press.

———. 1972. *Qualitative analysis: Historical and critical essays*. Boston: Allyn & Bacon.

Lazarsfeld, Paul F., Bernard Berelson, and Hazel Gaudet. 1944. *The people"s choice: How the voter makes up his mind in a presidential campaign*. New York: Duell, Pearce and Sloan.

Merton, Robert K. 1987. The focussed interview and focus groups: Continuities and discontinuities. *Public Opinion Quarterly* 51:550-66.

Morrison, David E. 1998. *The search for a method: Focus groups and the development of mass communication research*. London: ULP/John Libbey.

———. 2000. The late arrival of television research: A case study in the production of knowledge. In *Media power, professionals and policies*, ed. Howard Tumber. London: Routledge.

Neumann, Franz L. 1953. The social sciences. In *The cultural migration: The European scholar in America*, ed. W. Rex Crawford. Philadelphia: University of Pennsylvania Press.

Pooley, Jefferson D. 2006. An accident of memory: Edward Shils, Paul Lazarsfeld, and the history of American mass communication research. PhD diss., Columbia University, New York.

Pratt, S. 1954. In Service Training Program of the Bureau of Applied Social Research. Manuscript, Bureau of Applied Social Research (BASR) Library, Columbia University, New York.

Rogers, Everett M. 1994. *A history of communication study*. New York: Free Press.

Rossi, Peter H. 1980. The presidential address: The challenge and opportunities of applied social research. *American Sociological Review* 45 (6): 889-904.

Stein, Maurice R. 1964. The eclipse of community: Some glances at the education of a sociologist. In *Reflections on community studies*, ed. A. J. Vidich. New York: Wiley.

Sterne, Jonathan. 2005. C. Wright Mills, the Bureau for Applied Social Research, and the meaning of critical scholarship. *Cultural Studies ↔ Critical Methodologies* 5 (1): 65-94.

UNESCO. 1959. Questionnaire on "The administrative structure and working methods of selected social science research institutes." Manuscript, Bureau of Applied Social Research (BASR) Library, Columbia University, New York.

Vidich, A. J. 1964. *Reflections on community studies*. New York: Wiley.

Wright Mills, C. 1959. *The sociological imagination*. New York: Oxford University Press.

The Katz/Lowenthal Encounter: An Episode in the Creation of *Personal Influence*

By
GERTRUDE J. ROBINSON

This article traces the scholarly contacts between two important intellectual traditions: the historically based, Marxist Frankfurt school and the Lazarsfeld/Merton Bureau of Applied Social Research in New York between 1934 and 1956. In this account, the focus will be on the differential career stages of Leo Lowenthal and Elihu Katz and what that meant for their understanding of the mass culture critique. Three interrelated questions will be addressed: first, Lowenthal's preparation for his work at the Institute for Social Research in Frankfurt; then the Institute's transfer to Columbia and Lowenthal's role in developing a sociology of literature and popular culture; and finally, the implications of Lowenthal's mentorship of Katz at the beginning of his scholarly career.

Keywords: Frankfurt school; Bureau of Social Research; Lowenthal; Katz; mass culture critique

Rereading *Personal Influence* (Katz and Lazarsfeld 1955) fifty years after its creation is like entering a time capsule. How to re-create the empirical research traditions of the early 1930s, into which Paul Lazarsfeld's Bureau of Social Research created the innovation of "radio research"? One of the things one finds out when one enters this time capsule is that Lazarsfeld the European immigrant did not invent the field of radio research in the United States but rather that he "named" it. Daniel Czitrom (1982) noted that what the Research Committee on Recent Social Trends in 1933 called "agencies of mass impression" possessed an investigative history in American scholarship. Four empirical approaches were in use, only two of which Lazarsfeld embraced (pp. 122-26). They were propaganda analysis grounded in

Gertrude J. Robinson is an emeritus professor and past director of the Graduate Program in Communications at McGill University, Montreal, where the first Canadian PhD was developed. She became the first female president of the Canadian Communication Association (CCA) and the first female editor of the Canadian Journal of Communication. *She has written nine books and published more than fifty articles in national and international journals.*

DOI: 10.1177/0002716206293413

Harold Lasswell's *Propaganda Techniques in the World War* (1927); public opinion research, such as Walter Lippmann's two volumes, *Public Opinion* (1922) and the *Phantom Public* (1925); and the psychological approach spearheaded by the Payne Fund, which investigated the effects of motion pictures on children and adolescents. Added to these, there was a fourth precursor, marketing research, which received a substantial boost at the time of Lazarsfeld's arrival in the United States because the unseen radio audience was difficult to study. For Lazarsfeld, the outsider, psychological and market research provided opportunities to pursue his own methodological interests within the framework of the Vienna action tradition, in which he had been trained. The encounter between Elihu Katz and Leo Lowenthal is a topic worth investigating because it shows that the reification of the "administrative" versus the "critical" research traditions is not only oversimplified but also fails to acknowledge both groups' European intellectual roots and what they learned from each other after their "transplant" to the United States. Leo Lowenthal, it will be demonstrated, is one of the prime agents in this cross-pollination.

The encounter between Elihu Katz and Leo Lowenthal . . . shows that the reification of the "administrative" versus the "critical" research traditions is not only oversimplified but also fails to acknowledge both groups' European intellectual roots and what they learned from each other after their "transplant" to the United States.

Though Lowenthal had nothing directly to do with the production of *Personal Influence*, he was indirectly involved because he had been Katz's teacher at Columbia University. Katz noted that he had studied with a number of well-known scholars during his undergraduate and graduate years in New York. Among them were Robert Merton, Robert Lynd, Seymour Lipset, Herbert Hyman, and of course Lazarsfeld, for whom he wrote Part I of *Personal Influence* as his PhD project. In a December 6, 2005, interview Katz recalled,

As you know, Lazarsfeld helped Adorno, Lowenthal, Kracauer and other (Frankfurt refugees) to find work in New York. And it was my luck to find Leo—in an MA course—at the moment he was being groomed (by Paul, I suppose) for the unlikely position of Research Director of the Voice of America. To prepare himself for this job, he had some students—including me—analyze batches of radio fan mail and I did a batch of letters on the subject of "happiest day in February," written by housewife-listeners to a daytime radio "philosopher," named Ted Malone. . . . We worked very closely during this period, had cordial and even friendly relations, and we met again, once or twice, after he moved to Berkeley.

The feeling one gets from this account is that Katz knew little about his thesis director's life and activities when he was writing his master's thesis, titled "The Happiness Game," between 1948 and 1950.

To unravel the complex filiations between Katz's and Lowenthal's career stages, I shall use Merton's (1973) conceptualization of what is entailed in describing and reconstructing a scientific activity. He noted that any activity has at least three components: first, the individual motivation by which a scientist chooses his work; then there is the social setting in which this work is carried out and the collective use made of his findings; and finally, one has to look at the degree of autonomy that the actor enjoys in his or her career and the reference groups it addresses. Lazarsfeld (1975, 44) summarized that such a schema "provides what one might call the 'three-dimensional space' within which any concrete activity or organizational form can be located." Each of these contextual frameworks will now be applied to our two social actors to try to clarify not only what they "did" before their encounter but also what their life stages "meant" to them, as a phase in their respective careers.

Leo Lowenthal and the Institute for Social Research in Frankfurt (1926-1933)

To understand Leo Lowenthal's individual motivations for the role he played in the Frankfurt Institute, one has to go back to his family roots and educational background in Germany. Leo Lowenthal (1900-1993) was born in Frankfurt. His father was a medical doctor and an assimilated Jew, and the atmosphere at home was secular, enlightened, and antireligious. Politically, his father was a liberal democrat and a member of the Liberal People's Party (Freisinnige Volkspartei). Lowenthal remembers that his father encouraged him to think in a liberal rather than a nationalistic vein. He attended the Goethe Gymnasium, which was strong in the classics (Greek, Latin, and German literature). The high school had an international student body, and they read Freud, Zola, Balsac, and Dostoyevsky, to whom Lowenthal would later return to develop his literary sociology. He missed the final half of his senior year in 1918 because of military service in a Railway Regiment, but was nevertheless awarded the Abitur.

Lowenthal entered Frankfurt University in 1918 to study law but was soon sidetracked by student activism and helped found the Socialist Student group (USPD). When it split in 1920, he remained with the left wing. Meanwhile he had transferred to the University of Giessen, on the advice of Luise Habricht, a well-educated socialist, feminist, and pacifist, who, according to Lowenthal, "radicalized" him (Jay 1987, 34). At Giessen, Walter Kinkel suggested he study philosophy and literature, which would become his lifelong preoccupations, and in 1920, he finally found his permanent university niche, in Heidelberg. At the time, its faculty was still under the influence of Max Weber's prewar circle and thus provided him with an introduction to the classical thinkers, among them Alfred Weber, Karl Mannheim, Ernst Bloch, and Karl Jaspers. He also attended lectures by Karl Hempe in history and Emil Lederer in economics.

In 1923, Lowenthal married his first wife, Golde Ginsberg, who came from an orthodox Jewish family and was a Zionist; and the couple had a son, Daniel, in 1926. Under her influence, they became part of a Jewish group that formed around Rabbi N. A. Vogel. Lowenthal remembers that in his early married years, he gave adult education lectures in the Jewish Lehrhaus and functioned for a time as the editor of a Zionist weekly. However, that came to an end when he quit because he disagreed with Zionism's stand on the removal of Palestinians from their land. At about the same time, Lowenthal met Erich Fromm, who later married Frieda Reichmann, a friend of Golde's. She was a physician in a clinic near Dresden and in 1925 moved to Heidelberg, where she started a psychoanalytic treatment center. The friendship with Fromm, Lowenthal notes, introduced him to psychoanalysis and led the group of Marxist friends by the late twenties to consider psychological theory as the missing and mediating link between Marxism's base and superstructure (Jay 1987, 51).

Though he did not know it at the time, Lowenthal's age, Jewish social background, and interests in Marxism and literature provided the perfect preconditions for joining the Institute for Social Research in 1926. He started as a part-time research assistant to Max Horkheimer and Friedrich Pollock, while supporting his family as a high school teacher. Lowenthal was initially encouraged to continue his socioliterary analyses, some of which were developed for the League for Popular Lectures, offered at the Jewish Lehrhaus for an adult audience between 1928 and 1930. Lowenthal comments,

> I lectured on all areas of European literature, although my main interest was German literature. . . . Most of what I wrote or began to write in Germany before my emigration. . . . attempts to track down the decline and disintegration of bourgeois consciousness and to delineate a critique of ideology. . . . In my 1932 article "On the Social Situation of Literature," I argued that Germany (in contrast to France and England) lacked a significant carrier group for a liberal world-view, and consequently of political liberalism as well. . . . I stopped working on this material in 1930, because [I became full-time employed by the Institute] and was burdened with Institute business. (Jay 1987, 116-17)

The studies were ultimately collected and published as *Literature, Popular Culture and Society* (1961) thirty years later. The volume provides a critical reconstruction of bourgeois class-consciousness in terms of its most prominent literary representatives, such as Conrad Ferdinand Meyer, Dostoevsky (1934), and Ibsen (1936). It also contains a methodological program in which literary history is conceived as the critique of ideology. Dubiel summarized, "So literary sociology . . . means understanding literature as the material, along with other cultural documentation, in which social and cultural structures can be identified. (This) kind of a study uses literature as the medium and material for an analysis of society" (Jay 1987, 122).

When the labor historian Karl Grünberg fell ill, although it became clear that Horkheimer would take over the directorship of the Institute, he lacked the requisite scholarly status to apply for the position. Lowenthal aided him in completing his *Anfänge der bürgerlichen Geschichtsphilosophie* (Origins of Bourgeois Historiography; 1930), which gained him the professorship at the University of Frankfurt. In addition to Horkheimer and Pollock, the Institute's core members at the time were Herbert Marcuse, Leo Lowenthal, Theodore Adorno, Franz Neumann, Erich Fromm, and Karl Friedrich Wittfogel, all born around the turn of the century and thus of the same generation and Jewish social background. All of them, furthermore, revolted against the bourgeois complacency of their parents and called themselves Marxists, though most of them did not join the Communist or the Social Democratic parties during the Weimar Republic. In their optimism for the future, they hoped to elaborate a Marxist cultural critique of capitalist society in their newly founded *Zeitschrift für Sozialforschung* (*Journal of Social Research*), which they called "critical theory."

The euphoria engendered by the Institute's increased status did not last for more than one semester. On September 14, 1931, when 107 National Socialists entered the Reichstag, this group of Jewish intellectuals began to view themselves as "internal exiles" in a world that threatened to engulf them. In Lowenthal's recollection, "It became clear to us all, even before January 1, 1933, that political life had taken on a new quality. . . . Fascism creates a new political context, characterized by total mobilization of society, where everyone is a fellow prisoner, fellow culprit and conscious fellow traveler of the political order. That is why we emigrated" (Jay 1987, 79). The exit strategy developed by the group at the time was a branch research office in Geneva, which Horkheimer and Pollock, who had contacts there, asked Kurt Weil to fund. The idea of using this office for emigration purposes was not mentioned at the time, and the Institute ran a popular seminar on Hegel and Marx throughout 1931 and 1932. The seminar attracted not only left-wing students but well-known speakers such as Raymond Aron and Edmund Husserl. Meanwhile, Institute funds were transferred to the Netherlands, and only enough money was left in Frankfurt to cover running expenses. Frequent trips by both the professors and assistants paved the way for the exodus to Geneva. Lowenthal was the last to leave on March 2, 1933. Three days later the SA (Sturmabteilung, or Storm Troops) occupied the building but found no one on the premises.

Since only Horkheimer had Swiss residence papers, the idea of emigrating to the United States was not as far-fetched as it might seem. It came from Julian Gumperz, an American who was Pollock's assistant (Jay 1987, 56). Letters were written to various universities, requesting an organizationally and legally independent affiliation, similar to the Frankfurt setup. The University of Chicago and Columbia responded, and the group decided to accept the latter on the naïve grounds that New York was closer to Europe. No one, Lowenthal (1980, 72) mentioned, had any real knowledge of the United States at the time. The group's emigration occurred at different times as exit papers became available. Horkheimer and Marcuse moved in July 1934, followed by Lowenthal in August and Pollock in September with Wittfogel and the wives and children last. Fromm, in turn, had already been lecturing in Chicago since 1932 (Jay 1973, 39). Lowenthal offered this glowing assessment of his more than twenty-year association with the Institute (1926-1949): "The Institute affected my style, intellectual habits, theoretical approaches and permitted me to achieve a satisfactory synthesis of my philosophical, literary, sociological and hedonistic feelings. In a sense, I relived my student years there" (Jay 1987, 59). As they left the old continent for the new, the group believed that Hitler would continue to spread fascism, rather than precipitate a world war. Consequently, they conceived of the Institute's purpose in New York as an "island of German radical thought," which would maintain a link with the country's humanist past and be available for Germany's post-Nazi reconstruction. This was expressed in the *Zeitschrift*'s German language content and Marxist theoretical preoccupations. The extent to which the German language preference was a manifestation of what Lewis Coser (1984, 3) called the "exile mentality," rather than sheer necessity (because only Horkheimer and Pollock knew a bit of English, the rest did not), will become clear in the next section, which describes the social setting in which Lowenthal and the others did their work in the United States.

The Institute of Social Research in New York (1934-1949)

The Institute's physical transfer to New York with the support of Nicholas Murray Butler, president of Columbia, did not initially mean a complete break with Europe until the beginning of World War II. For the first six years, the Geneva, London, and Paris offices continued to function as liaison points between New York and the Librairie Félix Alcean, where the *Zeitschrift* was published through 1940. Paris was also an important way station for other Jewish Institute members on their exodus from Europe. Among these were Henryk Grossmann, a Polish economist and friend of Grünberg's; Otto Kirchheimer, a student of politics and law; Gerhard Meyer, the economist; and Hans Meyer, the Marxist literary critic. Walter Benjamin was the tragic exception. He did not leave the city in time, was placed into a detention camp by the Gestapo, and committed suicide when he tried to escape through Spain in 1940 but found the border closed (Jay 1973, 197-98).

On their arrival in New York, the Frankfurt group's financial independence allowed it to remain self-consciously German. At the time, the Institute's endowment brought in about $30,000, sufficient money to guarantee survival in a city still mired in a deep depression. Martin Jay (1973) noted that though the Institute funds were less than some of its petitioners expected throughout its New York *séjour*, it was able to offer support to some two hundred emigrés, whose names have never been conclusively tabulated. Among the known beneficiaries were Fritz Sternberg, Hans Meyer, Paul Lazarsfeld, Fritz Karsen, Gerhard Meyer, and A. R. Gurland. In the ten years between 1934 and 1944, furthermore, the Institute also provided approximately $200,000 to 116 doctoral candidates and 14 postdoctoral students, who were completing their degrees at Columbia University (pp. 39, 113-15).

In addition, by the midthirties, the Institute made itself useful by offering both guest lectures and courses through the Extension Division of Columbia University. European scholars such as Harold Laski and Morris Ginsberg, as well as Celestin Bouglé and Horkheimer, lectured to the larger university community. Daniel Bell remembers hearing the latter in 1940. In addition, extension courses were offered by August Wittfogel, Leo Lowenthal, and others on fascism and the role of culture in authoritarian regimes, two domains in which the core Institute members were well versed. Lowenthal, moreover, once again shouldered his administrative duties and became managing editor of the "Review Section" of the *Zeitschrift*, which required liaison with Paris until the German invasion of 1940. Beyond that, Lowenthal's administrative duties included editing work on an empirical study of workers in the Weimar Republic. The study, directed by Erich Fromm, had been conceived by Horkheimer in 1930 to explore the failure of traditional Marxism to explain the proletariat's reluctance to fulfill its historical vanguard role. In spite of its uncompleted status, the study had both an ideological and a practical outcome for the Institute's American work. Ideologically, it modified the Institute's understanding of "critical theory" and its mechanical acceptance of Marxist categories. It showed instead that the proletariat's revolutionary potential had to be historically contextualized and that in the United States what they called the "proletariat" had turned into a petit-bourgeois group with massive interests in the status quo (Lowenthal 1980, 61-64). Beyond that, the project led to further investigations on authoritarianism that included *Studien über Autorität und Familie* (1936) and Fromm's *Escape from Freedom* (1941), as well as Adorno et al.'s *The Authoritarian Personality* (1950). Fromm's book attracted much attention, because of its exploration of the kind of authoritarianism that America was going to fight in World War II, but sealed his split with the Institute, because of its psychoanalytic explanatory framework.

In its North American years, the Frankfurt group produced a total of sixteen books and ninety-one articles: 40 percent of these were studies in authority, 22 percent were philosophical treatises, and 18 percent were studies in literature, music, and art (Jay 1973, 342). The Institute employed two general approaches in its analysis of Nazi authoritarianism. One associated with Neumann, Gurland, and Kirchheimer followed a more orthodox Marxist line and stressed the centrality of monopoly capitalism and changes in legal, political, and economic institutions, with only a passing glance at social psychology or mass culture. The other major approach, followed by the group around Horkheimer and Lowenthal, saw Nazism as the most extreme example of a general trend toward irrational domination in Western countries. It no longer considered the economic substructure as the source of social cohesion but instead paid increasing attention to technological rationalization as an institutional force and instrumental rationality as a cultural imperative. In so doing, it explored the role of psychosocial mechanisms of obedience and violence in assuring the political domination of Nazism (Jay 1973, 166). Adorno introduced the concept of the "culture industry," and increasingly Institute members came to feel that the culture industry enslaved people in more effective and subtle ways than the crude methods of domination practiced in earlier years (Jay 1973, 216).

With the expansion of fascist power in Europe and America's entry into the war, the Institute's structure and goals had to be reevaluated. In 1941, the last of its capital was transferred from Switzerland and Holland and placed into the hands of the Kurt Gerlag- and Hermann Weil Memorial Foundations as well as the Social Studies Association. This association's board was composed of Jewish friends, among them Charles Beard, Robert MacIver, Robert Lynd, Morris Cohen, and Paul Tillich. The transfer showed that the endowment was no longer sufficient to continue all of the Institute's previous activities, especially since a series of disastrous real estate investments in upstate New York had further depleted the coffers. The results of these financial straits for the institution and its members were threefold. First, there had to be a reduction of support for the large number of part-time refugees who had been given work. Beyond that, senior staff were encouraged to look elsewhere for support. Fromm left to pursue his psychoanalytical practice, Gumperz became a stockbroker, and Wittfogel found other sponsors, while Horkheimer left the city for health reasons and moved to California in 1941, where he was joined by Adorno. This left Pollock and Lowenthal as codirectors in the New York office, where Marcuse, Kirchheimer, Gurland, Massing, and Felix Weil continued to work. In spite of their presence, the volume of activity declined substantially during the war years and in 1944 precipitated a move to smaller quarters in Columbia's Low Memorial Library and finally the complete closure of the Institute's New York office when Horkheimer and Adorno returned to Frankfurt in 1949 (Jay 1973, 168-69, 172, 222).

The second result of the financial stringency was the elimination of the *Zeitschrift*, which had been rechristened *Studies in Philosophy and Social Science* in 1939, but the volume (SPSS VIII:3) was not published until the summer of 1940. Horkheimer's foreword explained, "Philosophy, art and science have lost their home in most of Europe. . . . America . . . is the only continent in which the continuation of scientific life is possible. In publishing our journal (in English) we wish to give this belief its concrete expression" (Jay 1973, 167). Unfortunately, this promise was short-lived. Though the publication was initially reduced from a quarterly to a yearbook to save money, it had to be completely suspended in March 1942. In retrospect, it is clear that the closure did not negate the importance of the *Zeitschrift* in disseminating the Institute's research between 1930 and 1942. Lowenthal, who had been managing editor of the "Review Section," was now also under pressure to find additional sources of income. He, like other core members, except Horkheimer and Adorno who remained in California, worked in Washington. Between 1941 and 1943, Lowenthal had an advisory position in the Domestic Media Department of the Office of War Information and in 1944 evaluated German radio programs and press material for the Bureau of Overseas Intelligence. Marcuse, Neumann, and Kirchheimer were with the Office of Strategic Service, and Pollock was an adviser to the War Production Board. In his sessions with Dubiel, Lowenthal reminisced that "I remember my early time in Washington as a frustrating experience. There were too many people, and there was a great muddle of bureaucracy, professorial vanity, and phony intellectuals—I didn't find it satisfying . . . and therefore was not too unhappy to be called back to the Institute, to take an active part in a study on anti-Semitism among American workers" that commenced in 1943 (Jay 1987, 82).

Two massive studies in the forties restored the Institute's flagging finances and provided monetary security until its return to Germany in 1949. The first (1943-1945), for which Lowenthal returned from Washington, dealt with the degree of anti-Semitism in American labor. It was supported by the Jewish Labor Committee, a subgroup of the American Jewish Committee. The study was chaired by Adolph Held, who had contacts with the AFL, the CIO, and various unaffiliated unions, which facilitated the collection of data in New York, California, and Detroit. Because different types of unions were surveyed in the three locations, there were methodological problems from the start. Moreover, Horkheimer remembers that the conclusions of the study were so damaging to American labor that the Institute was hesitant to broadcast them and declared the report redundant in the light of the Institute's last important collaborative work (Jay 1973, 224-25). In the book *Studies in Prejudice*, Adorno and his colleagues explored the character types who would be most receptive to demagogic appeals and developed a series of anti-Semitic personality scales (Jay 1986, 94-95). The studies were paid for by the American Jewish Committee and constituted a collaborative effort with non–Institute members who were psychoanalytically trained and usually unfamiliar with critical theory. Without Horkheimer's unifying perspective, three of the five volumes dealt with prejudice as a basically subjective phenomenon. Among these are Bruno Bettelheim and Morris Janowitz's *Dynamics of Prejudice: A Psychological and Sociological Study of Veterans* (1950); Nathan Ackerman and Marie Jahoda's *Antisemitism and Emotional Disorder: A Psychoanalytic Interpretation* (1950); and T. Adorno, Else Frenkel-Brunswik, Daniel Levinson, and Nevitt Stanford's *The Authoritarian Personality* (1950). The fourth, Leo Lowenthal and Norbert Guterman's *Prophets of Deceit* (1949), analyzed the techniques of the demagogue; and the last, Paul Massing's *Rehearsal for Destruction* (1949), presented a straightforward historical account of anti-Semitism in Germany.

The Lazarsfeld/Merton Bureau of
Social Research (1941-1955)

While the Institute group settled into a Columbia-owned building on Morningside Drive, the members were unaware that another emigré scholar was also trying to establish a footing in the city. Paul F. Lazarsfeld, a Viennese social psychologist, trained in empirical research methods, lacked the endowment funds that cushioned the Frankfurt group's arrival. Lazarsfeld's idea to investigate radio effects fit in well with earlier U.S. empirical concerns of which Lazarsfeld was however unaware. Advertisers were interested in establishing national markets, while Roosevelt's and Goebbels's radio successes raised questions about radio's social and political implications. Harold Lasswell's propaganda work and Allport and Cantril's *Psychology of Radio* (1935) seemed to indicate that radio had stronger political impact than print (Lerg 1977, 74-76). To relate the behavior of actual people to the latent social structure became Lazarsfeld and Merton's cooperative research preoccupation throughout the forties and fifties, during which time Elihu Katz was a graduate student at Columbia (Lazarsfeld 1975, 45-48).

Using the Bühler's Vienna "Forschungsstelle" (Research Institute) idea, which supported itself through research commissions, Lazarsfeld commenced to reestablish his academic status by transferring this entrepreneurial model to New York. He accomplished the transplant in three rapid stages between 1937 and 1945, an exceptional feat for a Jewish emigré. First, Lazarsfeld created the Newark Research Center, where unemployment statistics were evaluated for the National Youth Administration. This organization was quickly transformed into the Princeton Radio Research Project (1937-1940), with Lazarsfeld as codirector along with Frank Stanton and Hadley Cantril. After the loss of its premises in Newark, and a year before Lazarsfeld and Merton were simultaneously appointed to the sociology department, the Radio Project was transferred to Columbia, where it became the Office of Radio Research (1940-1944) (Robinson 1990, 93). As of 1941, it was codirected by two "masters," whose relationship (according to Sills 1979, 421) was intense, personal, and deeply meaningful to each other. The final emergence of the Bureau of Social Research was not accomplished until 1945, when the administrative relationship to Columbia was regularized. The Bureau became a laboratory for the Faculty of Political Science, for which the university paid 10 percent of the annual operating budget (Lazarsfeld 1969, 333). In 1948, Lazarsfeld resigned the codirectorship to become chairman of the Sociology Department and was succeeded first by Kingsley Davis (1948-1950) and then by Charles Glock (1951-1956). Davis doubled the small budget of $90,000 to $180,000 of the early years and stabilized the Bureau's hand-to-mouth existence with a half-million-dollar grant from the Air Force to study the world's cities after World War II (Barton 1984, 1-3). By the late fifties, although they remained colleagues, both Lazarsfeld and Merton developed new research interests, the former in mathematical modeling and the latter returning to his original interest in the sociology of science (Barton 1982, 27).

In the Columbia school's functionalist framework, Lazarsfeld tended to focus on the character of motivation and Merton on the character of the structural context (Neurath 1988, 80-83). From the radio studies came three types of results: the theoretical underpinnings for survey analysis, the development of middle-range theory about mass communication processes in society, and an evaluation of the adequacy of the techniques used in the Bureau's research projects. Lazarsfeld was primarily associated with the first and Merton with the second set of accomplishments, while both contributed to the third (Converse 1987, 286). Examples of testing the adequacy of techniques are found in such early forties studies as Merton's analysis of the "Why We Fight" film series, for which he and Patricia Kendall helped to codify the "focused interview," while Lazarsfeld was creating the "program analyzer" with Stanton in New York. The former elaborated the stimuli involved in human action research, and the latter permitted listeners to immediately record their interest/disinterest in a radio episode. Lazarsfeld's own interests in the "effects" of media was explored through a variety of individual opinion formation, decision making, and behavioral actions studies, which were the focus of the Bureau's numerous marketing and voting studies. These prepared the way for the so-called limited effects paradigm, which emerged from Katz and Lazarsfeld's *Personal Influence* (1955) volume ten years later.

Merton's "middle range" theory contributions, which were never sufficiently recognized in comparison to Lazarsfeld's more numerous Bureau contributions, (Lazarsfeld 1975, 51-52) are brilliantly illustrated in two of his studies: *Mass Persuasion* (1946/1958) and "Patterns of Influence" (1949). The first was produced with the assistance of Marjorie Fiske and Alberta Curtis and analyzed the "Kate Smith War Bond Drive." It probed audience "gratifications" derived from media programming, such as a sense of participation in current events, and explored people's meaning-making strategies through rhetorical analysis. According to Peter Simonson (2004, XL-XLIII), the book makes three important theoretical contributions to the future field of media studies: it lays the foundations for understanding the "symbolic work" propagandists do; it demonstrates that audiences are "active" in interpreting programming; and it enunciates what James Carey would later call a "ritual" approach to mass media content, where message meaning is more important than its distributive characteristics. Merton's "Patterns of Influence: A Study of Interpersonal Influence and Communication Behavior in a Local Community" (1949), was based on eighty-seven in-depth interviews in an Eastern Seaboard town, codenamed "Rovere." Here, Merton focused on people and their social networks and discovered the media characteristics of what were then called "horizontal leaders." Merton renamed these individuals "influentials" and, after a restudy of their social activities, found that there were two kinds, based on their orientations toward the world. He called them "cosmopolitans" and "locals" and demonstrated that they used the media more than ordinary people and that other people sought their advice. By the end of the decade, Merton's magisterial *Social Theory and Social Structure* (1957) integrated all he had learned about manifest and latent functions, anomie and bureaucracy in modern life, at the level of the social structure. All these studies demonstrate Robert Merton's eclecticism, inventiveness, and ability to combine European with North American intellectual traditions. He had acquired these at Harvard, where he had studied with Pitrim Sorokin and Talcott Parson and explored the traditions of Marx, Weber, and especially Durkheim.

Contacts between the Frankfurt Institute and the Bureau in New York

Despite their ideological differences, the Frankfurt Institute and the Bureau had research contacts, exchanged personnel, and offered each other institutional help in New York. The most important research contacts were Theodore Adorno's "On Popular Music" (1941) and Leo Lowenthal's "The Triumph of Mass Idols" (1944), which highlighted both the inability of Adorno to work with Lazarsfeld as well as the compatibility of "critical theory" with evidential analysis. Though the "critical-administrative" debate has been well rehearsed by scholars like Hanno Hardt (1991, 65-85) and David Morrison (1978, 331-55), they view the historical context in which it was played out too narrowly. The missing elements are not only the deteriorating personal relationships between Lazarsfeld and Adorno, but also the Frankfurt group's total ignorance and disinterest in their New York colleagues' research agendas until the end of World War II, when their funds began to run out. In the summer of 1939, the Rockefeller-sponsored music project, in which Adorno had introduced the concept of a "culture industry," was cancelled. Lazarsfeld's letter mentions his extreme disappointment with the outcome of their association, commenting in the last paragraph, "You and I agree upon the superiority of some parts of your intellectual work, but you think because you are basically right somewhere, you are right everywhere" (Jay 1973, 223). In retrospect, it becomes clear that few men who knew Adorno doubted his intellectual brilliance, but fewer still, and here Horkheimer is the exception, found him an easy collaborator. In spite of the termination of the project, Adorno's "The Radio Symphony" (1941) was published in Lazarsfeld and Stanton's *Radio Research 1941* volume.

Lowenthal's "The Triumph of Mass Idols" (1944) followed the idea that the culture industry was subtly enslaving and that literature needed to be used to identify the social and cultural structures that promoted such enslavement in mass culture. Lazarsfeld, who knew about Lowenthal's unpublished biographical studies of Emil Ludwig and Stefan Zweig, wondered whether he could apply his insights to contemporary American literary productions. This request coincided with Lowenthal's discovery that the *Saturday Evening Post* and *Colliers*, two of the most popular American consumer magazines at the time, contained biographies. Lowenthal content analyzed all issues of the magazines between 1901 and 1940, "from the methodological viewpoint of their 'symptomatic' significance and reflected on the extent to which these market products might be indicators of social processes" (Jay 1987, 132). He found that in the first twenty years of the century, the heroes of the biographies were taken from the field of production: successful merchants, professionals, inventors, and entrepreneurs. The biographies thus seemed to function as politico-educational stimuli and to reinforce the Horatio Alger myth of personal success. The situation changed drastically at the end of the thirties, when the so-called heroes became people from show business: movie actors, radio stars, famous impresarios, singers, and sportsmen, whose sole function was to entertain the reader by portraying the entertainers' consumer habits and hobbies. Lowenthal concluded that these findings were evidence that in the stage of corporate capitalism, the rise of the entrepreneur increasingly turned into pure fiction; and second, that American bourgeois society had transformed itself into a consumer society in which people were interested only in consumption. Martin Jay (1973, 217) observes that the Institute's critique of mass culture and its related analysis of the American authoritarian potential had a greater impact on American intellectual life than their other studies, because by the fifties, local scholars like Clement Greenberg and Dwight MacDonald, through his influential journal *Politics*, began to disseminate similar critiques to a wider public.

Despite their ideological differences,
the Frankfurt Institute and the Bureau
had research contacts, exchanged personnel,
and offered each other institutional
help in New York.

The most interesting contacts between the Frankfurt and Bureau groups happened in 1944, when Lowenthal and Pollock's office had to move to smaller quarters, and their survival at Columbia seemed precarious because of their own financial woes. At the time, Lazarsfeld proposed that the Institute be integrated into his own Bureau of Social Research, where between 1944 and 1946, C. Wright Mills was overseeing the fieldwork and initial (unsuccessful) analysis of the Decatur data, which would ultimately become Katz and Lazarsfeld's *Personal Influence* (1955). Although the Sociology Department supported the plan, Horkheimer, who was working on the *Authoritarian Personality* (1950) with Adorno in California, ultimately declined the offer in 1946, citing health reasons (Jay 1973, 220). Yet at about the same time, Lowenthal reported to Horkheimer that there was encouraging news from Germany and that the Institute's desire to be available for post-Nazi reconstruction seemed to be coming to fruition. Members of the Frankfurt city community made the first concrete offer to return the Institute to its city of origin. Negotiations were concluded in July 1949, when the university chair taken away from Horkheimer was restored. With him went the Institute's endowment and library, although only two of the inner circle accompanied him—Adorno and Pollock—while the rest of the group, including Lowenthal, decided to remain in the United States (Jay 1973, 282-83).

The Katz/Lowenthal Encounter: An Attempt at Historiographical Reconstruction

In concluding this article, I once again come face to face with the initial question concerning Elihu Katz's encounter with Leo Lowenthal. What exactly were Katz and Lowenthal doing between 1946 and 1956 when Katz began his studies at Columbia? To unravel these complex filiations, it is necessary to revert to Merton's third moment in describing and reconstructing a scientific activity: the degree of autonomy of the actors involved and the difference in reference groups to which they belonged (Merton 1973).

Reviewing the individual motivations of the two protagonists and the social settings in which they were doing their work, I found surprising similarities as well as great differences. The similarities, it turns out, are found in their social backgrounds, while the differences are generational and thus affect the academic setting in which they meet. Elihu Katz was born in Brooklyn in 1926, into a family of East European Jewish immigrants. On his father's side, the family came from Poland, and on his mother's, from Galicia, then part of Austria (Katz interview, April 6, 2006). He commented, "We were a modern-orthodox family, in a community that pioneered the establishment of bi-lingual (Hebrew-English) schooling, which resulted in a good classic Jewish as well as secular education and a Zionist orientation. Father was head salesman of a large wholesaler of woolen cloth and mother was an activist in Jewish affairs" (Katz interview, March 20, 2006). This familial background has similarities to Lowenthal's early married years with Golde Ginsberg and their Zionist life in 1920s Germany. Yet the fact that Lowenthal was twenty-six years older than Katz meant that when they met at Columbia between 1948 and 1950, they were at very different stages in their careers. Katz, who had been drafted as an eighteen-year-old and had been an interpreter in Japan (1944-1946), returned to New York with the thought of studying journalism at Columbia. However, senior courses with Lazarsfeld encouraged him to switch into sociology with special emphasis on mass communication and public opinion.

The Katz/Lowenthal meeting, according to Katz, occurred in a course on the sociology of literature or popular culture, taught by Lowenthal as guest professor in 1948. Even though Katz believes "that he was 'rehearsing' for the job as

Research Director at the Voice of America" (Katz interview, March 20, 2006), the evidence shows that this interpretation is only partially correct. Yes, Lowenthal would be appointed to that post a year later (1949); however, his substantial content analytic work at the Bureau of Overseas Intelligence between 1941 and 1944 required no further "rehearsal" to demonstrate his research capacities. In 1948, he was supporting himself by combining his Columbia teaching with writing his *Prophets of Deceit* (1949) with Guterman, for which the American Jewish Committee was paying him $10,000. In this study, Lowenthal was once again utilizing content analysis methods similar to those that he had honed in the Lazarsfeld-commissioned "Biographies in Popular Magazines" (1944). Merton called this study "a rare and successful hybrid of European social theory and American style empirical research" (Merton 1957, 450). Yet in *Prophets of Deceit*, the focus was on the techniques of demagogic propaganda, including the rhetorical devices utilized in propagandistic language. To provide a larger historical context, the Nazi devices were compared with those of past propagandists, such as Savanerola and Robespierre. Katz had read both of these works and claimed that they "made a great impression on me."

Katz's own research competencies were acquired through participation in five Bureau studies between 1950 and 1954. They included the fan-mail project that earned him the MA in 1950 with "The Happiness Game" thesis, supervised by Lowenthal; and a chunk of the public opinion studies in Arabic countries, commissioned by Lowenthal at the Voice of America, for which Katz wrote a comparative report with Pat Kendall that was later used by Daniel Lerner in *The Passing of Traditional Society* (1958). The third Bureau project that Katz was involved in was called "engaged couples," which failed to receive funding, while the Decatur study offered material for his PhD dissertation on small-group dynamics and the two-step flow reported in *Personal Influence* (1955). Finally, there was the 1954 to 1955 work with Coleman and Menzel, designing, implementing, and analyzing a study on the diffusion of new drugs among medical doctors (Katz interview, March 20, 2006; Barton 1982, 46).

For the twenty-eight-year-old Katz, the "preparatory stages" for a scholarly career that would span positions in the United States and Israel would come to an end in 1954. At that time, he was offered an assistant professorship at Chicago, "which was suffering from depleted ranks and looked to Columbia for reinforcements. . . . Other Columbia people who came to Chicago slightly before and later, were Peter Rossi, Peter Blau, Jim Coleman, Rolf Meyerson, and Philip Ennis. This migration was rather dissonant with the Chicago tradition of Park, Burgess etc., and carried on by Janowitz, Anselm Strauss, Don Horton, Phil Hauser, Goffman . . . but most creatively, from my point of view, by Everett and Helen Hughes" (Katz interview, March 20, 2006). Interestingly, it is through Hughes that the Chicago tradition migrated to Canada, where his wife Helen had been born and where he founded one of the country's first sociology departments, at McGill University in Montreal.

For Lowenthal, in contrast, the 1946 to 1956 period constituted a major break in his intellectual life and ultimately in his career. In 1949, when Horkheimer,

Adorno, and Pollock returned to Frankfurt, his intimate involvement with the Institute ended. It had been both his "intellectual home" as well as his chosen place of work, where he had not only edited the *Zeitschrift* but been involved in the group's U.S. research projects and functioned as codirector of the New York branch office since 1941. What were Lowenthal's motivations for staying behind in North America, especially since he had not been satisfied with his wartime advisory position at the Office of War Information? His interviews with Dubiel suggest that there seem to have been at least three contributing circumstances: a challenging work opportunity, his integration into the U.S. intellectual milieu, and finally a new personal relationship (Lowenthal 1980, 113-18). The challenging work opportunity came in 1949, when he was encouraged to set up a research division for the Voice of America, after having analyzed German armed forces radio programs at the end of the war. Lowenthal mentions that he was free to choose his scientific colleagues. Among others, he chose the pollsters Joseph Klapper and Ralph White and the social-psychologist Marjorie Fiske. This group of researchers as well as their radio producers did pioneering work in developing new ways of analyzing media effects. In the Soviet Union and satellite countries' project, the researchers assessed the impact of "jamming techniques" on U.S. programming; and in the Near East studies, the focus was on communication habits in villages and cities and the formation of public opinion leadership (Jay 1987, 81-84). Throughout this period, Lowenthal traveled in war-damaged Europe (1949 and 1951) and through Spain, Portugal, and Greece for the study of cities (Jay 1987, 108-9). The Near East studies investigated who were the sources of public opinion, how it was disseminated in the rural areas, and by whom. Were the sources the café, the mule driver, or messengers traveling from the cities to the villages (Jay 1987, 84)? The Bureau, with Katz as a graduate researcher, was deeply involved with the Near East project, producing a total of nine reports for the Voice of America in the three years between 1949 and 1952 (Barton 1984, 20-21). These covered methods for identifying opinion leadership, estimating audiences to develop an intensity scale of listening to the Voice of America, content analysis and program classification, and a French study to develop a comparative approach for the study of foreign countries with different broadcast systems.

To Lowenthal's great surprise, his directorship of the Research Division came to an abrupt end in 1954, when the entire agency was transferred to the U.S. Information Agency as the Republicans took power. The ensuing McCarthy era, Lowenthal remembers, "made life very tough, broke up my department and reduced my research funding in order to gradually force me to quit" (Jay 1987, 86; Bogart 1993, 377). Dubin inquired whether the fact that he was suddenly no longer wanted in the post had something to do with his ideological and scientific background (Jay 1987, 89). Surprisingly, Lowenthal answered, "I hardly think so. More likely it coincided with a trend." He mentioned three reasons: "that the new administration wanted to fill the post with a Republican; that Congressional representatives objected to the scientific orientation of the methods used in the Research Division; and that there was a rivalry between the Congressional and federal bureaucracies" (Jay 1987, 90-91). According to Lowenthal, the McCarthy Committee was not at all liked by the members of the Senate Foreign Affairs Committee, which formed its own subcommittee (Hickenlooper), which "treated me with a great deal of respect" (Jay 1987, 90-91). To the accusation why people like himself, with a clear-cut intellectual, socialist tradition, had no qualms about entering the service of a power that just one generation later was seen as unequivocally imperialistic, Lowenthal had the following answer: "Governmental service did not compromise either Marcuse or me. For practical (financial) reasons, as mentioned above, I was forced to find suitable employment. . . . Furthermore, in the post-war period I never had the feeling I was working for an imperialist power. At that time, American foreign policy was (still) essentially reactive and in no respect active" (Jay 1987, 93-94). Lowenthal was never called before the McCarthy Committee, because they could not find anything to hold against him, and he refused to resign, instead taking a leave of absence from the Voice of America from 1954 to 1955 to assess his options.

Once again, Lazarsfeld provided crucial advice and in 1955 arranged for an invitation to the Stanford Center for Advanced Studies. He suggested, "In this research year you have the alternative of either embarking on what the Americans call 'having a good time,' and at the end of the year you become a dog-catcher in Palo Alto; or you can write a few books and subsequently become a professor" (Jay 1987, 138). Lazarsfeld's advice proved to be sound, and Lowenthal wrote his *Literature and the Image of Man* (*Das Menschenbild in der Literatur*; 1957) based on a revision and rewrite of older articles that had appeared in the *Zeitschrift* and a new section on Goethe as well as a study on the relation of art and popular culture in eighteenth-century England. In the fall of 1956, Lowenthal was appointed professor in the Department of Sociology at the University of California, Berkeley, where he became an early supporter of the Free Speech Movement and a leading member of the 1968 Muscadine Committee, which reconceptualized education at Berkeley.

Lowenthal's intellectual integration into the American milieu was perceptively analyzed by Lewis Coser (1984), using the notion of barriers to the transfer of prestige. He noted that immigrants, because they leave their country voluntarily, expect to integrate into their new country to rebuild their prestige. Exiles, in contrast, are forced to leave and therefore usually wish to return to their country of origin, where their prestige remains intact (p. 4). The majority of the Frankfurt group were certainly exiles when they arrived in New York, yet the younger members like Lowenthal, who were at the beginning of their careers, were not as reluctant as their elders to learn new ways. Lowenthal had furthermore benefited from the group's initial financial security and his contacts with Lazarsfeld. Lazarsfeld, according to Neumann, epitomized the ability to integrate new experiences with the old traditions (as cited in Coser 1984, 12). Lowenthal's integration is evidenced by the already mentioned quantitative methods he learned and employed in "Biographies in Popular Magazines" (1944) and his coauthored *Prophets of Deceit* (1949). Integration was also enhanced through collaboration with such Bureau personnel as Seymour Lipset and Joseph Klapper, who were involved with the Near East modernization studies (Hughes 1974, 102). Dubiel concluded in wonder, "In Germany you're perceived as a German professor who lives and works abroad . . . while here . . . both in the literature and in conversational remarks, your colleagues perceive you as an American intellectual" (Jay 1987, 141). Lowenthal responded that this was partially a result of the fact that in his career he had been forced to deal with concrete things and that the key areas of his work, both theoretical and applied, lay in the field of mass communication, which for a long time was one of the most important themes of American social science (Jay 1987, 140).

In spite of their generational differences, the careers of Katz and Lowenthal have one great similarity: both are "border travelers," and they have consequently contributed to the geographical transfer of ideas.

The new personal relationship, finally, which attached Lowenthal to America after the departure of the Frankfurt group, was Marjorie Fiske (1914-1992), whom he must have met at the Bureau and married in the late forties. Fiske had received her BA from Mount Holyoke and her MA in psychology from Columbia, where Lazarsfeld had hired her, like Katz, as a promising student researcher. By the time Lowenthal met her, Fiske was one of the accomplished female researchers at the Bureau, whose seventeen years' worth of contributions (1939-1955)— along with those of others such as Herta Herzog, Lazarsfeld's second wife—needs urgent reconsideration to provide a more balanced picture of their professional contributions. In the Bureau, Fiske had worked on fifteen psychology of radio projects and another five concerned with the effects of motion pictures and comics and coauthored two books with Robert Merton, *Mass Persuasion* (Merton, Fiske, and Curtis 1946) and *The Focused Interview: A Manual of Problems and Procedures* (1956). Between 1950 and 1952, she had furthermore been part of Lowenthal's Voice of America research team, which attempted to learn more about the efficacy of American official communications at the beginning of the cold war era (Barton 1982, 55). In 1953, she was finally promoted to executive director of a new Bureau division, the Planning Committee on Media Research. Fiske's 1955 move to Stanford with Lowenthal thus constituted a new career stage, for her as well as him, and they commenced with a joint study titled "The

Debate over Art and Popular Culture in Eighteenth-Century England" (Lowenthal and Fiske 1957). On her arrival, she taught in the Department of Sociology and the School of Librarianship, where she authored a report *Book Selection and Censorship* (1959) for which she received the Library Literature Award of the American Library Association in 1960. From 1958 to 1984, she directed a series of interdisciplinary studies on adult development and aging in the Department of Psychiatry and wrote nine books for which she received the Kleemeier Award from the Gerontology Society (1973) and the Distinguished Research Award from the American Psychological Association (1987) (see "In Memoriam" 1992).

Although officially retired since 1968, Lowenthal remained active in departmental and university affairs in Berkeley until virtually the end of his life. The celebrated private graduate seminar in the sociology of literature attracted a post-Vietnam crowd, eager to learn about the Frankfurt School. Lowenthal's publications were collected during the 1980s, both in Germany by Suhrkam Verlag and in America by Transaction Press. As a result, his *Literature and the Image of Man* (1957); *Literature, Popular Culture and Society* (1961); and his autobiographical reflections with the German sociologist Helmut Dubiel, *An Unmastered Past* (1987) became available to a large new readership. In the last decade of his life, he was awarded the Berkeley Citation and the Federal Republic of Germany's Distinguished Merit Cross as well as Frankfurt's Goethe Medal and Adorno Prize, as the final survivor of the Frankfurt School's inner circle and symbol of its remarkable collective achievement (Jay 1992, 2-3). His obituary notes that he is survived by his son Daniel and his third wife, Susanne Hoppmann, director of Berkeley's German Cultural Center (Bogart 1993, 378).

In spite of their generational differences, the careers of Katz and Lowenthal have one great similarity: both are "border travelers," and they have consequently contributed to the geographical transfer of ideas. In Katz's case, the transfer is from America to the young state of Israel. Starting in 1950, when he was still a graduate student at Columbia, he visited Jerusalem as national president of the Intercollegiate Zionist Federation of America. His wife Ruth had been assigned as *shaliach* (emissary, ambassador) by the World Zionist Organization to accompany him (Katz interview, April 6, 2006). For Lowenthal, the transfer, as we have seen, was from Germany to the United States in the midthirties. As border travelers, Katz and Lowenthal also played key roles in setting up new research institutions, which would utilize their scholarly expertise. For Katz, the geographical "commuting" commenced between 1956 and 1958, when he took a leave from Chicago and started to work at the Israel Institute of Applied Research, set up by Louis Guttman. Not only did he direct this institution in the coming decade, but he also founded Hebrew University's Communication Institute, where he trained faculty and students, just as Lazarsfeld had done at the Bureau. Finally, Katz's and Lowenthal's expansion of their theoretical horizons as a result of their cross-border engagement is well documented in their scholarly work. For Lowenthal, this involved coauthorship with Frankfurt scholars such as Horkheimer, Marcuse, and Guterman; while for Katz it involved work with a new generation of Israeli and

British scholars (see www.asc.upenn.edu/asc/Application/Faculty/BioDetails.asp [accessed March 13, 2006]). British collaboration in the seventies tackled such theoretical issues as gratification research (1974) with J. Blumler, comparative broadcast issues (1977) with F. Wedell, the new genre of late night news (1980) with B. Zelizer et al., and the role of mass media in social change (1981) with T. Szecsko. Copublications in the nineties brought in newly trained Israeli scholars whose work addressed Israeli concerns. Among them: a collection of live broadcast history programs (1992) with D. Dayan; reading *Dallas* cross-culturally (1993) with T. Liebes; cultural policy in Israel (1999) with H. Sella; and volumes on popular culture in 1999 and 2000, with I. Yanovitzky and H. Haas, respectively. All of these activities demonstrate that both Katz and Lowenthal kept alive the important research traditions of the Bureau and the Frankfurt group for a new generation of scholars at Hebrew University and at Berkeley. Yet in their careers, both men also embodied something else. Through their outgoing personalities, integrity, and deep engagement with the world, they demonstrate that scholarly transfer "matters" in the globalized twenty-first century and that insightful scholarship from the past, including their own, provides bridges for the future.

References

Adorno, Theodore W. 1941. The radio symphony. In *Radio research 1941*, ed. P. F. Lazarsfeld and F. Stanton, 110-39. New York: Duell, Sloan & Pearce.

Barton, Allen H. 1982. Paul Lazarsfeld and the invention of the University Institute for Applied Social Research. In *Organizing for social research*, ed. Burkhard Holzner and Jiri Nehnevajsa, 17-83. Cambridge, UK: Schenckman.

Barton, Judith S., ed. 1984. *Guide to the Bureau of Applied Social Research*. New York: Clearwater.

Bogart, Leo. 1993. In memoriam: Leo Lowenthal, 1900-1993. *Public Opinion Quarterly* 57:377-79.

Converse, Jean M. 1987. *Survey research in the United States: Roots and emergence, 1890-1960*. Berkeley: University of California Press.

Coser, Lewis A. 1984. *Refugee scholars in America: Their impact and experiences*. New Haven, CT: Yale University Press.

Czitrom, Daniel. 1982. *Media and the American mind: From Morse to McLuhan*. Chapel Hill: University of North Carolina Press.

Fiske, Marjorie. 1992. *In memoriam*. 1992. University of California. http://dynaweb.oac.cdlib.org:8088/dynaweb/uchist/public/inmemoriam1992/@Generic_BookTextView/918;pt=948 (accessed February 23, 2006).

Hardt, Hanno. 1991. The conscience of society: Leo Lowenthal. *Journal of Communication* 41 (3): 65-85.

Hughes, H. Stuart. 1974. *The sea change: The migration of social thought, 1930-1965*. New York: Harper & Row.

Jay, Martin. 1973. *The dialectical imagination: A history of the Frankfurt school and the Institute of Social Research, 1923-1950*. Boston: Little, Brown.

———. 1986. *Permanent exiles: Essays on the intellectual migration from Germany to America*. New York: Columbia University Press.

———, ed. 1987. *An unmastered past: The autobiographical reflections of Leo Lowenthal*. Berkeley: University of California Press.

———. 1992. In memoriam: Leo Lowenthal. *Berkeley Journal of Sociology* 37:1-3.

Katz, E., and P. F. Lazarsfeld. 1955. *Personal influence: The part played by people in the flow of mass communication*. Glencoe, IL: Free Press.

Lazarsfeld, Paul F. 1969. An episode in the history of social research: A memoir. In *The intellectual migration: Europe and America 1930-1960*, ed. Donald Fleming and Bernard Bailyn. Cambridge, MA: Harvard University Press.

———. 1975. Working with Merton. In *The idea of social structure: Papers in honor of Robert K. Merton*, ed. Lewis Coser, 35-66. New York: Harcourt Brace Jovanivich.

Lerg, Winfrid. 1977. Paul Felix Lazarsfeld und die Kommunikationsforschung: Ein biobibliographisches Epitaph. *Publizistik* 1:72-87.

Lowenthal, Leo. 1944. The triumph of mass idols. In *Radio research 1942-1943*, ed. Paul F. Lazarsfeld and Frank Stanton, 516-28. New York: Duell, Sloan & Pearce. Repr., *Literature and mass culture*, chap. 6, New Brunswick, NJ: Transaction Books, 1984.

———. 1980. *Mitmachen wollte ich nie: Ein autobiographisches Gespräch mit Helmut Dubiel.* Frankfurt, Germany: Suhrkamp Verlag. 1980. (Repr., *An unmastered past*, translated by Martin Jay, University of California Press, Berkeley, 1987)

Lowenthal, Leo, and Marjorie Fiske. 1957. The debate over art and popular culture in eighteenth-century England. *Common Frontiers in the Social Sciences*, pp. 33-112.

Merton, Robert K. 1949. Patterns of influence: A study of interpersonal influence and communication behavior in a local community. In *Communications in research, 1948-49*, ed. Paul F. Lazarsfeld and F. Stanton, 180-219. New York: Harper & Bros.

———. 1957. *Social theory and social structure.* Glencoe, IL: Free Press.

———. 1973. *The sociology of science.* Edited by Norman Storer. Chicago: University of Chicago Press.

Merton, Robert K., Marjorie Fiske, and Alice Curtis. 1946/1958. *Mass persuasion: The social psychology of a war bond drive.* New York: Harper.

Morrison, David. 1978. Kultur and culture: The case of Theodore Adorno and Paul F. Lazarsfeld. *Social Research* 45 (2): 331-55.

Neurath, Paul. 1988. Paul Lazarsfeld und die Institutionalisierung der empirischen Sozialforschung. In *Exil, Wissenschaft, Identität: Die Emigration deutscher Sozialwissenschaftler 1933-1945*, ed. Ilja Srubar, 67-105. Frankfurt, Germany: Suhrkamp.

Robinson, Gertrude J. 1990. Paul Felix Lazarsfeld's contributions to the development of US communication studies. In *Paul Lazarsfeld*, ed. Wolfgang Langenbucher, 89-111. Munich, Germany: Verlag Ölschläger.

Sills, David, ed. 1979. *International encyclopedia of the social sciences.* Vol. 18, Biographical supplement. New York: Free Press.

Simonson, Peter. 2004. Introduction. In *Mass persuasion: The social psychology of a war bond drive*, ed. R. K. Merton, XI-XLV. New York: Howard Fertig.

The Part Played by Gentiles in the Flow of Mass Communications: On the Ethnic Utopia of *Personal Influence*

By
JOHN DURHAM PETERS

Personal Influence is not only a landmark study within the sociological literature on networks, influence, and decision making. It is also an allegory of Jewish-ethnic identity in mid-twentieth-century America and a sideways commentary on modern Jewish involvement in communications. The book participates in a utopian imagination of society in which Jews and Gentiles alike would be centrally involved in the flow of communications. It turns from Gentile-style status toward Jewish-style connectivity as the basis of social power; defends socially grounded conceptions of mental life against Gentile individualism; insists in its notion of the two-step flow on the rabbinic principle that a text without a commentary is meaningless; and performs some amazing intellectual-moral-historical footwork with the most inconspicuous of all its central terms, "people." In all these things, it can be read as a "Jewish" text in some sense.

Keywords: communication research; Jewish studies; American democracy; intellectual history; social science; sociology; ethnicity

It is only the setting that is Jewish; the core belongs to humanity in general.
—Sigmund Freud on Jewish jokes

I want to argue that *Personal Influence* (Katz and Lazarsfeld 1955) is not only a landmark study within the sociological literature on networks, influence, and decision making. It is also an allegory of Jewish-ethnic identity in mid-twentieth-century America and a sideways commentary on modern Jewish involvement in communications.

NOTE: I thank Menahem Blondheim, Daniel Dayan, Elihu Katz, Ruth Katz, Samuel Z. Klausner, J. Kenneth Kuntz, Tamar Liebes, Michael Schudson, Peter Simonson, and Joseph Turow for citations, comments, criticisms, encouragement, and warnings. Here more than usual, I alone bear responsibility for this article.

DOI: 10.1177/0002716206292425

The Jewish Question in Communications

Reading *Personal Influence* as a "Jewish" text immediately raises a number of vexatious problems. To say that a text is Jewish might seem like a category mistake, sort of like the "diabetic ice cream" one can buy in grocery stores. Just as ice cream cannot have a malfunctioning pancreas, so texts do not have ethnicities. Furthermore, to read the book in this way might seem redolent of the anti-Semitic reduction of works of art and science to crude authorial variables. In the era in which *Personal Influence* was written, personal identity was not a scholarly topic for personal disclosure or public analysis. Nazism's use of the slur of "Jewish" science (to slander psychoanalysis and Marxism especially) was only one example of the problems of tying the "background" of scholars to their work. Indeed, Robert K. Merton (1942) had made the irrelevance of biography a norm of science and democracy, and midcentury positivist philosophy of science suppressed the personal dimension. According to interviews conducted by Peter Simonson with Merton before his death, Merton and Lazarsfeld never discussed their Jewishness. The WASP-ishly named Merton, born Meyer Schkolnick, went public with his Jewish identity only in his ninth decade (Merton 1994), though it may have been well known among colleagues and students. The treatment of ethnicity in *Personal Influence* is one of the book's most telling silences. The book is a muted response to a century stained by the worst anti-Semitic violence in history. The absence of any explicit discussion of Jewishness in *Personal Influence* is, I argue, not an oversight: it is an aspiration. The book participates in a utopian imagination of society in which Jews and Gentiles alike would be centrally involved in the flow of communications.

The part played by Jews in the flow of mass communications is plain to see historically. They have been leaders and innovators in wire services, the press, Hollywood, radio, television, recorded music, computers, and the Internet, not to mention related areas such as banking, retailing, and the liberal professions. Jews have shown remarkable talent at building institutions that involve interfaces and networks of all kinds. To list some: in wire services, there is Charles-Louis Havas, founder of Agence France-Presse, the first wire service, and Paul Julius Reuter, founder of Reuters; in publishing, Joseph Pulitzer, Adolph Ochs, Alfred Knopf, Richard Simon and Max Schuster, Samuel Irving Newhouse, Walter Annenberg, Robert Maxwell and Conrad Black; broadcasting boasts RCA's David Sarnoff, CBS's William Paley, ABC's Leonard Goldenson, and more recently, Viacom's Sumner Redstone, not to mention a host of producers, writers, and talent. The high technology business has Intel's Andrew Grove, Microsoft's Steve Ballmer, Oracle's Larry Ellison, Dell's Michael Dell, and Google's Sergey Brin. The most

John Durham Peters is the F. Wendell Miller Distinguished Professor of Communication Studies at the University of Iowa. He is the author of Speaking into the Air *(Chicago, 1999) and* Courting the Abyss *(Chicago, 2005), as well as a coeditor of* Canonic Texts in Media Studies *(Cambridge: Polity Press, 2003) and* Mass Communication and American Social Thought: Key Texts, 1919-1968 *(Boulder, 2004).*

famous arena, of course, is Hollywood film, where Jews such as William Fox, Samuel Goldwyn, Carl Laemmle, Marcus Loew, Louis B. Mayer, the Warner Brothers, and Adolph Zukor built celluloid dreams about an America in which they remained partial outsiders—a history told in too conspiratorial a fashion for my taste by Gabler (1988). A similar demographic persisted in the next generation of Hollywood moguls such as David O. Selznick and Irving Thalberg and continues today with Dreamworks' Steven Spielberg, Jeffrey Katzenberg, and David Geffen; Miramax's Weinstein Brothers; Disney's long-time CEO Michael Eisner; and Seagrams' Edgar Bronfman Jr. One should not forget Edward Bernays, inventor of public relations, or Emile Berliner, inventor of the gramophone. The list could go on—and this one focuses almost exclusively on the United States.

In addition to managing communications institutions themselves, Jews have played a vastly influential role in the intellectual interpretation of communications—as judges interpreting laws about public communication (such as Louis Brandeis, Benjamin Cardozo, and Felix Frankfurter), activists agitating on behalf of civil liberties (including much of the American Civil Liberties Union), and media scholars and critics. Fully half of the authors of a recent collection of leading twentieth-century texts on mass communication and American social thought are Jews (Peters and Simonson 2004).

More than any other group in history, Jews have made enormous contributions to the channels, interpretation, and content of communication. Personal Influence *is one chapter in this story.*

More broadly, Jews have arguably been the most successful communicators in history, providing a treasure trove of content to world culture. It is incontestable that the Jewish tradition has some kind of elective affinity with the arts of communication. Once a small Middle Eastern tribe among many rivals, their sacred literature has become the scripture for—and their god worshipped by—more than half of the world's population. The Hebraic conception of history as a meaningful story with an ending has shaped history itself. Their national story of bondage and exodus is one of the key political narratives of the modern world, transformed for wildly diverse purposes by puritans, communists, abolitionists, Rastafarians, and anti-imperialists among many others—not to mention, of course, Zionists (Walzer 1985). In the United States and elsewhere, a great percentage of personal and place names are still of Hebrew origin; four out of the six most popular boy's names in the United States since 1880, for example, are David, Jacob, John, and Michael (the other two are James and Robert). In the past two centuries, an extraordinary explosion of Jewish creativity has shaped modern thought and culture, both high and popular, from Marx, Freud, and Einstein to Hollywood, the Broadway musical, and *Seinfeld*. Modern science, medicine, painting, philosophy, social science, literature, theater, cinema, music, humor, law, and politics would be dreadfully impoverished without the leaven provided by the people of the book. More than any other group in history, Jews have made enormous contributions to the channels, interpretation, and content of communication. *Personal Influence* is one chapter in this story.

Writing such paragraphs as the previous three raises haunting methodological worries. The observation that communications industries are staffed by a larger number of Jews than a chi-square test would predict has been abused so often and so cruelly for anti-Semitic purposes that one dares to make it with fear and trembling lest one be grouped with the thugs or give comfort to their schemes. From *The Protocols of the Elders of Zion* up to fantasies that are all too easy to find with a simple Google search, notions of Jewish control of the media have been used for pogroms, paranoia, and persecution for much of the past two centuries. Anyone with the slightest acquaintance with the internal divisiveness of Jewish culture, history, and politics, of course, should be instantly cured of conspiracy theory. Perhaps no culture has ever so actively cultivated internal variation and dissent. (Of course, one could read such diversity as another kind of unity, arguing that adaptability in interfacing with difference is perhaps one of the group's most distinctive cultural competences.) Prejudice, however, is quite immune to evidence and logic—a finding we owe, not incidentally, to the famous "Mr. Biggott" studies on prejudice (Cooper and Jahoda 1947; Kendall and Wolf 1949) done in Lazarsfeld's Bureau of Applied Social Research, which, in case there was any doubt, was clearly involved in studying, and fighting, anti-Semitic attitudes at midcentury. Though one will find no discussion of the sample or setting in these two published articles, the Bureau Archives at Columbia University make clear that many, if not all, of the interviews were done in Decatur, Illinois.

The overwhelming evidence for Jewish involvement in the arts of symbolic mediation cannot be neglected by the historical sociologist of communication, though one must be careful to demarcate the generalizing ambitions of the scholar from the superficially similar schemas of the anti-Semite. Any study of Jewishness will perhaps inevitably, and tragically, risk casting a dangerous shadow: "for much of the twentieth century . . . antisemites have been setting the terms of the debate over the role of Jews in popular culture" (Most 2004, 7). Few scholars today trust the old-fashioned assurance that research is immune from responsibility for its uses. Sociologist George Lundberg's 1929 assertion rings hollow nearly eight decades later: "It is not the business of a chemist who invents a high explosive to be influenced in his task by considerations as to whether his product will be used to blow up cathedrals or to build tunnels through the mountains" (quoted in Merton 1938/1996, 283). On the other hand, there is something to be said for wagering that the results of free inquiry will outweigh the risks. Foolish ears can find warrant for folly in almost anything, and self-censorship out of fear for bad side effects is one of the chief dangers of the third-person effect (Davison 1983). In any case, we know from research done at Columbia that audience responses are variable and unpredictable. The best course is to gird up one's loins and forge ahead with care and constant self-inspection. (For encouragement in this enterprise, see Hollinger 2004.)

Some lessons for studying the history of Jewish involvement in communications can be drawn from the checkered history of explaining the related question of "the intellectual pre-eminence of the Jews," as Thorstein Veblen (1919) put it. The problem of Jewish success, intellectual and otherwise, has been on the agenda for well over a century, and it has proven very difficult to treat—intellectually, politically, and ethically—since some of the earliest and most enduring answers were explicitly anti-Semitic and thus contributed to some of the most odious events of the age. One can see this dangerous interpretive-moral ambiguity in the work of early-twentieth-century sociological economists such as Veblen and Werner Sombart, who tried to tackle the extraordinary success of Jews in science and business, respectively. Veblen found an answer in the liminal social status of the Jewish renegade: "It is by loss of allegiance, or at best by force of a divided allegiance to the people of his origin, that he finds himself in the vanguard of modern inquiry" (p. 38). The Jews could serve as "disturbers of the intellectual peace" (p. 39) and join "the uneasy gild of pathfinders and iconoclasts" (p. 34) because of their symbiotic relationship vis-à-vis the Gentile host culture. (Veblen feared that Zionism, by dissolving the productively dissonant conditions of the diaspora, would stunt Jewish intellectual preeminence.) Sombart, an unjustly forgotten scholar who coined the word "capitalism," wrote *Die Juden und das Wirtschaftsleben* (1911; translated as *The Jews and Modern Capitalism*) as a riposte to his friend Max Weber's *Protestant Ethic and the Spirit of Capitalism* (1904-1905/1958). Read in its day as philosemitic, Sombart's book, like his work in general, has since fallen on harder interpretive times, thanks to his failure to condemn Nazism before his death in 1941. Certainly, he was no outspoken Nazi, as were Martin Heidegger or Carl Schmitt, his contemporaries whose intellectual brilliance continues to be refracted through clouds of biographical idiocy, but neither was he a fan of modern capitalism or of the people he most associated with it (Slezkine 2004, 55-56). In any case, the problem he raised, that of the uneven occupational distribution of ethnic minorities in the modern world, if not all of his answer, remains relevant in the twenty-first century. Though much would be gnarled and difficult in the project, one hopes that one day a volume might be written on *The Jews and Modern Communications*.

One recent and ambitious effort to solve the puzzle is Yuri Slezkine's *The Jewish Century* (2004), a brilliantly provocative book arguing the following striking thesis: "Modernization is about everyone becoming urban, mobile, literate, articulate, intellectually intricate, physically fastidious, and occupationally flexible. . . . [It], in other words, is about everyone becoming Jewish" (p. 1). (Implicit here is a rather contentious view about the borrowing of ethnic identity to which we will return.) Slezkine's wide-ranging history seeks to show how Jewish experience has been the paradigm case of modern experience, ranging from the extremes of scientific discovery, capitalist success, revolutionary over-throw, alienated suffering, and abject persecution; his particular historical contri-bution is to explore the remarkable quadruple destiny of Russian Jewry in Soviet communism, American liberalism, Israeli Zionism, and German death camps.

Of particular value for interpreting the network theory of *Personal Influence* is Slezkine's (2004) chapter on what he calls "Mercurian" people and activities. Borrowing the name from the Roman god Mercury (the Greek Hermes)—who as the patron of rogues, travelers, liars, and messengers, was also the god of communications—Slezkine surveyed a great variety of ethnic groups who have historically taken advantage of their liminal status to serve as professional go-betweens, "technicians of transgression," or cultural mediators. Parsees in India, Chinese in Southeast Asia, Germans in Russia, Lebanese in Latin America, Indians in East Africa, or Gypsies in Europe, as well as a wide range of less well-known groups, are all examples of "service nomads" who consciously cultivate their outsider status so as to specialize in tasks of transfer and mediation that local sedentary populations (called "Apollonians" by Slezkine) prefer not to—or cannot—do themselves. Such features as literacy, endogamy, dietary restrictions, tribal solidarity, demographic dispersion, and distinct (or secret) languages posi-tion Mercurians to play key roles in commerce, education, politics, and culture—and also put them at risk of resentment and persecution. As "internal strangers" Mercurians can say things, traffic in substances, and perform services forbidden to the host population. They are specialists of the threshold, border-crossers between purity and danger, and this trickster status can make them both enor-mously useful and enormously threatening to those who employ them. Mercurians are consequently the target of fantasies and projection, sexual and otherwise, hostile and friendly. The Jews, in Slezkine's view, are simply the *primus inter pares* of service nomads—the most literate, global, ancient, and influential of all mediating tribes. Their accomplishments, and their persecution, are part of their productive difference. Cultural brokers and operators, masters of writing media in all their forms, Jews have usually been "at the switch" in Menahem Blondheim's words. To twist one of the central concepts of *Personal Influence*, Jews have long served as "intervening variables."

Problems of Interpretation

The connection between ethnic identity and cultural production is enor-mously subtle. Answering the question, What is a Jew? is just as difficult as answering the question, What is a human being? (Both are, of course, the same question.) Similar issues have been faced in cultural studies more generally about other forms of racial, ethnic, gender, sexual, and national identity. The large ques-tion of relating cultural artifacts to their social environments of production and reception was central, of course, though in a different way, to the Columbia tradition of research on media effects. Elihu Katz, in his teaching, has suggested—with characteristic prepositional magic—a handy sorting device. A cultural artifact can be *of*, *by*, or *for* the people. This phrase captures the three main wings of media studies: content (of), production (by), and audience (for) research. These are also the three distinct dimensions that identify minority cultural artifacts. A "black" television show can be about blacks, made by blacks, aimed at a black viewership, or some mix of them. A "French" film can have French themes, be produced in France, or appeal to a Francophone audience. (Diabetic ice cream is *for* diabetics.)

The "by" of *Personal Influence* is obviously Jewish, but this fact, necessary but not sufficient for my reading, is not particularly significant for it. The twentieth century has seen an astonishing variety of methods for interpreting texts, including psychoanalysis, phenomenology, hermeneutics, critical theory, pragmatism, the new criticism, audience-response, and deconstruction—few of which will leave us in peace if we try to keep the "background" innocent. Most of these reading strategies, however, also make authorial biography the weakest explanatory link, focusing instead on structures and gestures of allegiance and affiliation that exist objectively, if unconsciously, in the text (or intertext) rather than subjectively in the head of the author. In a similar way, my reading looks for elective affinities and has no interest in attributing any conscious intent to Katz and Lazarsfeld. My method might be parodied as interpretation by zeitgeist. *Personal Influence* is part of a historical moment and a project whose traces and anxieties are in as plain sight as Poe's purloined letter. Texts are plastic things whose meaning is given and taken in acts of reading. The key question is how hospitable is the text to the reading: Does it sustain or entertain it? What defenses has the text against the reading? *Personal Influence*, I argue, all but courts the reading I will give it.

The "for" of *Personal Influence* is obviously—and interestingly—Gentile, but its "of" is the most interesting of all. Its argument for a network vision of social order manages an ecumenical translation between Jewish authorship and Gentile readership. The book performs a communication linkage at the same time that it theorizes one. As outsider observers of the Gentiles, Jews historically developed cultural resources for special sight in social analysis (Cuddihy, 1974). Cuddihy's (1974) argument resonates with what liberation theology, race theory, and feminism like to call "the epistemological privilege of the oppressed." *Personal Influence* provided sedentary Apollonians a fresh way to see their society: as a Mercurian network of relays, communicators, switches, and influences. The book turned from Gentile-style status toward Jewish-style connectivity as the basis of social power; defended socially grounded conceptions of mental life against Gentile individualism; and performed some amazing intellectual-moral-historical footwork with the most inconspicuous of all its central terms, "people." (Who said the two-step was not a dance?) We might add that two-step flow is also an applied point from the history of Jewish hermeneutics. Against the propaganda model of a lone text broadcast to the world that changes people's minds, *Personal Influence* reasserts the rabbinic principle that no text signifies without a commentary: oral debate, such as the face-to-face interchange of *chavruta* that prevails to this day in the yeshiva, is what brings the text to life and gives it meaning in people's lives. The principle that a (media) text without an (interpersonal) oral commentary has no meaning fits equally Talmud study and the two-step flow. In all of these traits, *Personal Influence* belongs to the world of Jewish modernity and its engagement in the arts of communication.

Networking as Democracy

The epigraph to *Personal Influence*, taken from John Stuart Mill's *On Liberty* (1859/1975), tells more than it wants to: "And what is still a greater novelty, the mass do not now take their opinions from dignitaries in Church or State, from ostensible leaders, or from books. Their thinking is done for them by men much like themselves, addressing them or speaking in their name, on the spur of the moment." Thus, the themes of the book are put in the voice of an illustrious predecessor who announces a shift from institutions and leaders to the spontaneity of everyday talk as the chief source of opinion and influence. In fact, this is a bowdlerized Mill that is missing the last three words of his sentence: "through the newspapers" (Mill 1859/1975, 62). This citational legerdemain sums up a host of ambiguities about the book. *Personal Influence*'s Mill seems to be endorsing a shift of emphasis from media to personal influence, when the historical Mill was referring to the power of media to magnify influence. In *Personal Influence*, people channel media influence; for Mill, media channel personal influence. Katz and Lazarsfeld think that the newspapers speak through people; Mill thinks that people (at least a few of them) speak through the newspapers. What sounds like a defense of populism in the epigraph is, in its original context, a lament about people whose "thinking is done for them." Mill's previous sentence states that the public is "always a mass, that is to say, a collective mediocrity"; and elsewhere the same paragraph asserts the lonely thesis: "At present individuals are lost in the crowd." Mill states the fear, which he borrows explicitly from Tocqueville, that the intellectual effects of democratic leveling will be a massive dumbing down. In the mid-nineteenth century, this fear centered on the newspaper and other agencies of public opinion rather than radio, television, or film as in the mid-twentieth. The specter of mass society was as clearly faced by John Stuart Mill as by C. Wright Mills, in the 1850s as well as the 1950s. (Had I space, I would show that Katz's career-long interest in the linkage of media, conversation, opinion, and action owes as much to Mill's liberal philosophy as to Gabriel Tarde.) Here Mill, the arch-Gentile, is circumcised of the argument that media have structural power. Psychoanalysis is the art of reading mauled texts, and as such it is often accused of overreading. Even so, *Personal Influence*'s treatment of Mill suggests something subtle: a neutralization of the argument that media are controllable by a small cabal and can work nefarious effects. I am not saying that the Jews control the media; I am saying *Personal Influence* can be read as a response to that paranoia. Its epigraph serves as a prophylactic gesture in which a Gentile spokesman is ventriloquized as endorsing the relative power of face-to-face talk vis-à-vis the media.

I am not saying that the Jews control the media; I am saying Personal Influence *can be read as a response to that paranoia.*

The point here is not to quibble about accuracy of quotation but to explore a central ambiguity in the project of *Personal Influence*: its blurring of the distinction between media and personal influence, and its debt to the anxieties of liberal democracy. As is well known, *Personal Influence* is a gambit within a larger intellectual debate at midcentury to which we can give the convenient if loose label of mass society theory (Gitlin 1978; Peters 1989; Simonson 1996). The book has a Tocquevillean picture of how individualism creates new conditions for both choice and conformity—at least this is the "picture of society" against which it reacts. Its famous account of the intellectual history of communications research begins with what is really the second step in modern social thought: modern society in all its impersonality and atomization. The accompanying methods of social research on "'representative' individuals lifted from the context of their associations" (p. 18) only reproduce this picture of a vast lonely crowd of individualists without anchor. Katz and Lazarsfeld criticize "the idea of the mass" as it is used in phrases such as *mass production, mass communication*, and *mass society*. This notion "is associated with the newly 'independent,' newly individuated, citizen of the modern industrial age, and, at the same time, for all his individualism, the person who is subject to the remote control of institutions from which he and the myriad of his 'unorganized' fellows feel far removed" (p. 40). The person is conceived as "a worker attuned to individualistic economic incentive in the competitive race for maximizing gain; an anonymous urban dweller trying to 'keep up' with anonymous Joneses; a radio listener shut in his room with a self-sufficient supply of the world outside" (p. 40). Such mass thinking, the book argues, infested economy, society, and communications. To the 1950s specter of a rat race of organization men in gray flannel suits, *Personal Influence* answers with better news: the roiling world of community has not gone away; nor have the social ties that anchor opinions, attitudes, and values. They reverse the direction of modern social thought: starting in the ocean of what Tönnies called *Gesellschaft* or Durkheim called "organic solidarity" they swim home like salmon to *Gemeinschaft* and mechanical solidarity. They make it halfway there.

Central to their affirmation of community amid modernity is the famous claim that mass and interpersonal communication are structurally homologous. "The individual person . . . needs to be studied in his two-fold capacity as a communicator and as a relay point in the network of mass communications" (p. 1). *Personal Influence* makes a reparative move: just as it moves from modern, anonymous society back to the honeycomb of face-to-face relationships, so it moves from the mass media to human communicators as the chief purveyors of influence. "Behind the design of this study was the idea that persons, and especially opinion leaders, could be looked upon as another medium of mass communication, similar to magazines, newspapers, and radio" (p. 11). People can be mass media. "Some of the communications roles played by people . . . may be relevant even in a mass media society such as ours" (pp. 28-29). The mass media do not "hollow out" the intimate sphere as Habermas, borrowing from 1950s American debates about media and society (including Mill) famously claimed a few years later in his 1962 book, *Structural Transformation of the Public Sphere* (Habermas 1962/1989); rather, the media feed and complement it. The picture of personal influence here is notably brighter than in other works of the period; in *The Lonely Crowd*, Riesman (1950, 85) put the basic idea of the two-step flow with considerably less cheer: "The mass media are the wholesalers; the peer groups, the retailers of the communications industry."

The shift from vertical to horizontal, from status to connection, as the source of influence can be read twice: as a move within 1950s intellectual politics to divert attention from the amassed institutional power of mass communication, as Gitlin (1978) argued, and as a defense of the role of those actors who work outside of the bounds of status and official legitimacy, strangers, traders, Mercurians, Jews. Indeed, the whole book can be read in two ways: as a social-scientific study advancing knowledge of the social psychology of influence and as a gambit in the drama of Jewish assimilation in mid-twentieth-century America. The two readings complement each other. *Personal Influence* is a "democratic apologia," as Simonson (1996) argued, but it is also a Jewish defense of the social self, connected and connecting to others amid the Gentile-genteel picture of the solitary and rational individual. The "image of society" as anonymous social atoms could be read as a parody of the possessive individualism of the Gentile liberal tradition. Gentile social psychology—from the philosophical psychology of Hobbes, Locke, and J. S. Mill to their more empirically minded heirs such as William James and B. F. Skinner—insists on cognitive conservatism, the great inertia and miserliness of all cognition. From Freud to Leon Festinger to Daniel Kahneman and Amos Tversky, one might discern a lineage of Jewish social psychologists who treat mental processes in a similar way, but with a key spin: they feature the ironies of rational individualist decision making, thus tweaking the Gentile bourgeoisie's dearest self-image, the free-standing reasonable self. For Katz and Lazarsfeld, the picture of decision making is less ironic, but the anti-individualist social grounding remains clear: choice is never a private act. "Ostensibly private opinions and attitudes are often generated and reinforced in small intimate groups of family, friends, or co-workers" (p. 8, cf. p. 59). "Even an individual's seemingly personal opinions and attitudes may be by-products of interpersonal relations" (p. 65). Individual choice is always woven into intergroup relations. To be sure, similar views are also clear in Protestant social thought in the United States, especially in the communitarian legacy of Dewey, Mead, Royce, and Cooley—and Cooley is discussed at length in *Personal Influence*.

As Cuddihy (1974) argued, echoes of the *shtetl*, with its simultaneously suffocating and cozy social life, recur throughout twentieth-century American sociology. Does Decatur, chosen to be a plain vanilla American community, become a shtetl, buzzing with female busybodies, playing distinct roles that we might recognize as updates from the stories of Sholom Aleichem or Isaac Bashevis Singer? That the private sphere is only "ostensible" can be read as a critique of the Gentile self in favor of a ruder and deeper communal form of social life in which there are no secrets from the community. I do not want to overread the relevance of the shtetl, which was clearly remote from the experience of Lazarsfeld's assimilated family in Vienna, but rather to point to a communal way of thinking, a scent for community even amidst anonymous society. Lazarsfeld was famous for community studies: Marienthal, Sandusky, Decatur, Elmira. His inspiration for the Marienthal study was Robert and Helen Lynd's *Middletown*, which he read in Austria after it appeared in 1929. But compare the Lynds' picture of Muncie, Indiana, with Katz and Lazarsfeld's picture of Decatur, Illinois: in Middletown, the great majority of people are passive Apollonians, earning a living, raising children, going to church, and consuming leisure, while the women of Decatur are abuzz with talk and influence. The picture of middle-range America in *Personal Influence* is not one of smug complacency or narrow-minded contentment; it is a beehive of communicative activity. The cultural resources honed by centuries of living in the ecological niche of the margin are here applied to the women of "Central City," as it was known in the documents of the Bureau.

Personal Influence endows a huge cast of characters with Mercurian traits, including the following figures culled from its literature review: "adolescents, alcoholics, beauty operators, boy scouts, children, college students, factory foremen, fans, fathers, gangs, girls, Greek villagers, housewives, husbands, immigrants, Jews, Lebanese radio listeners, minorities, mothers, Negroes, neighbors, salespersons, secretaries, soldiers, Soviets, traveling salesmen," and many more. This almost Whitmanesque list bulges with the multitudes it contains. Just about everyone gets to be a communications trader in the world of *Personal Influence*, including, above all, "girls, wives, and matrons." Opinion leaders are obviously such, but the influencees are also understood as full participants in the flow of communication. Everyone gets to take part in the betwixt-and-between of exchange. Katz and Lazarsfeld conceive of interpersonal and group relations as networks of exchange instead of as closed bubbles. Society is understood as capillary flows of influence instead of as standing relations of power or status. *Personal Influence* partakes in a kind of communications imagination of the social, generalizing from the shared capacity for speech to the larger social order. (In this, it shares a structural similarity to Habermas's theory of communicative competence without the accompanying critical theory of society.) Its genius is to uncouple status from influence. The book is not only a political defense of American democracy as thriving in an era of mass communication but also an ethnic-cultural defense of influence and networking as worthy activities, indeed the vital center of democratic life.

The Discovery of People

Personal Influence achieves a brilliant inversion: the white-bread provincials of Decatur are discovered to be "people" (this all too bland category of postwar social science) who also participate in networks of influence; its subtitle might read, "The Part Played by Gentiles in the Flow of Mass Communications." In the drama of Jewish assimilation, Katz and Lazarsfeld provided the people of the heartland of America, found in a community especially chosen to be free of "sectional peculiarities" (appendix A), the greatest gift possible: it made them Jews. Even the categories of influence studied in Decatur are ones in which Jews have had remarkable success: film, marketing, fashion, and politics. *Personal Influence* puts everybody at the switch. It generously shares a subcultural attitude and practice distilled for centuries with a population that almost seems to have been chosen to be an ethnic blank slate. In conception and interpretation, *Personal Influence* is fruitfully read as a cross-cultural study in which Jewish cosmopolitans laid out their go-between network theory onto the Protestant locals, and everyone came out a happy family of white communicating Americans.

The generosity to Middle America was perhaps, as Gitlin (1978) suggests, misguided. Gitlin vigorously contests the happy fusion of interpersonal and mass communication in *Personal Influence*—and Katz (1987) contests back just as vigorously. The leveling of concentrated media power and everyday chit-chat was, according to Gitlin, an ideological maneuver that cloaked a class society in the garb of a pluralist democracy. He laments, in effect, an affirmative politics that effaces the structural differences between the literally Jewish captains of industry—such as David Sarnoff and William Paley, whom he mentions—and the metaphorically Jewish activities of everyday people. To restate Gitlin's critique: you cannot say everyone is Jewish without losing hold of the crucial difference in power between industrial control and audience interpretation. My reading is structurally similar to Gitlin's: beneath the innocuous surface of *Personal Influence* important political business is being conducted. Where Gitlin sees an apology for American capitalist media, I see a utopian gambit in an ethnic story about a world in which everyone can finally, at long last, be people—at least in Decatur. Gitlin's focus on class politics reads the book as a sellout; my focus on ethnic politics reads it as having a secret messianic mission. How different are these readings? The whole dialectical tradition from Marx to Habermas has taught us to understand the utopian politics of liberal inclusion—and these are the politics of *Personal Influence*—as both a sociological lie and a normative necessity. Our two readings ride different sides of the dialectic: Gitlin emphasizes demystification of the actual, and I emphasize what Walter Benjamin called "redemptive criticism" of the possible.

There is a certain gaiety or lightness to the text of *Personal Influence*, especially in its various "discoveries"—the small group, interpersonal relations, and above all, people. It is a delicious irony that mass communication researchers wrote a book announcing the discovery of interpersonal communication. It is even better that it took social scientists to discover people. (We should not overlook the book's implicit humor.) This discovery is richer than most readers typically suspect. "People" has never meant "everybody"—it is a concept with an internal split. Many nations call themselves with names that mean "the people" (such as the German *Deutsch* or the Navajo *Dine*)—as opposed to all the others out there. *Personal Influence* bends over backwards to make "people" generic. "People" here have an anodyne quality, being stripped of all markers of particularity. There are no structures, no history, no trauma: just busy women talking, buying coffee for their husbands and cereal for their children, reading books, magazines, and newspapers, and incessantly dealing in all kinds of decisions. All discussion of larger structures is confined to Appendix A—which frankly outlines the quest for the most vanilla town possible. The study was explicitly designed to take place in a kind of ethnic tabula rasa. The methodological choice goes together with a fantasy of a world in which people would no longer have any particular markings. What is most striking about the book is precisely its plainness, its flat picture of people.

It is a delicious irony that mass communication researchers wrote a book announcing the discovery of interpersonal communication. It is even better that it took social scientists to discover people.

"People," the most generic of all the terms in social science, is actually a word with a long and rich history. The apparently most neutral of all social terms is not really so neutral. "The people" has a resonant history in American political culture, appearing in the preamble to the Constitution and serving since as the repository of hopes and despair about democracy itself. It has a split legacy. In eighteenth-century Britain, "the people" was a contentious concept, usually meaning a select group of property holders who were authorized to act and not the whole populace indifferently; by the 1770s, the newfangled idea that "the people" should include all adult males was considered quite radical (Gunn 1983, 73-88). The "people" of the U.S. Constitution of course did not include women and notoriously counted slaves as three-fifths of a person. It is a privilege and massive historical achievement for some groups, including Jews, to be "people" at all. As Hegel (1821/1970) notes, to be a "person" is to be granted a layered set of rights to property, opinion, and personal inviolability. Until the abolition of slavery and attenuation of patriarchy, "people" and the human species have been very different things. This most neutral of all categories of social science indeed needed to be "invented," and *Personal Influence* is doing so in a richer and more layered way than is obvious. The word "people" has hardly ever meant "every-body," and almost all large-scale projects of communication have sought to include the outcaste portion. The flow of mass communication has always been about reaching the scattered remnants.

In a sense, the founding question of modern social theory is, How do Jews fit into modern society? What is their place among the nations? Jewish struggles to define their own peoplehood have provided stories about modern people and society in general. Marx, whose notorious essay on the "Jewish question" established the genre, deployed an entire critique of capitalism that can be read as an effort to resolve Jewish difference—precisely by abolishing Judaism altogether. Under communism, all of the activities he notoriously classed as Jewish—exchange, lending, brokering, networking—would be dissolved in a world of "purely human" flourishing. Indeed, his utopia was rather sedentary and rural—people would fish in the morning, hunt in the afternoon, and be critics after dinner. Postprandial literary endeavor was the closest one got to anything cosmopolitan. For Durkheim, descendent of a long line of rabbis, society itself should become the proper object of our religious energies. In contrast to Veblen, Durkheim thought that Jewish intellectual preeminence owed to the ability to maintain traditional communal solidarity in the midst of modern upheaval: Jews have "all the intelligence of modern man without sharing his despair" (Durkheim 1897/1951, 167-69). Weber, the only non-Jew in the holy trinity of modern social theory, in turn nominated curiously Judaizing Protestants as the movers of modern capitalism (and Sombart, as noted, soon tried to put things back on their Jewish footing). Freud is probably the most explicit of all foundational figures of modern social thought to grapple with Jewish themes, ranging from his book on jokes (Freud 1905/1989), which is among other things a compendium of Jewish humor, to the practice of psychoanalysis, which allowed his endless supply of neurotic Jewish patients a safe haven, which looses the Id, or Yid as Cuddihy puns, to speak in puns, make off-color comments, and free associate without the supervisory sanction of Gentile propriety. The psychoanalytic session was a protected space in which to be Jewish—to mix sex, God, and language in impolitic or impolite streams of talk and fantasy without fear of goyish censure (Cuddihy 1974).

"People" of course is a central concept in the Jewish tradition, where it also has a split legacy. The Hebrew Bible uses two words for people: "am" (Jew) and "goy" (Gentile). The *am* is a "peculiar" people, set apart by the covenant it has made with God; the *goyim* (nations) comprise the rest of the people of the earth, the non-Jews or Gentiles. "Am" suggests a relation built on kinship, while "goy" has a political flavor, but the terms have diverse and overlapping meanings in Hebrew (Speiser 1960). Agamben (2000, 85) argues that "the term 'people' is always already divided, as if crossed by an original theological-political fault-line." When the Septuagint translators rendered the Hebrew Bible into Greek, an act that catapulted Jewish culture into the world language of the era, they chose the word "laos" for "am" and the word "ethnos" for "goy" (curiously avoiding the more prestigious word *dēmos*, the root for terms such as democracy). In ancient Greek, "laos" meant the common folk (in contrast to leaders), and is the source of such terms as "lay" and "laity," contrasting common or average people with specialized or professional classes; in modern Greek, *laikos* means popular or even folksy. "Ethnos" (plural "ethnē"), in contrast, meant a race or tribe, and pointed to a particular rather than general class of human beings. This tilt to the peculiar or unique lives on in "ethnic," a term that suggests social difference or marking. For both the Hebrew Bible and the Septuagint, Jews are the people, and the others are literally ethnics. The unmarked pole, in other words, was from a Jewish perspective the Jews.

In the New Testament, "ethnē" sometimes expanded to include all who are not Jewish or Christian. The grafting in of the Gentiles into Israel was a dream of ancient prophecy, and the most ambitious (and successful) executor of this project was Paul of Tarsus. In a rather surprising recent intellectual development, Marxists and poststructuralists (among others) have become fascinated with Paul. Once the exclusive property of theologians, he has been reclaimed as a subversive who helped undermine the Roman empire from within and, thus, as a model for how to cope with the economic empire of capitalism and military-cultural empire of the United States (Agamben 2000; Badiou 1997; Boyarin 1994; Žižek 1999; for what I call Franciscan Marxism, see Hardt and Negri 2000). This reinterpretation yields a Paul who, as a devout Jew, is also a universalist proclaimer of a message that the distinction of Jew and Gentile no longer matters. (Paul in fact invokes the contrast of *laos* and *ethnos* in Romans 10:19-20, arguing that the *ethnē* can also be the *laos* of God.) More relevant for us is the discovery that Paul's massive missionary efforts, and those that came after him, were all essentially efforts at mass communication, specifically at announcing the good news (Simonson 2006). The Christian message for the deeply Jewish Paul (as opposed to some of his anti-Semitic followers later) was both a religious redemption and a social program of transforming and universalizing Jewishness: the God of the Jews had become the god of the entire earth. In the church that he proclaimed, there is no Jew or Gentile, slave or free, male or female. The God of Abraham, Isaac, and Jacob, via Jesus Christ, became a world citizen. Missionary work as Paul conceived and conducted it was a massive communications enterprise turning on the two axes of religious conviction and social incorporation—of the *ethnē* or Gentiles. The point is not that the authors of *Personal Influence* had any awareness of Paul but that the project of broadcasting starts in early Christian history as the task of grafting Gentiles into the Jewish family tree (see Romans 11). Paul, in his epistolary writing and itinerant preaching, wedded textual and oral communication, and this blurring of interpersonal and mass media went together with his political-social program of joining in-groups and out-groups in a cosmopolitan, universal community. Since Paul, the task of communication theory has been to make everyone "people." (It is at least convenient that Lazarsfeld's first name was Paul.)

Personal Influence achieves what structuralists call a "markedness reversal." Whether Katz and Lazarsfeld were conscious of the rich history of "people" as a term or not, the Jewish fascination with interpreting the puzzling ways of "the peoples" (the goyim) serves as a rich context for understanding the otherwise unmarked notion of "people" that social scientists study or, in the case of this book, "discover." *Personal Influence* might be read as reversing the notion that Jews are people and the rest are ethnics. It may seem like a wry bit of inside humor—it would take a social scientist to discover "people"—but the gesture is magnanimous: the people (goyim) are discovered as people (am). Even the women of Decatur are envisioned as experts at networking and trading information. (That women were the projecting screen might point to the historic link of Jews and women as twin alternatives to dominant models of masculinity: Boyarin 1997.) The Jews run the media network, and the Gentiles run the interpersonal network, and the processes of communication studied in this book happily scramble their roles together. Hooking up the interpersonal network with that of mass communications is, as above, a cross-cultural gesture: Jew and Gentile meet in the two-step flow.

Personal Influence is also an American story. In the United States, the story of a chosen people making an exodus from captivity to the Promised Land was invoked by Puritans, abolitionists, African Americans, and waves of immigrants. The native peoples of the Americas were understood by a diverse range of Jewish and Christian theologians alike as descendents of the house of Israel (Bushman 2004). The Judaic story of people formation has served a wide range of identity projects in American history by peoples white, black, red, and more rarely yellow. Just as ethnics used Jewish stories to become Americans, so Jews used ethnic stories to become Americans, especially in early- to mid-twentieth-century musical theater and film. Jewish actors and narratives—most famously in *The Jazz Singer* (play 1925, film 1927)—performed racial stereotypes such as blackface as if to demonstrate the contingency and plurality of all racial identity (Rogin 1996; Most 2004). *Personal Influence* might be read alongside *The Jazz Singer* as two distinct approaches to how Jews might lay claim to membership in liberal America. In the play and film, produced during an era when Jews in America were still widely considered to be a distinct race and discrimination was still quite overt, Jews played the parts of groups more racially marked on the color spectrum so as to suspend or background their own marked status or, more pointedly, to demonstrate that identity categories are no more binding than theatrical roles. In the book, published when their status in America was more secure, Jews studied the performances of the provincials of Central City and discovered them to be people (Jew-ish) too. *The Jazz Singer* whitened Jews; *Personal Influence* Judaized whites. The notion that ethnic identity can be freely performed, loaned, and bor-rowed is, of course, the essence of liberal pluralism, and it is one of the great cul-tural creations of mid-twentieth-century American Jews and their Gentile partners. *Personal Influence* played a part in building this culture.

In their book, Katz and Lazarsfeld unite mobile purveyors of the text and sedentary channelers of word of mouth—and they are all discovered to be peo-ple. The two-step flow performs an impressive piece of cultural work: writing and orality, text and interpretation, mobile and sedentary, mass and interpersonal, Jew and Gentile all shake hands within it. In its muted way, the book announces the messianic age in which everyone has finally become a Jew in *America*. The future when all people will be God's people (i.e., Jewish) that the prophets fore-told (e.g., Isaiah 56:6-8) comes to pass, of all places, in Decatur, Illinois. (The Messiah alights in surprising places.) There is a hidden utopian force to *Personal Influence's* discovery of people. The book announces the long-awaited moment prophesied by Hosea and repeated by Paul when God will say "to them that were not my people, you are my people" (Hosea 2:23, Romans 9:25-26). In his new introduction to *Personal Influence*, Katz (2006, xxv) says that Lazarsfeld belonged to the prophetic tradition. Katz only didn't make clear which one.

References

Agamben, Giorgio. 2000. *Le temps qui reste: Un commentaire de l'Epitre aux Romains*. Translated by Judith Revel. Paris: Éditions Payot et Rivages.

Badiou, Alain. 1997. *Saint Paul: La fondation de l'universalisme*. Paris: Presses universitaires de France.

Boyarin, Daniel. 1994. *A radical Jew: Paul and the politics of identity*. Berkeley: University of California Press.

———. 1997. *Unheroic conduct: The rise of heterosexuality and the invention of the Jewish man*. Berkeley: University of California Press.

Bushman, Richard Lyman. 2004. The Book of Mormon and its critics. In *Believing history: Latter-day Saint essays*, 107-42. New York: Columbia University Press.

Cooper, Eunice, and Marie Jahoda. 1947. The evasion of propaganda: How prejudiced people respond to anti-prejudice propaganda. *Journal of Psychology* 23:15-25.

Cuddihy, John Murray. 1974. *The ordeal of civility: Freud, Marx, Lévi-Strauss and the Jewish struggle with modernity*. New York: Basic.

Davison, W. Phillips. 1983. The third-person effect in communication. *Public Opinion Quarterly* 47:1-15.

Durkheim, Emile. 1897/1951. *Suicide: A study in sociology*. Translated by John A. Spaulding and George Simpson. Glencoe, IL: Free Press.

Freud, Sigmund. 1905/1989. *Jokes and their relation to the unconscious*. New York: Norton.

Gabler, Neal. 1988. *An empire of their own: How the Jews invented Hollywood*. New York: Crown.

Gitlin, Todd. 1978. Media sociology: The dominant paradigm. *Theory and Society* 5:205-53.

Gunn, J. A. W. 1983. *Beyond liberty and property: The process of self-recognition in eighteenth-century political thought*. Kingston, Canada: McGill-Queen's University Press.

Habermas, Jürgen. 1962/1989. *Structural transformation of the public sphere*. Cambridge, MA: MIT Press.

Hardt, Michael, and Antonio Negri. 2000. *Empire*. Cambridge, MA: Harvard University Press.

Hegel, G. W. F. 1821/1970. *Philosophie des Rechts*. Frankfurt, Germany: Suhrkamp.

Hollinger, David A. 2004. Rich, powerful, and smart: Jewish overrepresentation should be explained instead of avoided or mystified. *Jewish Quarterly Review* 94:595-602.

Katz, Elihu. 1987. Communications research since Lazarsfeld. *Public Opinion Quarterly* 51 (50th Anniversary Supplement): S25-S45.

————. 2006. Lazarsfeld's legacy: The power of limited effects. In *Personal influence: The part played by people in the flow of mass communications*, 2nd ed., xv-xxv. New Brunswick, NJ: Transaction Press.

Katz, Elihu, and Paul F. Lazarsfeld. 1955. *Personal influence: The part played by people in the flow of mass communications*. Glencoe, IL: Free Press.

Kendall, Patricia L., and Katherine M. Wolf. 1949. The analysis of deviant cases in communications research. In *Communications research, 1948-1949*, ed. Paul F. Lazarsfeld and Frank N. Stanton. New York: Harper and Brothers.

Lynd, Robert S., and Helen Merrell Lynd. 1929. *Middletown: A study in contemporary American culture*. New York: Harcourt, Brace.

Merton, Robert K. 1938/1996. Science and the social order. In *On social structure and science*, ed. Piotr Sztompka. Chicago: University of Chicago Press.

————. 1942. A note on science and democracy. *Journal of Legal and Political Sociology* 1:115-26.

————. 1994. *A life of learning*. American Council of Learned Societies Occasional Paper no. 25. http://www.acls.org/op25.htm (accessed October 8, 2005).

Mill, John Stuart. 1859/1975. *On liberty*. New York: Norton.

Most, Andrea. 2004. *Making Americans: Jews and the Broadway musical*. Cambridge, MA: Harvard University Press.

Peters, John Durham. 1989. Democracy and American mass communication theory: Dewey, Lippmann, Lazarsfeld. *Communication* 11:199-220.

Peters, John Durham, and Peter Simonson. 2004. *Mass communication and American social thought: Key texts, 1919-1968*. Boulder, CO: Rowman & Littlefield.

Riesman, David. 1950. *The lonely crowd: A study of the changing American character*. With Reuel Denney and Nathan Glazer. New Haven, CT: Yale University Press.

Rogin, Michael. 1996. *Blackface, white noise*. Berkeley: University of California Press.

Simonson, Peter. 1996. Dreams of democratic togetherness: Communication hope from Cooley to Katz. *Critical Studies in Mass Communication* 13:324-42.

————. 2006. Visions of mass communication: An unorthodox history from Paul of Tarsus to the county fair. Manuscript, University of Colorado.

Slezkine, Yuri. 2004. *The Jewish century*. Princeton, NJ: Princeton University Press.

Sombart, Werner. 1911. *Die Juden und das Wirtschaftsleben*. Leipzig, Germany: Duncker & Humblot.

Speiser, E. A. 1960. "People" and "nation" of Israel. *Journal of Biblical Literature* 79:157-63.

Veblen, Thorstein. 1919. The intellectual pre-eminence of the Jews in modern Europe. *Political Science Quarterly* 34:33-42.

Walzer, Michael. 1985. *Exodus and revolution*. New York: Basic Books.

Weber, Max. 1904-1905/1958. *Protestant ethic and the spirit of capitalism*. Translated by Talcott Parsons. New York: Scribner's.

Žižek, Slavoj. 1999. *The ticklish subject*. New York: Verso.

This article offers an exogenous historical analysis of
Personal Influence, arguing that it offers an engaged
response to a fundamental change taking place at that
time in the world economy as it moved from scarcity to
abundance. The ten year delay in the publication of the
book after the original field work was done in Decatur,
Illinois, in 1945 suggests that the sociology of mass
communication had difficulty in making sense of the
data that work produced. It needed the new sociology
of interpersonal communication to interpret it. In
accounting for the fusion of these two different sociologies in the work that was finally published, this article indicates the passing of the time of the masses and
the coming of the time of everyday life.

Keywords: history; sociology; the end of the masses;
everyday life; sociability

Personal Influence and the End of the Masses

By
PADDY SCANNELL

The Historiography of Academic Fields

Intellectual fields have two histories: the internal, endogenous history of their formation and
development as an academic discipline, and an
external, exogenous history of what summoned it
into existence in the first place. Endogenous histories take themselves for granted. They accept
as given their foundational concerns and attend
to the development, modifications, and changes
of direction of those concerns. The endogenous
history of sociology turns out to be a series of
national histories, all with the same narrative
structure and agenda: the history of the formation

*Paddy Scannell is now a professor in the Department of
Communication Studies at the University of Michigan
after many years at the University of Westminster,
London. He is a founding editor of* Media Culture &
Society. *He is the author, with David Cardiff, of* A
Social History of British Broadcasting, 1922-1939
(Blackwell, 1991); editor of Broadcast Talk *(Sage, 1991)
and author of* Radio, Television and Modern Life
*(Blackwell, 1996). Scannell is currently working on a
trilogy, the first two volumes of which will be published
by Sage in 2007:* Media and Communication *and*
Television and the Meaning of "Live".

DOI: 10.1177/0002716206292528

of sociology in Germany, France, the United States, and so forth. Within each national sociology, there are founding fathers, institutions, and agendas; and there are, of course, complex, interesting cross-connections with other national sociologies in these developments. There is a well-established body of literature about the Chicago School, for instance, while the current work of Peters and Simonson (2004) has reconstructed the historical field of "mass communication" as a distinctive genre of American social thought. Within that history, key individual texts also have their own internal history, which is of relevance both for understanding the particular project as well as its significance within the subfield to which it contributes.

It is now commonly recognized that *Personal Influence* (Katz and Lazarsfeld 1955) was a key text in the then new and exciting field of mass communication, itself embedded in the larger field of American sociology. Endogenous accounts of Katz and Lazarsfeld's collaborative work attend first to its internal history: the etiology of the Decatur study in 1945 and its roots in the Ohio County study of voting behaviors in 1940. They note the reasons for its temporary lapse and subsequent rescue by Elihu Katz, then a postdoctoral associate of Paul Lazarsfeld, in the early 1950s. They engage with the disjuncture between the first part of the book, based on Katz's doctoral thesis (group theory) and the second part, which collates the earlier work of the original workers on the Decatur field study. They may then go on to evaluate the ways in which *Personal Influence* defined the history of the study of the mass media thus far in terms of "effects" and proceed to trace the afterlife of its findings and conclusions and its continuing, contested significance through to this day. Such is a core concern of this collection of articles and especially the historical contributions by Jefferson Pooley, John Summers, and David Morrison.

What, by way of contrast, would an exogenous history of this famous sociological text look like? I will attempt a brief sketch map in the rest of this article. There are two key considerations. What in the first place called forth the question of the media as a concern for sociology, and how was it raised? And second, and subsequently, What set of circumstances produced the Decatur study, its results, and its conclusions? From this perspective, *Personal Influence* is not so much a sociological text that resonates within the field of sociology as a historical text that resonates within its own historical, changing time and place. This change of footing allows us to consider sociology and its sociological texts not in their own and taken-for-granted terms but rather as a set of responses to the impact of history whose status is symptomatic rather than diagnostic. But symptomatic of what exactly? I would like to propose that all modern university disciplines are hailed into existence by the pathologies (the disorders) of modernity and the contemporary unease to which they give rise.[1] From this perspective, then, it is first a question of *why* sociology in response to what, where, and when, and, within that question, why a sociology of *mass communication*. The root answer to both questions is the same, namely, that a logos of the social (an academic discourse calling itself sociology) arose in the first place in response to the question of the masses, for that *was* the "social question" from the late eighteenth century through to the mid-twentieth century in Europe and North America. From this perspective the question of communication, as and when it arose, was an extension of sociology's basic question—hence a sociology of *mass* communication in which the emphasis falls on the first rather than the second term.

Mass Communication

Today, no one speaks of the masses, but the first half of the past century could well be defined as the time of the masses—of mass production, mass politics, mass society, mass culture, and hence, inter alia, of mass communication. There is a tendency nowadays to claim that the masses never existed. In his robustly enjoyable broadside against *The Intellectuals and the Masses, 1875-1939,* John Carey (1992, 1) begins by briskly dismissing "the masses" of the late nineteenth and early twentieth centuries as a fiction, the product of the rancid, class-ridden snobbery of the European bourgeois intelligentsia of that time who nearly all, to a man and a women, despised the uneducated, unwashed urban working classes. But while I have some sympathy with Carey's knockabout treatment of the intellectuals, it has to be said that the masses were no fiction. They were the defining political and economic reality of those times, in Europe and North America. The question of "the masses" became *the* social question ever since the French revolution; it was more exactly to do with the politicization of poverty. That, Hannah Arendt (1963/1990, 62) has argued, is the conclusion that Karl Marx drew from it: "He interpreted the compelling needs of mass poverty in political terms as an uprising not only for the sake of bread or wealth, but for the sake of freedom as well. What he learned from the French Revolution was that poverty could be a political force of the first order." It ceased to be a natural fact and became an historical fact that entered into, indeed determined, the politics of Europe and North America from the nineteenth century through to the mid-twentieth century. It was the driver of history because the newly created urban working class was the essential wealth creator for the mass produced goods of factory capitalism. The structural economic antagonism between capital and organized labor, so clearly and presciently analyzed by Marx, gave rise to continuing industrial unrest and conflict whose resolution required the increasing intervention of the state: the length of the working day and week, the appalling abuse of child labor, health and safety in the work-place, wage bargaining, the unionization of labor and the rights of unions . . . a host of issues requiring continuous political management to keep the economy going and defuse the fear (always in the background) of insurrection from below. And in all this the nature of the state itself was gradually reformed and redefined in the direction of mass representative democracy, a new kind of politics that only came to fruition in Europe in the early twentieth century.

The question of the masses, then, defined and determined economic and political life in the first decades of the past century. It acquired new significance and urgency in two key moments: the Bolshevik Revolution in Russia in 1918, which coincided with fierce industrial unrest in all the advanced economies, and the Wall Street crash of 1929 whose consequences defined the next decade. This—the interwar period—was the moment of "mass communication" and "mass culture." In the writings of those years, "mass" and "masses" were taken-for-granted, unmarked, uninterrogated terms, used as natural descriptors of natural facts. To be sure, the words meant different things in Europe and North America: the masses in Europe were the urban proletariat. In America, they were the atomized individual components of the lonely crowd. But in neither case could they be regarded as the imaginary constructs of contemporary intellectuals looking at social phenomena through the wrong end of a telescope. They were real, insistent social facts. The politics of poverty returned to haunt the 1930s and to drive the world into war. It was called, lest we forget, the *hungry* thirties.

The study of mass communication in North America was driven not so much by fear of the revolutionary potential of the masses as anxiety about their well-being.

The study of mass communication in North America was driven not so much by fear of the revolutionary potential of the masses as anxiety about their well-being. What was the effect of powerful new communication technologies on the ordinary man? Was he not vulnerable to manipulation because he was ill informed through lack of education and psychologically suggestible through economic insecurity? Such were the underlying assumptions of the first important case study of the impact of the first great, and then very new, technology of broadcast communication, radio. Hadley Cantril's (1940) study *The Invasion from Mars* was subtitled *A Study in the Psychology of Panic*. The fact that large numbers of people were so frightened by a spoof scary play for Halloween—an adaptation of *The War of the Worlds* by H. G. Wells—that they fled their homes and took to the road seemed to confirm the power of radio and the vulnerability of "the common man." It was the task of intellectuals "to spread knowledge and scepticism more widely among common men" so that they might be "less harassed by the emotional insecurities which stem from underprivileged environments" (p. 205). That important task was addressed in Paul Lazarsfeld's (1940) key study of *Radio and the Printed Page*, published in the same year, whose aim was to answer the question "uppermost in the minds of many citizens: what will radio do to society?" and to provide those concerned with mass education with an analysis of the conditions in which the "masses" would or would not expose themselves to education by radio (p. 133). The theme of *Mass Persuasion* was addressed at exactly this time, in Robert Merton's (1946/2004) elegant study of audience responses to Kate Smith's marathon radio broadcast to promote the purchase of government war bonds.

The End of the Masses

All these studies of the impact of radio in the late thirties and early forties presupposed its direct and powerful impact on powerless masses. It *did* make people flee in fear. It *did* make them buy $40 million dollars worth of war bonds in a single day. But when we get to the other side of the forties and into the early fifties, the masses have faded away along with the power of the media. Why? An answer is provided by one of the readers of the draft manuscript of the first part of *Personal Influence* and a later collaborator with Lazarsfeld, David Riesman. Riesman was at the time the celebrated author of the best-selling work of American sociology ever, *The Lonely Crowd* (1950/1976). It was written in the late forties and published in 1950, roughly the moment of the Decatur fieldwork. In it, Riesman argued that a structural transformation of the American soul was taking place at that very moment, a transition from the inner-directed to the other-directed individual. This restructuring of the self was not an internal (endogenous) reorganization of the American psyche but was brought about by exogenous social, historical forces, most fundamentally and pervasively the transformation of the economy from the production of primary heavy industrial goods to the manufacture of secondary, light domestic products. It was the then-accelerating transition from an economy of scarcity to an economy of abundance that forged a new kind of individual in its own image and likeness. The life circumstances of individuals were changing from work-defined patterns of existence to new leisure-defined ways of living. The coercive time of work and the workplace no longer dominated individual life and experience, which were now oriented toward free time. The pendulum was swinging from production to consumption. It was a decisive change of gear in the long, still-continuing world historical process of societal modernization in which subsistence economies and the forms of life developed in adjustment to them give way to unprecedented surplus economies of abundance and new forms of life defined, for the first time, by economic choice and freedom. This is the moment of the dissolution of the masses and the discovery of "people," proclaimed in Katz and Lazarsfeld and interpreted by Riesman. It is the moment of transition from the first to the second historical phase of world modernization, from modernity to postmodernity. This transition shows up, of necessity, in America first because it had the most advanced economy in the world. It shows up later in the past century in Europe and at present in India and China, whose economies are at this moment changing from scarcity to abundance.

The people in the Decatur study, then, are not the atomized, anomic individuals of the lonely crowd so memorably portrayed in the iconic American painting of the 1940s, *Nighthawks* by Edward Hopper (1942). They are found to be and are shown without comment as Riesman's other-directed individuals. There was much discussion at the time about the moral significance of the inner- and other-directed character types. The Weberian inner-directed WASP was dear to the American self-imagination whose rugged individualism cast him in the heroic mold of the cowboy, the sheriff, and the captain of industry. It was of course a profoundly gendered, masculine typology. And it is a fascinating, unaccountable, unexamined fact about the Decatur study that it was exclusively concerned with women. (This point is examined by Susan J. Douglas 2006 [this volume].) Is the typology of the other-directed individual essentially feminine? Does that account for something of the ambiguity in Riesman's own view of the types with its decided hint of a nostalgic preference for the old, now-vanishing, self-motivated, self-driven American male of the previous century? The other-directed type can be interpreted negatively as lacking moral depth of character in comparison with the inner-directed individual. That is suggested by Riesman's two metaphors of the gyroscope and the radar to characterize the workings of the two types: the inner-directed individual's in-built gyroscope (set there by his parents) keeps him unswervingly on track while the other-directed individual uses the then-state-of-the-art "new" technology of radar to constantly scan the environment for possible external threats to his sense of self. The new postwar, postmodern woman is "exceptionally sensitive to others: she is shallower, freer with her money, friendlier, less certain of herself, more dependent on the approval of others" than the older, independent icon of modernity, the inner-directed individual (Riesman 1950/1976, 190).

[T]he study of the two-step flow, which endogenously checks "personal influence," exogenously discloses the rise of sociability in postwar, postmodern society.

I have deliberately switched gender in the quotation in the last sentence not only to highlight the unexamined gender assumptions in Riesman's book but also those in Katz and Lazarsfeld. It could indeed be argued that the transition from modernity to postmodernity—from work- and production-defined forms of life to leisure and consumption—also implicates an historical realignment of the gendered self: from the valorized masculinity of the inner-directed individual to the valorized femininity of the other-directed individual. At all events, the implicit characterization of the women in the Decatur study is in perfect accord with Riesman's other-directed typology. That indeed was the point of the study: to identify the influence of others on the individual's shopping purchases, fashion tastes, movie choices, and news-related opinions. It is a key argument in Riesman (1950/1976) that the new character type is, by definition, more involved in relations with other people than the old self-possessed (self-absorbed), inner-directed type. The rise of *sociability* is the manifest sign of the new people-minded social type. Almost as if to confirm this point, a key factor identified and examined in the Decatur study is the "gregariousness" of the women as defined by two key indicators checked in the interviews and questionnaires: membership of local associations and friendship networks. Thus, the study of the two-step flow, which endogenously checks "personal influence," exogenously discloses the rise of sociability in postwar, postmodern society. This in turn indicates the beginnings of a revaluation of leisure and consumption as the basis of new forms of social life, no longer determined by the coercive compulsions of economic necessity but freed from this and based on families, friends, and friendship. In such newly recovered *personal* relationships (relations between people as persons in their own right), the values that pertain to such relationships—intimacy, trust, sincerity, and authenticity—take on new meaning and significance. The rise of the "merely sociable" heralds the fundamental transformation of the conditions of life in postwar America that now appears as focused on the ordinary and the everyday. In short, what Riesman perceives and what Katz and Lazarsfeld so convincingly "prove" is the emergence into history of something that is now recognized and identified as "everyday life." The discovery of "people" in the Decatur study is, in a larger sense, the discovery of everyday life.

The Sociology of Everyday Life

Both parts of *Personal Influence* explore the sociology of everyday life. The Katzian first part is drawn from the then new field of interpersonal communication. Mass communication sociology, as Katz points out, regarded interpersonal communication either as nonexistent or irrelevant to its concerns (Katz and Lazarsfeld 1955, 34). But Lazarsfeld saw that it might help to explain the role of what he thought of as "opinion leaders" in his two-step flow hypothesis, and so he recruited Katz's aid in another attempt to make something of the Decatur material. Katz begins with a robust criticism of "the traditional image of the mass persuasion process." It took no account of "people." It was no use thinking of "opinion leaders" as if they were a group apart and as if leadership was a trait that some possessed but others did not. It was essential to begin to think of opinion leaders as "an integral part of the give-and-take of *everyday interpersonal relationships*" (ibid., 33, italics added). The new field of interpersonal communication, if we consider it exogenously, can be seen as a response precisely to the historicization of everyday life, which, so to speak, summoned it into existence as its sociological interlocutor. I do not mean, of course, to suggest that everyday life did not exist until this moment—that would be absurd—but rather that hitherto it lacked any historical and sociological significance. Previously, it was *beneath* history and *below* the radar of sociology. Now, in 1950s America and elsewhere in Europe, everyday life begins to achieve visibility and recognition as something distinctive and meaningful in its own terms and for its own sake. It becomes a good in itself, an end in itself, and not merely the means whereby labor reproduces itself as the instrument of capital. That was its marginal marginalized role in the work-defined lives of the masses under the dull economic compulsion of factory capitalism in the nineteenth and early twentieth centuries.

It is one of the historical ironies of World War II that it solved immediately the prolonged economic crisis of the 1930s. In America and Britain, unemployment disappeared overnight. More and more people were recruited to the labor force.

All those in work achieved an absolute rise in their standard of living, and for the first time, blue collar workers saw theirs rise faster than that of white collar workers. For women, especially, it was a moment when they were massively recruited into work and, as *Rosie the Riveter* showed so charmingly and poignantly, ordinary women briefly achieved a new economic independence and greater purchasing power than had ever previously been possible for them. It did not last. When the war ended, they were told to get back home and breed while the men, returning from the far-flung fighting fronts, replaced them in the work-place. This, remember, was the moment of the Decatur study, undertaken in the final stages of the war. Coming out of the war, the American economy entered into a long period of continuous growth and expansion, in which life for many if not most Americans was better than ever before and the hungry thirties became no more than a rapidly receding trace memory.

This is the emerging world explored by *Personal Influence*, which, in this exogenous reading, is a pioneering study of the *sociable* character of everyday life in mid-twentieth-century America. A richly patterned quilt-work of relations within and between younger and older, married and unmarried women of differing socioeconomic status emerges from the data. When it comes to moviegoing, it is the young single girls across all status levels who are the influentials, but in the matter of choosing breakfast cereals, the mothers of young families are opinion leaders. High-status women are more informed about public affairs because they have more time for it: their lives are less taken up with household drudgery than their less-well-off contemporaries. Fashion, like moviegoing, is more determined than the others by life cycle position: young single girls across all status levels are the fashion influentials, and unsurprisingly, fashion opinion leaders are highly gregarious. However, while there are fewer fashion opinion leaders (as might be expected) among low-status young women, it turns out that there are just as many middle-status fashion leaders as there are high-status opinion leaders, and this is in spite of the fact that a significantly greater proportion of high-status women have a high interest in fashion than middle-status women. Why the discrepancy? Why are there not proportionately more opinion leaders among young, rich, single women? An intriguing answer is suggested: they simply talk less about fashion. They *are* the fashion, and perhaps it is not fashionable to talk about it (ibid., 266).

Thus, the role of personal influence in the formation of tastes, attitudes, purchases, and media consumption is convincingly established: it is an "almost invisible, certainly inconspicuous, form of leadership at the person-to-person level of ordinary, intimate, informal, everyday contact" (ibid., 138). It is "casually exercised, sometimes unwittingly and unbeknown, within the smallest grouping of friends, family members and neighbor" (ibid.). This is a very different picture of everyday life and its texture of social relations to that described and analyzed in, for instance, Robert Merton's slightly earlier classic study of *Mass Persuasion* (1946/2004). In a celebrated section of the book, Merton interprets contemporary America as characterized by pseudo-gemeinschaft. If gemeinschaft stands for a genuine community of values, pseudo-gemeinschaft is its negation: "the feigning of personal concern with the other fellow," as Merton puts it, "in order to get the better of him." Urban Americans (or men, at least) live in a climate of reciprocal distrust. Anomie, pseudo-gemeinschaft, and cynicism are the psychological effects of a society that, focused on capital and the market, tends to instrumentalize human relationships.

We might note, again, that this is presented as the world of men and reflect, again, on the fact that the Decatur study describes a world of women. We must, moreover, recall that in fact the Merton study was also a study of women: of the impact, on one hand, of a female singer, Kate Smith, the best-known, highest-paid radio performer of her day and, on the other hand, of the response of a multitude of female listeners to her marathon broadcast. Again, the profoundly gendered nature of the study is unremarked and unaccounted for in the original study. And yet it is surely a key, if not *the* key, to the central theme and problem of the study, namely, the question of sincerity. What drew so many (female) listeners to Kate Smith, what kept them with her through the whole long day of the broadcast, was, as they heard and reported it, her undoubted genuineness and sincerity. They experienced her broadcast as a personal, intimate thing: "She was speaking straight to me"; "You'd think she was a personal friend. I feel she's talking to me" (Merton 1946/2004, 61). Merton evidently found it difficult to make sense of this. He reads American society as characterized by Durkheimian anomie: that is his interpretative frame for the study. "Only against this background of skepticism and distrust stemming from a prevalently manipulative society were we able to interpret our subjects' magnified 'will to believe' in a public figure who is thought to incarnate the virtues of sincerity, integrity, good fellowship and altruism" (ibid., 10-11). But the fragments of data included in the text do nothing to support this interpretation of listener responses as a "will to believe," nor a view of Kate Smith as the incarnation of anything. She was simply heard as a genuine person in her own right, something that Merton found hard to acknowledge or accept. For male intellectuals, the whole thing was "obviously" phoney—"pseudo," to borrow a word that was then commonly used to describe many aspects of contemporary life. Lazarsfeld saw the Kate Smith episode as "almost as bizarre as the 'Invasion from Mars' " (Simonson 2004, xix).

History and Sociology

In drawing attention to the gendered aspects of mass communication research in the period under discussion, some of the differences (and tensions) between sociology and historiography rise to the surface. Is it permissible to "read" from the perspective of today the politics of gender in the past? The gendered aspects of the work of Lazarsfeld and his colleagues were unremarked by them. Is it not an incidental fact that most of the listeners to Kate Smith's broadcast were women? The reason that the people in the Decatur study were all women could be explained, simply and innocently, by the fact that the research was commissioned by a publisher of women's magazines. Thus, the commercial sponsor of the research got useful details about the tastes, preferences, and opinions of contemporary American female consumers of popular culture, while Lazarsfeld could equally usefully apply the same data in a quite different way to explore the two-step flow hypothesis. This may show the effective double-sidedness of the administrative research pioneered by Paul Lazarsfeld, which allowed him to satisfy the external demands of corporate sponsors and at the same time get something of intellectual, academic value to the field of sociology. But are we, today, entitled to find different issues to those addressed in the original research and to interpret and evaluate them from perspectives that are markedly different to those of the original researchers?

It depends on who "we" are, of course: whether, in this case, we are historians or sociologists. One way of understanding the difference between these two not unrelated disciplines is in terms of the different temporalities in and with which they operate. By and large, sociology operates within what Luc Boltanski (1999, 191-92) has called "the politics of the present." Thus, all the sociological research under discussion in this article was commissioned and executed in response to immediate issues as they showed up in contemporary America. Likewise, the results and findings were constrained within the same order of time: the present, the more or less immediate "now." Effects studies, as both Katz and Lazarsfeld generally insisted, operate within the short term. Methodologically and in principle, the long-term effects of short-term sociology must always elude its grasp. It has no resources from which to begin to consider the long-term implications of research commissioned and undertaken in the now-of-concern that elicited it. How could it? None of us can jump over our own shadow. The work of history begins only as the past begins to appear distinct from the present. Today, looking back to the time of the publication of *Personal Influence,* we can see aspects of that work, unremarked and unremarkable at the time, that would shortly emerge into historical significance.

The immediate moment of *Personal Influence* is the date of its publication. But as we have seen, its internal history goes back to the study of voting behaviors in the presidential election campaign of 1940 and what was learned from that study. *The People's Choice* (Lazarsfeld, Berelson, and Gaudet 1944), in turn, reflected foundational concerns of the emerging sociology of the media of mass communication. Thus, a historical interpretation of the significance of *Personal Influence* must regard its impact in 1955 as the outcome, indeed the culmination, of twenty years of work on the impact of mass communication on American society. What shows up, historically, in this time span—the time of the genesis of the two-step flow hypothesis and its testing from the midthirties to the midfifties—is, I have argued, a fundamental sea change in the long and still unfolding process of world historical modernization. If this is so, the significance of *Personal Influence* extends beyond the field of sociology as embedded in American contemporary historical life with which I have thus far been concerned. It remains to consider this classic text of American sociology in relation to similar developments in Europe at the time, events that also disclose the same historical transformations discussed above.

Conclusions

Let me summarize those transformations at this point. The 1940s, defined by the world-shattering event of World War II, were the historical hinge of the past century. The first half of the century—up to and going into the war—was "the time of the masses." The second half of the past century, coming out of the war, appears as the "time of everyday life." The world of the 1950s, in the United States, Britain, and the advanced economies of Europe, was simply a different world to that of the 1930s. This change is the historical effect of the restructuring of the global economy as it shifted decisively from scarcity to abundance. In Europe and North America, the politics of poverty defined the first half of the past century; in the second half, it was displaced by the politics of plenty, which was and remains, more exactly, the politics of everyday life.

The new mass media showed the consequences of poverty to contemporary audiences but were themselves part of a new culture of leisure and consumption underpinned by the rapidly developing economy of abundance.

I have thus far emphasized the social question of the masses and the politics of poverty to which it gave rise as a core concern of "classic" sociology in Europe as well as in North America. The prewar sociology of mass communication was hailed into existence by current concerns with the vulnerability of the urban masses to manipulation by new technologies of social communication. But the interwar period was also the moment when new, modern forms of entertainment that would define the rest of the century (radio, cinema, and the music industry) were decisively established. While millions endured hunger, unemployment, and squalid living conditions in Europe and North America, millions more were beginning to enjoy a marginal surplus of disposable time and money that they spent on the newly emerging culture of consumption and entertainment. The postwar culture of everyday life was formed in the interwar period. The new mass media showed the consequences of poverty to contemporary audiences but were themselves part of a new culture of leisure and consumption underpinned by the rapidly developing economy of abundance. The sociology of mass communication across a twenty-year span from the midthirties to the midfifties tracks this transition taking place in American society. Read as a key sociological text, *Personal Influence* resolves a riddle within the field. Read as a key historical text, it points to the fading of the politics of poverty and the question of the masses and the emergence of a politics of plenty and the question of everyday life. The social question no longer presents itself only in terms of economic and political concerns. It now appears and begins to be recognized as a cultural concern. The cultural turn in the humanities and social sciences, clearly evident from the 1970s onward, was evident in the 1950s.

A key text in which this "turn" became explicit appeared in Britain in 1958. The very title of *Culture and Society* by Raymond Williams makes explicit the newfound link between the social and the cultural. The development of cultural studies as a new academic field took place in Britain in the 1970s but had its origins years earlier when Williams along with Richard Hoggart (1957/1992) and Edward Thompson (1963) reconfigured the meaning of culture. Whereas hitherto culture was thought of in terms of literature and the arts and the taste cultures of privileged minorities, it was now rethought as the mundane, common culture of ordinary people in everyday life. *Culture and Society* was the key text that not only redefined culture but emphasized its quite new significance. Central to Williams's concluding discussion of the meaning of culture in contemporary fifties Britain was an attempt to break out of older habits of thought and crucially the then-prevalent tendency to think of others as "the masses." In a celebrated passage, Williams claimed, "There are in fact no masses; there are only ways of seeing other people as masses":

> I do not think of my relatives, friends and neighbors, colleagues, acquaintances, as masses; we none of us can or do. The masses are always the others, whom we don't know, and can't know. Yet now, in our kind of society, we see others, regularly, in their myriad variations; stand, physically, beside them. They are here, and we are here with them. And that we are with them is of course the whole point. To other people, we are also masses. Masses are other people. (Williams 1958/1966, 289)

Just as Katz and Lazarsfeld discovered real people living in social networks of relatives, friends, neighbors, colleagues, and acquaintances in Decatur, so too in England at exactly the same time the masses have melted away and in their place are "other people" similarly inscribed in their sociable networks of everyday life. Richard Hoggart's (1957/1992) ethnography of everyday, working class life and culture in fifties Britain revealed to a middle-class readership "the 'real' world of people" and their "full rich life" (pp. 102-31, 133-68).

The postwar academic discovery of everyday life first appears from the rubble of war-torn France in Henri Lefebvre's quite remarkable *Critique of Everyday Life* (1947/1992). In the United States, it achieves definitive recognition in Erving Goffman's *Presentation of Self in Everyday Life* (1959), which takes for granted that the self in question is indeed the new "other-directed" type identified by Riesman (1950/1976). In Britain along with the work of Hoggart and Williams, who redeem the ordinary and the everyday from the condescension of

Literary Studies, I want to emphasize the quite different, but no less important work of J. L. Austin, who pioneered the philosophy of ordinary language on the stony soil of Oxford philosophy in the 1950s.[2] His work was fundamental to establishing ordinary language and its everyday (nonacademic) usage as a valid object of academic enquiry, thereby making possible the beginnings of an adequate understanding of human communication. Finally, at the start of the 1960s, but firmly rooted in Germany of the 1950s, Jurgen Habermas published *Strukturwandel der Offentlichkeit* (The Structural Transformation of the Public Sphere), a key work that argued for the political opinions of ordinary people and the ways in which these were arrived at as the historical and normative basis of modern democracy (Habermas 1962/1989).[3]

These academic developments are one indicator of the quite new importance of everyday life in postwar North America and Europe. But it shows up in all sorts of ways. It is there in the theatre, novels, and films of the decade but nowhere more so than television, which now becomes the definitive new medium of everyday life. And most significantly of all, it begins to show up as a new kind of politics, as the politics of the masses gives way to the politics of everyday life. The first stirrings of the new politics show up in the United States: the civil rights movement, the women's movement, and, a little later, the student movement. This was not a politics produced or led by established organizations and their representatives. It came from ordinary people, and what they wanted was something other than what traditional politics offered. Foucault has distinguished between three forms of oppression: exploitation, domination, and subjection. The first is economic and concerns the struggle for subsistence, the second is ideological and concerns the struggles over imposed political and religious authority, and the third is social and cultural and concerns the struggle to be allowed to be oneself in public (Foucault 1982). The new social movements, as they began to articulate their own self-understanding, were concerned with this third claim. The politics of recognition, as it was aptly called by Charles Taylor (1994), has grown in global significance in the past half century. In many ways, its defining moment was the refusal of Rosa Parks to give up her seat to a white passenger on a bus in Montgomery, Alabama, on December 10, 1955. Her action, in the same year that *Personal Influence* was published, perfectly encapsulated the emerging politics of everyday life.

That emergent politics was prefigured in the sociological literature reviewed above. It may have been an unnoticed aspect of the research projects at the time, but what the data disclosed about the position of women as consumers of popular culture can now be seen as a pointer toward the politicization of gender relations that developed as a core concern of the politics of everyday life in the late 1950s. Moreover, the position of women working within sociology—their marginal status in relation to male colleagues, their lack of career opportunities, their largely hidden and subordinate contributions to the work in progress—becomes clearly visible when we attend to the small print of who did what in the acknowledgements of the published works. The fate of Helen MacGill Hughes, whose pioneering research into the human interest story in the newspapers was one of the very few studies in the 1930s to take seriously the attitudes and opinions of the *demos* and to write of ordinary people without condescension, is exemplary (Hughes 1940). Her husband (whom she met at graduate school) became a professor while she never progressed further than part-time editorial work on the *American Journal of Sociology*. Hughes was able at last to address the fate of her own generation and its far wider ramifications in her edited report on *The Status of Women in Sociology 1968-1972*, which she presented to the American Sociological Association in 1973. The report was inspired by "the movement which bears the general name of 'Women's Liberation' " (Hughes 1973, 2) and still makes troubling reading. Thus, what became an articulate politics within sociology many years later we now can see, looking back from our own present day, was beginning to appear in the 1930s.

It is the argument of this article that the full significance of *Personal Influence* cannot be grasped by a purely immanent sociological reading. The exogenous historical reading that I have essayed necessarily starts from the internal history of the text and its position (at the time and since) within the field of sociology, both of which are crucial to its understanding. But moving outwards from this, we must think of it as embedded in the economic, political, social, and cultural determinants of its own and present times as these impinged upon and shaped the concerns of sociological work in progress. In attending to the historical gestation of *Personal Influence*, I have offered a symptomatic reading of it as a response to a profound sea change in the world with which it engages—the passing of the time of the politics and culture of the masses and the emergence of the politics and culture of everyday life. Thus, what the book discloses both in its internal history *and* as a response to the historical process of its own time (its inner and outer dialectic, so to speak) is the passage from modernity to postmodernity, if by that is meant the structural transformation of the global economy from scarcity to abundance and the corresponding reconfiguration of the form and content of contemporary political, social, and cultural life. As a contribution in its own day to its own times, *Personal Influence* was a prescient work, a work of real discovery and a pointer to social change. Its long-term impact and effect could not then be foreseen and would only become apparent in the silent passage and slow working through of historical time itself. The simple fact of this collection of articles, written fifty years after its publication, offers ample testimony to its enduring sociological and historical significance, then and now.

Notes

1. For a fuller discussion of this proposition, from which historiography is not excluded, see Scannell (forthcoming).

2. The key text is Austin's *How to Do Things with Words*, given as a series of lectures at Harvard in 1955 (the year of *Personal Influence*) and first published, posthumously, in 1962.

3. See Scannell (forthcoming) for a much fuller discussion of the authors mentioned in this paragraph.

References

Arendt, H. 1963/1990. *On revolution*. London: Penguin.

Austin, J. L. 1962. *How to do things with words*. Oxford: Oxford University Press.

Boltanski, L. 1999. *Distant suffering*. Cambridge: Cambridge University Press.

Cantril, H. 1940. *The invasion from Mars: A study in the psychology of panic*. Princeton, NJ: Princeton University Press.

Carey, J. 1992. *The intellectuals and the masses, 1880-1939*. London: Faber and Faber.

Douglas, Susan J. 2006. *Personal influence* and the bracketing of women's history. *Annals of the American Academy of Political and Social Science* 608: 41-50.

Foucault, M. 1982. The subject and power. In *Michel Foucault. Beyond structuralism and hermeneutics*, ed. H. Dreyfus and P. Rabinow. Brighton, UK: Harvester.

Goffman, E. 1959. *The presentation of self in everyday life*. Harmondsworth, UK: Pelican.

Habermas, J. 1962/1989. *The structural transformation of the public sphere*. Cambridge: Polity.

Hoggart, R. 1957/1992. *The uses of literacy*. London: Penguin.

Hughes, H. M. 1940. *News and the human interest story*. Chicago: Chicago University Press.

———, ed. 1973. *The status of women in sociology 1968-1972*. Washington, DC: American Sociological Association.

Katz, E., and P. Lazarsfeld. 1955. *Personal influence*. Glencoe, IL: Free Press.

Lazarsfeld, P. 1940. *Radio and the printed page*. New York: Duell, Sloan and Pearce.

Lazarsfeld, Paul F., Bernard Berelson, and Hazel Gaudet. 1944. *The people's choice: How the voter makes up his mind in a presidential campaign*. New York: Duell, Sloan and Pearce.

Lefebvre, H. 1947/1992. *Critique of everyday life*. London: Verso.

Merton, R. 1946/2004. *Mass persuasion*. New York: Howard Fertig.

Peters, J. D., and P. Simonson, eds. 2004. *Mass communication and American social thought, 1919-1968*. Lanham, MD: Rowman & Littlefield.

Riesman, D. 1950/1976. *The lonely crowd*. New Haven, CT: Yale University Press.

Scannell, P. Forthcoming. *Media and communication*. London: Sage.

Simonson, P. 2004. Introduction to *Mass persuasion*, by R. Merton. New York: Howard Fertig. (Originally published 1946)

Thompson, E. P. 1963. *The making of the English working class*. London: Pelican.

Taylor, C. 1994. *Multiculturalism*. Princeton, NJ: Princeton University Press.

Williams, R. 1958/1966. *Culture and society*. London: Pelican.

Fifteen Pages that Shook the Field: *Personal Influence*, Edward Shils, and the Remembered History of Mass Communication Research

By

JEFFERSON POOLEY

Personal Influence's fifteen-page account of the development of mass communication research has had more influence on the field's historical self-understanding than anything published before or since. According to Elihu Katz and Paul Lazarsfeld's well-written, two-stage narrative, a loose and undisciplined body of pre-war thought had concluded naively that media are *powerful*—a myth punctured by the rigorous studies of Lazarsfeld and others, which showed time and again that media impact is in fact *limited*. This "powerful-to-limited-effects" story line remains textbook boilerplate and literature review dogma fifty years later. This article traces the emergence of the *Personal Influence* synopsis, with special attention to (1) Lazarsfeld's audience-dependent framing of key media research findings and (2) the surprisingly prominent role of Edward Shils in supplying key elements of the narrative.

Keywords: Paul Lazarsfeld; Edward Shils; Elihu Katz; media research; history of social science; disciplinary memory

The bullet model or hypodermic model posits powerful, direct effects of the mass media. . . . Survey studies of social influence conducted in the late 1940s presented a very different model from that of a hypodermic needle in which a multistep flow of media effects was evident. That is, most people receive much of their information and are influenced by media secondhand, through the personal influence of opinion leaders (Katz and Lazarsfeld 1955).

—Joseph Straubhaar and
Robert LaRose (2006, 403)

Jefferson Pooley is an assistant professor of media and communication at Muhlenberg College. His research centers on the history of media research, as the field's emergence has intersected with the twentieth-century rise of the other social sciences. He is currently revising his dissertation (An Accident of Memory: Edward Shils, Paul Lazarsfeld and the History of American Mass Communication Research) *for publication.*

NOTE: Thanks to Peter Simonson for extensive and insightful suggestions.

DOI: 10.1177/0002716206292460

The main thread of American mass communication research holds that the scholars who surrounded Paul F. Lazarsfeld in the years during and after World War II dispelled the conventional wisdom that media marinate the defenseless American mind. According to the story, a loose and undisciplined body of prewar thought had concluded naively that media are *powerful*—a myth punctured by the rigorous studies of Lazarsfeld and others, which showed time and again that media impact is in fact *limited*.

If we were to trust the first chapter of *Personal Influence*—the landmark 1955 study by Elihu Katz and Lazarsfeld[1]—the whole of pre-World War II research would seem to us naïve in its methods and crude in its conclusions. Katz and Lazarsfeld's well-written, fifteen-page synopsis of the "ideas with which mass media research began" ascribes to past scholarship one of "two opposite inclinations": the interwar body of work either decried the mass media as "instruments of evil design" or else heralded those media as a "new dawn for democracy" (pp. 15-17). Both approaches—the fearful *and* the ebullient—described the media message as a "direct and powerful stimulus" (p. 16). Swept up by popular alarm or blinded by utopian rhetoric, both groups of scholars based their judgments on intuition or folk wisdom or speculative European theory. None of this will do, write Katz and Lazarsfeld. Fortunately, a new body of work has emerged that rejects the folk wisdom and spurns the Europeans and opts instead for a sober and quantitative approach. Katz and Lazarsfeld conclude their fifteen pages with a review of the new research—much of it generated by Lazarsfeld's Bureau of Applied Social Research—whose "greater precision" has generated "increasing skepticism about the potency of the mass media" (p. 24).

In one short chapter, the field's untidy past was neatened. A naïve, intuitive prehistory—given over to the mistaken belief that radio and film wield enormous power—got displaced by a calmer, *scientific* appraisal: these media, according to the new evidence, have only "limited" effects. This *Personal Influence* history is simple, direct, and meagerly sourced. Its clean narrative is resolved by the second act. And it was believed: fifty years later, the "powerful-to-limited-effects" story line remains textbook boilerplate and literature review dogma.[2] Katz and Lazarsfeld's fifteen pages have had more influence on the field's historical self-understanding than anything published before or since.

All of the historiographical clichés of the decades to come—the interwar "magic bullet theory," for example, or the idea of a "hypodermic needle" model—trace their origins to those fifteen pages. They themselves do not employ these terms.[3] But Katz and Lazarsfeld lay out the Whiggish two-stage history that would become the common reference point—the default citational authority—for the many later elaborations of the "powerful-to-limited-effects" story line.

Katz and Lazarsfeld's narration is all the more striking for its departure from the many *other* ways that Lazarsfeld, before *Personal Influence*, had presented the same bundle of findings. Over the fifteen years or so that he conducted media research—culminating in *Personal Influence*—Lazarsfeld had framed a fairly stable set of findings in a number of distinct and resourceful ways, depending especially on the main *audience* that any particular study was intended for. He took a set of findings that were, initially, disappointing in scientific terms and *repackaged* them repeatedly according to the intended audience. His core findings—that short-term, mass-mediated persuasion attempts often fail, that face-to-face efforts seem more successful, and that the two persuasion types may be connected— were most often, for example, put forward as *technical advice* to would-be persuaders in government, industry, and public advocacy. The findings were framed, moreover, one way when the audience was composed of socially concerned liberal intellectuals and another when the audience featured fellow media academics. Lazarsfeld was a masterful *packager*, chameleon-like in his audience adaptability. His last word was *Personal Influence*, and it is the only one we remember.

o o o

It is a fitting irony that the sociologist Edward Shils, a mandarin theorist and intellectual maverick with no interest in the empirical study of media, supplied the coalescing field of mass communication research with its usable past. It was Shils who furnished, without intending to, *Personal Influence*'s basic plot.

While it is possible to discern inchoate gropings toward the "limited effect" story line *before* Shils's unwitting intervention, these were scattered and inconsistent, without narrative tightness. As early as 1942, Lazarsfeld and others started to note the difficulty of bringing about attitude change through media persuasion (Lazarsfeld 1942; see also Lazarsfeld and Merton [1943] and Merton and Kendall [1944]). But this observation—repeated often during the next ten years—was not yet framed as a claim of minimal media impact, nor as a happy repudiation of precursor overreach. Indeed, the discovery of the obstinate audience was typically discussed as a *technical* problem, as an obstacle in the design of effective propaganda. Occasionally, especially in the years immediately after the war, the failure of straightforward persuasion *was* treated in broad, media-impact terms, but almost always in tension with the ongoing search for careful propaganda design.[4] This two-track, schizophrenic framing—a concern, on one hand, for finding out how to make persuasion *work*, and on the other, an effort to draw sweeping conclusions about media impact—made it hard to formulate a clean, coherent statement of limited effect. With the cold war dramatically hotter by 1949, Joseph Klapper, one of Lazarsfeld's students, finally makes a muscular case for minimal media impact in free, plural societies in his influential synthesis of research to date (Klapper 1949).[5] There is, in Klapper's summary, a palpable tone of relief that anticipates the upbeat, celebratory cadence of the full-fledged "limited effects" story line.[6] But there is still no *plot* in Klapper, no clear account of the triumph of careful observation over alarmist conjecture. This Shils would supply.

Shils's help with the narration came in two installments. He provided, first, an account of the disappearance and reemergence of "small-group" research that proved vital to *Personal Influence*'s powerful-to-limited-effects account (Shils 1948, 40-52; Shils 1951). Drawing on his authority as a major exegist of European sociology, Shils attributed the temporary small-group research falloff to the influence of the misguided European tradition. "The great stream of [European] sociological thought in the nineteenth century," he wrote in the crucial 1951 paper, developed a wrong-headed picture of the transition to modernity (p. 44). For the Europeans—he mentions only Tönnies and Marx—that transition was a great unraveling of old communal bonds, a shucking off of tradition, to be replaced by an atomized and disoriented populace bound only by contract and mutual expediency. The Europeans greatly underestimated, Shils insists, the persistence of custom and primary ties in the modern world.

Shils stressed the Europeans' influence on the younger American field. Though American sociologists, and Charles Horton Cooley in particular, had generated their own rich tradition of thought on primary groups in the early twentieth century, they regrettably succumbed to the European obsession with *Gesellschaft*: "As a living trend in sociological research, the primary-group studies stimulated by the writings and teachings of Cooley . . . had come to an end by the early 1930s" (ibid., 47). It was left, Shils concludes, to scattered research groups to start anew; their unwitting "convergence" on the small group had, by the late 1940s, fortuitously reclaimed an abandoned current of American sociology (ibid., 59).

The more measured finding of limited *effect . . .*
has its roots in an image of society that
recognizes the endurance of primary ties and
a rich associational life.

Katz and Lazarsfeld, in *Personal Influence*, embraced Shils's fall-and-rise account with alacrity.[7] But as it happened, the contrast between the pictures of society that Shils invoked—between the mistaken European view of impersonal isolation as against his view, that *Gemeinschaft* elements endure—had even greater influence. The distance between the "potent" and "minimal" media impact stances, Katz and Lazarsfeld argue, is the distance between these contrasting pictures of modernity. Those with the superceded belief in media potency clung to that image of breakdown and anonymity of "the late 19th century European schools" (p. 17). The more measured finding of *limited* effect, by contrast, has its roots in an image of society that recognizes the endurance of primary ties and a rich associational life. The wrongness of the interwar media analysts, in other words, rested on their warped view of modern life: "Their image, first of all, was of an atomistic mass of millions of readers, listeners and movie-goers prepared to receive the Message" (p. 16).

Katz and Lazarsfeld acknowledge their debt to Shils's "excellent" essay early and often.[8] Their narrative contrast between interwar media analysts' naïve belief in media potency and their own, more sober conclusions *relies* on the parallel distance between the two camps' social image.[9] And with this grounding, Katz and Lazarsfeld had elegantly narrated the history of the field, retroactively drafting Lazarsfeld's body of communication research to the "limited effects" position. Shils's treatment of small-group research, and especially his embedding of that story in terms of societal imagery, was essential to the field.

Shils's own personal influence derived from his unusual, border-spanning perch. He had become an empirical social scientist with a penetrating knowledge of social thought in a social scientific milieu in which such knowledge was scarce.[10] He was already, in 1951, claiming an interpretive authority in intellectual historical matters that was only to swell in the years to come. With one foot in social theory and the history of social thought, and the other in the world of postwar empirical social science, Shils was able to take his knowledge of the former—with all of its self-validating prestige—and redeploy it to a besotted field.

Shils had his own intellectual reasons for narrating the history in the manner that he did (first in 1948 and again, with more clarity, in 1951)—reasons rooted in his evolving and deeply engaged search for the underpinnings of modern social order (Shils and Janowitz 1948; Shils 1948, 1951).[11] In a sense, however, his reasons did not matter once the narrative itself was released to the American sociological public; Lazarsfeld and Katz had *their* own reasons for adopting the historical picture that Shils put forward—reasons largely centered on scholarly competition and norms of originality. The powerful-to-limited-effects narrative in *Personal Influence*, in turn, was so widely embraced in the late 1950s for a still-different set of reasons—because of the scholarly support it lent to the public intellectual defense of American popular culture, in the context of an evolving cold war liberalism. (In these same debates, Daniel Bell [1956, 1960] and Shils [1957a, 1961, 1962] introduced the complementary "mass society theory" pejorative, which later merged with the powerful-to-limited-effects story, in, for example, Bauer and Bauer [1960]; Bramson [1961]; Gans [1966]; and, above all, DeFleur [1966].)[12] The staying power of this limited-effects narrative was ultimately guaranteed, however, by the newly institutionalized, would-be discipline of "communication"—which retained the story line as a usable, and teachable, past.

There was nothing smooth or linear about the chain of distinct purposes and contexts that led, eventually, to a standard "disciplinary" history for mass communication research. In this case at least, the memory got formed, altered, adopted, modified, and readopted in disjointed succession. What was for Shils an intellectual coming to terms was for Katz and Lazarsfeld an artful repackaging; for the mass culture debates it was scholarly ammunition and for the communication discipline an origin myth and internal cohesive. That Shils would indirectly draft the lecture notes of journalism school instructors in 2006—this was an accident.

* * *

Shils's 1948 *Wehrmacht* paper, written with Morris Janowitz, was to become one of the most frequently cited in the emerging postwar literature of "communication research," both for its substantive findings but also for its clear framing. Shils and Janowitz's stress on the relative insulation of primary groups from generalized propaganda confirmed, with new and different evidence, an emerging research truism. A diverse body of wartime survey research on propaganda effectiveness— including studies on war bond publicity conducted for the Department of the Treasury and Lazarsfeld's own 1940 election study *The People's Choice* (Lazarsfeld, Berelson, and Gaudet 1944)—had suggested that mass-mediated persuasion appeals, on their own, tend not to change behavior, unless supplemented with personal, face-to-face attempts.[13] Even the well-known experimental studies of the "Why We Fight" films (Hovland, Lumsdaine, and Sheffield 1949), conducted by the Army's Research Branch—which provided more evidence of mass-mediated persuasion—had nevertheless pointed to a series of qualifications and conditions that made for more or less effectiveness.[14] The many social scientists who had mobilized for propaganda service came away from their wartime experience with a basic consensus: persuasion, especially the mass-mediated kind, is not a simple affair, but instead only works under certain conditions that should be heeded in future propaganda work. Social scientists' conclusions about the complexity of mass persuasion were put forward, that is, in the unambiguous context of an ongoing project to design effective propaganda.

This context is very often forgotten because the limited effects narrative, when it emerged in the mid-1950s, retroactively reframed the wartime and postwar findings as proof that mass media influence is happily inconsequential. For the wartime scientists, however, there were no sighs of relief at the failures of propaganda—and, indeed, these partial failures prompted the researchers to search for the particular conditions under which propaganda would work. (As it happened, the search for effective propaganda would remain a core research concern for mass media scholars until the mid-1960s. From the mid-1950s on, in the context of the cold war shift to the campaign for third world allegiance, domestic media research summaries stressed minimal impact. However, international media research, in its front-stage published work, tended to point to positive media impact on economic development, while its backstage unpublished reports remained focused on the search for effective propaganda strategy.[15])

Shils's *Wehrmacht* article was, in line with the other wartime research, fundamentally concerned with workable propaganda design. This should hardly be surprising since the major mission of Shils and Janowitz's military unit—the Psychological Warfare Division's Intelligence Section—had been to assess the effectiveness of Allied propaganda. But the article's unambiguous concern with propagandizing *well* still comes off as startling, mainly because the term has since recaptured its appalling connotations. As the article's brief editorial foreword in *Public Opinion Quarterly* states, "This study thus provides an example of the sociological and psychological analysis which the propagandist must make if he is to obtain maximal response to his communications" (Shils and Janowitz 1948, 280). From this angle, the Shils and Janowitz paper is an attempt to explain the largely indifferent reaction of German soldiers to Allied propaganda, especially when appeals were made to systems of belief or general symbols (ibid., 281).

With this failure in mind, Shils and Janowitz report that on the basis of their unit's early findings, a series of air-dropped leaflets were designed with the aim to undermine primary groups, without recourse to such secondary symbols (ibid., 314). Propaganda tailored to address these small-group bonds, the authors stress, is more effective than broader appeals.

Shils and Janowitz, in short, framed their findings in much the same way as other social scientists emerging from the war—as technical lessons for a complicated task. But the authors also narrated their conclusions, and in a way that prefigured the "powerful-to-limited-effects" story line that would become, years later, the standard history of mass communication research. Shils and Janowitz, that is, contrasted their sober and realist findings with a naïve belief in media omnipotence that, they claim, had been widely held, even recently: "At the beginning of the second world war, many publicists and specialists in propaganda attributed almost supreme importance to psychological warfare operations," they wrote (ibid., 314). The "legendary success" of World War I efforts and the "tremendous expansion" of advertising and public relations in the interwar years "had convinced many people that human behavior could be extensively manipulated by mass communications" (ibid., 314). They were wrong, the authors wrote. Propaganda, in fact, only works under specific conditions, and even then its impact is narrower than once thought. "The erroneous views concerning the omnipotence of propaganda," they wrote, "must be given up and their place must be taken by much more differentiated views as to the possibilities of certain kinds of propaganda under different sets of conditions" (ibid., 314).

The *Wehrmacht* paper, in light of the later, mid-1950s emergence of a full-fledged "powerful-to-limited-effects" narrative, was important in a number of overlapping ways. It provided, first, one of the empirical anchors for the notion that face-to-face contact trumps more general, impersonal appeals like those issued by mass media. Though this was treated in the paper itself, and by early commentators, as a lesson for propaganda design—take advantage of personal networks, the paper instructs; tailor propaganda to address small-group solidarity—the article's finding of relative small-group imperviousness would be repackaged later as evidence for the thesis that media impact is fortuitously negligible. The other substantive contribution made by the *Wehrmacht* article is its stress on the primary group itself. The explanations that had already been put forward for the failures of direct propaganda tended to stress social psychological verities about cognitive consistency and selective perception; to the extent that these filtering tendencies were placed in a social context at all, as in *The People's Choice*, they were related to socialization and to larger categories of socioeconomic background and group membership on the order of "Catholic" and "urban."[16] Very little attention had been paid, before Shils and Janowitz's article, to the importance of small-group ties as an ongoing buffer between persuaders and their targets.

But the paper's more crucial contributions, arguably, were not empirical so much as historical and imagistic. The article's scholarly narrative, that a mistaken belief in media omnipotence has given way to a more qualified, scientific finding, prefigured the decisive element of the *Personal Influence* emplotment of mass communication research. Shils's narrative influence, in this respect, came through his friend and intellectual dependent Bernard Berelson, but also directly through Lazarsfeld himself.

Berelson was an ambitious operator who managed to transform a lowly post in the University of Chicago's library school in the late 1930s into the directorship of the Ford Foundation's Behavioral Sciences unit by the early 1950s. He had, in 1940, joined Lazarsfeld's Office of Radio Research at Columbia, where he coauthored *The People's Choice*. In 1946, he returned to the University of Chicago as the dean of its Library School, but he remained affiliated with Lazarsfeld's research organization, by then renamed the Bureau of Applied Social Research. He directed the second major Bureau election study, of the 1948 presidential race as it played out in Elmira, New York, published in 1954 as *Voting* (Berelson, Lazarsfeld, and McPhee 1954), with Berelson as first author.

The Shils-Berelson relationship was an important one for many different reasons. Here, it is enough to point to Shils's, and the *Wehrmacht* article's, influence on a crucial paper that Berelson wrote later the same year, "Communications as Public Opinion" (Berelson 1948). In the paper, Berelson attempted to summarize the extant research findings on the effects of mass media.[17] In line with most writing on this issue during and after the war, Berelson (1948) explicitly framed his contribution in terms of the search for effective propaganda—and, in this instance, with code-worded allusions to the heating-up cold war:

> Of the importance of this topic it is hardly necessary to speak. If the defenses of peace and prosperity, not to mention other desirable political conditions, are to be constructed in men's minds, then the critical position of communications and public opinion for that defense is evident. (p. 167)

The paper, published in 1948 and reprinted in the field's first two, widely influential readers (Schramm 1949; Berelson and Janowitz 1950), became known and often-cited for its pithy statement of qualified effect: "Some kinds of *communication* on some kinds of *issues*, brought to the attention of some kinds of *people* under some kinds of *conditions*, have some kinds of *effects*" (p. 172).[18]

Like the Shils and Janowitz paper, Berelson's article contrasts the field's mature, measured conclusions with a naïve interwar belief in media potency: "To speak roughly, in the 1920's propaganda was considered all-powerful—'it got us into the war'—and thus communication was thought to determine public opinion practically by itself" (Berelson 1948, 171). In a manner similar to Shils and Janowitz, but with a stronger claim to represent an emerging scientific consensus, Berelson continues,

> In the 1930s the Roosevelt campaigns "proved" that the newspaper had lost its influence and that a "golden voice" on the radio could sway men in almost any direction. Now, in the 1940's, a body of empirical research is accumulating which provides some refined knowledge about the effect of communication on the public and promises to provide a good deal more in the next years. (Ibid., 171)

In Berelson's account, a mistaken and questionably scientific interwar conviction that mass media are all-powerful has been displaced by a more sophisticated understanding of the particular conditions that make for effective influence.

Berelson consulted both the *Wehrmacht* article and Shils himself as he drafted his paper, though it is impossible to demonstrate that Berelson's statements of qualified effect, or his claim for the interwar belief in propaganda potency, derive exclusively from Shils or Shils's writings.[19] The idea that persuasion only works under certain conditions, after all, was a rather widely held tenet among the war-service social scientists. But Berelson's narrative contrast to the interwar belief in media potency does seem closely linked to Shils's similar, earlier statement. The *Wehrmacht* article was, after all, the first published source to narrate the history in this two-stage manner; and Berelson's was the second. Neither version offers any evidence, citational or otherwise, for its historical claims. Given this Shils-Berelson sequence, given the linguistic and substantive overlap between the two narratives, given Berelson's admitted consultation with Shils and the Shils-Janowitz article, and given Berelson's ongoing and demonstrable dependence on Shils for intellectual advice, it seems likely that Berelson's "all-powerful" historical formulation derived from Shils's.[20]

Berelson's few lines of history ended up as the *only* cited source for the repeated claim, in Katz and Lazarsfeld's *Personal Influence*, that interwar research had fixated on media omnipotence. Needless to say, this was a crucial borrowing: Katz and Lazarsfeld's characterization of interwar media research is a paraphrase, with credit, of the passage in Berelson's 1948 paper:

> First the newspaper, and later the radio, were feared as powerful weapons able to rubber-stamp ideas upon the minds of defenseless readers and listeners. In the 1920's, it was widely held that the newspapers and their propaganda "got us into the war," while in the 1930's, many saw in the Roosevelt campaign "proof" that a "golden voice" on the radio could sway men in any direction. (Katz and Lazarsfeld 1955, 16)[21]

Recall that Berelson's nearly identical claims offered no source or citation—nor did, in keeping with Shils's usual practice, the account in the *Wehrmacht* paper. The interwar "powerful effects" portrayal, for all its longevity and mnemonic traction, was built atop a solid-seeming but really quite hollow foundation.

Shils would later provide Katz and Lazarsfeld, in his 1951 account of the "rediscovery" of the primary group, with another foundation stone that was, like the "powerful effects" characterization, quite porous. This was the idea of an underlying contrast between two pictures of society, one that mistakenly stressed anonymous and isolated masses, superseded by another that correctly perceived the endurance of meaningful small-group ties. Katz and Lazarsfeld, in *Personal Influence*, would go on to fuse Shils's image-of-society contrast with the powerful-to-limited-effects progression, by ascribing the anonymous-masses picture to the interwar media analysts, and the small-group vitalism to postwar social scientists like themselves. Shils's *Wehrmacht* paper already sets up this contrast in social imagery, albeit only in passing and without the clear narrative signposts that appear in his 1951 article.

Even before the straightforward 1951 narration, Lazarsfeld recognized in the *Wehrmacht* paper—and in Shils's *Present State of American Sociology* (1948)—a framework with which to make sense of the Bureau's findings, in *The People's Choice* and elsewhere, that interpersonal influences appear more effective than mass-mediated appeals. The Shils and Janowitz article made enough of an impression to feature prominently in a little-known 1948 lecture, "What Is Sociology?" which Lazarsfeld delivered in Oslo during a semester-long visit (Lazarsfeld 1948c).[22] His remarks on sociology, in that postwar moment when he had finally warmed to the disciplinary label, are in themselves unremarkable. But the Oslo lecture is a crucial record of Shils's early and pivotal role in Lazarsfeld's embrace of the small group as an interpretive frame.

Shils would . . . provide Katz and Lazarsfeld [with] . . . the idea of an underlying contrast between two pictures of society, one that mistakenly stressed anonymous and isolated masses, superseded by another that correctly perceived the endurance of meaningful small-group ties.

The lecture is full of postwar breathlessness; the field, Lazarsfeld proclaims, is in "transition from social philosophy to empirical sociology" (Lazarsfeld 1948/1990, 14). Some of Lazarsfeld's nomothetic language—the references, for example, to a "system of general laws"—bears the textual imprint of Shils's *Present State* (ibid., 19). But it is the Oslo lecture's focus on primary groups—the *Wehrmacht* findings are brought together with the Hawthorne studies and Lazarsfeld's own *People's Choice*—that is unmistakably indebted to Shils.

Shils, in *The Present State*, had included a short version of the small-group-reemergence thesis that would, in the 1951 "Study of the Primary Group," take center stage. Under the heading "The Small Group," Shils had, in 1948, identified a "new focus of interest on the small group in American empirical sociology" (p. 40). As in 1951, Shils described a "rediscovery" of a native sociological tradition rooted in Charles Horton Cooley and a few early Chicago School monographs (p. 40). With the same narrative arc that he would deploy in 1951, Shils described a regrettable abandonment of the "primary group" theme in the interwar years: "the whole trend of American sociology, despite its fruitful point of origin, moved away from a preoccupation with this subject, as in the development of urban sociology and community studies, spatial patterns and the larger neigh-borhood and urban community came to the foreground of attention" (p. 41).[23]

Shils, as evidence for the resurgence, points to the Hawthorne studies of Mayo and Whitehead, and their accidental discovery that "productivity was to a large extent the function of morale, which in turn was the function of small group sol-idarity" (ibid., 41). Crucially, he also identifies Lazarsfeld's *The People's Choice* as another "instance of the unexpected re-emergence of this problem" (ibid., 41). This retroactive designation by Shils is of profound significance, given that *The People's Choice* itself is silent on the topic of "small" or "primary" groups;[24] the book's claims for voter intransigence, after all, are grounded in, and explained through, category-wide demographic variables like "rural" and "Protestant."

The Oslo lecture is plainly dependent on Shils's *Present State* and the *Wehrmacht* study, though neither is explicitly credited. "Sociologists," Lazarsfeld (1948/1990) observes in the lecture, "have developed the notion of a primary group":

> By this they want to indicate that most people are not affected in their daily lives by the larger community in which they live. They are so to say embedded in very small groups, their families and a few friends and coworkers. The affection they can get from these small primary groups, the influence which is exercised by these few people, and the reactions which help them adjust to this little world of their own, is what explains a great part of their behavior. (p. 23)

Lazarsfeld proceeds to illustrate this "notion" with three examples that, though unnamed, are clearly the Hawthorne experiments, the *Wehrmacht* study, and *The People's Choice*, respectively (p. 23).

In language that closely tracks Shils's own synopsis of the Hawthorne experi-ments, Lazarsfeld (1948/1990) refers to "studies . . . on how to increase the pro-ductivity of workers." After glossing over, like Shils, researchers' expectation that external factors like lighting would boost morale, Lazarsfeld observes that "all these technical factors are of some importance but much more important turned out to be the personal relations the workers had with each other and with their foreman" (p. 23).

The "same importance of the primary groups was found," Lazarsfeld (1948/1990) continues, "when social scientists investigated why the German army in the last war fought so well at a time when no one could doubt any more even in Germany that the Germans had to loose [*sic*] the war" (p. 23). With clear reference to Shils and Janowitz's *Wehrmacht* article, Lazarsfeld adds,

> The soldiers were not much affected by the general political situation of Germany, and not even by general military events in which the whole army was involved. As long as the small primary groups, of which the German army was carefully built up, kept intact, the moral [*sic*] of the German soldiers was not destroyed. (p. 23)

Lazarsfeld's own *People's Choice*—though again without direct reference—rounds out the social scientific triptych. "Sociologists," he observes, "turned toward making empirical studies of politics and actual behavior of voters," and found that the parties have a "great stability" (p. 23). In an unannounced departure from the analysis in *The People's Choice* itself, Lazarsfeld claims here that political opinion is "something which develops in small primary groups": "A person is surrounded by other people who look at public affairs just as he does himself" (p. 23).

[T]he Personal Influence *story line to come,
in which barriers to propaganda get
repackaged as safe-for-democracy proof
that media impact is thankfully minimal,
has plain roots in Lazarsfeld's 1948 embrace
of Shils's primary group arguments.*

Shils's artful reframing of *The People's Choice* has, in the Oslo lecture, become Lazarsfeld's reframing.[25] And the *Personal Influence* story line to come, in which barriers to propaganda get repackaged as safe-for-democracy proof that media impact is thankfully minimal, has plain roots in Lazarsfeld's 1948 embrace of Shils's primary group arguments. Shils himself recognized Lazarsfeld's linked borrowings in 1948 and 1955: "I was heartened . . . by the invocation by Professor Paul Lazarsfeld in a lecture which he delivered in Oslo in 1948 very shortly after our paper appeared," he wrote in a 1975 memoir, "and then a few years later by his adoption of this hypothesis in his and Professor Elihu Katz's *Personal Influence*" (Shils 1975, xxv).

* * *

Lazarsfeld, in his and Katz's *Personal Influence* narrative, characterized his own body of media research as the progressive unfolding of a counterintuitive insight: that the media have only minimal effects. Todd Gitlin, in *his* Lazarsfeld narrative of the late 1970s, portrayed the Bureau findings for limited effect as a payment-in-absolution to its media industry patrons (Gitlin 1978). Timothy Glander and Christopher Simpson have since challenged Lazarsfeld's self-description more fundamentally: the Bureau was hardly concerned to show that media impact is limited since it was in the business of making persuasion *work* for its commercial and especially government clients (Glander 2000; Simpson 1994). Elihu Katz and Peter Simonson, most recently, have asserted that Lazarsfeld's media research was far more sophisticated and even *critical* than his detractors ever admit (Katz 2001; Simonson and Weimann 2003).

None of them is wrong. Lazarsfeld's published research on mass media was all of these—and more still. Indeed, to read through his 1940s media scholarship is to invite disorientation. This is not on account of the research findings themselves, which were relatively stable over time. No, the dizzy feeling comes from the sheer variety of sense-making scaffolds that Lazarsfeld erected *around* the findings. Lazarsfeld, in these pages, comes off as a deeply serious scholar, an industry apologist, a public-information campaigner, an advertising strategist, an unblushing propagandist, and even an industry critic. On occasion, he is more than one of these in the same article.

This presentational flux stands out so markedly because the *same* core evidence is marshaled to such diverse argumentative ends. Ever since the initial 1941 data analysis of what would become, in 1944, *The People's Choice*, Lazarsfeld discovered—against his expectations—that short-term media persuasion does not, on its own, change minds or behavior very easily (Lazarsfeld, Berelson, and Gaudet 1944).[26] From the same data, he realized that face-to-face influence works better than the mediated sort. He also surmised that the two kinds of persuasion may be complementary, or at least relatable in some way.

During the next decade, Lazarsfeld would take this basic bundle of findings and give it variable shape—not randomly, but according to the particular *audience* he was to address. If educational broadcasters were the target, he might stress the importance of local, face-to-face promotion as a means to build a broadcast audience. If he was addressing scholars, he might concede the limits of short-term campaign studies and call for elaborate research into *long-term* effects. If his audience was the fretting public, he might highlight the reassuring finding that propaganda often fails. If he was writing for government propagandists, he might strategize about the most effective mix of interpersonal and media tactics—turning his *People's Choice* findings into a complicated blueprint for two-step manipulation.[27]

Thus Lazarsfeld, with Merton as coauthor, presented wartime communicators with a sort of technical manual in their 1943 "Studies in Radio and Film Propaganda." A similar bundle of research-derived tips was offered to antiracist campaigners, in Lazarsfeld's 1947 "Some Remarks on the Role of Mass Media in So-Called Tolerance Propaganda." The stress, in these papers, was on how to harness face-to-face and predispositional factors to the act of persuasion.

When the audience was more public—citizens groups, industry critics, the industry itself, and the academics of the public opinion field—the message shifted to emphasize the counterintuitive innocuousness of the mass media. Lazarsfeld's eve-of-war address at a Rockefeller-sponsored University of Chicago conference in 1941, for example, downplayed the threat of media string pulling, with reference to the same principles of self-selection and personal influence

(Lazarsfeld 1942). The emphasis, in these more public essays, was on the mass media's limited effects.

When the audience was more exclusively academic and, in particular, sociological, the Bureau's media research findings were placed in more complicated frames. In certain cases—as with Lazarsfeld's famous 1941 essay for the Frankfurt School's *Studies in Philosophy and Social Science*—the audience was very select indeed, and the framing was highly particularized. In papers directed at broader academic publics—including the 1948 essays "Communication Research and the Social Psychologist" (Lazarsfeld 1948a) and "Mass Communication, Popular Taste and Organized Social Action" (Lazarsfeld and Merton 1948)—the stress on limited effects coexisted, albeit awkwardly, with the propaganda advice. These papers tended to be lively, fecund, and more judgmental than his other work—and, indeed, it is on their bases that various Lazarsfeld defenders have built a case for his status as a critical scholar manqué. Methodological ambitions, the limits of existing data, the need for long-term measures of media impact—all these themes were touched upon in the essays written for fellow social scientists.

It is important to stress that nearly all of Lazarsfeld's studies of media impact would, like the original *People's Choice* research, assume a shape called for by Lazarsfeld's interest in the psychology of the decision act. It was a peculiar shape: Bureau media inquiries were designed, in most cases, to test short-term persuasion campaigns' effects on individuals' attitude or behavior. Given the initially crude psychological model that Lazarsfeld worked with, effects were conceived in terms of change—in terms, that is, of conversion. Set up in this way, the studies were almost guaranteed to produce "disappointing" findings. The failure to find media "effects" in Erie County and in the other Bureau studies was, in other words, a predictable result of narrow research design—which itself derived from a very particular question that, moreover, got posed with little concern for the broader issue of media impact on society. Lazarsfeld's curiosity was, as many others have observed, confined to methodology and decision making, and the Bureau's media effects research program tracked those interests. As Todd Gitlin (1978), Kurt and Gladys Lang (1996, 2006 [this volume]), and others have argued, the findings that would get summarized under the "limited effects" banner were, from the start, methodologically determined: the quantitative study of short-term, media-induced attitude or behavior change was, time and again, to produce only minimal evidence for conversion. This, in itself, proved to be an important finding indeed, especially for would-be propagandists. But the Bureau model, first deployed in Erie County, could hardly produce results adequate to the wider and much more complex question of, for example, long-term media "influence."

Occasionally, Lazarsfeld conceded that his media campaign studies could only support very qualified conclusions (Lazarsfeld 1948a, 1949). But the inherent limitations of the Bureau-style campaign study did not, however, stop him from making sweeping (and contradictory) claims about media impact elsewhere—and never with more confidence, nor with more lasting impact on the field, than in the first fifteen pages of *Personal Influence*. There and elsewhere, the finding that direct, broadcasted appeals only infrequently bring about observable change (on their own) was boldly redeployed to support a much farther-reaching assertion: that media have only limited effects. Lazarsfeld's truth-seeking commitments were, so to speak, otherwise occupied; in the case of media influence, his entrepreneurial cunning was left to steer his findings into various interpretive molds. The result was a decade-long framing drift that culminated in *Personal Influence's* immodest history narration.

Over Lazarsfeld's media-research career, the contrasts in framing were dramatic, especially in evaluative terms. It is possible, however, to isolate two dominant frames, with the caveat that not all of Lazarsfeld's media-research studies during the 1940s cleanly fit either. The striking thing about the two claims is that they are, in evaluative terms, diametric opposites of one another. In much of the published media research, the findings are framed, first, in terms of *effective propaganda design*. The limits of direct media persuasion, in this frame, are presented as a challenge for persuaders that, however, can be got around through messages that appeal to audiences' preexisting interests and through supplementary face-to-face persuasion. In this first frame, then, the selectivity and interpersonal influence findings are packaged as advice to the would-be propagandist. The overriding message: persuasion is complicated, so here's how to navigate around the obstacles.

The other prominent frame—less often deployed than the first, but (with *Personal Influence*) granted the definitive last word—takes the same basic findings, but treats them as evidence, instead, that the impact of media is *happily negligible*. Selectivity and interpersonal influence, in this second frame, are treated as reassuring buffers between man and media. Public fretting about movie-made children is an overreaction that neglects—to quote the *Personal Influence* subtitle—the "part played by people." Here, the message is a populist one, that media persuasion is very often ineffective.[28]

If, employing the first frame, Lazarsfeld counseled the propagandist in her art, in the second frame, he reassured the targets of propaganda that they need not worry. In both frames, direct media appeals are described as relatively ineffective *on their own*. But in the effective propaganda frame, face-to-face influence is portrayed as a *strategic complement* to media-based propaganda campaigns. In the limited effects frame, by contrast, face-to-face persuasion and self-selection are re-deployed as *obstacles* to successful media appeals.

If this is Jekyll and Hyde, it is in keeping with Lazarsfeld's penchant for rhetorical expediency. His legendary resourcefulness revealed itself in any number of *other* ways—in his contract-to-scholarship alchemy, in his reanalytic zeal for layabout raw data, in his ability to harness particular student interests to larger Bureau goals. None of this was wasted. His tenacious ingenuity in securing funds, for example, made possible the Bureau's awe-inspiring scholarly output—much of it his own and much of it abundant with insight.

But that same adaptive cunning could also *impede* the pursuit of knowledge. This happened in the case of mass communication research—and probably because his own interests lay elsewhere. To some extent, media research was a *means* to other ends: a source for reputation and resources, a testing ground for new methods, but in other respects an intellectual afterthought. His relative indifference was expressed, in part, through his rather plastic treatment of the research findings. The decade-long framing drift—the audience-dependent packaging of his media studies—reveals that this research was an instrument for other goals. When stature and funding opportunities permitted, he moved on.

Personal Influence was, as a result, his narrative last word—a final occasion to make the case for his media research legacy. The book, unlike some of his other published reflections, was addressed to his scholarly peers, more of whom than ever were sociologists. The fall and rise of the small-group account that Shils supplied was in many respects a perfect sense-making device. Some of *The People's Choice* findings that had already been put to various use—the better performance of face-to-face over mediated persuasion in short-term campaigns, the hypothesis of a two-step flow—could be brought together in one coherent narrative. And the findings could also be assimilated into an exciting research field, the small group, which was, moreover, definitively sociological. Shils's idea that the primary group had been abandoned on account of a mistaken, European-derived image of society helped, first, to place the narrative in terms of scientific progress. And "the *Gemeinschaft* after all" framing provided a legitimating link to the discourse of learned social theory.

In the few years after Personal Influence, *the "power-to-limited-effects" narrative was solidly established as* the *remembered history of mass communication research.*

The first chapter scene setting that Katz and Lazarsfeld produced was very cleanly written and delivered with confidence. It was, for all of its inaccuracies, an impressive feat of intellectual agility. They had managed to convert the disappointments of *The People's Choice* data into a convincing claim to original insight. The ahistorical culture of empirical sociology and survey research, and other related conditions, helped to secure the claim's uncritical embrace. In the few years after *Personal Influence*, the "power-to-limited-effects" narrative was solidly established as *the* remembered history of mass communication research.

The story line's extraordinary staying power—it remains the bedrock account in most mass communication textbooks[29]—was helped along by the new "discipline" of communication, busy colonizing journalism schools in the 1950s. With its own comparatively meager research traditions, the new discipline, under Wilbur Schramm's guidance, inherited and adapted the account as a usable past.[30] The discipline's field-borrowing disconnect with its own remembered history *contributed*, ironically, to the narrative's widespread adoption. There were few remnants of contradictory memory to stir up questions about its validity.

Lazarsfeld's "limited effects" story line did not, in the end, just blot out the many strands of interwar media analysis through the ascription of naïve and unscientific "powerful" findings. He also retroactively cast the Bureau's media research in such a way that most of *its* contributions—Lazarsfeld's included—have long since been forgotten. Most of the Bureau tradition's media inquiries could not fit comfortably under the "limited effects" banner, and very few, as a result, live on in the collective memory of mass communication researchers. The exceptions all have particular explanations. The 1948 "Mass Communication, Popular Taste and Organized Social Action" paper by Lazarsfeld and Merton survived because of its sheer conceptual brilliance as well as the combined prestige of its authors. The Bureau's rich, proto-functionalist "gratifications" studies—those by Herta Herzog (1940, 1944a, 1944b), Rudolf Arnheim (1944), and Berelson (1949) especially—were named predecessors to the "phenomonalist" functionalism called for by the Bureau's Charles Wright, Joseph Klapper, and, under the later "uses and gratifications" label, Elihu Katz. (The late 1950s, early 1960s call by Wright [1959, 1960] and Klapper [1963] was, fittingly, a direct outgrowth of the limited effects finding: Now that we know that media do not do much to people, let's study what the *people* do with media.) Leo Lowenthal's 1944 "Biographies in Popular Magazines" essay has lingered in the field's memory too, certainly for its superb and still-relevant historical analysis, but also because it was incorporated into the Frankfurt-and-Bureau intellectual historical drama that, especially from the 1970s on, has gained a large interdisciplinary audience. Each of these "survivors," for some of the reasons cited above, were included in early "readers"—which played an especially crucial role in establishing their mnemonic resilience.[31]

But nearly all the rest of the Bureau's media research has been assigned to the academy's overflowing dustbin. Even *Mass Persuasion*, Merton's (1946) brilliant Kate Smith war bond study, has barely limped along in semiobscurity.[32] The "limited effects" narrative, of course, cannot account for all of this forgetting; there are many other factors at work. But Lazarsfeld's retroactive characterization of his own tradition was narrow enough that much of it got excluded by default.

* * *

When Elihu Katz and Paul Lazarsfeld set out to establish a sense-making basis for mass communication research, they might have borrowed from any number of available story lines that surfaced during the decade that *Personal Influence* gestated.[33] Or they might have framed the Decatur findings using any one of the several illustrative scaffolds that Lazarsfeld had, over the previous fifteen years, employed himself—many of which were not cast in historical terms. But he and Katz chose to adopt the narrative packaging that *Shils* had generated. Why was the story line that Shils put forward, under his name, the framing that Lazarsfeld and Katz selected for *Personal Influence*? Shils's story *was* selected, but why?

For a tentative answer, it is important to examine Lazarsfeld, to be sure, but also the academic context around him. The best way to understand Lazarsfeld's choices about *Personal Influence* is, first, to recognize that the quest for scientific *distinction*—for peer respect—was one of Lazarsfeld's fundamental academic stimuli. This motivation coexisted profitably with two genuine intellectual interests, methodology and the psychology of decision making—interests that were, however, well suited to the generation of the claims to *novelty* that underwrite scholarly reputation. The other crucial aspect for understanding Lazarsfeld is the *field* in which he staked his claims to credit; when he came to America in the early 1930s, he stumbled into the extremely peculiar and fast-evolving field of *public opinion research*. The cluster of public opinion research became, for Lazarsfeld, an intellectual frame of reference, but also served as the institutional context in which he made his highly entrepreneurial career. The interwar world of public opinion research was both extradisciplinary and interdisciplinary, *Gemeinschaft*-like in its personal networks; tethered to foundations, commercial firms, and even the lay public; and centered intellectually on a set of evolving *methods*. With Lazarsfeld's prominent help, these methods and the research shops to service them would, after World War II, somewhat improbably establish themselves at the center of empirical sociology more broadly.

From the beginning, the study of mass media was the opinion cluster's most pronounced topical research area—to such an extent, in fact, that the various "communication"-related labels that emerged before and during the war were often paired, or used interchangeably, with the "public opinion" moniker.[34] But this was an accident of funding and world crisis, and not the result of a conscious intellectual program or a received tradition of study. The field's mass communication focus was a straightforward outgrowth, rather, of media- and advertiser-sponsored research, Rockefeller Foundation intervention, and the federal government's wartime propaganda mobilization.[35] Lazarsfeld's own deep immersion in media research almost perfectly tracked these three successive, somewhat overlapping, funding windows. Like the rest of the field's, only more markedly, Lazarsfeld's engagement with the study of media was opportunistic. This he freely admitted on a number of occasions: the topic was attractive not for its own sake but because funds were available—and because such studies were easily fitted to his *real* interests in methodology and the psychology of the decision act. One of the ironies of this disinterest is that it contributed to his ignorance and lack of curiosity about those currents of media analysis that had *preceded* his own. This ignorance, of course, was a fundamental precondition for the taut, denuded two-stage narrative that he and Katz put forward in *Personal Influence*. The same is true, in a slightly different sense, for the public opinion field more broadly. One of the reasons that it failed to correct the "powerful effects" construal was that it, too, was largely cut off from, and uninformed by, its media research predecessors.

It is useful here to establish an analytic contrast that, in the Lazarsfeld-Shils case at least, helps to clarify the mnemonic transfer that took place—the distinction between the *raw findings* of any given research and the *framing* within which these are placed. (This contrast is especially artificial since "raw findings" do not meaningfully exist independent of *some* attempt at sense making in language.) For historically specific reasons, the interwar public opinion cluster, as well as postwar empirical sociology, tended to be meticulous and attentive to research design and process, but rather loose and instrumental with contextual framing. The *packaging* of any given study—the attempt to explain wider significance—was by default an important but late-stage afterthought. If anything, it became acceptable, and the typical practice, to invoke research predecessors without much care for faithful renderings. There were many explanations for this, but one of them was the basic lack of historical knowledge, which conditioned both the initial thinness of the research histories *and* their widespread acceptance. The field was at the same time in a state of relative *reputational flux*. Narrated claims to originality, for the reputation savvy, were crucial instruments for earning prominence, even especially because such claims were, in historical terms, rather poorly "policed." For specific reasons, research *framing* was a vital reputation-building instrument that was, moreover, relatively flexible. The conditions, in short, were felicitous for mnemonic intervention.

Lazarsfeld's context-dependent credit seeking helps explain not just his research program in mass communication but also his and Katz's particular *Personal Influence* shaping of the field. Over the fifteen years or so that Lazarsfeld conducted media research, he framed a fairly stable set of findings in a number of distinct and resourceful ways, depending especially, as we have seen, on the main *audience* that any particular study was intended for. He used, in particular, book-length studies like *The People's Choice* and *Personal Influence* to make the reputational case to his broadest academic frame of reference—the increasingly coterminous fields of public opinion research and empirical sociology. The book-length studies were used, that is, to advance carefully framed claims to *originality*, in both substantive and methodological terms.

Personal Influence, published after he had effectively left the field of media research, was in this sense a last-word reputational sealant—a chance to establish, retroactively, the novelty and relevance of his fifteen-year effort.[36] Claims for originality are easiest to make in narrative terms, especially with before-and-after contrasts. The powerful-to-limited-effects story line was deployed in just these terms, as a summative and retroactive claim to the novelty and coherence of his body of media research. The Shils small-group story, in this context, became an irresistible aid. It provided a ready-made narrative contrast that helped, moreover, to reframe the failures of media persuasion as, instead, a constitutive contribution to an exciting research trend. The fact that Shils, as perhaps only he could plausibly do with confidence, set his narration in broad form—with reference to the history of the American field, the century-old European theoretical influence, the big-picture contrast of clashing *images* of society—rendered his story all the more attractive in novelty-establishing, reputational terms.

Lazarsfeld's zeal for distinction, the public opinion field's specific contours, the features of Shils's narratives—these combined to produce the most influential fifteen pages ever written in American media research.

The story line would go on to supply glue to an emerging "communication" field with bricks but no mortar. Scholars oriented themselves, and their graduate students too, on its foundations. Disputes within the field were framed with appeals to its authority. The world outside communication studies—the world of deans and the established social sciences, in particular—was exposed to its plot. The story of the discipline's past became a common idiom in a field without much else in common. Even leftist detractors in the late 1970s took the history as the main thing to detract *from*.[37]

The story has such staying power *because* it is a great story, containing dramatic clarity, the frisson of breakthrough, vivid (and violent) metaphors like "magic bullets" and "hypodermic needles"—the elements, in short, that make for riveting narrative. It has also proven *plastic*, flexible enough to bend without losing its form. And it has benefited from a kind of self-reinforcing mnemonic inertia.

Like all narratives, the story that communication studies has told itself is *partial*—bashed at and edited down. And like other narratives, the field's chronicle has, in turn, doubled back on the reality that it ostensibly describes. The history drafted by Shils, Lazarsfeld, Katz, and the others, to put it more bluntly, helped shape the emerging field itself—marked off its boundaries, plotted its future. That history, after all, was drafted in a specific context: early cold war American social science, with its cocksure scientism and choose-the-West assurance. Even as the cold war cooled off—and even as faith in cross-tabulated renderings of the world flagged—the story line had already anchored in the field's consciousness.

Notes

1. The question of *Personal Influence* authorship is a complicated one. The original data were collected in 1945 and proceeded, over the next decade, to pass through the hands of a number of Bureau associates and students. Notoriously, C. Wright Mills was one of the first. Accounts of the fascinating Lazarsfeld-Mills encounter are somewhat thin—in part because Mills's three-hundred-plus-page write-up of the Decatur data apparently does not survive. John Summers (2006 [this volume]), surveys extensive evidence from the Bureau archives, and from Mills's and Lazarsfeld's letters, to piece together the most exhaustive picture yet. But Mills was not the only Bureau figure to attempt an analysis of the Decatur data. David Gleicher, Peter Rossi, and Leo Srole all wrote extensive analyses, some of which appeared, in modified form, in part II of *Personal Influence* (see Katz and Lazarsfeld 1955, xiii; Katz 2005, xvii). It is, however, undisputed that Elihu Katz, then a young graduate student, drafted part I of *Personal Influence* (including the crucial "Images of the Mass Communications Process"). Katz had prepared an earlier version of what became part I as a 1953 Bureau report, commissioned by the Implementation Committee on Television (Katz 1953). (Peter Simonson brought this report to my attention.) In a series of personal communications in 2005 and 2006, Katz has acknowledged that Lazarsfeld must have known of Shils's small-group account, but Katz expressed doubt that Lazarsfeld explicitly urged him to bring small-group and mass communication research into mutual dialogue. Based on evidence presented here—including clear proof that Lazarsfeld, by 1948, was already reframing *The People's Choice* in small-group terms, with Shils as his guide—I have elected to treat the crucial *Personal Influence* historical narrative as jointly authored.

2. The story of the "powerful-to-limited-effects" narrative, as it became firmly established in the field's memory, is complex and deserves much greater study. Here, I can only point to a few crucial early adoptions.

Elihu Katz himself repeated the story in a number of follow-up publications, including Katz (1957, 1960) and Katz and Foulkes (1962). Lazarsfeld himself reaffirmed the narrative in, for example, Lazarsfeld and Menzel (1963). Bureau student Charles Wright, in his 1959 textbook (one of the first), devoted a full chapter to the "limited effects" story line (p. 50). Joseph Klapper, another Bureau student, is also an important figure here; his influential 1960 literature review is a book-length defense of the "limited effects" finding (p. 5). Leon Bramson (1961) (as had Bauer and Bauer [1960] at around the same time) merged the "limited effects" story with explicit reference to the now-stock "mass society theory" (pp. 96, 100). The crucial adoption of the narrative, however, was DeFleur (1966); this early textbook was deeply influential, and is frequently *the* cited source for the "limited effects" story line (pp. 101, 121).

3. Though Katz and Lazarsfeld do not refer to "magic bullets" or "hypodermic needles" in *Personal Influence* itself, the "hypodermic" image *does* appear in a 1953 Bureau report written by Katz—a report, moreover, that formed the basis for part I of *Personal Influence*. On the 1953 Katz report, see note 1. Lazarsfeld's onetime colleague at the Bureau, Bernard Berelson, also used the "hypodermic" term in his 1954 *Voting* study (Berelson, Lazarsfeld, and McPhee 1954, 233). Lazarsfeld, of course, is the study's second author. Deb Lubken, whose (2005) unpublished paper on the adoption of the "hypodermic needle" is masterful, brought my attention to the *Voting* passage with the "hypodermic" reference. Berelson, the student of library information turned Lazarsfeld associate turned Ford Foundation social science rainmaker, is a fascinating but neglected figure in the history of social science research.

4. Two classics of media research from the immediate postwar years—Merton's *Mass Persuasion* (1946) and Lazarsfeld and Merton's "Mass Communication, Popular Taste and Organized Social Action" (1948)—display this tension in acute form.

5. In a fascinating foreword, however, Lazarsfeld (1949) is at pains to emphasize the limits of short-term persuasion studies to answer wider questions about media impact, which, he argues, must occur over time and through a complex back and forth with the social environment. Klapper, as in his crucial and much better known 1960 update to the 1949 summary, argues throughout that *reinforcement* of preexisting beliefs and norms is the main, and salutary, effect of mass media (Klapper 1960). His synthesis, published after he had assumed the chief research post at CBS, incorporated the "limited effects" narrative in full, and contributed hugely to the diffusion and establishment of that history.

6. Klapper (1949, I-1, I-23, I-29): "the research of several months suggests that allegations of public taste being thus lowered are far more prevalent among casual observers than among the more formal social scientists. The latter, who are not numerous, treat the subject with extreme caution. . . . It seems no exaggeration to say that by and large people like what they read or hear because they read or listen to what they know they will like. . . . A host of related objective studies and careful conjectures indicate that mass media can and occasionally do contribute to development of better taste in individual members of the audience."

7. Katz and Lazarsfeld (1955, 33): "We might say, perhaps, that as a result of investigating and thinking about the opinion leader, mass communications research has now joined those fields of social research which, in the last years, have been 'rediscovering' the primary group." The footnote to the passage relates that this "rediscovery" is "an accepted term by now, referring to the belated recognition that researchers in many fields have given to the importance of informal, interpersonal relations within situations formerly conceptualized as strictly formal and atomistic. It is 'rediscovery' in the sense that the primary group was dealt with so explicitly (though descriptively and apart from an institutional context) in the work of pioneering American sociologists and social psychologists and then was systemically overlooked by empirical social research until its several dramatic 'rediscoveries'. . . . For an account, see Shils 1951." There was, too, a local source for Katz and Lazarsfeld's "rediscovery of the primary group" narrative: Robert K. Merton. In the same footnote (p. 33), Katz and Lazarsfeld quote the phrase from Merton's (1948/1949) "Manifest and Latent Functions" essay. Merton's reference, however, is merely a passing one—a footnote on page 114, along with a brief discussion of the Hawthorne studies on pages 120-21. Indeed, the second reference is anchored by a long quote from Shils's (1948) *Present State of American Sociology*, referring to the interwar drop-off in small-group research (p. 121). It is possible, as Peter Simonson suggested to me, that Merton expounded on the "rediscovery of the primary group" in lecture—in what Merton referred to as an "oral publication." On Merton and the importance of "oral publication," see Simonson (2005).

8. For example, "Several sections of this and the following chapter will draw extensively on Shils' excellent essay" (Katz and Lazarsfeld 1955, 17). See also ibid., 28, 33, 37, and 45. Shils, Katz and Lazarsfeld write

in another note, "in his excellent discussion of the antecedents, as well as the contemporary flowering, of small group research" (ibid., 45).

9. Katz and Lazarsfeld (1955, 17). Shils is extensively credited in the footnote: "In 'The Study of the Primary Group,' Shils (1951) discusses this main trend in nineteenth-century European sociology which was reflected in the notion that 'any persistence of traditionally regulated informal and intimate relations was . . . an archaism inherited from older rural society or from a small town handcraft society.' Discussing early American sociology, Shils indicates that there was a comparatively greater interest in the primary group as a subject for study. He points out, however, that Cooley's well-known contribution and the interest displayed by American sociologists in voluntary associations, pressure groups, etc. were counterbalanced by an emphasis on the disintegration of the primary group in urban society such as may be found in the work of W.I. Thomas, Park and his associates, and others. Several sections of this and the following chapter will draw extensively on Shils' excellent essay."

10. Shils has a remarkably small place in the memory of American sociology. As it is, there are only traces, scattered fragments, of Shils's life and influence registered in larger histories, supplemented by a few surprisingly insubstantial essays and memorials by a small circle of admirers. There's no biography or book-length study of his work, though both are richly deserved. For a much more exhaustive treatment of Shils and his intellectual context, see Pooley (2006, 25-184).

11. Though Shils's concern with the constituents of social order comes out, in the *Wehrmacht* essay (Shils and Janowitz 1948), only in its last few lines, his clear fixation on this, the problem of order, is clearly on display in other published essays from these years. His survey of American sociology, for example, explicitly recommends the "fundamental problem of consensus" as the central research agenda for the field (Shils 1948, 55). In his 1949 reflective essay on the philosophy of social science, he proposes that the understanding of social order become the explicit value-relevant theme, in Weberian terms, that guides the selection and design of research projects (Shils 1949, 239-40).

12. For a brief discussion of the post-*Personal Influence* uptake of the "powerful-to-limited-effects" story line, see note 2.

13. The Treasury war-bond studies were conducted by Rensis Likert's Division of Program Surveys at the Department of Agriculture, under Dorwin Cartwright's direction. On the studies and their personal-influence findings, see Converse (1987, 174, 225) and Cartwright (1949). Merton and Lazarsfeld were consulting for Likert's outfit at the time, and Merton's classic study of the eighteen-hour Kate Smith radio war bond drive, *Mass Persuasion* (1946), was a piece of the Program Surveys' Treasury studies, and Lazarsfeld's suggestion (see Converse 1987, 174).

14. The studies were conducted by the Army's Research Branch, under the direction of the young psychologist Carl Hovland, who was to continue his experimental studies of media influence at Yale until his death in 1961. The wartime studies were collected and reanalyzed as part of the Carnegie-funded *American Soldier* series; Hovland's mass communication research was summarized in volume 3 (Hovland, Lumsdaine, and Sheffield 1949).

15. On secret propaganda work overseas, see, for example, Samarajiva (1987), the flawed but informative Simpson (1994), and Gilman (2003).

16. For example, "There is a familiar adage in America folklore to the effect that a person is only what he thinks he is, an adage which reflects the typically America notion of unlimited opportunity, the tendency toward self-betterment, etc. Now we find that the reverse of the adage is true: a person thinks, politically, as he is, socially. Social characteristics determine political preference" (Lazarsfeld, Berelson, and Gaudet 1944, 27).

17. Berelson's paper was delivered at a 1948 conference organized by Wilbur Schramm, who would become the key figure in the institutionalization of "communication" as a quasi-discipline. The conference, held at the University of Illinois, was funded by the Rockefeller Foundation and organized around the founding of Schramm's new Institute of Communication Research (see Chaffee and Rogers 1997, 139-40). Lazarsfeld's (1948b) own contribution to the conference is a revealing, advice-filled meditation on the communication researcher's "tightrope walking" between criticism of, and dependence upon, the media industry. The conference talks were published in a collection edited by Schramm (1948), who, as dean of the College of Communication at the University of Illinois, directed the University of Illinois Press.

18. The two readers, one edited by Wilbur Schramm (1949), and the other edited by Berelson himself along with Shils's coauthor Janowitz (1950), were especially important given the complete absence of mass communication textbooks at the time. Berelson's paper was included in the two additional editions of

Schramm's reader, in 1960 and 1972; and included, too, in the three additional editions of Berelson and Janowitz's reader, in 1953, 1966, and 1981.

19. Shils, Janowitz, and Berelson had close contacts from 1946 on. The three worked together to form the University of Chicago's short-lived Committee on Communication ("Current Items" 1949, 429; on the Committee, see Wahl-Jorgensen's [2004] flawed but revealing history). And there is ample evidence that Berelson was dependent on Shils for intellectual guidance. Berelson's 1952 presidential address to the American Association of Opinion Researchers, and the last, theoretical chapter of *Voting* were written with Shils's significant help (see the acknowledgments: Berelson [1952, 313]; Berelson, Lazarsfeld, and McPhee [1954, 305]). Shils (1957b) himself referred to the help on *Voting* (p. 143). Berelson and Shils, moreover, planned to cowrite a volume on mass communication standards, for Lazarsfeld's *Foundations of Communication Research* series (see Berelson 1948/1952, 52).

20. A piece of possible counterevidence is that Shils, in his statement, refers especially to the social scientists in the early days of the war—those who would go on to design the war's psychological warfare efforts—while Berelson's vague, passive formulation could imply a scholarly or more public set of beliefs, or both. Shils does, however, refer to the social scientists' early-war belief as an extension of the wider post–World War I faith in propaganda potency in such a way that Berelson's statement might be read as a sloppy restatement.

21. The footnote, which is appended to the passage above, is to the 1950 reprint of Berelson's 1948 article (in Berelson and Janowitz 1950, 51).

22. The lecture (Lazarsfeld 1948c) was published in Norway in pamphlet form. It was later reprinted in a Norwegian sociology journal (Lazarsfeld 1948/1990). My page references are to the 1990 reprint.

23. Shils (1948, 42) continues, "This original and indeed central problem of sociology has come once more into the very center of attention, not through deliberate, conscious pursuit of the phenomena, but as an incident in the failure of other methods of study to provide answers for hypotheses regarding variables which were originally thought to have little connection with small (primary) group membership. In none of the following instances has the rediscovery of the problem been stimulated by direct descent from its earlier formulation in the work of Cooley—indeed the history of the study of primary groups in American sociology is a supreme instance of the discontinuities of the development of this discipline: a problem is stressed by one who is an acknowledged founder of the discipline, the problem is left unstudied, then, some years later, it is taken up with enthusiasm as if no one had ever thought of it before."

24. Indeed, the phrases "small group" and "primary group" do not appear in the text.

25. Indeed, Lazarsfeld, along with coeditor Merton, commissioned a lengthy Shils reanalysis of primary group data from the *American Soldier* studies for their *Studies in the Scope and Method of the American Soldier* (see Shils 1950). The Shils paper included an explicit restatement of the "rediscovery" of the primary group (Shils 1950, 16, 19).

26. Former Bureau student Peter Rossi, based on interviews with Lazarsfeld, reports that Lazarsfeld and his coauthors set aside the 1940 data for a full year after conducting the preliminary analysis, on account of their disappointment at the lack of media persuasion findings (Rossi 1959, 16).

27. For a complementary analysis of Lazarsfeld's rhetorical expediency, see John Durham Peters, "The Part Played by Gentiles in the Flow of Mass Communications" (2006 [this volume]). It is worth, also, quoting Lazarsfeld's introduction to his friend and colleague Samuel Stouffer's collected papers. There, Lazarsfeld gently reprimands Stouffer for not understanding the sociology of academic labeling: "When you go through Stouffer's papers, you find at every point an interesting new contribution, but it is never tagged. . . . While Sam and I worked on various similar matters, most of the time in complete agreement, he did it and I added a slogan to it . . . he didn't recognise, so to say, the important things he did, and therefore impeded in a way his role in the history of sociology" (quoted in Platt 1996, 32).

28. Katz himself, in a follow-up essay (1957, 61), referred to *Personal Influence*'s populism: "The [two-step flow] hypothesis aroused considerable interest. The authors themselves [referring to Katz and Lazarsfeld] were intrigued by its implications for democratic society. It was a healthy sign, they felt, that people were still most successfully persuaded by give-and-take with other people and that the influence of the mass media was less automatic and less potent than had been assumed." Compare this to the altogether different tone in *The People's Choice*, in which the finding of limited media effect was recruited to the book's thesis that the democratic ideal falters in practice: "The real doubters—the open-minded voters who make a sincere attempt to weight the issues and the candidates dispassionately for the good of the

country as a whole—exist mainly in deferential campaign propaganda, in textbooks on civics, in the movies, and the minds of some political idealists. In real life, they are few indeed" (Lazarsfeld, Berelson, and Gaudet 1944, 100). The fact that the same bundle of evidence can be so easily put forward as reassuring evidence of media noninterference in the democratic process—the claim, in *Personal Influence*, that the American political system is not ridden with top-down manipulation but instead richly endowed with face-to-face discussion—is a startling testament to interpretive plasticity. For a more detailed discussion of *The People's Choice*, see Pooley (2006, 283-94).

29. See epigraph. See also, for example, Wood (2005, 303), Wimmer and Dominick (2006, 8), Grossberg et al. (2005, 302), and McQuail (2005, 65).

30. In the early 1960s, Schramm, champion of the new stand-alone discipline of "communication," would add Harold Lasswell, Carl Hovland, and Kurt Lewin to the roster of "founding fathers," but in such a way that their contributions were largely incorporated into the "limited effects" story line. See, for example, Schramm (1963, 1980, 1997).

31. Lazarsfeld and Merton (1948) is in Schramm (1949); Berelson (1949) and Herzog (1944b) are reprinted in Schramm (1954); Lowenthal (1944) and Herzog (1944b) reappear in Berelson and Janowitz (1950); and Arnheim (1944) and Berelson (1949) are reprinted in Daniel Katz et al. (1954).

32. Peter Simonson has, fortunately, brought out a reprint edition with an excellent introduction (Merton 1946/2004).

33. The Decatur field research for what would become *Personal Influence* was completed in 1945; the book was published in 1955. See note 1.

34. See, for example, Shils's (1948) own postwar survey of American sociology, with its subheading: "Communications Analysis and Public Opinion" (p. 34).

35. Educational and antidiscrimination groups were also important, though secondary, funders.

36. It is true that Lazarsfeld continued to publish intermittently on mass communication issues even after *Personal Influence* (see, for example, Lazarsfeld 1961, 1963; Lazarsfeld and Menzel 1963). But the bulk of his research energies had, by *Personal Influence*'s publication in 1955, long since been redirected to other areas, especially research methodology and its academic history.

37. Gitlin's 1978 critique of the Lazarsfeld "dominant paradigm" is an important case in point (p. 207).

References

Arnheim, Rudolf. 1944. The world of the daytime serial. In *Radio research 1942-1943*, ed. Paul F. Lazarsfeld and Frank N. Stanton, 43-81. New York: Duell, Sloan and Pearce.

Bauer, Raymond A., and Alice Bauer. 1960. American, mass society, and mass media. *Journal of Social Issues* 10:3-66.

Bell, Daniel. 1956. The theory of mass society: A critique. *Commentary* 22:75-83.

———. 1960. *The end of ideology: On the exhaustion of political ideas in the fifties.* Glencoe, IL: Free Press.

Berelson, Bernard. 1948. Communications and public opinion. In *Communications in modern society*, ed. Wilbur Schramm, 167-85. Urbana: University of Illinois Press.

———. 1948/1952. *Content analysis in communication research.* Glencoe, IL: Free Press.

———. 1949. What missing the newspaper means. In *Communications research, 1948-1949*, ed. Paul F. Lazarsfeld and Frank N. Stanton, 111-28. New York: Harper and Brothers.

———. 1952. Democratic theory and public opinion. *Public Opinion Quarterly* 16:313-30.

Berelson, Bernard, and Morris Janowitz, eds. 1950. *Reader in public opinion and communication.* New York: Free Press.

Berelson, Bernard, Paul F. Lazarsfeld, and William N. McPhee. 1954. *Voting: A study of opinion formation in a presidential campaign.* Chicago: University of Chicago Press.

Bramson, Leon. 1961. The American critique of the theory of mass society: Research in mass communications. In *The political context of sociology*, 96-118. Princeton, NJ: Princeton University Press.

Cartwright, Dorwin P. 1949. Some principles of mass persuasion: Selected findings of research on the sale of United States war bonds. *Human Relations* 2:253-68.

Chaffee, Steven H., and Everett M. Rogers. 1997. Wilbur Schramm, the founder. In *The beginnings of communication study in America: A personal memoir*, ed. Steven H. Chaffee, Everett M. Rogers, and Wilbur Schramm, 126-76. Thousand Oaks, CA: Sage.

Converse, Jean M. 1987. *Survey research in the United States: Roots and emergence, 1890-1960*. Berkeley: University of California Press.

Current items. 1949. *American Sociological Review* 14:426-30.

DeFleur, Melvin L. 1966. *Theories of mass communication*. New York: David McKay Company.

Gans, Herbert. 1966. Popular culture in America: Social problem in a mass society or social asset in a pluralist society? In *Social problems: A modern approach*, ed. Howard S. Becker. New York: Wiley.

Gilman, Nils. 2003. *Mandarins of the future: Modernization theory in cold war America*. Baltimore: Johns Hopkins University Press.

Gitlin, Todd. 1978. Media sociology: The dominant paradigm. *Theory and Society* 6:205-53.

Glander, Timothy. 2000. *Origins of mass communications research during the American cold war: Educational effects and contemporary implications*. Mahwah, NJ: Lawrence Erlbaum.

Grossberg, Lawrence, Ellen Wartella, D. Charles Whitney, and J. McGregor Wise. 2005. *Mediamaking: Mass media in a popular culture*. 2nd ed. Thousand Oaks, CA: Sage.

Herzog, Herta. 1940. Professor quiz: A gratification study. In *Radio and the printed page: An introduction to the study of radio and its role in the communication of ideas*, ed. Paul F. Lazarsfeld, 64-93. New York: Duell Sloan and Pearce.

———. 1944a. On borrowed experience. *Studies in Philosophy and Social Science* 11:65-95.

———. 1944b. What do we really know about daytime serial listeners? In *Radio research 1942-1943*, ed. Paul F. Lazarsfeld and Frank N. Stanton, 3-33. New York: Duell, Sloan and Pearce.

Hovland, Carl I., Arthur A. Lumsdaine, and Fred D. Sheffield. 1949. *Experiments on mass communication*. Princeton, NJ: Princeton University Press.

Katz, Daniel, Dorwin Cartwright, Samuel Eldersveld, and Alfred McClung Lee, eds. 1954. *Public opinion and propaganda: A book of readings*. New York: Holt, Rinehart and Winston.

Katz, Elihu. 1953. *The part played by people: A new focus for the study of mass media effects*. Bureau Report B-0482-3. New York: Bureau of Applied Social Research.

———. 1957. The two-step flow of communication: An up-to-date report on an hypothesis. *Public Opinion Quarterly* 21:61-78.

———. 1960. Communication research and the image of society: On the convergence of two traditions. *American Journal of Sociology* 65:435-40.

———. 2001. Lazarsfeld's map of media effects. *International Journal of Public Opinion Research* 13:270-79.

———. 2005. Introduction to the Transaction edition. In *Personal influence: The part played by people in the flow of mass communications*, by Elihu Katz and Paul F. Lazarsfeld. New Brunswick, NJ: Transaction Publishers. (Orig pub. Glencoe, IL: Free Press, 1955)

Katz, Elihu, and David Foulkes. 1962. On the use of the mass media as "escape": Clarification of a concept. *Public Opinion Quarterly* 26:377-88.

Katz, Elihu, and Paul F. Lazarsfeld. 1955. Images of the mass communications process. In *Personal influence: The part played by people in the flow of mass communications*, 15-42. Glencoe, IL: Free Press.

Klapper, Joseph T. 1949. *The effects of mass media*. New York: Columbia University Bureau of Applied Social Research.

———. 1960. *The effects of mass communication*. New York: Free Press.

———. 1963. Mass communication research: An old road resurveyed. *Public Opinion Quarterly* 27:515-27.

Lang, Kurt, and Gladys Engel Lang. 1996. The European roots. In *American communication research*, ed. Everette E. Dennis and Ellen Wartella. Mahwah, NJ: Lawrence Erlbaum.

———. *Personal influence* and the new paradigm: Some inadvertent consequences. *Annals of the American Academy of Political and Social Science* 608:157-78

Lazarsfeld, Paul F. 1941. Remarks on administrative and critical communications research. *Studies in Philosophy and Social Science* 9:2-16.

———. 1942. The effects of radio on public opinion. In *Print, radio, and film in a democracy: Ten papers on the administration of mass communications in the public interest*, ed. Douglas Waples, 66-78. Chicago: University of Chicago Press.

———. 1947. Some remarks on the role of mass media in so-called tolerance propaganda. *Journal of Social Issues* 3:17-25.

———. 1948a. Communication research and the social psychologist. In *Current trends in social psychology*, ed. Wayne Dennis, 218-73. Pittsburgh, PA: University of Pittsburgh Press.

———. 1948b. Role of criticism in management of mass communications. In *Communications in modern society*, ed. Wilbur Schramm, 186-203. Urbana: University of Illinois Press.

———. 1948c. *What is sociology?* Oslo, Norway: Skrivemaskinstua Universitets Studentkontor.

———. 1948/1990. What is sociology? *Sosiologi i dag* 20:11-26.

———. 1949. Foreword. In *The effects of mass media*, ed. Joseph T. Klapper, 1-9. New York: Columbia University Bureau of Applied Social Research.

———. 1961. Mass culture today. In *Culture for the millions? Mass media in modern society*, ed. Norman Jacobs, ix-xxiii. Princeton, NJ: Van Nostrand.

———. 1963. Afterword. In *The people look at television: A study of audience attitudes*, ed. Gary A. Steiner, 409-22. New York: Knopf.

Lazarsfeld, Paul F., Bernard Berelson, and Hazel Gaudet. 1944. *The people's choice: How the voter makes up his mind in a presidential campaign*. New York: Duell, Sloan and Pearce.

Lazarsfeld, Paul F., and Herbert Menzel. 1963. Mass media and personal influence. In *The science of human communication*, ed. Wilbur Schramm, 94-115. New York: Basic Books.

Lazarsfeld, Paul F., and Robert K. Merton. 1943. Studies in radio and film propaganda. *Transactions of the New York Academy of Sciences* 6:58-78.

———. 1948. Mass communication, popular taste and organized social action. In *The communication of ideas*, ed. Lyman Bryson, 95-118. New York: Harper.

Lowenthal, Leo. 1944. Biographies in popular magazines. In *Radio research 1942-1943*, ed. Paul F. Lazarsfeld and Frank N. Stanton, 507-49. New York: Duell, Sloan and Pearce.

Lubken, Deb. 2005. Reconsidering the straw man: Who said "hypodermic" first, how we forget, and why we should remember more about the theory that never existed. Paper presented at the annual meeting of the National Communication Association, Boston.

McQuail, Denis. 2005. *McQuail's mass communication theory*. 5th ed. Thousand Oaks, CA: Sage.

Merton, Robert K. 1946. *Mass persuasion: The social psychology of a war bond drive*. New York: Harper & Brothers.

———. 1946/2004. *Mass persuasion: The social psychology of a war bond drive*. New York: H. Fertig.

———. 1948/1949. Manifest and latent functions. In *Social theory and social structure*, 37-59. Glencoe, IL: Free Press.

Merton, Robert K., and Patricia Kendall. 1944. The boomerang response. *Channels* 21:1-7.

Peters, John Durham. 2006. The part played by gentiles in the flow of mass communications: On the ethnic utopia of *Personal influence*. *Annals of the American Academy of Political and Social Science* 608:97-114.

Platt, Jennifer. 1996. *A history of sociological research methods in America*. Cambridge: Cambridge University Press.

Pooley, Jefferson. 2006. An accident of memory: Edward Shils, Paul Lazarsfeld and the history of American mass communication research. PhD diss., Columbia University, New York.

Rossi, Peter. 1959. Four landmarks in voting research. In *American voting behavior*, ed. Eugene Burdick and Arthur J. Brodbeck, 5-54. Glencoe, IL: Free Press.

Samarajiva, Rohan. 1987. The murky beginnings of the communication and development field: Voice of America and the passing of traditional society. In *Rethinking development communication*, ed. Neville Jayaweera, Sarath Amunugama, and E. Tâi Ariyaratna, 3-19. Singapore: Asian Mass Communication Research and Information Centre.

Schramm, Wilbur, ed. 1948. *Communications in modern society*. Urbana: University of Illinois Press.

———, ed. 1949. *Mass communications: A book of readings selected and edited for the Institute of Communications Research in the University of Illinois*. Urbana: University of Illinois Press.

———, ed. 1954. *The process and effects of mass communication*. Urbana: University of Illinois Press.

———. 1963. Communication research in the United States. In *The science of human communication*, ed. Wilbur Schramm, 1-16. New York: Basic Books.

———. 1980. The beginnings of communication research in the United States. In *Communication yearbook(4)*, ed. D. Nimmo, 73-82. New Brunswick, NJ: Transactions.

———. 1997. *The beginnings of communication study in America: A personal memoir*. Thousand Oaks, CA: Sage.

Shils, Edward. 1948. *The present state of American sociology*. Glencoe, IL: Free Press.

———. 1949. Social science and social policy. *Philosophy of Science* 16:219-42.

———. 1950. Primary groups in the American army. In *Studies in the scope and method of the American soldier*, ed. Robert K. Merton and Paul F. Lazarsfeld. Glencoe, IL: Free Press.

———. 1951. The study of the primary group. In *The policy sciences: Recent developments in scope and method*, ed. Daniel Lerner and Harold D. Lasswell. Stanford, CA: Stanford University Press.

———. 1957a. Daydreams and nightmares: Reflections on the criticism of mass culture. *The Sewanee Review* 65:587-608.

———. 1957b. Personal, primordial, sacred, and civil ties. *British Journal of Sociology* 8:130-45.

———. 1961. Mass society and its culture. In *Culture for the millions? Mass media in modern society*, ed. Norman Jacobs, 1-27. Princeton, NJ: Van Nostrand.

———. 1962. The theory of mass society. *Diogenes* 39:45-66.

———. 1975. Introduction. In *Center and periphery: Essays in macrosociology*, vii-xliii. Chicago: University of Chicago Press.

Shils, Edward, and Morris Janowitz. 1948. Cohesion and disintegration in the *Wehrmacht* in World War II. *Public Opinion Quarterly* 12:280-315.

Simonson, Peter. 2005. The serendipity of Merton's communication research. *International Journal of Public Opinion Research* 17:277-97.

Simonson, Peter, and Gabriel Weimann. 2003. Critical research at Columbia: Lazarsfeld's and Merton's "Mass communication, popular taste, and organized social action." In *Canonic texts in media research: Are there any? Should there be? How about these?* ed. Elihu Katz, John Durham Peters, Tamar Liebes, and Avril Orloff, 12-38. Cambridge, UK: Polity.

Simpson, Christopher. 1994. *Science of coercion: Communication research and psychological warfare, 1945-1960*. New York: Oxford University Press.

Straubhaar, Joseph D., and Robert LaRose. 2006. *Media now: Understanding media, culture, and technology*. 5th ed. Belmont, CA: Thomson, Wadsworth.

Summers, John H. 2006. Perpetual revelations: C. Wright Mills and Paul Lazarsfeld. *Annals of the American Academy of Political and Social Science* 608:25-40.

Wahl-Jorgensen, Karin. 2004. How not to found a field: New evidence on the origins of mass communication research. *Journal of Communication* 54:547-64.

Wimmer, Roger D., and Joseph R. Dominick. 2006. *Mass media research: An introduction*. 8th ed. Belmont, CA: Thomson, Wadsworth.

Wood, Julia T. 2005. *Communication mosaics: An introduction to the field of communication*. 4th ed. Belmont, CA: Thomson, Wadsworth.

Wright, Charles R. 1959. *Mass communication: A sociological perspective*. New York: Random House.

———. 1960. Functional analysis and mass communication. *Public Opinion Quarterly* 24:605-20.

Personal Influence and the New Paradigm: Some Inadvertent Consequences

By
KURT LANG
and
GLADYS ENGEL LANG

An examination of the reception given *Personal Influence* when first published points to highly selective interpretations of the findings. The claims reviewers made for the influence of interpersonal communication relative to the mass media, especially in the political process, went even beyond those advanced by the authors. They overlooked not only the very restricted conceptualization of "effects" that guided the Decatur research but also previously accumulated evidence on multiple kinds of media influence. This article argues that the new conventional wisdom pitting personal versus mass media effects associated with this and previous studies in the Columbia tradition discouraged, however inadvertently, a coming generation of sociologists from researching the effects—particularly long-range effects—of mass communication. As a consequence, academic sociology came to cede much of the high ground it once occupied in media studies to political science and to more professionally oriented departments or schools of communication.

Keywords: mass media effects; interpersonal communication; concept of mass

Ideas have consequences, sometimes even contrary to those intended by their protagonists. Rarely do our observations about the world, its people, how they behave, and the things they produce quite speak for themselves. Meanings rest on interpretation, on what we read into them, even if unwittingly. This caveat applies even more strongly to our self-conscious search for significance in the sciences and in the arts, where creative individuals are always reaching out for something yet unknown, than it does for those aspects of everyday life taken for granted. Only the unfamiliar demands explanation. As to new findings from research—the accompanying rhetoric can elevate them into the kind of discovery eagerly seized on by peers and likely to affect the direction of future inquiries. In what follows, we examine how the rediscovery of personal influence during the 1940s and the elaboration of this finding in subsequent studies by Columbia University sociologists diverted many of their

DOI: 10.1177/0002716206292614

colleagues, at least for a while, from further exploration into the effect of mass communication on public opinion.

No one questions that *Personal Influence: The Part Played by People in the Flow of Mass Communication* by Elihu Katz and Paul F. Lazarsfeld (1955) was a major milestone in the development of communication research. Many researchers associated with the Columbia University department of sociology and the Bureau of Applied Social Research (BASR) had a hand in the planning and execution of the surveys in Decatur, Illinois, on which this book is based. The fieldwork was conducted in 1945 just as World War II was coming to an end and several years before television emerged as the dominant medium it was to become in the next decade. The punch cards with the coded responses, we have been told, lay around for several years because of sharp disagreement about the analysis between Lazarsfeld and C. Wright Mills, who had supervised the fieldwork.[1] No one was quite sure about how best to proceed until Katz found a way to mine this lode of data. Now some fifty years later, we are reexamining and acknowledging the conclusions that Katz and Lazarsfeld drew from the study and the reception of these findings.

We begin by briefly tracing the strongly positive reception of *Personal Influence*, and then explain how the findings accorded with trends in communication research. Next, we compare the conclusions the authors themselves drew from the Decatur study with how others interpreted them. Finally, we elaborate on the consequences, suggesting that the apparent downgrading of mass communication effects relative to personal influence dissuaded a generation of sociologists from addressing the role of the mass media in politics and government. The subject was ceded to other disciplines. If theory and research are still struggling over the relative power of the individual, the media, and interpersonal influence, something Katz (2006, xxxiii) now finds "ironic," it is because the issue came to be defined in these terms. While this article makes no attempt at a final answer to the question, it will have something to say about why that struggle has lasted so long.

Kurt Lang is a professor emeritus of sociology and communications at the University of Washington. His introduction to public opinion and communication research came as a research analyst for the U.S. military government immediately after World War II. Relevant publications (all with Gladys Engel Lang) include Politics and Television *(1968, 1984, 2002) and* The Battle for Public Opinion: The President, the Press, and the Polls during Watergate *(1983). Their first study of television (1952) received a one-time award from the American Sociological Society and the distinguished career award of both the American Association for Public Opinion Research (1989) and the Political Communication section of the American Political Science Association (1994).*

Gladys Engel Lang is a professor emerita of communications, political science, and sociology at the University of Washington. Her first introduction to communication research was with the Office of War Information (OWI) in Washington, D.C., studying, for example, what information radio soap operas were disseminating to the public. Thereafter, she spent some years with the Office of Strategic Services (OSS) as a research analyst in England and Italy. Returning to academia after a year in China as a press analyst, she met and married Kurt. Since then, they have frequently collaborated, producing the books listed above as well as others on collective behavior, voting and nonvoting, broadcasting, and artistic reputations.

FIGURE 1
RECEPTION OF PERSONAL INFLUENCE (FIVE-YEAR INTERVALS)

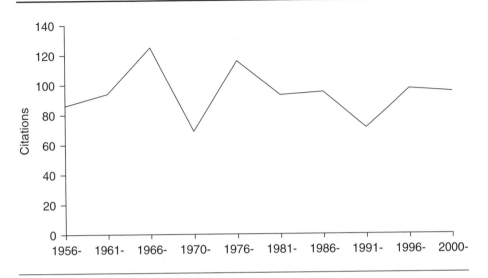

The Reception

Personal Influence, with Katz, still a year away from receiving his PhD, listed as first author (hereafter annotated as Katz), was immediately tagged as a major work when published. Already much talked about before, once in print it attracted instantaneous attention and was widely reviewed. Since then, it has been frequently cited in the peer-reviewed social science literature, counts of which serve as one of the standard indicators by which researchers in the sociology of science estimate the "importance" of a discovery and of its discoverer. For 1956, the year after publication, the *Social Sciences Citation Index* lists 17 citations and a cumulative total of 84 in the five-year period to 1960 (see Figure 1).[2] That the number appears to have peaked in the years 1966 to 1970 should not be interpreted as a sign of progressive inattention. For some major discoveries, to be sure, there comes a point in time when their validity is so widely accepted that scholars no longer feel obliged to cite their source, leading to what Merton (1946) called "obliteration by incorporation"—a fate that has not, or at least not yet, befallen *Personal Influence*. Quite to the contrary: the book keeps being widely cited right down to the present. By July 20, 2005, the day we undertook this count, there had been 941 citations, a number that, especially with the publication of this second edition, is soon bound to pass the 1,000 mark.

To make the count more meaningful, we searched for a yardstick by which to compare the fate of this book with that of similar books published during the

1950s but, to our dismay, found no more than one classified by the Library of Congress as "Mass Media and Public Opinion," the category in which *Personal Influence* was placed. That lone other book was *Mass Communication: A Sociological Perspective* by Charles R. Wright (1959), another Columbia University PhD. It takes note of the findings about "personal influence" in its overview of the field. This much-adopted short text, which went through three editions, with a fourth scheduled for 2005, hardly qualifies as a competitor; nor was it ever intended to be.

The yield of truly comparable books was hardly higher when we expanded our search to those listed under the rubric of "Mass Communication." Still, one has to work with whatever one finds, so we selected, because it seemed to make sense, the following five in addition to the Wright text. They are, by order of publication date, Paul F. Lazarsfeld, Berelson, and Gaudet, *The People's Choice* (1944/1968); Robert K. Merton, *Mass Persuasion* (1946); C. Wright Mills, *The Power Elite* (1956); Joseph T. Klapper, *The Effects of Mass Communication* (1960), and William N. McPhee, *Formal Theories of Mass Behavior* (1963). Every one of these six was authored by a sociologist associated with Columbia University, and all of them, even when not classified as mass communication research—such as those by Mills and by McPhee (who was in the same cohort of graduate students working with Lazarsfeld and Katz)—did touch on issues relevant to that subject.

The citation counts shown in Table 1 are limited to the period 1969 (the year the citation index went online) through 2005. Judged by this indicator of "importance," *Personal Influence* definitely lags behind *The Power Elite*. This is no surprise since it was the book through which Mills extended his visibility far beyond conventional disciplinary boundaries. He became somewhat of a guru for the political left and a lightning rod for conservatives within and outside professional sociology. More striking perhaps, given Merton's subsequent star standing among social scientists, is how close to oblivion his once well-known study of the drive by Kate Smith, a highly popular songstress, to sell war bonds via radio seems to have sunk. Dealing with little more than a short campaign, the study of Smith was, to be sure, more limited in scope than the other five books, but one would think that scholars would have retained interest in this diagnosis of the persuasive potential of celebrity, when coupled with a carefully crafted self-presentation, to deliver an effective message.[3] A second factor accounting for the relatively swift demise of *Mass Persuasion* is that the themes it played did not quite fit the paradigm of the not-so-powerful media beginning to emerge in the 1940s with the publication of *The People's Choice* and more fully developed over the next two decades. As to the McPhee volume, his proposals for a new *opus operandi* fared more poorly yet, possibly for being similarly out of tune with the times, even though in recent years there has been—judging from citations—somewhat of a revival of interest in this work but not primarily among those specializing in the study of mass communication.

Judged by these counts, *Personal Influence* did remarkably well over the years. It certainly holds its own against the two other landmark books on mass communication: *The People's Choice*, which introduced the concept of the two-step flow into social

TABLE 1
CITATIONS, 1969-2005

Mills, *Power Elite* (1956)	1,144
Lazarsfeld, Berelson, and Gaudet, *People's Choice* (1944/1968)	856
Katz and Lazarsfeld, *Personal Influence* (1955)	652
Klapper, *Effects of Mass Communication* (1960)	512
Wright, *Mass Communication* (1959)	133
McPhee, *Formal Theories* (1963)	103
Merton, *Mass Persuasion* (1946)	78

science, and Klapper's 1960 review of the extant literature on the effects of mass communication, where he highlighted personal influence as one of the factors intervening between content and audience response. In this respect, the Klapper book as well as the text by Wright were part of the secondary literature that helped to reinforce interest in the findings and conclusions laid out in the book by Katz.

What about *Personal Influence* accounts for its sustained reception? For one thing, Lazarsfeld's name being on the title page, albeit as second author (*K* does, after all, precede *L*), guaranteed it immediate attention. Furthermore, the study came out of Columbia University at a time when the network of scholars around Lazarsfeld, trained in or otherwise connected to the BASR, formed one of those "invisible colleges," as Diana Crane called them, whose members remain in contact over the years, sharing ideas and supporting one another in building careers. To point to these extraneous factors is not, of course, to overlook the qualities of the work itself. Writing in a clear expository style, Katz put the data collected as part of a marketing survey in a small Midwestern city into a solid theoretical framework.

Most important of all for the strongly positive reception was the elaboration of an explicitly sociological perspective—one that looked beyond demographics—into audience research. No longer could it be seen as made up of individuals receiving messages independently of one another. The new view put the emphasis on the multiple social relationships through which the media content was filtered, reinterpreted, and/or reinforced. Reviewers were downright jubilant. David Gold (1956) hailed the theoretical essay that took up roughly the first third of *Personal Influence* as "the most lucid and sophisticated discussion of the mass communication process that has appeared up to date . . . [and] an exposition which is a model of clarity and exposition, to develop the significance and relevance derived from small group research." He quoted approvingly what he saw as its major methodological conclusion—"no longer can mass media research be content with a random sample of disconnected individuals as respondents . . . they must be studied within the context of the group or groups to which they belong or have 'in mind' " (p. 792). Other reviewers for major social science journals praised the book for similar reasons: as "aiming toward a theoretical model of research" in mass communication (M. W. Riley 1956, 101) and as making a strong case for "the necessity of taking group phenomena into account in any adequate analysis of the [mass] communication process" (J. W. Riley 1956, 355).

To expand a bit: in his wide-ranging survey of the small-group and sociometric literature, Katz expounded on a wide range of studies to underline the fact that attitudes and opinions are social in character, that people develop their ideas and preferences in communication with peers, and that the concept of an audience consisting of lone individuals within an anonymous mass does not conform to the living reality. He invoked these findings to question the adequacy of the previously reigning paradigm associated with the name of Harold D. Lasswell in connection with propaganda studies: Who? says What (including How)? to Whom? with what Effect? To understand how campaigns did—or failed to—persuade, this formula at the minimum had to be supplemented by a new variable, one that took account of the social setting in which messages were received, interpreted, passed on, and used. Experimental studies on persuasive communication carried out at the University of Iowa by Kurt Lewin (1947/1958) and by the group around Carl I. Hovland at Yale had already been moving in this direction (cf. Kelly and Volkart 1952), but these studies, confined as they were to the laboratory, never directly inquired into network structure and channels of influence as the defining characteristics of real audiences.

[Personal Influence] *put the emphasis on the multiple social relationships through which the media content was filtered, reinterpreted, and/or reinforced. Reviewers were downright jubilant.*

The influence of scholarly works is not self-perpetuating. Their impact and even more so their longevity are highly contingent on their place within an emerging tradition—in this instance, that of the Columbia "school" of communication research. Or, to put it somewhat differently, it was not just the coauthorship of Lazarsfeld that attracted attention to *Personal Influence* but also its fit with the kind of research conducted under his leadership at the BASR. The "applied" in the name of the Bureau expresses its original raison d'etre. Many of its projects, including the Decatur study, were designed to answer questions primarily of practical interest to commercial and other sponsors. It was they who supplied the funds that made it possible to explore potentially useful but not yet fully tested methodologies for such studies, thereby paving the way for more "theoretically oriented" studies that foundations and other public interest organizations were willing to underwrite. Taken together, the various projects generated some inter-esting findings, among them the serendipitous discovery of the frequency and effectiveness of personal influence during the 1940 presidential campaign, which its authors stipulated to be part of a hypothesized two-step flow of mass communi-cation by way of "opinion leaders [who] were the most responsive to campaign events" (Lazarsfeld, Berelson, and Gaudet 1944/1968, 51). Opinion leaders, they observed, engaged in political discussion more often than others and cited the mass media as a more effective source of influence on themselves than personal relations (ibid., 151). "The person-to-person influence reaches the ones who are more susceptible to change, and serves as a bridge over which formal media of communications extend their influence" (ibid., 152). This was their theory. Years later, in his introduction to the third edition of *The People's Choice*, Lazarsfeld recalled his surprise at what seemed a great deal of person-to-person interaction, which, at the time, they were unable to "document . . . very specifically because our primary efforts were directed toward establishing the role of the formal media" (ibid., vi).

This finding about the importance of "person-to-person" interaction clearly indicated a major path that research at Columbia was about to follow for the fore-seeable future. Building on *The People's Choice*, the Decatur surveys were planned with two related objectives in mind: first, to examine how informal lead-ers exerted influence horizontally within their immediate surroundings; and second, to give a firmer grounding to the "two-step flow" hypothesis, according to which mass media reach well-informed opinion leaders, who then act as trans-mitters or relays of information and influence.

Interpreting the Findings

Reviewers of *Personal Influence* were distinctly less enthralled by the data part of the book, the one that dealt with the flow of everyday influence in a Midwestern community, than they were by the theoretical formulation. Gold (1956) was dis-appointed that "the empirical research did not match the expectations of beauty aroused" by the theoretical formulation; and Roy F. Carter (1956, 383), review-ing for *Social Forces*, found that there was "more theory here than evidence," with his harshest criticism directed at deficient support for the two-step flow of mass communication. These comments were on target insofar as they underline that, in the analysis of the data, the part played by people and the question of who influenced whom came to take precedence over the original purpose of the Decatur study, which had been, at least according to Mills,[4] to document the flow of media influence through interpersonal networks. Apparently unexpected dif-ficulties encountered in reaching persons whom respondents named as "having influenced them" made it impossible to trace the "flow of information" all the way back to its original sources (Katz and Lazarsfeld 1955, 362ff.). This failure, freely acknowledged, caused the analysis to be limited to *"specific influence inci-dents* [italics added], and our heroes, the specific influentials" and the assessment of the different kinds of influence—personal and mass media—on "decisions" that involved a change in food brands, or fashions, or political opinions, or whether to see a particular movie in place of another (ibid., 160). Except for the one chapter, to quote Katz again, "where we were interested in the relationship between opinion leaders and the media, we have been concerned almost exclusively with the flow of influence from person to person" (ibid., 321).

This last statement is not altogether accurate in view of the frequency with which comparisons are drawn between the "effectiveness" of face-to-face communication and communication via the mass media. On this issue, let us now separate the claims about the supposed "ineffectiveness" of mass communication derived from the comparisons of influence on "decisions" in the four areas from what the data, as reported in the book, actually show.

To begin with, findings are based on what respondents—all of them women— *recalled* when questioned about conversations and exposure to media content relevant to recent everyday decisions or choices concerning the three areas of consumption—food, fashion, and cinema. This is where, we are told, the "dominant role of personal contacts . . . comes out fairly clearly. . . . [Of these three areas,] fashion . . . is the only exception to the general conclusion that the impact of personal contact is greater than that of any other sources [i.e., the formal mass media] investigated in this study" (ibid., 183f.).

A second caveat relates to the ease with which the above "one-out-of-three" generalization glosses over findings about opinion leadership in the "public affairs area" that suggest a rather different relationship between personal influence and media influence. Of 619 reported changes of opinion, 58 percent were—to quote—"apparently made without involving any remembered personal contact, and were, very often, dependent upon the mass media" (ibid., 142). In seeming contradiction to the relative *un*importance of personal influence is the observed relationship between knowing someone who could be trusted and relied on for guidance about public affairs and being an influential for other persons, a relationship that becomes sharper as one moves up the ladder from the designators of influentials contacted in the original sample to those they designate along the chain of interpersonal influence through its second, third, and subsequent links. The higher one goes the stronger this relationship (281f.). Since the higher level "public affairs" experts also turn out to be more informed (judged by the measure used in this study), one may conclude, as Katz does in connection with the two-step flow, that "the effect of the media in public affairs would be more clearly visible if we traced the networks of interpersonal influence further back; in other words, we are likely to find that those on the next step— that is, the opinion leaders of the opinion leaders—are the ones who form opinions in more direct response to the media. Or, it might be that we would have to go back several steps before we found the link between the interpersonal networks of public affairs opinion and disproportionate mass media effect" (ibid., 319). In short, the study failed to demonstrate its hypothesized link between mass media and personal influence.

Third, the only support for the two-step flow comes from the general finding that the persons identified as "opinion leaders tend to be both more generally exposed to the mass media, and more specifically exposed to the content most closely associated with their leadership" (ibid., 316). While presumably information from the media enhances the influence of these leaders on others, all the attention here is on the second step. In part, this was mandated by the lack of success in identifying all the links in the chain of influence emanating from an original media source. But it was also a deliberate choice. The initial research design aimed at studying "not historical episodes but *specific incidents* . . . [by collecting] a large number of reports on concrete situations where people made *minor* decisions" (ibid., 166, italics added). This leaves a lot of room for mass communications of a different kind and with a different focus.

Finally, Katz himself appended a strong qualification to his argument that future research into *short-run* media effects on individuals ought to build on investigations of the processes elucidated in *Personal Influence*. He did this in a long footnote, wherein he urged that "what should not be lost in all this, however, is the idea that there are other kinds of mass media effects—which have not been much studied—where the impact of the mass media on society may be much greater" (ibid., 133, fn. 20). Subsequent reactions to *Personal Influence* provide ample evidence, if such is needed, that many scholars skip the footnotes in which such qualifications tend to be buried—or it may be that the fault lies with their overworked graduate assistants. The backward look Katz takes on the Decatur study in his introduction to the Transaction edition of *Personal Influence* contains a similar hint of limits beyond which one cannot generalize its findings: "Together with the concept of 'selectivity' in exposure, perception, and recall of media messages," he writes, "the 'two-step' hypothesis points to a shift in the balance of power between media influence and audiences, *at least as far as short-run persuasion is concerned*" (Katz 2006, xv, italics added). These findings, limited to self-reported impact, should not have kept anyone from ruling out the existence of other kinds of effects.

Personal Influence *heralded a clear shift in the rhetoric surrounding sociological research concerning the effects of mass communication.*

With the ground prepared by previous studies in the Columbia mold, *Personal Influence* heralded a clear shift in the rhetoric surrounding sociological research concerning the effects of mass communication. Examples surfaced immediately in reviews of the book in academic journals. John Riley (1956, 356) cited it as having found "personal influence, relative to the various mass media, [to be] the most important factor in accounting for decision making in the four [*sic*] areas";[5] Gold (1956, 793) for finding it "more frequent and more effective in specific influencing incidents"; and Carter (1956, 383) as showing that it has "more 'impact' . . . on decisions." Of eight reviews we examined, the one by Matilda Riley (1956) was the only one to express a somewhat more qualified view of this finding about personal influence. She noted that a research design that "restricts 'personal influence' to the giving of recent, specific advice of a nature which respondents can remember and report . . . [e]xcluded . . . studying long-range influence and that which operates below the level of awareness" (p. 102), a comment that refers not to the influence of mass communication but to extended relationships of each person with the significant others that shape everyone's personality and have affected all of our lives.

All in all, it was less the theoretical discussion in the first part of *Personal Influence* than the techniques used to identify opinion leaders, findings about how they functioned, the importance of personal influence, and the hypothesized two-step flow that sustained its relevance. A perusal of nearly one hundred articles in which the book was cited turned up an unsurprising number containing no more than a perfunctory reference serving as a pro forma fulfillment of the mandatory literature review. More surprising—only two among the other articles focused on its underlying conceptualization. One by Todd Gitlin (1978) published in the British journal *Theory and Society* offered a methodological and ideological critique of the Lazarsfeld tradition, while the other by Heinz Eulau (1980, 210) in *Social Science History* faulted the Decatur study from a "network perspective" for failing to distinguish clearly between "group structure" and "communication flow." However, the clear majority of articles sought to link up with the line of interest in "the part played by people in the flow of mass communication" pioneered by Columbia University, to strengthen its foundation, to fill knowledge gaps.

The tendency to downplay media effects kept surfacing. Looking back at the first two decades of public opinion study, William Albig (1957, 20) referred to this trend as a "necessary reassessment of the overestimation of the effects of the mass media." George Fisk (1959, 87), in an article with the broad title "Media Influence Reconsidered," pointed to a finding from his own study that "roughly confirms [the conclusion of Katz and Lazarsfeld] that personal influence may be more effective than influences stemming from the mass media" with no qualification as to the concrete circumstances in which that proposition might hold. About the same time, Klapper (1957), another influential exponent of the Columbia tradition, was advancing some tentative generalizations about the effects of mass communication. Ordinarily, he averred, mass communication "does not serve as a necessary and sufficient cause of audience effects, but rather functions among and through a nexus of mediating factors and influences." These factors and influences, among which he included opinion leadership, "typically render mass communication a contributory agent, but not the sole cause, in a process of reinforcing the existing conditions" (p. 458). Except for their role in decision-making episodes, where they function as agents of change, he wrote in another context, opinion leaders personify group norms. Consequently, when acting as gatekeepers or transmitters of mass communication content, for example, they "might readily transmit or approve material in accord with group norms, and might fail to transmit, or inveigh against, material opposing such norms" (Klapper 1960, 36).

The first time we ourselves ran up against a strongly entrenched "minimalist" view of media effects was in 1956, when Eugene Burdick, a political scientist soliciting essays for a collection on American voting behavior (Burdick and Brodbeck 1959), sent us a letter about difficulties he had finding someone among his colleagues at Berkeley who thought mass communication mattered very much. "One thing that stands out in all [the recent voting studies]," he observed, "is the relative insignificance of the mass media in influencing the voter's decision. . . . It occurs to me that much of the alleged impotence of the mass media may be due to the fact that the studies were not specifically set up to catch this aspect of voting" (personal communication, 1956). Others were less circumspect. Tom Burns (1977/1995, 259), a sociologist at Edinburgh, referred unabashedly to the "accumulation of *almost entirely* [italics added] negative findings from research over thirty-five years into the extent to which broadcasting actually influences opinion and voting behavior" and then went on to chide those who, like Denis Quail and the Langs, argued otherwise and sought to develop research designs governed by an alternative conception of media influence. Or, as Finkel (1993, 3) was to put it half a lifetime after our initial experience, the results from voting studies "quickly became part of the core of the emerging 'minimal effects' model in campaign, media, and mass communication research."

Inadvertent Consequences

The downplay of mass media influence in this wave of assertions had consequences, however unintended. In changing the focus away from influences that occur en masse and over time toward the concrete responses of individuals, assessments like the above undercut a long-standing concern, dating back to the early 1920s, and even before, about the role of mass circulation newspapers, of film, and of radio. It put into question the value of further inquiries into the new worlds these media had opened. After all, if research had convincingly demonstrated that mass communication had only minimal effects compared with face-to-face influences, then what payoff could one expect from spending valuable time and energy to tease them out? Young budding scholars hoping to make a name for themselves were unlikely to advance a career by searching for effects that they were being told barely existed. Of course, the dissuasion is not solely attributable to *Personal Influence* but, more accurately, the culmination of a whole genre of studies in the tradition pioneered at the Office of Radio Research and later at the BASR, which gave rise to the mantra about a paradigmatic shift away "from the all-powerful media toward a limited effects" model.

One casualty of this reorientation was the sociological, as opposed to the ideological, concept of mass. The incontrovertible fact that the members of media audiences do not live their lives in total isolation from other people, that they do not constitute some mass of anonymous individuals without any local attachments, shared ideals, and common ideas does not render the concept of mass as related to mass communication obsolete. What matters, as Eliot Freidson (1953), a Chicago sociologist, made clear in an article that anticipated a theorem put forth in *Personal Influence*, is whether one looks at the media-created audience in its entirety or at the very concrete local audiences, whose members sift, evaluate, discuss, and bring past experience to bear on the media content. That very compelling fact does not obviate in any way the other equally compelling fact, namely, that the mass media make it possible that people all over a country and even around the world will react to some of the same events. The kind of large audience, called into being by these media, "is more or less a mass. . . . There is no well-organized bond between different local audiences and in this sense the type of social experience presupposed by such a bond need not be taken into account." The concept of mass, Freidson points out, falls short only insofar as "one cannot *explain* the behavior of its [individual] members except by reference to the local audiences to which they belong. It is their experience as members of local audiences that determines how they act, not the fact that there happen to be members of other local audiences whom they do not know, who are not necessarily similar to them, do not interact with them and do have well-organized relationships with them. . . . Thus, so long as one treats the national audience as an aggregate body, the concept of mass is not inaccurately applied" and can be useful for other areas of research (p. 317).

The implications for the role of interpersonal influences are obvious. In deciding to try a new brand or what movie to see, people will exercise old-fashioned common sense to compensate for their own limited experience by seeking advice from whoever, as they have reason to believe, knows more than they do. Let us also recognize, however, that consumer and media choices are less than fully autonomous but constrained by what is available, actively promoted, and/or in line with prevalent taste. A too exclusive focus on how individuals choose has been at the expense of research on the larger aggregate patterns, whose dynamics, as in the movement of fashion, cannot be directly inferred from "who influences whom" just as to understand how an electorate becomes polarized or produces a landslide one has to look beyond the individual voter at the point of decision.

One can argue, with good justification, that the link between personal influence and outside influence from mass media at different points and stages in the diffusion process was more fully explored in subsequent research by Katz and others at the BASR (cf. Katz 1957; Coleman, Katz, and Menzel 1966). Yet the emphasis in these follow-up studies was still on the individual making a choice or reaching a decision, a strategy that excluded many responses to mass communication not easily elicited in self-reports of things done or left undone. Some influences of exposure may be too subtle for respondents themselves to take note of. Inability to name a specific item of information that caused them to "change your mind" does not rule out the existence of such media influences as framing, priming, sleeper, reinforcement, and others attributable to the day-to-day flow of news. To cite these is not to imply that audiences respond like a herd of sheep doing what-ever the media tell them to do or to accept uncritically whatever opinions or ideas are disseminated. Messages have been known to boomerang. Equally undeniable is that people do form pictures of the larger world beyond the experience of the orbits within which they move, and even when nothing very much is happening, a cumulation of impressions, each by itself of little consequence, can result in a significant movement of opinion. Still other effects, such as those on political leaders, on institutions, and those imputed to "third persons" (Davison 1983), which though operating more circuitously and unobtrusively have been fairly well established, similarly fall outside this line of inquiry.

The superior effectiveness of personal influence, compared to mass commu-nication, found in these studies may lie, Katz theorizes, in the different charac-teristics of the two kinds of media. Formal (mass) media exert their "influence mainly by representation or by indirect attraction, that is *by what they tell*" whereas other persons "can influence both this way and by *control*" (Katz and Lazarsfeld 1955, 185). In other words, "persons have *two* major avenues of influ-ence while formal mass media, like radio and print, have only one" (ibid., 186). This speculation may be true in the abstract but, one is tempted to ask, is there really firm ground for assuming that advice on consumer choices—trying a new brand or deciding which movie to see—are "controlling" in the above sense? Most exchanges about such things occur when people are trying to reduce uncer-tainty by checking with someone who may already have tried the new product or seen the widely advertised movie and, even if they have not, can be expected to have useful information. The explanation carries no greater weight in the area of public affairs. Few citizens, including those identified as opinion leaders, have useful *firsthand* knowledge about the government in Washington or what City Hall is up to. All depend, directly or indirectly, on what goes out over the "news." Thus, in critical events, such as the assassination of President Kennedy, the media were found to have played a primary role in the diffusion of knowledge with per-sonal influence assuming only a secondary role. Not only were the media the first source of information for great numbers of people, but even where people first heard the news from others, they immediately turned to radio or television for confirmation (cf. Greenberg 1964).

There is a fundamental difference between direct media influence on every-day decisions and opinion formation on public issues. People hold political opin-ions but actually make decisions only when specifically called upon to cast a vote. Vote decisions are rather complex acts; the practical consequences facing the individual casting a ballot are often hard to fathom. The ideas and imagery that go into a vote develop as part of an ongoing discourse, with both influential and influencee oriented to what the media carry and/or have highlighted over the years. Viewed from this macro-perspective, the longer-term influence of mass communication on public opinion looms as relatively more important than it does when examining specific influences on private consumption. At least this much was admitted by Lazarsfeld when, speculating about the apparent lack of media influences in the 1940 presidential campaign in the introduction to the third edition of *The People's Choice*, he acknowledged that this must have been "because most arguments were formulated either for or against Roosevelt and had become stereotyped through two previous campaigns" (Lazarsfeld, Berelson, and Gaudet 1944/1968, vi).

Public opinion is not just what individuals think but more like an ever-evolving collective representation (cf. Blumer 1948). We may be able to trace the networks through which an innovative idea or concrete proposal spreads, but then, as it encounters opposition, issues arise. A one-way diffusion model does not adequately catch this confluence. Unlike specific items of information, products, or behavior whose adoption one can track, issues do not come ready-made. They are socially constructed, largely from grievances and competing demands that get public recognition from the media—as, for example, the well-documented "blue-collar" rally back to Harry S. Truman during the 1948 presidential campaign (Berelson, Lazarsfeld, and McPhee 1954)—and are then elaborated, modified, or even sidetracked through further discussion, not only in associations and neighborhoods, but also among political leaders, spokespersons for various interests, and journalists. The mass media provide the most open forum for this discourse that takes place on all levels of the polity. More and more, it has been the media that, by granting public recognition to whatever they choose to cover, legitimate its importance. They are also a major channel of communication among political leaders and from them to their following.

To illuminate the question of "media versus personal influence" from yet another angle, the media create the symbolic environment that serves as the background against which interpersonal discussion takes place and/or decisions are made. Katz, in a later seminal work about media events in collaboration with Daniel Dayan, has granted full recognition to the role of the media in creating the appropriate atmosphere, that "sense of occasion," as they call it, that marks the celebrations, conflicts, and coronations with which their book deals (Dayan and Katz 1992). Experience of these spectacles may be modified by interpersonal discourse, but they remain *media* events. We worked from precisely this assumption in our earlier study of the public welcome given to General Douglas MacArthur. The effect of exposure to the TV broadcast of this kind of public event, we wrote at the time,

> cannot be measured most successfully in isolation. For the influence on one person is communicated to others, until the significance of the video event overshadows the "true" picture of the event, namely the impression of someone physically present at the scene of the event. The experience of spectators may not be disseminated or may be discounted as the biased version of a specially interested participant. Or, again, a spectator's interpretation of his own experience may be reinterpreted when he finds the event in which he participated discussed by friends, newspapermen, and radio commentators. If the significance of the event is so magnified, even casual spectatorship assumes importance. The fact of having "been there" is to be remembered—not so much because the event, in itself, has left an impression, but because the event has been recorded by others. (Lang and Lang 1953, 3)

including the media and history books.

What all too often got lost in the shift to the new paradigm with its emphasis on the part played by people is the simple and obvious fact that without a first step as the initial impetus in the two-step flow there might never have been a second or further step.

The notion of the "all-powerful" media was a convenient straw man, too easy to demolish to have ever been taken seriously by other than pop sociologists. For better or worse, the media have become the arena on which many political controversies are fought out. Although television has made these conflicts distinctly more visible, its ability to cover the full range of relevant facts remains limited and the willingness of owners to invest in the effort highly questionable. Some important media effects have less to do with what the big media convey than with what they leave out. The topics, events, facts, issues, arguments, personalities, and political figures that never make it into this public forum have consequences, short-term and long-range. All kinds of groups, and not only those outside the mainstream of opinion, are forever at work to attract the "right" kind of coverage.

Katz himself, unlike other sociologists who abandoned research on mass communication effects, remains an untiring advocate for new inquiries; his many students are still carrying the flag.

We are not suggesting that Lazarsfeld or his associates were oblivious of the monopolistic power of media conglomerates or of changes accompanying the introduction of a new medium of communication. Lazarsfeld himself made this clear in an article published a few years after *The People's Choice*. The four-by-four matrix of communication effects he presented contains only one box for the responses of individuals to specific messages but makes full allowance for effects of the medium and of its control structure on masses of people and on society as a whole—effects that are especially pertinent today in anticipating the long-term effect of the Internet (Lazarsfeld 1948). One has at least to allow for the possibility that this most recent communication innovation, with its capacity for expanding the range of personal conversation, will shift the balance away from television and toward grassroots conversation just as the evasion of censorship through cheaply printed pamphlets helped undermine absolute monarchy. The medium may not be the message, but it does affect how people think and act.

The consequences of the shift in paradigm on the direction of sociological research is more than difficult to document within the framework of this article.[6]

Investigations into the effects of mass media certainly did not come to an abrupt halt with the publication of *Personal Influence.* Our rummaging through *Sociological Abstracts* for a trajectory of the decline and growth in communication research turned up nothing really conclusive. It shows that the number of peer-reviewed articles classified under 0828—"mass phenomena/communication," which, upon inspection, struck us as the most appropriate category, has increased exponentially since 1956 (when Leo Chall launched the abstracts), but so did the volume of sociologically relevant literature as the number of journals kept growing and some of the older ones adopted peer review. Proportions in the classification fluctuated from year to year but did not decline. Katz himself, unlike other sociologists who abandoned research on mass communication effects, remains an untiring advocate for new inquiries; his many students are still carrying the flag. Still, Bernard Berelson, Lazarsfeld's close associate, proved a true "influential" when in 1958 at the annual meetings of the American Association for Public Opinion Research he declared during a roundtable on the "State of Communication Research" that it was "withering away." Many of its innovators had taken up other interests and most of their students had either left the field or were not going much beyond their masters' ideas. In sum, he concluded (and later wrote), the " 'great ideas' that had given the field of communication research so much vitality ten or twenty years before had to a substantial degree worn out. No ideas of comparable magnitude had appeared to take their place" (Berelson 1959, 6).

Berelson's pronouncement did not go unchallenged. Yet whether his assessment was right or wrong or merely a rhetorical flourish, there is no question that the new stress on the insignificance of media effects played into Berelson's pessimism and dissuaded some students of politics from pursuing this line of inquiry. Suggestive of this abandonment is the choice of questions included—or excluded—in the National Election Studies conducted at four-year intervals at the University of Michigan. Having observed that television had been the most important source of information during the 1952 presidential election, the Survey Research Center did not thereafter try to ascertain what difference this may have made or to explore the effects of the mass media on the election in general. Its "funnel" model of electoral decision making focused on the general allegiances, identities, and perceptions of individual voters as they moved toward closure during the course of the campaign until election day. The one relevant entry in the index for 558 pages of text in *The American Voter* (Campbell et al. 1960) is for "mass media and political participation." There is none for "television" or for any other subject related to mass communication. With possible media influences having fallen outside their purview, all they could report about the effects of the first televised debate between Kennedy and Nixon—a critical event in the 1960 presidential campaign—was that "the relative small proportion of the population who failed to see any of the television debates . . . was made up of voters less likely to have revised their previously stated vote intention before their final decisions than people who had watched the debates" (Converse 1962/1967, 147). The perspective and commitment to a particular survey design kept the Michigan group from collecting interesting effects not directly reflected in the final vote.

The hiatus in studies about mass media and voting proved only temporary. Among sociologists outside the United States, this interest seems never to have waned. What reawakened interest among American researchers were a series of controversies outside the normal election season that highlighted the role of the media in political conflicts. First were the televised Army-McCarthy hearings in 1954, which highlighted the role of the media in any kind of political conflict. What then followed were the heated, often violent disputes of the 1960s, first over civil rights, then over the Vietnam War, with attention peaking during the "long nightmare" of Watergate. Blacks demonstrating peaceably against segregation played well on television, while the troopers confronting them seemed less than concerned about the reactions of viewers. In retrospect, there is little reason to doubt that the vivid pictures of state troopers' attacks on unarmed marchers undercut the legitimacy of Southern resistance to their demands, yet there is only the flimsiest evidence from a few surveys to support this proposition (cf. Tumin 1958). Speculation about the possible role of the news media in precipitating riots in the black ghettoes of America and of white reaction induced the National Advisory Commission on Civil Disorders (1968) to commission a study of the television coverage, but it was unable to draw any firm conclusion about its effects. A study by Benjamin Singer (1970) of blacks arrested during the riots in Detroit suggests that news coverage of rioting contributed to its spread. In another study, a combination of content analysis of Los Angeles newspapers over several decades with surveys of blacks and of whites in that area, the emphasis was on the differences in the reactions of the two groups to the rioting (Johnson, Sears, and McConahay 1971).

As regards Vietnam, Peter Braestrup's (1977) bold assertion, in his magnum opus about the Tet Offensive, that its television coverage had turned public opinion against the war was repeatedly challenged, most directly by Hallin (1986), who conducted his own content analysis of the coverage devoted to the Vietnam War, and by others who noted that support for the war had started to decline before Tet when the coverage was still essentially favorable. Despite the erosion of popular support, antiwar protests, many of them student-led, did not find great favor among the public. The reactions of activists, especially of leaders spotlighted by the media, were analyzed by a sociologist who had played an active role in the peace movement (Gitlin 1980).

The climate generated by these issues also helped revive interest in studying such subjects as the production of news (e.g., Gans 1979; Tuchman 1978; Roshco 1975; Fishman 1980) and the interactions between political actors and those in the media who cover them (e.g., Molotch and Lester 1974; Lang and Lang 1983), topics that had once commanded attention but had been overshadowed by recent findings about the limited persuasive potential of the media. All are illustrative of research modes that antedated the entrepreneurial data-collecting activities in whose development Lazarsfeld and the BASR had played a critical role and that, with unprecedented opportunities for funding from industry, government, and foundations, had become the gold standard for measuring media effects.

An examination of *Sociological Abstracts* reveals still another trend, namely, the growing importance of specialized journals linked to a profession, such as *Journalism Quarterly*, and even more to the expanding scholarly endeavor under such rubrics as communication or media studies rather than sociology. The list includes the *Journal of Communication, Journalism Quarterly, Media Culture and Society, Communication Research*, and more. Specialization is inevitable, and the breakup of professional associations into sections is a common phenomenon. The American Sociological Association accommodates sections for just about every subject pursued by its members but—and this is indicative—has none specifically dedicated to mass communication. Nor have there been in recent memory many sessions at its annual conference devoted to the subject. Substantive interest in the media has not disappeared but is more likely to show up in connection with studies of popular culture, gender, and children rather than the political scene. In this last area, it seems, American sociologists have ceded much ground they once occupied to political scientists, whose association does have a political communication section, organized in cooperation with the International Communication Association. Many members in one association are also members of the other, but multiple membership is not a requirement. That few of the younger American sociologists participate in either is yet another indication of the extent to which communication research has moved out of sociology and of the parallel exodus of sociologists specializing in this area into communication departments and institutes. We can only wonder how many departments of sociology still list a course on mass communication and, if they do, whether such a course has more than a marginal place in their curriculum and is taught by a regular member of the faculty, by an adjunct, or by someone whose primary professional pedigree is in sociology.

The main exception to this turning away by sociologists from media research has been a growing recognition over the past two decades by students of collective behavior and social movements of how dependent demonstrators and movement activists are on the amount and quality of media coverage as their major point of entry into the public discourse. It is in this connection that a lot of earlier work on the news media, long ignored, gains new relevance. A field such as communication research stands to gain maturity not only through discovery but also by reflecting on an ancestry that includes critics as well as exponents of the "golden age" at Columbia University.

Afterthoughts

Now to return to questions raised by Katz in his introduction to the anniversary edition of *Personal Influence* (Katz 2006): First, why has the struggle over the relative power of the individual, the media, and interpersonal influence lasted so long? Part of the answer lies in the promotional themes for the book, which emphasized the superior power of personal influence. Sorry to say but Katz and Lazarsfeld, in their introduction to the original edition, invited exactly this kind of reading by their reiteration of the finding from *The People's Choice* that, in 1940, "the effect of the mass media was small as compared to the role of personal influence" (Katz and Lazarsfeld 1955, 3) and went on to assert that the "crucial issue, we wanted to know was how influences stemming from other people compared with the mass media influences in their decision making experiences" (ibid., 5). These formulations became major selling points for the book. But by no stretch of imagination were the findings ipso facto quite so definitive. Commenting on the early election studies, Ithiel de Sola Pool (1959) paid deference to the concept of opinion leadership as a real step forward in communication research but went on to "affirm the probable importance of some direct media impacts, although we do not know what they are. After all, the opinion leader selects material from the mass media. This is an impact of the media, and certainly he is not alone in being susceptible to such influence" (p. 241). An interview method that relies on the respondent's own perception of influence is "not well suited to measuring the relationship between the stimulus and [the] response to them. . . . Responding to a smile on TV does not depend on recalling the fact of the smile" (p. 239). Personal and media influence obviously affect people in different ways.

Second, possibly the most "irate" critique of *Personal Influence* has come from Gitlin (1978), who argued, as Katz puts it, that "the opinion leader idea was mere camouflage for the direct effects of the media" (Katz 2006, xvi). As for "objections" imputed to the Langs (cf. Lang and Lang 1979), they are not specified but coupled to those of Theodor Adorno and Marshall McLuhan. More to the point, we do not consider the attention given informal opinion leadership as camouflage. But Gitlin's criticism does accord, at least to some extent, with our contention that the "new paradigm" diverted researchers' attention from the power of the mass media. As a result, many questions about media monopolies and chummy relationships between journalists and the establishment were not asked as often as they should have been. Nor can one ignore the fact that financing of the Decatur study came largely from Macfadden Publications, a very conservative publishing empire. Its research director, according to the introduction to *Personal Influence*, had been alerted by findings about the 1940 election study to the importance of opinion leaders and, apparently, recognized the implications for his firm, especially the ones with regard to the "crystallization of opinion"— whatever may have been meant by this phrase (see Morrison 2006 [this volume]). Elements of the study design did indeed reflect the interests of commercial sponsorship: the sample was confined to women and questions were geared to marketing. Notwithstanding these obvious constraints, Lazarsfeld has repeatedly argued, with some justification, that the analysis of consumer behavior would yield insights whose implications extended to more general patterns of human behavior. It certainly has—but within limits previously outlined.

A third point, more or less a corollary to the second, stems from the fact that commitments made to sponsors of the Decatur study limited the leeway researchers had to add questions of special interest to themselves. They had more control over the analysis and how to write up their findings. We think they would have been better served had they made a sharper separation between findings bearing on the three marketing areas and findings in the public affairs or political realm. Concrete consumer choices should never have been conflated, as they were too often in this book, with the formation and expression of political opinions.

Fourth, nothing ever remains quite the same. How similar was the role of a woman living in a middle-sized city in 1945 to that of most women today? A lot has happened to make women more independent and less subservient in their political opinions to their male spouses. The evidence lies in the gender gap of opinion on many matters. Not that personal influence no longer operates, but a rising level of evidence shows that the average woman has become more sensitive to what the formal media convey. The other big change is in the ubiquity of television. The Decatur study was, after all, the product of the late radio era. Today, even politically disinterested consumers of television find it hard to avoid all political content, particularly the advertisements by the parties and candidates that have saturated the media in recent campaigns.

Finally, the long-term and society-wide consequences of any new medium are difficult to demonstrate by methods based on the individual as the unit of observation. None of this is to deprive Katz of the credit he deserves for being among the first to focus on the dyad as the unit of observation in survey research. This methodological innovation has borne fruit. But to understand the full range of media effects requires us to look beyond specific person-to-person relationships and take in the entire fabric that holds society together. Knowledge is power, and its uneven distribution as a rule affects the normal course of politics more than conversation at the grassroots level, except during periods of massive unrest when large segments of the people take things into their own hands. This is not a refusal to acknowledge the part played by people, only a plea to recognize how much more there is yet to know about the long-range and society-wide effects of the media.

Notes

1. See Summers (2006 [this volume]).

2. Social science citation index starts in 1956. *Web of Science* machine-readable counts are available from 1969. Because of incomplete entries for the first year or two, figures for the three five-year periods 1956 to 1960, 1961 to 1965, and 1966 to 1970 are based on manual counts.

3. It was republished in 2004 with an introduction by Peter Simonson under the imprint of Howard Fertig, New York.

4. Personal conversation with C. Wright Mills in 1956.

5. Riley overlooked that the finding applied to only two of the four areas.

6. This subject is treated in greater detail by Pooley (2006 [this volume]).

References

Albig, William. 1957. Two decades of opinion study: 1936-1956. *Public Opinion Quarterly* 21:14-22.

Berelson, Bernard. 1959. The state of mass communication research. *Public Opinion Quarterly* 23:1-6.

Berelson, Bernard, Paul F. Lazarsfeld, and William N. McPhee. 1954. *Voting: A study of opinion formation in a presidential campaign*. Chicago: University of Chicago Press.

Blumer, Herbert. 1948. Public opinion and public opinion polling. *American Sociological Review* 13: 542-49.

Braestrup, Peter. 1977. *Big story: How the American press and television reported and interpreted the crisis of Tet 1968 in Vietnam and Washington*. Boulder, CO: Westview.

Burdick, Eugene, and Arthur J. Brodbeck Jr., eds. 1959. *American voting behavior*. Glencoe, IL: Free Press.

Burns, Tom. 1977/1995. The organisation of public opinion. In *Description, explanation and understanding: Selected writings, 1944-1980*, 258-88. Edinburgh, UK: Edinburgh University Press.

Campbell, Angus, Philip E. Converse, Warren E. Miller, and Donald E. Stokes. 1960. *The American voter*. New York: Wiley.

Carter, Roy F. 1956. Review: Katz and Lazarsfeld, *Personal influence. Social forces* 34:383.

Coleman, James S., Elihu Katz, and Herbert Menzel. 1966. *Medical innovation: A diffusion study*. Indianapolis, IN: Bobbs-Merrill.

Converse, Philip E. 1962/1967. Information flow and the stability of partisan attitudes. In *Elections and the political order*, ed. P. E. Converse, W. E. Miller, and D. E. Stokes, 136-57. New York: Wiley.

Davison, W. Phillips. 1983. The third-person effect in communication. *Public Opinion Quarterly* 47:1-15.

Dayan, Daniel, and Elihu Katz. 1992. *Media events: The live broadcasting of history*. Cambridge, MA: Harvard University Press.

Eulau, Heinz. 1980. The Columbia studies of personal influence: Social network analysis. *Social Science History* 4:207-28.

Finkel, Steven E. 1993. Re-examining the "limited effects" model in recent presidential campaigns. *Journal of Politics* 55:1-21.

Fishman, Mark. 1980. *Manufacturing the news*. Austin: University of Texas Press.

Fisk, George. 1959. Media influence reconsidered. *Public Opinion Quarterly* 23:83-91.

Freidson, Eliot. 1953. Communication research and the concept of the mass. *American Sociological Review* 18:313-17.

Gans, Herbert J. 1979. *Deciding what's news: A study of CBS Evening News, NBC Nightly News, Newsweek, and Time*. New York: Pantheon Books.

Gitlin, Todd. 1978. Media sociology: The dominant paradigm. *Theory and Society* 6:205-53.

———. 1980. *The whole world is watching: Mass media in the making and unmaking of the New Left*. Berkeley: University of California Press.

Gold, David. 1956. Review: *Personal influence* by Katz & Lazarsfeld. *American Sociological Review* 21:792-93.

Greenberg, Bradley S. 1964. Diffusion of news of the Kennedy assassination. *Public Opinion Quarterly* 25:225-32.

Hallin, Daniel C. 1986. *The "uncensored war": The media and Vietnam*. New York: Oxford University Press.

Johnson, Paula B., David O. Sears, and John B. McConahay. 1971. Black invisibility, the press, and the Los Angeles riot. *American Journal of Sociology* 76:698-721.

Katz, Elihu. 1957. The two-step flow of communication: An up-to-date report on an hypothesis. *Public Opinion Quarterly* 21:61-78.

———. 2006. Introduction to *Personal influence: The part played by people in the flow of mass communication*, by Elihu Katz and Paul F. Lazarsfeld. New Brunswick, NJ: Transaction Publications. (Orig. pub. 1955)

Katz, Elihu, and Paul F. Lazarsfeld. 1955. *Personal influence: The part played by people in the flow of mass communication*. Glencoe, IL: Free Press.

Kelly, Harold H., and Edmund H. Volkart. 1952. The resistance to change of group-anchored attitudes. *American Sociological Review* 17:453-65.

Klapper, Joseph T. 1957. What we know about the effects of mass communication: The brink of hope. *Public Opinion Quarterly* 21:453-74.

———. 1960. *The effects of mass communication*. Glencoe, IL: Free Press.

Lang, Gladys Engel, and Kurt Lang. 1979. Mass communications and public opinion. In *Social psychology: Sociological perspectives*, ed. M. Rosenberg and R. H. Turner, 653-82. New York: Basic Books.

———. 1983. *The battle for public opinion: The president, the press, and the polls during Watergate*. New York: Columbia University Press.

Lang, Kurt, and Gladys Engel Lang. 1953. The unique perspective of television and its effect: A pilot study. *American Sociological Review* 18:3-12.

Lazarsfeld, Paul F. 1948. Communication research and the social psychologist. In *Current trends in social psychology*, ed. W. Dennis, 218-73. Pittsburgh, PA: University of Pittsburgh Press.

Lazarsfeld, Paul F., Bernard Berelson, and Hazel Gaudet. 1944/1968. *The people's choice*. New York: Columbia University Press.

Lewin, Kurt. 1947/1958. Group decision and social change. In *Readings in social psychology*, 3d ed., ed. Society for the Study of Social Issues, 197-211. New York: Holt.

McPhee, William N. 1963. *Formal theories of mass behavior*. New York: Free Press.

Merton, Robert K. 1946. *Mass persuasion: The social psychology of a war bond drive*. New York: Harper.

Mills, C. Wright. 1956. *The power elite*. New York: Oxford University Press.

Molotch, Harvey, and Marilyn Lester. 1974. Accidental news: The great oil spill as local occurrence and national event. *American Journal of Sociology* 81:235-60.

Morrison, David E. 2006. The influences influencing *Personal influence*: Scholarship and entrepreneurship. *Annals of the American Academy of Political and Social Science* 608:51-75.

National Advisory Commission on Civil Disorders. 1968. *Report*. New York: Dutton.

Pool, Ithiel de Sola. 1959. TV: A new dimension in politics. In *American voting behavior*, ed. E. Burdick and A. J. Brodbeck Jr., 236-61. Glencoe, IL: Free Press.

Pooley, Jefferson. 2006. Fifteen pages that shook the field: *Personal influence*, Edward Shils, and the remembered history of mass communication research. *Annals of the American Academy of Political and Social Science* 608:130-56.

Riley, John W., Jr. 1956. Review: *Personal influence* by Katz & Lazarsfeld. *Public Opinion Quarterly* 20:355-56.

Riley, Matilda White. 1956. Review: *Personal influence* by Katz & Lazarsfeld. *American Journal of Sociology* 62:101-3.

Roscho, Bernard. 1975. *Newsmaking*. Chicago: University of Chicago Press.

Singer, Benjamin D. 1970. Mass media and communication processes in the Detroit riot of 1967. *Public Opinion Quarterly* 34:236-45.

Summers, John H. 2006. Perpetual revelations: C. Wright Mills and Paul Lazarsfeld. *Annals of the American Academy of Political and Social Science* 608:25-40.

Tuchman, Gaye. 1978. *Making news: A study in the construction of reality*. New York: Free Press.

Tumin, Melvin. 1958. *Desegregation: Resistance and readiness*. Princeton, NJ: Princeton University Press.

Wright, Charles R. 1959. *Mass communication: A sociological perspective*. New York: Random House.

As Time Goes By . . .

Published in 1955, *Personal Influence* is a study of how middle America made political and consumer decisions in small primary groups and how ordinary people were both influenced and influencing. The Vietnam War challenged the paradigm as a new generation of scholars turned to larger units—state and society—and the power the media might have in reinforcing class structure. Part II of this article examines the application of the paradigm in voting studies from Walter Lippmann as the prototypical cosmopolitan to the locals of Decatur. The conclusion raises questions about the future based on globalization and the decline of the nation-state. Drawing on Dayan and Katz's work in studying televised events, this article shares their perspective based on aesthetics, which would give more attention to culture.

Keywords: decision making; primary groups; nation-state; globalization; culture

By
THELMA McCORMACK

I

Paradigm shifts are often difficult to discern in their early stages, and even more so when we are tracking subparadigms. However, their primary purpose is to help us understand that modern science does not develop in some linear, cumulative, and continuous way; its changes, which are often abrupt, represent a major discontent with "normal" science and a disconnect with other theories. Science does not make itself, Kuhn (1962) argues; we make it by creating new holistic models without waiting for the older ones to die.

Thelma McCormack is a professor of sociology and women's studies emerita at York University and currently a research associate at the Institute for Social Research. While a graduate student at Columbia, she worked as an intern at the Bureau of Applied Social Research. From 1980 to 1995, she served as senior editor in the JAI series in Studies in Communication. Her work has been primarily in political sociology, communications, and women's studies. She has just completed a paper on Ariel Sharon v. Time Magazine and is currently working on a book-length essay on Rosa Luxemburg.

DOI: 10.1177/0002716206292526

Personal Influence (Lazarsfeld and Katz 1955) crossed several thresholds. From the study of journalism as a craft to a profession; from the study of individuals, acting and thinking alone to the study of small groups; from the study of affinity groups to the study of factions and differences within them or, as Converse (1975) said, hierarchies within groups; from the study of policies to the study of the formation of consensus. Most important of all was the move from the study of technology—telephone, press, radio, television—and naive theories of technological determinism to the study of the social construction of meaning. Process, groups, divisions within groups, the formation of consensus, and interpretation are the key ideas that together constitute a matrix, a paradigm that opened a floodgate of new research, new both substantively and methodologically.

Still, older inquiries persisted. There was a time, not long ago, when you could not pick up a quality magazine or opinion journal without finding Herbert Schiller or Leo Bogart warning us of the information juggernaut with its monopolistic structure and manipulative intentions speeding in our direction without regard to our privacy, civil liberties, or the public interest. Former Attorney General Janet Reno may have had this in mind when she undertook an antitrust action against Microsoft (*United States of America v. Microsoft Corporation*, C.A. 98-1233 [June 2000]). The government won its case but nothing comparable in scale has been repeated, and it would require a different administration and one less politically conservative for it to occur.

---

*With one foot in the physical sciences
and the other in the humanities,
the social sciences were different from
each and belonged to neither.*

Personal Influence was both a beginning and an end. Its roots were in the early study of voting behavior and grassroots democracy; its future, I am going to suggest, lies in political activism, on one hand, aesthetics, on the other, or what Walter Benjamin (1968) called "the aestheticization of politics." But in 1955 the configuration of ideas reflected a range of the new social sciences—sociology, cultural anthropology, political science, economics, and social psychology—areas of scholarship that were no longer embedded in nineteenth-century philosophy and had achieved some degree of autonomy and professional acknowledgment.

With one foot in the physical sciences and the other in the humanities, the social sciences were different from each and belonged to neither. Some practitioners preferred quantitative measurement and experimental designs; others, narrative, metaphor, image, rhyme, and the use of qualitative methods. The tension between these polarities attracted a diverse group of students who engaged in endless discussions about causality, materialism, determinism, probability, and other abstract concepts. But in this lively ongoing dialectical process we were laying a foundation for "communication" as a uniquely interdisciplinary perspective open to many different ways of inquiry and with high expectations of combining analytic rigor with insight.

Personal Influence was published in 1955, the same year Stouffer published *Communism, Conformity and Civil Liberties* (1955). Both were studies of middle-range politics and complemented each other. Stouffer was interested in the American fear of communism and the social psychological factors that contributed to intolerance, that is, a fear of dissent and a hostility toward social differences. More broadly, intolerance was the predispositional foundation of (1) a rejection of egalitarian values and a fear of social values, (2) the reenforcement of dogmatic thinking, and (3) behavioral conformity. Out of this mix came the "authoritarian personality" (Adorno et al. 1950). Persons who scored high on the authoritarian personality scale could only further jeopardize the quality of life, corrupt public discourse, as well as undermine the secular basis of liberalism and modernization.

Progressive education would be a major step forward, toward a culture of entitlement and toward the civil rights movement. These not only changed the opportunities for African Americans but also the demography and social structure of the South. Tolerance (especially of race, class, and gender) and critical thinking with respect to ideas were at the other end of the continuum from intolerance, bias, class conflict, and the status quo.

Personal Influence examined the process of influence among individuals, from person to person, and recognized two things: first, all of us, in varying degrees, could be both influenced and influencing others. Second, the group itself was an actor not just the tabula rasa that would passively record the attitudes, opinions, and ideas of others. But the thread running through *Personal Influence* was the deeply held American belief in the "local" as the foundation of democracy and public life. Small government and big business would create communities that would be safe and trustworthy. Ideally, no one would be left out. It combined all the best characteristics of *Gemeinschaft*, while the big-city metropolitan perspective symbolized social problems, crime, corruption, deception, opportunism, dissent, divorce, family instability, and in general a lack of roots and self-discipline.

The locals who were less transient in their lifestyles looked at life more innocently and with little desire to change institutions and cultural expression. Church and the nuclear family held a privileged position. The naiveté and vulnerability of people were reflected in beliefs that were closer to faith or tradition than to science. Festinger's *When Prophecy Fails* (Festinger, Ricker, and Schachter 1956) studied how people who were in every sense normal and reasonably well-educated handled the contradiction between their convictions and reality. In Festinger's example, a group of people came to know each other through their common interests in the occult and specifically flying saucers. Eventually, they were receiving messages from the other world predicting an imminent flood. Fortunate to be informed of this catastrophe ahead of time, the group could be saved by leaving the doomed planet with the help of those who were already on the other side, friends who would conduct them to their new homes. A date for this transfer was established.

During the waiting and preparation period, there was no proselytizing since most of the people understood and accepted the communications received from the other side. A few had minor doubts but did not need convincing about what would happen or the basic plan. Members disposed of their property, terminated their employment, and were ready to depart. However, on the scheduled date for their departure, their transportation did not arrive. Understandably disappointed, they tried to understand what happened. They were not inclined to doubt the larger scenario. Perhaps they had the wrong information about the date and place? And there were other very reasonable ad hoc rationalizations. Most of the group remained convinced that sooner or later there would be a catastrophic flood and they would be rescued as they had expected. Their skepticism, if they had any, was not too deep. They remained confident that their destiny would be with other true believers.

The term used to describe this phenomenon is "cognitive dissonance," the need of overcommitted people to justify contradictions or deny evidence that fails to confirm their original belief, the pressure we all feel in varying degrees to keep our beliefs consistent with each other and with reality. Take away the bizarre narrative here and one sees commonplace behavior where we frequently remain firmly attached to certain ideas and expectations despite internal contradictions, changes, and denials.

When we combine *Personal Influence* with *Communism, Conformity and Civil Liberties* and *When Prophecy Fails* and include Eric Fromm's *Escape from Freedom* (1941) along with Karl Polany's *The Great Transformation* (1944), Karl Mannheim's *Ideology and Utopia* (1936), John Dewey's *Human Nature and Conduct* (1922), and Daniel Lerner's *The Passing of Traditional Society* (1958), we have more or less the liberal intellectual framework of the 1950s, which shaped a professional identity and became the foundation of a new scholarship for the next four decades.

Many liberal intellectuals voted for Adlai Stevenson, but General Eisenhower won the presidential election; Gandhi, who had sensitized a generation to poverty and became a moral model throughout the world, was assassinated. The pendulum swung among academics to problems of development. Economists, historians, and political scientists explored new development theories rejecting earlier evolutionary models. The United States was a case in point. Was its development at the expense of poorer countries and peripheral underdevelopment? And was American development the norm within reach of many countries or an exceptional model? On these points, development theorists were not in agreement among themselves. Nevertheless, they were convinced that literacy was a key factor and the print media had something to do with development.

But suppose the development was a circulation of elites and not part of a much deeper reform? "Think tanks" became part of universities, and governments addressed these problems. Development was high on the agenda, but academics were still applying for grants from the various foundations and government agencies, designing samples, and interviewing and analyzing the data to study long-range, short-range, or comparative studies. Maslow (1968) and the culture of California had taught this generation to self-actualize and appreciate "peak experiences," while the civil rights movement had persuaded the oppressed in the American South that they would "overcome."

When the United States became involved in the Vietnam War in the late 1950s, college-age groups demonstrated, protested, boycotted, marched, and performed various types of civil disobedience. It became the cornerstone of a counterculture and a new activism that went all the way from sit-ins to guerrilla warfare. New media were created and circulated. *Mother Jones, Rolling Stone, The New Left Review,* and other publications overshadowed some of the older and more respectable ones. *The Public Opinion Quarterly,* which had begun in 1937, was beginning to look too conventional. Fifty years after Walter Lippmann wrote *Public Opinion,* Pierre Bourdieu (1972) challenged it. "Public Opinion," he wrote, "Does Not Exist."

Much of this was subsumed under the heading of the New Left as distinct from the Marxist Old Left. It was an alternative paradigm based more on macro communities and secondary groups, mainly the state and class structure, and the processes of exploitation and modern imperialism. It captured the anger and frustrations of older colonial countries and stimulated the ideas of Chairman Mao. Many of the intellectuals turned to a new "critical theory" that Herbert Marcuse and other members of the Frankfurt School brought to American universities. Maoism and critical theory both attracted the imagination and in many cases, the devotion and allegiance of graduate students, especially those who were themselves refugees from European totalitarianism or third world dictatorships. Others were becoming dissatisfied with American positivism in the classrooms and American aggression/imperialism elsewhere. Ariel Dorfman's *How to Read Donald Duck: Imperialist Ideology in the Disney Comic* (1984) and Herman and Chomsky's *Manufacturing Consent* (1988) had enthusiastic followers.

The support for the Dorfman (1984) book was, in part, its style—a mix of irony and content analysis. But more significantly, it and others like it marked a shift in the way sociology studied social movements (Adams 1993; Gusfield 1994; Handler 1992; Knoke and Wisely 1990; Hess and Torney 1967). Earlier sociology textbooks located social movements under the heading of collective behavior and included cults, fads, fashions, and various forms of group hysteria and collective pathology. The new social movements—antiwar, environment, sustainable development, human rights, holistic medicine, feminism, organic agriculture, home births assisted by midwives—were presented as being sound, credible, rational alternatives to the dominant techno, industrial models of culture and social welfare. Clients and consumers who were critical of high-tech were not regarded as nostalgic or backward; nor were they suspect as being left-of-center captives of

Maoism. Instead, they were perceived as acceptable, normal, legitimate critics who were not overwhelmed by the new "new." But the politics of this period moved to Latin America, Asia, and the Middle East where a younger generation turned to "resistance" and violence.

"Uses and gratifications," this very understanding and tolerant doctrine implicit in *Personal Influence,* was being displaced by more impersonal and analytic discussions of statutory entitlement, law, and rights. The criminal justice system was also becoming part of the scene as police arrested student demonstrators and pacifist protestors. "Distributive justice" became a law school underground course and was reflected in a new style of practice, the drop-in storefront clinic. Various faith-based conservative groups were challenging our relativism in values and putting pressure on newspapers, magazines, and broadcasting to become part of a more restrictive cultural environment. Their opposite numbers explored postmodernism and chose to raise the consciousness of their sympathizers without jeopardizing the First Amendment.

The Vietnam War, France in 1968, the New Left in Europe and North America, liberation theology in the Southern Hemisphere, the draft evaders in Canada and the revival of Marxism on the West Coast, environmental groups (Greenpeace, in particular), and second-wave Feminism all contributed to a generation who found in the mainstream media the symptoms of alienation and, in turn, the cause of it. Either way, cause or effect, the media were culpable. There was a new focus on the media as texts that could through bias, editing, and self-censorship manipulate their audiences. Marshall McLuhan notwithstanding, the medium was not the message (McCormack 1964).

There was more interest, too, in the media as a type of formal organization. The Glasgow Group's *Bad News* (1976) was a study of newspaper employees, from managerial executives and professionals to the semiskilled in lower ranks. *Bad News* examined the proletarianization of journalists, the role of unions, and the vertical lines of managerial authority.

What was becoming clear from these and other studies was that the media and the study of communication fell between our understanding of the material base—the means of production—and superstructure as ideologies. Journalists were ideologues writing about ideologues claiming an arm's-length distance.

Todd Gitlin's *The Whole World Is Watching* (1980) was setting its own agenda. Gitlin traced the emergence of Students for Democratic Society, a university-based antiwar movement, as it was "constructed" in the quality media, the *New York Times*, and the Columbia Broadcasting System. The disparity between Gitlin's own version as an insider of the movement and the version generated by the media was, he said, a "shock of non recognition." But which one was objective, and did we want objectivity or authenticity?

Putting aside these questions, the point Gitlin raised was the distinction between understanding of events by insiders and outsiders. The dilemma for methodological inquiry was locating a hypothetical boundary, a constantly shifting line separating research from advocacy, how to be simultaneously *engagé* and detached without sacrificing integrity or quality.

Personal Influence studied the way people made decisions about consumer goods including the decision to see a movie. Film was becoming a major part of our mass and middlebrow culture. Movie reviews were printed in newspapers, which also kept their readers informed about Hollywood gossip and the private lives of well-known stars. Further up the cultural scale, film theory and film criticism were creating their own place in avant-garde bookstores and university courses. Leni Riefenstahl's film *Triumph of the Will* produced in 1934 evoked enormous criticism outside of Germany in part because the Nazi propaganda was so blatant and in part because of its cinematic techniques. Audiences who had known only entertainment film began to study the documentary and the ability of the camera to penetrate beneath the surface. Kracauer's *From Caligari to Hitler* (1947) traced the images and themes in art films revealing still deeper trends in our collective unconscious.

With Kracauer and other film theorists in mind, I invited a group of academics with different specializations—ethnomethodology (Albert 1982), symbolic interaction (Hewitt 1982), Marxism—to analyze Martin Luther King Jr.'s "I Have a Dream" speech (McCormack 1981). The variations and richness of the interpretations broadened our understanding of the text, opening it up rather than narrowing it. But all of us were inferring things about the people who heard the speech on site and those who heard about the speech, and still others who appropriated it for themselves. The differences were easy to recognize, not unlike what goes on in literary studies, where our colleagues teach courses on *Crime and Punishment, A Tale of Two Cities*, Dante's *Inferno*, the works of Ernest Hemingway or Gertrude Stein. No probability sample nor frequency distribution to cope with, each scholar looked at one text, the same text, but constructed its meaning differently and its probable impact.

Looking back, then, we can see the communication paradigm emerging in academic life at a certain time in this history, a period when other older disciplines were changing as well. Initially, most scholars were print-oriented with some interest in film and news photography. They stumbled through radio and were speculating about television before they had seen it. But the interdisciplinarity of communications gave it a special distinction and provided a new road map. World War II underwrote and stimulated major research. Some of this will become clearer when we turn next to a major concentration in the field: studies of the electoral process and public opinion polls.

II

When Walter Lippmann wrote *Public Opinion* in 1922, women in Britain, the United States, and Canada had just won the vote. It was a new and larger electorate. Women had been active in various peace movements, civic reform, and public health. They had campaigned hard to get the vote and were successful. Yet no one knew what the outcome would be. Or why.

Neoessentialists like Carol Gilligan (1982) think that gender creates its own political discourse so that there is no cognitive basis for consensus or a discourse between men and women, although for other reasons they might agree on the same candidate. Simone de Beauvoir, (1953) on the other hand, recognized gender differences but attributed them to the result of oppression reinforced by the patriarchal state. And still others—and I am one—saw the new female electorate being socialized into the male party system and its culture, occasionally turning to the judiciary for a redress of grievances (McCormack 1991).

Whichever explanation fits best, the results are not in dispute. Women were marginalized. And that was as true for women in left-wing parties as it was for the mainstream. Women in the Communist and Socialist parties, women who were often very well educated, remained quietly behind the scenes as a kind of half-hearted protest against the false claims of what Lenin (1913) called "bourgeois parliamentarianism."

It was a brilliant decision by Lazarsfeld and Katz to study consumption, recognizing the importance of women and opening the way to later studies of women as consumers.

This gendered reality was largely overlooked by the research community. The truth is that the early studies of behavioral politics showed more interest in the political socialization of children than in the adult female electorate (Greenstein 1965; Connell 1971; Hess and Torney 1967). It was a brilliant decision by Lazarsfeld and Katz to study consumption, recognizing the importance of women and opening the way to later studies of women as consumers who had their own charge accounts, women who became heads of departments in department stores, and, in their own right, opinion leaders. It was to the authors' credit that they did not use the image of "economic man" who was central to classical theories. Was this market research or was it a way of establishing priorities in a planned economy?

Lippmann, of course, was not the only writer who gave little or no attention to women voters. But he was the cutting edge in the transition from philosophy to social science. He was, I believe, the first to use the term "stereotypes" ("pictures in our heads") in connection with political knowledge. And it was Lippmann who recognized from the new knowledge in psychology and sociology that there was no such thing as "self-interest" because, as he said, we have several selves. How could we be governed by self-interest, he asked, if we had several selves? So, "while it is true," he said, "so true as to be mere tautology that self-interest determines opinion, the statement is not illuminating," he continued, "until we know which self out of many selects and directs the interest so conceived" (1922, 132). Lippmann's warning about oversimplifying self-interest is still valid and continues to be largely unheeded.

Lippmann also anticipated a problematic future. He sensed that the intellectual responsibilities carried on the voters' shoulders might become too heavy. Despite the growth of literacy and public education, the new citizen in this New Jerusalem might never acquire enough knowledge to act wisely (Delli Carpini 1996). It was not a problem of short range or long range, particulars or abstractions, but a deeper kind of cultural distortion. Lippmann saw the naive and well-intentioned voter gazing out at an increasingly complex world through the eyes of a provincial small-town citizen, a voter who, Lippmann said, "looked at a complicated civilization and saw an enclosed village." That village could have been Decatur, Illinois; Sandusky, Ohio; or Muncie, Indiana.

Cosmopolitans like Lippmann left a legacy of distinguishing between themselves and the hometown locals in which the latter lacked the sophistication to contribute wisely to Rousseau's *volonté générale*. The disparity between what we know and what we ought to know remains. It is one of those existential disparities in a complex social structure that applies to almost everyone and everything despite an education and well-intentioned efforts to close it. That said, what needs to be emphasized is that it was an article of faith in American society that voting was itself educational.

The public opinion poll was one of the extraordinary innovations of our research. The rapid development of polls and their improvement in terms of sampling, question construction, interviewing, and interpretation has been remarkable. Almost too good, for polls were also becoming reified, ends in themselves, and becoming, as things so often do in American life, commodities. Despite some of the failures of polls to predict electoral outcomes, these incidents were not catastrophic enough to discredit them completely. As Converse (1975) observed, no political candidate can entirely disregard the polls either. Often, they are used more for measuring trends than predicting outcomes.

Critics, on the other hand, Foucault in particular, regarded polls or any similar measuring device as part of a system of social control, one of the ways of "managing consensus," a strategy for manipulating the public and justifying the establishment. Others, like Habermas, recognized that polls were a two-edged sword; they could be part of a managerial function of the state but also part of a critical dialogue eventually transforming the state, making it more responsive and empowering citizens. But it was not either/or, not Foucault or Habermas. And that became clear in Noelle-Neuman's work on German voters (1984).

Noelle-Neuman (1984) attributed a different function for opinion polls. They were, she said, a standard that voters consulted not because they were undecided or unsure of themselves but because they wanted to be certain they were in the mainstream. Her typical voter is a person who deeply and unconsciously fears isolation. The regular publication of polls during an election campaign provides these alienated voters with a baseline against which they could measure themselves in relation to others and the extent of their own deviation from the norm. If it widens, the voter may drop out and not vote or may adjust his or her vote to the trend. Thus, the final election reflects a well-established and, in her opinion, a desirable consensus. Too much dissent, too much disparity, she claims, undermines a necessary cohesion of the modern state.

Noelle-Neuman was, as Splichal (1999) said, a midcentury functionalist; she was convincing to many despite very unconvincing evidence from American studies (Simpson 1996; Scheufele and May 2000; Glynn, Hayes, and Shanahan 1997; Taylor 1982; Mullen et al. 1984; Katz 1983).

But neither her admirers nor critics recognized the new reality in which the nation-state was losing its place in the new global economy. If globalization is carried to its logical conclusion, it will so drastically diminish the importance of national sovereignty that elections will become the program notes of the concert.

The voter of *Personal Influence* stood between Hamlet and Sisyphus: chronically undecided and destined never to get his stone to the top of the hill. In contrast, the voter of rational choice theory presents us with a strategic voter who thinks and behaves differently. Our new literature urges us to think of ourselves as one of the actors in "the prisoner's dilemma."

Rational choice theory is the convergence of three theoretical models: cognitive psychology (decision making), numbers theory (calculating the logical outcome), and self interest.

Rational choice theory is the convergence of three theoretical models: cognitive psychology (decision making), numbers theory (calculating the logical outcome), and self-interest. Neither Hamlet nor Sisyphus, the individual voter is a loner who evaluates each situation in terms of the best outcome without regard for the opinions of others or their material or social interests. This voter looks only at the possible consequences and is not driven by a political ideology or by motivation. An egocentric voter does not build on community discussions or the opinions of opinion leaders. Social policy is similarly impersonal. Its goal is to reduce the number of "free riders," for example, the unmarried mothers living on social assistance.

James Coleman (1990), influenced by Max Weber and Talcott Parsons, was one of the few sociologists urging us to think in terms of rational choice theory. If the starting point for sociology was the family, childhood, and socialization, it was now displaced by institutions—schools, government departments, business news, hospitals, and housing developments—or what Coleman called corporate units. "Opinion leaders" are banished to some outer ring. Coleman had confidence in think tanks where complex decisions could be formally debated and finally made by highly credentialed, invisible, and unelected elites. Public opinion in his opinion is of little consequence and may confuse the processes of genuinely rational decision making.

Rational choice theory is a radical change from sociology based on community, neighborhoods, social interaction, and gradualism. Its starting point is elsewhere, in the boardrooms of the corporate unit. It has made a significant contribution to studies of formal organization, offering scholars a more direct route to studies of administration as the key process in a developed modern society. Whether it is the taproot its followers believe remains to be seen, but if nothing else it has given legitimation to studies in formal organization. Herbert Simon (1997), one of its strongest advocates, calls this microeconomics, and it has more to do with the upwardly mobile middle managers than the rank-and-file employees whose career lines are relatively horizontal and relatively short. And it is remote from earlier theories of leadership based on biology or status succession. I do not want to dwell further on rational choice theory except to suggest that it is the theoretical shadow of a highly rationalized global economy. It is light years away from the humanism of *Personal Influence*, which was instrumental in the development of the nation-state and an economy moderated by compromise and social legislation.

In retrospect, I think we can see the extent to which *Personal Influence* and the research it both inspired and influenced was embedded in a different political economy, one that was based on sovereignty and a mixed economy, on the aspirations of liberal social democrats and their welfare state sometimes called market socialism.

In recent years, there has been a revival of studying small informal groups influenced largely by Habermas (1991), who in turn was influenced by the literature on coffee houses and similar gathering places of the eighteenth century. The modern public sphere, he pointed out, is an outgrowth of modern capitalism and can be manipulated by the mass media and popular culture in general. Nevertheless, there is the possibility of developing a new public sphere that is autonomous. Habermas is under no illusions about the resistance of the new public sphere, but he nevertheless regards it as a future hope.

Like many people, Habermas is enthusiastic that the new communications technology can offer significant progress. But for academics who have been studying communications, we have heard all this before. (FM radio was my introduction to this theme.) And in the end, it is the Katz-Lazarsfeld concept of the informal group that proves more resilient. *Personal Influence* remains a better model of participatory democracy than Habermas's floundering "public sphere" or the NGOs.

Neither Katz nor Lazarsfeld had been a journalist, although at a later time Katz spent some time with the British Broadcasting Corporation; both had come up through the ranks of academe and academic sociology. They were interested in social capital of the citizen and brought to their work insights about how ordinary people in small communities go about the business of making micro and macro decisions. These decisions could come from the heart or from guilt and a variety of other motives, but the process was different from that described by rational choice theorists. Amartya Sen (1982), an economist whose focus has been on development, inequality, and poverty, has a word for these rational choice economists: "Rational Fools." Middle America of *Personal Influence* moved on a different track, more Main Street than Wall Street.

Personal Influence turned a spotlight on the social psychology of small groups and their empowerment, looking at a frangible process that moved erratically toward a resolution. There was no "selfish gene" driving us; rather, it showed us turning to friends, family, and neighbors for practical advice on how to vote, buy winter clothes, discipline children; where to vacation; how to give and receive medical advice. The subjects of *Personal Influence* were very practical and pragmatic folk who were confident about the direction they were going and rarely questioned the larger system or beyond it. And although our economy has changed toward a more privatized and competitive one, a new economy that takes pride in its ability to move information at incredible speed, the earlier Keynesian economy of the 1950s remains part of our heritage—and nowhere more than in academia, where despite the hierarchical structure of administration there is an informal alternate culture of communitarianism.

As long as we have an open society, we will have elections; and as long as we have elections, we will have polls; but neither may be as important in the long run as the larger international power structure. Nevertheless, elections are rituals. And polls function in them in a more dramaturgical way like the Chorus in Greek drama, sustaining our interest in the plot, building suspense, hinting about the outcome, and predicting everything and nothing. I share Dayan and Katz's (1992) thesis that we are moving toward the study of events—the wedding of Charles and Diana, the visit of Sadat to Israel, and other similar events that elicit the attention of the entire nation, if not the Western world. They are events that engage the public's attention beyond the level of politics as usual, and, eventually, they become part of a system of markers that are internalized to become part of our collective memory.

Fifty years from now, scholars will still be reading *Personal Influence,* not as a study of persuasion or influence nor as a way of confirming or disconfirming an hypothesis; not to clarify variables and develop scales nor to look at frequency distributions and chi-squares, all of which have served us well; but rather as a study in social philosophy—a way of exploring the human condition.

References

Adams, Barry D. 1993. Post Marxism and the new social movements. *Canadian Review of Sociology and Anthropology* 30:316-36.

Adorno, T. W., E. Frenkel-Brunswick, D. J. Levinson, and R. N. Sanford. 1950. *The authoritarian personality.* New York: Harper.

Albert, Edward. 1982. The audience that "knows" the speech, "discovers" it. In *Studies in communications*, vol. 2, *Culture, code and content analysis*, ed. Thelma McCormack, 91-110. Greenwich, CT: JAI.

Benjamin, Walter. 1968. The work of art in the age of mechanical reproduction. In *Illuminations*, 217-51. New York: Harcourt Brace & World.

Bourdieu, Pierre. 1972. Public opinion does not exist. In *Communication and class struggle*, vol. 1, *Capitalism, imperialism*, ed. Armand Mattelart and Seth Sieglaub, 124-30. New York: International General.

Coleman, James S. 1990. *Foundations of social theory*. Cambridge, MA: Belknap Press.

Connell, R. W. 1971. *The child's construction of politics*. Melbourne, Australia: Melbourne University Press.

Converse, Philip E. 1975. Public opinion and voting behavior. Non governmental politics. In *Handbook of Political Science*, vol. 4, ed. Fred I. Greenstein and Nelson W. Polsby, 75-169. Reading, MA: Addison-Wesley.

Dayan, Daniel, and Elihu Katz. 1992. *Media events: The live broadcasting of history*. Cambridge, MA: Harvard University Press.

de Beauvoir, Simone. 1953. *The second sex*. Translated by H. M. Parshley. New York: Knopf.

Delli Carpini, Michael X. 1996. *What Americans know about politics and why it matters*. New Haven, CT: Yale University Press.

Dewey, John. 1922. *Human nature and conduct*. New York: Carleton House.

Dorfman, Ariel. 1984. *How to read Donald Duck: Imperialist ideology in the Disney comic*. New York: International General.

Festinger, Leon, Henry W. Ricker, and Stanley Schachter. 1956. *When prophecy fails*. New York: Harper.

Fromm, Eric. 1941. *Escape from freedom*. New York: Farrar & Rinehart.

Gilligan, Carol. 1982. *In a different voice*. Cambridge, MA: Harvard University Press.

Gitlin, Todd. 1980. *The whole world is watching*. Berkeley: University of California Press.

Glasgow University Media Group. 1976. *Bad news*. London: Routledge & Kegan Paul.

Glynn, Carroll J., Andrew F. Hayes, and James Shanahan. 1997. Perceived support for one's opinions and willingness to speak out. A meta-analysis of survey studies on *The spiral of silence. Public Opinion Quarterly* 61:452-63.

Greenstein, Fred I. 1965. *Children and politics*. New Haven, CT: Yale University Press.

Gusfield, Joseph R. 1994. The reflexivity of social movements, collective behavior and mass society theory revisited. In *New social movements from ideology to identity*, ed. Enrique Larana, Hank Johnston, and Joseph R. Gusfield. Philadelphia: Temple University Press.

Habermas, Jürgen. 1991. *The structural transformation of the public sphere. An inquiry into a category of bourgeois society*. Cambridge, MA: MIT Press.

Handler, Joel F. 1992. Postmodernism, protest and the new social movements. *Law and Society Review* 26 (4): 697-735.

Herman, Edward S., and Noam Chomsky 1988. *Manufacturing consent*. New York: Pantheon.

Hess, Robert D., and Judith Torney. 1967. *The development of political attitudes in children*. Chicago: Aldine.

Hewitt, John P. 1982. Symbolic interactionism and the study of communication. In *Studies in communications*, vol. 2, *Culture, code and content analysis*, ed. Thelma McCormack, 1-37. Greenwich, CT: JAI.

Katz, Elihu. 1983. Publicity and pluralistic ignorance. Notes on *The spiral of silence. Mass Communication Review Yearbook*, Vol 4, pp. 89-99.

Knoke, David, and Nancy Wisely. 1990. Social movements. In *Political networks: The structural perspectives*, 57-84. Cambridge: Cambridge University Press.

Kracauer, Siegfried. 1947. *From Caligari to Hitler. A psychological history of the German film*. New York: Noonday Press.

Kuhn, Thomas S. 1962. *The structure of scientific revolutions*. Chicago: University of Chicago.

Lazarsfeld, Paul F., and Elihu Katz. 1955. *Personal influence*. New York: Free Press.

Lenin, V. I. 1913. *National culture*. Vol. 20 of *V. I. Lenin Collected Works*. Moscow: Progress Publishers.

Lerner, Daniel. 1958. *The passing of traditional society*. Glencoe, IL: Free Press.

Lippmann, Walter. 1922. *Public opinion*. New York: Penguin.

Mannheim, Karl. 1936. *Ideology and utopia: An introduction to the sociology of knowledge*. New York: Harcourt, Brace & World.

Maslow, Abraham H. 1968. *Toward a psychology of being.* New York: Van Nostrand.

McCormack, Thelma. 1964. Innocent eye on mass society. *Canadian Literature* 22 (autumn): 55-60. (Reprint, in Raymond Rosenthal, ed., *McLuhan: Pro and con*, New York: Funk and Wagnals, 1968)

———. 1981. Revolution, communication and the sense of history. In *Mass media and social change*, ed. Elihu Katz and Tamas Szecsk. Beverly Hills, CA: Sage.

———. 1991. *Politics and the hidden injuries of gender. Feminism and the welfare state.* Ottawa: Canadian Research Institute for the Advancement of Women.

Mullen, Brian, Jennifer L. Atkins, Debbie S. Champion, Cecelia Edwards, Dan Hardy, John E. Story, and Mary Vanderklok. 1984. The false consensus effect: A meta-analysis on 115 hypotheses tests. *Journal of Experimental Social Psychology* 21:262-83.

Noelle-Neuman, Elisabeth. 1984. *The spiral of silence.* Chicago: University of Chicago Press.

Polany, Karl. 1944. *The great transformation.* New York: Farrar & Rinehart.

Scheufele, Dietram A., and Patricia May. 2000. Twenty-five years of *The spiral of silence:* A conceptual review and empirical outlook. *International Journal of Public Opinion Research* 12 (1): 3-28.

Sen, Amartya. 1982. Rational fools: A critique of the behavioural foundation of economic theory. In *Choice, welfare and measurement*, 84-106. Oxford: Basil Blackwell.

Simon, Herbert A. 1997. *An empirically based microeconomics.* Cambridge: Cambridge University Press.

Simpson, Christopher. 1996. Elisabeth Noelle-Neuman "Spiral of silence" and the historical context of communication theory. *Journal of Communication* 46 (3): 149-75.

Splichal, Slavko. 1999. *Public opinion.* Lanham, MD: Rowman & Littlefield.

Stouffer, Samuel A. 1955. *Communism, conformity and civil liberties.* New York: John Wiley.

Taylor, D. Garth. 1982. Pluralistic ignorance and the spiral of silence: A formal analysis. *Public Opinion Quarterly* 46:311-35.

The Troubling Equivalence of Citizen and Consumer

By
MICHAEL SCHUDSON

As Todd Gitlin observed in his 1978 critique of *Personal Influence*, Elihu Katz and Paul Lazarsfeld (1955) in that work treated consumer choices and political choices at the voting booth as methodologically equivalent. Many critics since have identified this purported equivalence as a flaw in American social science that reduces politics to consumer behavior. But is it a flaw? This article contends that consumer choices can be and have often been political; that political choices can be and often have been consumer-like; and that the distinction between citizen and consumer, intended to uphold the superiority of the citizen's role, in fact may itself be damaging to public life. It calls for a reconsideration of what the differences between the worlds of politics and consumption really are.

Keywords: citizen; consumer; choice; boycott

A feature of *Personal Influence* that has troubled readers, at least since Todd Gitlin's blistering critique in 1978, is that Elihu Katz and Paul Lazarsfeld (1955) treated their research subjects' choices of consumer products, movies, fashions, and political candidates equivalently. They were writing their book just as Adlai Stevenson was complaining that the effort to merchandise presidential candidates like cornflakes was "the ultimate indignity to the democratic process" (Westbrook 1983, 156). This has been a theme in cultural criticism ever since, that there is something sacred about civic or political life in a democratic society that should not be sullied by confusion with or treatment as consumerism. Marketers may romanticize consumers, but social critics are

Michael Schudson is a professor of communication and an adjunct professor of sociology at the University of California, San Diego. He is the author of six books and many articles concerning the history and sociology of the American news media, advertising, cultural memory, and civic and political participation. Recent works include The Good Citizen: A History of American Civic Life *(Free Press, 1998) and* The Sociology of News *(Norton, 2003).*

DOI: 10.1177/0002716206291967

unlikely to. The consumer, in fact, is as inauthentic and as "manufactured" as the products the corporations are selling them. "In a simpler time," Christopher Lasch (1978, 72) wrote, "advertising merely called attention to the product and extolled its advantages. Now it manufactures a product of its own: the consumer, perpetually unsatisfied, restless, anxious, and bored."

Gitlin (1978) identified in *Personal Influence* an assumption of "the commensurability of buying and politics" (p. 215). For him, this "blithe assumption" was "never explicitly justified, never opened up to question," and it "hung over the entire argument of *Personal Influence* like an ideological smog" (p. 215). As Gitlin observed, Lazarsfeld himself recalled that as a young socialist in Austria, he had noticed "the methodological equivalence of socialist voting and the buying of soap" (p. 241). The question that brought Lazarsfeld to social science was, in fact, the problem of why the socialists were not winning converts or, as he put it, "why our propaganda was unsuccessful" (p. 242).

Gitlin (1978) acknowledged the factual basis for Lazarsfeld's recognition of an affinity between casting votes in a democratic election and buying soap at the supermarket—in each case, it is possible for the individual who chooses to be "both sovereign and passive." But for Gitlin, this is not something that a democrat should accept without comment. He added an important sentence: "When the consumers choose, they confirm the legitimacy of the suppliers" (p. 243); and this is true whether they are implicitly affirming the values of consumer capitalism by buying soap or implicitly affirming the values of mass democracy by voting. What the consumer and the voter tacitly confirm is just what Gitlin wants to deny—that "choice among the givens amounts to freedom." In both cases, there may be only an illusion of freedom. Does choice among gas-guzzling cars repress the possibility of mass transportation? Is the choice among car models then really a "free" choice? Does electoral choice between Tweedle-Dum and Tweedle-Dee negate the possibility that more worthy alternatives have been excluded?

Elections, like markets, limit choices. In a way, this is precisely the purpose of elections. Early modern political theorists took for granted, themselves borrowing directly from Aristotle, that elections are a quintessential institution of oligarchies or aristocracies, not democracies. The way to select leaders in a full-bodied democracy is to do what the Athenians did, at least for some offices—select officeholders by lot. Citizens do not choose, but any citizen has an equal chance to be chosen. Elections are not as democratic as this. Montesquieu wrote, "Selection by lot is in the nature of democracy, selection by choice is in the nature of aristocracy." When James Harrington complained that the Athenian senate was chosen by lot rather than by election, his objection was that a "natural aristocracy" could not be returned to office or sit long enough to understand the problems of government. Harrington expected—as did James Madison and the other American founders—that with elections people would invariably choose representatives better than themselves (Manin 1997, 27, 67, 70).

Ironically, Gitlin's critique may be stronger than he intended: the passive sovereignty of most consumers most of the time is matched by the passive sovereignty of most voters most of the time. The commensurability of buying and voting is less a philosophical presupposition of Katz and Lazarsfeld than an empirical generalization.

And then there is another irony: once Katz and Lazarsfeld (1955) got into the empirical details, they found that political attitude change operates differently from changes in consumer choices. When the eight hundred Decatur, Illinois, women the *Personal Influence* team studied looked to other people for advice on fashion, movies, or consumer goods, they overwhelmingly turned to other women. However, when these same women turned to other people for advice on public affairs, they overwhelmingly turned to men. With public affairs more than marketing or fashion, Katz and Lazarsfeld reported, women "are free to decide whether or not they will participate or even take an interest. Without endangering their self-respect or the respect of others, women can, to a greater extent than men, get through life without participating in, or having opinions about, public affairs" (p. 270). Women more than men, they found, express ignorance about current events, talk less about them, and claim less interest in politics. By the way, this remains true today, and there is a political science literature that tries to understand why (Burns, Schlozman, and Verba 2001; Pew Research Center 2004).[1]

With public affairs opinion change, in contrast to consumer preference changes, fewer women designated specific individuals who influenced their changed opinion. There were therefore less data for Katz and Lazarsfeld (1955) to follow up. Even so, what they found suggested to them the following:

- In public affairs, women were more likely to be influenced by men than in the other domains; the influence came primarily from men inside the family, husbands for married women and fathers for unmarried women (p. 276).
- In the relatively few cases where public affairs influencing took place outside the family, a smaller percentage of influentials for the women were of the same status as the women than in marketing and fashions—46 percent compared to 60 and 57 percent, respectively. In this area only, Katz and Lazarsfeld wrote, "Upper-status people become accessible to people lower down in status. Activities such as electioneering, health and community welfare campaigns, civic and political concerns, and the like immediately come to mind as examples of how such cross-status contact might take place" (p. 278). Of course, it could be said just as accurately that this is the area where lower-status people become accessible to upper-status people.
- When women were asked to name someone in the area of public affairs they turned to for advice, 67 percent selected a male. When the authors followed up with the "experts," so identified to find out whom they went to for public affairs advice, 95 percent of the men named other men while only 52 percent of the women named males as the expert they consulted. And in yet a further wave of follow-up, when the experts' experts were asked who they sought out for public affairs advice, again 95 percent of the men named other men, while only 49 percent of the women named men (pp. 282-83).
- The public affairs opinion leader's place in the life cycle mattered less than it does for marketing and fashion, but the social status mattered relatively more, flowing from higher-status to lower-status people, with gregariousness mattering more than status does and "seem[ing] to be the major key to leadership in public affairs" (p. 295).

Katz and Lazarsfeld (1955) also sought to confirm from the named conversational partner that that person acknowledged having a conversation with the person who designated him or her. If the contact was confirmed, they also tried to ascertain if the conversational partner acknowledged the direction of influence (from him or her to the other person), reported that it was the other way around, or could not confirm the direction of influence. What they found was that there were notably fewer confirmations in the area of public affairs than in the other areas. With consumer goods, they got 70 percent confirmation of the contact from "influencees," with fashion 67 percent, but with public affairs only 50 percent. With "influentials," there was 76 percent confirmation in marketing, 69 percent in fashion, and 59 percent in public affairs (p. 159).

Why should this be? Katz and Lazarsfeld (1955) speculated that "men may be unwilling to admit having been influenced by a woman; or they may even fail to acknowledge talking to a woman about public affairs because they do not feel that such conversations with women are serious enough to warrant the status of two-way 'discussion' " (p. 160). Probably more important than male chauvinism, however, they suggested, is "the simple fact that politics is a touchier matter about which to question. . . . It is easier to confirm personal influence for a new brand of peaches than what someone said to you about Communists" (p. 160). And then they added another possibility: "Influencing a marketing change may more often take place during a single contact than influencing a change in political attitude. One may be a much more discrete, and recollectable, incident than the other" (p. 160). I find this last possibility particularly striking since it is a strong suggestion that buying and voting are not commensurable choices, that the process of decision making about politics is qualitatively, not just quantitatively, different from consumer choices.

It is hard not to be impressed with the authors' attentiveness to their data. They looked at it. They looked at it again. They turned it around in their heads and looked at it from another angle. They separated conclusions from speculations, but that did not keep them from speculating. Unless I am mistaken, they were having a good time speculating.

What Is the Difference between Political Choices and Consumer Choices?

There is an old joke about the couple celebrating their fiftieth wedding anniversary and their friends ask them, how do you do it? How have you kept up this loving relationship for so long? And the wife replies, "I think it really has to do with the division of labor we worked out. I took care of the little things, like where to send the kids to school or who to have over for dinner and what to serve them, or when to replace the furnace, those sorts of things, and John attended to the big problems, like whether to admit Red China to the UN."

The joke plays on the very contrast I have been talking about, but, of course, it puts it in a different light. The wife in this case deals with matters over which her expertise and her attention make a real difference, while the husband handles opinions pretty much for their own sake, not because he has any passion for the issue at hand or expects to make one whit of difference in what national policy will be. Her job is to run the household and his is to have political opinions. In fact, the joke suggests, this exhausts his obligation. As Lazarsfeld and Merton wrote in their celebrated 1948 paper on "Mass Communication, Popular Taste, and Organized Social Action," "The interested and informed citizen can congratulate himself on his lofty state of interest and information and neglect to see that he has abstained from decision and action . . . he has all sorts of ideas as to what should be done. But, after he has gotten through his dinner and after he has listened to his favored radio programs and after he has read his second newspaper of the day, it is really time for bed" (p. 106).

In contrast to this old joke, the more common rhetorical use of the contrast between citizen and consumer elevates the citizen and puts down the consumer. Take the concluding discussion of Elizabeth Cohen (2003) in *A Consumers' Republic:* "As much as I might prefer a public sphere inhabited by voting citizens rather than demanding consumers, by public-spirited taxpayers rather than self-interested tax cutters, and by communities committed to cooperation rather than wrapped in isolated localism or destructive competition, I fear that such an alternative hopelessly resides in an unregainable past—if it ever existed at all" (p. 409). There you have it—citizens vote, consumers demand; citizens are public-spirited and consumers are self-interested; citizens inhabit cooperative communities and consumers live in isolated locales.

The usual contrast suggests a pathological interplay between consumer desire and political obligation, the former displacing the latter like bad money driving out good or tabloid television drowning out "The Newshour with Jim Lehrer." You can see the contrast in John Dewey's *The Public and Its Problems* in 1927:

> Man is a consuming and sportive animal as well as a political one . . . the movie, radio, cheap reading matter and motor car with all they stand for have come to stay. That they did not originate in deliberate desire to divert attention from political interests does not lessen their effectiveness in that direction. The political elements in the constitution of the human being, those having to do with citizenship, are crowded to one side. In most circles it is hard work to sustain conversation on a political theme; and once initiated, it is quickly dismissed with a yawn. Let there be introduced the topic of the mechanism and accomplishment of various makes of motor cars or the respective merits of actresses, and the dialogue goes on at a lively pace. (p. 139)

But there are reasons to believe that the contrast between consumer and citizen is neither as flattering to political choice nor as favorable to a strong civic life as those who uphold the distinction imagine. There are three reasons to complicate the consumer/citizen contrast. First, sometimes consumer choice is political in even the most elevated understandings of the term. Second, sometimes political choices are—and have long been—complex matters of family, ethnic, and religious tradition, emotional links to one brand rather than another, based on limited information and limited experience, and expected by the individual to have limited personal impact, not unlike a great many consumer decisions. Third, the elevation of politics to the realm of the highly intellectualized, highly instrumentalized, and highly public-regarding does not encourage political participation and may not even increase the quality of reasoning in voting or the intensity of political commitment and action of voters. The contrast between citizen and consumer stands not outside our civic life but is a constitutive element of it. On the whole, I think it may have made it marginally more difficult for ordinary people to become politically engaged and it certainly has made it more difficult for journalists, critics, and scholars to understand everyday political life.

> *[T]here are reasons to believe that the contrast between consumer and citizen is neither as flattering to political choice nor as favorable to a strong civic life as those who uphold the distinction imagine.*

Consumer Choice Can Be Political

This is the easiest point to make. If you have ever boycotted grapes to support the United Farm Workers union or decided to drive a hybrid car to help conserve the earth's resources, if you have ever "bought green" or paid extra to purchase "fair trade" coffee, you know perfectly well that consumer decisions can be directly political. Sometimes these individual choices at the point of purchase are planned ahead and direct you to some stores rather than others; patronage at these stores—the health foods store, for instance—may lead you to informal associations that are not as random or nonpolitical as those you would have at the neighborhood market.

To add some symbolic weight to this point, the historian T. H. Breen (2004) has argued that consumer choice was a critical element in the American Revolution. Without going into his whole argument, his general point is that the issues of political theory that agitated some of the colonial leaders did not agitate anybody else. A revolution could not be mounted unless it had some popular support, and what brought along that popular support was the experience of ordinary people in joining up in the nonimportation movement that began with the Stamp Act in 1765. In the nonimportation effort, citizens would sign their names to a publicly circulated and posted list testifying to their commitment not to purchase consumer goods imported from Britain. By 1773, "the experience of being a consumer in Britain's great empire of goods provided a powerful link between everyday life and political mobilization" (p. 19). This public affirmation of commitment to a boycott of British goods was conceived at a Boston town meeting on October 28, 1767, and brought ordinary people, women as well as men, into the public realm as never before. By the time of the Boston Tea Party, British goods had "invited colonists to think radical new thoughts about empire. British manufactures came to symbolize dependence and repression" (p. 299). What the American colonists learned in the 1760s, Mahatma Gandhi would reinvent as the central tactic of the Indian independence movement in the 1920s and 1930s.

Political Choices Can Be Consumer-Like

This is also a fairly obvious point. Voters are not simply or mechanically pocketbook voters, but "it's the economy, stupid" is a plausible first approximation of voters' moods and preferences. Voters often look at candidates in terms of what benefits in the way of social programs or punishments in the way of taxes the candidate will be likely to inflict on the individual and his or her family. This is a kind of price comparison shopping. Voters are also very much influenced by past experience with a candidate, as they are with past experience with a product, and voting is often what political scientists call "retrospective" voting, a judgment on how the incumbent has done in office. If voters are faced with an open seat where two or more candidates vie for a position where there is no incumbent in the race, party label—the closest politics offers to a brand name—may weigh very heavily.

Critics have complained for a century about Americans' lack of passion for politics. John Dewey found it all but impossible to get a discussion going on political topics in the 1920s, and Robert Dahl wrote in 1961 that "food, sex, love, family, work, play, shelter, comfort, friendship, social esteem, and the like" and "not politics" are "the primary concerns of most men and women." (p. 279). As I have observed before, every one of the areas Dahl mentioned has in the past forty years been politicized, including self-esteem, notably with the California Task Force to Promote Self-Esteem and Social Responsibility published by the state's Department of Education in 1990. But concern about laws, regulation, and litigation about matters like schoolyard bullying is now a part of local politics across the country. This is not so much a drive of bureaucrats to become national nannies— I suspect this is the last thing bureaucrats desire. It is a response to what voters feel passionate about. And as with the citizens of Boston who did not read Montesquieu but did drink tea, matters close to home for reasons close to home bring people into the political arena.

This is not the same thing as saying that voters are self-interested. It is to say that self-interest is motivating and mobilizing. It can be educative. It can be transforming. You may wind up leading an effort to change school policy about bullying after your own child has been traumatized on the playground, even after that child has graduated, so that other children are not harmed in the same way. It is highly unlikely that reading the California report on self-esteem would have led you down the same path.

Curiously, liberal critics of consumer culture, though disparaging of consumer behavior, are often inclined to wish voters acted more like consumers, not less.

I have in mind American liberals who believe that if only the broad middle class and working-class voters knew what was good for them economically, they would realize that Republican promises of lower taxes and smaller government would be financially harmful to them. Yes, they would save a few hundred dollars in taxes, but the public schools they depended on would have fewer teachers, the school nurse and the art program would be let go, and parents would have to pay for the bus service for the field trip or there would be no field trip. There would be charges for garbage collection that government once provided free. Bus fares would increase and the frequency of buses would decline. The lines at the Social Security office or the Motor Vehicles Department would be longer because the number of employees would be reduced. Public library hours would be cut, book purchases would drop, and the city or county's recreation centers and pools would be closed or their hours reduced. After-school care or before-school care that made life more economically and socially possible for working parents would close. Why, the liberals wonder, can people not read the bookkeeping on the wall and vote their pocketbooks—for the Democrats?

Making political choice less consumer-like is a task democracies undertake at their peril.

The Citizen/Consumer Distinction May Itself Be Damaging to Public Life

Making political choice less consumer-like is a task democracies undertake at their peril. I make this claim with a glance back to the Progressive Era political reforms that took place between 1890 and 1920. Reformers of that day were not crusading against consumerism but against a mindlessness or thoughtlessness in political life that was controlled and exploited by political parties for their own ends. American political life in the late nineteenth century was more participatory and more enthusiastic than at any other point in our history, with election turnouts routinely in the 70 to 80 percent range. Vast numbers of people participated in election campaigns in torchlight processions, brass band concerts, parades, picnics, pole raisings, and other activities that shocked visitors to our shores. When Jules Verne's fictional hero, Phileas Fogg, arrives in San Francisco, he is literally swept up in an election rally, a rally that turns into a brawl. Barely escaping, Fogg later asks someone what all the commotion was about. Just a political meeting, he is told. For "the election of a general-in-chief, no doubt?" Fogg asked. "No, sir; of a justice of the peace," was the reply (Verne 1962, 180).

This is just what the Progressives sought to phase out. They wanted electoral campaigns focused on issues, not on the military-like recruitment of long-standing partisans. They urged secret ballots, rather than the standard public distribution of party tickets at the polls for voters to place in the ballot box in return for a convivial reward at the party's favorite saloon thereafter. They fought for primary elections to remove from party hacks the power to choose candidates. They sponsored laws for initiatives and referenda to place complex legislative matters directly before the voters, providing a new check on the power of party-controlled legislatures from doing whatever they pleased. What they accomplished with these reforms was to reduce voter turnout from more than 70 percent in the 1880s and 1890s to less than 50 percent by the 1920s. This sharp decline was no doubt a product of many forces, but these included what we might think of as the de-branding or unbranding of politicians, forcing individual voters to read the package ingredients rather than just the party logo on the package. The reformers pressed individuals to rely on information and not on personal influence and social pressure. They protected the individual conscience at the expense of separating the act of voting from the fraternity it had once expressed.

All of these reforms offered American politics a kind of Protestant Reformation, removing the idols and the incense from the political church; offering a politics cleansed of the souvenirs, the sensuous experience, and the small everyday rewards that once enhanced political life. No more election day hooliganism, or at least a lot less; no more festivity, no more emotionalism and soccer-team-style loyalties. The new voter should be motivated by ideas and ideals and information, not by social pressure or the social pleasure of a free drink and an extra dollar in the pocket (Schudson 1998, 144-87).

There is an alternative reading of this Progressive Era reformation. Michael McGerr's (1986) excellent history emphasized that the new information-centered era, having swept aside the participatory emotionalism of nineteenth-century party politics, led quickly from the "educational politics" the reformers had sought to what he called an "advertised politics." In advertised politics or "merchandising" politics, as historian Richard Jensen (1969) put it, campaigning centered increasingly on promoting the image of the candidate as a personality rather than the issues of the party as public policy. I agree, but I do not agree with McGerr's implication, as in Robert Westbrook's (1983) earlier essay, that the new politics was a diminished and morally inferior politics. It is important to keep in mind what the contrasting politics was like. Jensen contrasted "merchandising" politics with "military" politics. McGerr contrasted "advertised" politics with "enthusiastic" politics. The reformers of the day self-servingly, but not without cause, contrasted honest politics with corruption. The nineteenth-century politics that was being supplanted was one of emotional, partisan manipulation and mobilization that had more to do with feelings of fellowship and teamwork and rivalry, and the good feeling engendered by alcohol, than it did with considerations of policy or the public good. The new politics may have led to superficiality in presenting candidates to the public and may have been the avenue that would one day lead high-minded leaders to complain of being marketed like breakfast cereal, but the old politics was no closer to the sort of "rational-critical" public discussion that political philosophers like to think is the heart of democracy (see also Marvin and Simonson 2004).

Conclusion

Is there a way to take politics seriously without making political interest severe? Is there a way to identify the distinctive value of public affairs without dismissing or demeaning the ordinary experience of private life, including the life of consuming? One of the virtues of a liberal society is, presumably, that private life is indeed private. In an age of e-mail, it is worth recalling that one of the great advantages of the postal system in the new American nation, in contrast to the French and the British, is that it was the exception and not the rule that government officials would open and read letters entrusted to the postal service (John 1995, 42-44). Is there a way to recognize that the high political theory and publicly legitimated political knowledge used to draw in very narrowly the circle of the politically adept now confront a politics broadened and loosened in ways that are, I think, largely to the good? That people are "doing politics" not only when they vote but when they choose in which hotel or which state to hold the annual meeting of their trade union or professional association, when they come out to their family or friends or workmates, when they buy a ticket to a benefit concert or donate their frequent flyer miles to tsunami relief organizations, when they urge their church leaders to go on record against any judge who might uphold *Roe v. Wade?* When they sue for admission to the University of Michigan because affirmative action policies have discriminated against them on the grounds of the color of their skin?

[W]e will not enhance the value of public affairs by positing the moral weakness of consuming.

Political choices and consumer choices are not just the same. But I find the commensurability between consumer and political choices that Katz and Lazarsfeld (1955) posited more of an enduring provocation than a fault in their study. I still do not know exactly where or how to draw the line. My conclusion at this point, and I know it is a boring one, is only that we will not enhance the value of public affairs by positing the moral weakness of consuming. Better, I think, to find strategic opportunity in consuming to enlarge the points of entry to political life and to underline the political dimensions of our world with cases in point. I would love to see someone write, for instance, about the politics of the morning bathroom ritual—what political choices and public investments have been required for there to be clean running water in sink and shower and toilet? What regulation of the licensing of plumbers, of housing inspections, of water filtration, of waste disposal, of fluoridation, of the ingredient labeling on the toothpaste or the trustworthiness of the claims on the shampoo that no animals were used in testing—not to mention that the bathroom light turned on reliably when you walked into the bathroom this morning in the first place? In a day when even Democrats will not talk about raising taxes, is this in part because the infrastructure of our everyday consumer and private lives that government provides has become invisible to us? There are ways for the consumer and the citizen in each of us to meet.

I have been trying to wrestle with this problem since 1981 when I wrote an essay critical of the very thinkers who had drawn me to the study of consumption in the first place—Vance Packard and John Kenneth Galbraith, popular and very smart critics of consumer society (Schudson 1981). Years later, having written a book on how the advertising industry works, I wrote a more sophisticated critique of a wider range of popular and academic views of what is wrong with consumer culture and found the various views inconsistent with one another, often not quite honest with themselves, and unsatisfying in their efforts to judge consumption an unworthy feature of human behavior (Schudson 1984, 1999).

Still, I have not yet nailed what troubles me about the elevation of "the citizen" over "the consumer," apart from the tone of piety that often accompanies it. Even so, as Ruth Katz remarked to me at the conference where this paper was presented, "If there isn't a distinction between citizens and consumers, there should be!" Indeed, there should be. One should have to step *up* to the political stage and be a little better than oneself, whereas in consuming it is normally enough to be oneself and not step on the toes of others. It is not that in consuming one looks out only for oneself—so much of consuming, done so often by wives and mothers, is for others, not for oneself. It is only that in the ordinary act of consuming, the circle of people one thinks about tends to be small; in the ordinary act of politics, the circle of people one *should* be thinking about should extend to the boundary of whatever polity one is acting in—if not further! Consuming feels good not only because it may provide material pleasures but because it is enacted largely within a comfortable social circle (which is not to say that it does not arouse anxieties about how one's house, car, dinner party, or gift will be received by others). Politics feels tense and dangerous, even under relatively peaceful circumstances, because it is performed in the midst of and because of significant conflict with others (which is not to say that there are no pleasures in displaying one's great good sense or great good heart or oratorical powers in the political arena). But just what the most salient differences are between the world of politics and the world of consumption seems to me far from obvious and, in an age of environmentalism, consumer boycotts, and political regulation of the safety of cars and toys and pajamas, ripe for reconsideration.

Note

1. See Burns, Schlozman, and Verba (2001). Young women are the population group least likely to say that "keeping up with the news" is important to them. While 47 percent of men in a 2004 Pew Research Center poll regularly attend to newspapers, only 37 percent of women do so; 33 percent of men regularly get news online, 25 percent of women. Women outpoll men only when it comes to local TV news, nightly network news, network news magazines, and TV morning news shows. See Pew Research Center (2004, 15).

References

Breen, T. H. 2004. *The marketplace of revolution: How consumer politics shaped American independence*. New York: Oxford University Press.

Burns, Nancy, Kay Lehman Schlozman, and Sidney Verba. 2001. *The private roots of public action: Gender, equality, and political participation*. Cambridge, MA: Harvard University Press.

Cohen, Elizabeth. 2003. *A consumer's republic: The politics of mass consumption in postwar America*. New York: Knopf.

Dahl, Robert. 1961. *Who governs?* New Haven, CT: Yale University Press.

Dewey, John. 1927. *The public and its problems*. New York: Henry Holt.

Gitlin, Todd. 1978. Media sociology: The dominant paradigm. *Theory and Society* 6:205-53.

Jensen, Richard. 1969. Armies, admen, and crusaders: Types of presidential election campaigns. *History Teacher* 2:33-50.

John, Richard. 1995. *Spreading the news*. Cambridge, MA: Harvard University Press.

Katz, Elihu, and Paul Lazarsfeld. 1955. *Personal influence*. New York: Free Press.

Lasch, Christopher. 1978. *The culture of narcissism*. New York: Norton.

Lazarsfeld, Paul F., and Robert K. Merton. 1948/2004. Mass communication, popular taste, and organized social action. Reprinted in *Mass communication and American social thought: Key texts 1919-1968*, ed. John Durham Peters and Peter Simonson. Lanham, MD: Rowman & Littlefield.

Manin, Bernard. 1997. *The principles of representative government*. Cambridge: Cambridge University Press.

Marvin, Carolyn, and Peter Simonson. 2004. Voting alone: The decline of bodily mass communication and public sensationalism in presidential elections. *Communication and Critical/Cultural Studies* 1:127-50.

McGerr, Michael. 1986. *The decline of popular politics*. New York: Oxford University Press.

Pew Research Center for the People and the Press. 2004. Online News Audience Larger, More Diverse: News Audiences Increasingly Politicized. *Pew Research Center Biennial News Consumption Survey*. June 8. Washington, DC: Pew Research Center for the People and the Press.

Schudson, Michael. 1981. Criticizing the critics of advertising. *Media, Culture and Society* 3:3-12.

———. 1984. *Advertising, the uneasy persuasion*. New York: Basic Books.

———. 1998. *The good citizen: A history of American civic life*. New York: Free Press.

———. 1999. Delectable materialism: Second thoughts on consumer culture. In *Consumer society in American history: A reader*, ed. Lawrence Glickman. Ithaca, NY: Cornell University Press.

Verne, Jules. 1962. *Around the world in 80 days*. New York: Heritage Press.

Westbrook, Robert B. 1983. Politics as consumption: Managing the modern American election. In *The culture of consumption: Critical essays in American history, 1880-1980*, ed. Richard Wightman Fox and T. J. Jackson Lears. New York: Pantheon.

This article analyzes the relationship between citizenship and consumption posited by the Decatur Study and developed in the influential book *Personal Influence* by Katz and Lazarsfeld. It shows that they understood a close relationship between the two. It also contrasts the Katz/Lazarsfeld understanding of the relationship between citizenship and consumption with that of contemporary consumer activists to show that, for scholars of "effects," Katz and Lazarsfeld, who focused exclusively on the "inputs" of consumer choice, paid surprisingly little attention to the social impact of consumption.

Keywords: citizenship; consumption; consumer activism; Decatur Study

The Consumer and the Citizen in *Personal Influence*

By
LAWRENCE B. GLICKMAN

I

Personal Influence makes a number of fascinating claims about consumption and citizenship in the mid-twentieth-century United States. By suggesting that there was a relationship between the two, the book was part of a postwar discourse that highlighted consumption as a form of citizenship. But Katz and Lazarsfeld (1955) treated this relationship differently than many of the celebrants of what Lizabeth Cohen (2004) called the "Consumers' Republic" of postwar America. In the first part of this article, I will take up the nouns in the title, focusing on the nature of the seeming equivalence between consumers and citizens raised by the book; and in the second part, I will deal with the definite articles and ask who exactly are *the consumer* and *the citizen* treated in *Personal Influence*.

Lawrence B. Glickman teaches American history at the University of South Carolina. He has published A Living Wage: American Workers and the Making of Consumer Society *(Cornell University Press, 1997) and* Consumer Society in American History: A Reader *(Cornell University Press, 1999). He is currently writing* Buying Power: Consumer Activism in American History from the Boston Tea Party to the Twenty-First Century *(University of Chicago Press, forthcoming).*

DOI: 10.1177/0002716206292366

As a scholar of American consumer society, in general, and of the history of political consumerism, in particular, I was struck by the many parallels and overlaps between the Katz/Lazarsfeld model of communication and theories of the meaning and power of consumption held by contemporary consumer activists. (Equally significant, we will see, are the differences between these models of consumption and communication.) To make this claim is not to impose an alien or anachronistic framework onto Lazarsfeld's research agenda or onto *Personal Influence*. Throughout his career, Lazarsfeld posited homologies between consumption and communication, between marketing and politics, and between choice and freedom. In his memoir, for example, Lazarsfeld described the "origin" of his "market research studies" in the "methodological equivalence of socialist voting and the buying of soap" (Lazarsfeld 1969, 279). In *Personal Influence*, too, political topics and items of consumption are tantalizingly, sometimes jarringly, juxtaposed, as in the mention of "nail polish/price control, etc" on page 153; the book also treats "campaigns" of all sorts—from rolling out new candidates to rolling out new products—as analogous processes. The "advertiser, or the radio executive, or the propagandist, or the educator," Katz noted in part I, are all "interested in the effect of their message upon the public" (Katz and Lazarsfeld 1955, 18). The book establishes a similarity in the interactions among the message, the media, and people in these and other realms.

To say that politics and consumption are related or even homologous processes, however, is not automatically to reduce the one to the other, or to demean the political.

Such equivalences between electoral politics and quotidian consumption may seem at first glance to be flip and/or politically suspect, and critics, at least since Todd Gitlin in 1978, have been wary of this linkage. To say that politics and consumption are related or even homologous processes, however, is not automatically to reduce the one to the other, or to demean the political. To link consumption and politics is not necessarily to lament the degradation of politics as another site of passive, therapeutic meaninglessness, as Christopher Lasch and his followers would have it. Nor is it necessarily to accept the view that all acts of consumption are potentially subversive, as some cultural studies scholars assume (Glickman 1999). Indeed, scholars and consumer activists have noticed similarities in the structure of the two at least since the Progressive Era, and the normative valence assigned to this relationship has varied a good deal. For the pundit Walter Lippmann, both consumers and citizens were ignorant of the complex workings of the world: hence the need for scientifically trained experts to provide what he called a "map" of this world. Though she shared his concerns about the analogous complexities of the two, Lippmann's contemporary, Florence Kelley of the National Consumers League (NCL), saw consumption as a site for the exercise of citizenship, particularly by women, who until 1920 were excluded from the franchise. Kelley and other members of the NCL believed that consumers held the key to ensuring both that workers were treated well and that products sold in stores were not only safe but in accord with the promises of their marketing and packaging. Kelley was concerned that most consumers did not take their responsibilities as consumers seriously but held out hope that through the leadership of the NCL Americans would understand the causal impact of consumption and would gain information about the true content of their purchases as well as the working conditions of those who grew and made the foods they ate and the clothing they wore (Glickman 2004). Activists ever since, whatever their ideological inclinations, have traded on the assumption of overlap between politics and consumption. In his memoir, we should remember, Lazarsfeld (1969) claimed that his interest in the study of consumption came about as a result of his youthful interest in left politics, which, he believed, needed better advertising and marketing to succeed.

Lazarsfeld and his colleagues located the links between consumption and politics, and indeed other social practices, along a number of axes. An underlying assumption of Lazarsfeld's studies is that people make choices, not autonomously, but in the context of a variety of networks. In this view, communication and consumption networks, while distinct, operate in analogous ways. Notwithstanding the ubiquity and power of these networks, Katz and Lazarsfeld sought to show that individual agency was central to what they called the "flow of mass communications" and also to what we can call the flow of mass production and consumption. A key challenge posited by Katz and Lazarsfeld—indeed it is the first claim in chapter 1 (p. 15)—is to question conventional wisdom about the supposed relative powerlessness of shoppers in the web of consumption and of individuals in the web of communication. Less explicitly argued but, nonetheless, assumed is the significance of citizens in the web of political discourse. In both cases, "opinion leaders" serve as important nodes on these information and material circuits, not only passing on but interpreting and shaping the meaning of information and goods.

Lazarsfeld claimed that the pivot of his research agenda—the reason for the convergence of marketing and politics in his work—was his interest in *handlung* or action, which the intellectual historian Daniel Czitrom defined as "how people make choices between available alternatives" (see Lazarsfeld 1969, 281; Czitrom 1982, 127). Commercial markets and a communications infrastructure provide those alternatives and are thus a crucial aspect of handlung. But it is people's choices within those networks that Katz and Lazarsfeld sought to emphasize. An unstated element of their argument is that choice is an essential part of what characterizes a free society.

In comparison with propaganda and the command economy that were the dominant forces in totalitarian societies, the fact of choice is a symbol of freedom in democracies. Moreover, in showing that the media were only part of the "two-step" flow of communication, they argued against the prevailing "inoculation" thesis, in which media propaganda shaped popular consciousness. As John Durham Peters and Peter Simonson (2004, 266) summarized, for Katz and Lazarsfeld "interpersonal relations offer evidence for the ongoing health of American society against the influence of the media." It is interesting to note that Ernest Dichter, another founder of motivation research, was, like Lazarsfeld, raised in Vienna and trained in that city's school of socially oriented psychology, which placed a special emphasis on handlung. Dichter too was intrigued by the structures of choice, albeit from a more individualistic psychological angle than from Lazarsfeld's socially inflected understanding of handlung (Horowitz 2004, chap. 2).

In the book, Katz and Lazarsfeld carefully, indeed brilliantly, analyze factors in decision making, with a special emphasis on changes in fashion, shopping trends, political beliefs, and movie selections. Despite the manifold ways in which Lazarsfeld and his group considered the meaning of consumption, there were a few blind spots in their approach. Sociologist Andrew Abbott has called consumption "the most studied single phenomenon in American life," and many scholars have traced the source of this interest to the midcentury social research of Lazarsfeld (quoted in Easton 2001). But too often scholars have focused on the question of, as in the article in which Abbott is quoted, "Why people buy stuff?" Of course, the answers to this seemingly straightforward question are extraordinarily complex; furthermore, it would be reductionist to claim that this is the research question at the heart of *Personal Influence*. However, it is true that the book, for all its typologizing of the process of decision making, focuses only on certain aspects of choice. The same is true for Lazarsfeld's pioneering studies of working-class consumption: he examined what workers like to buy and what attracts them; he focused on the social causes, as opposed to the social impact, of their consumption (Lazarsfeld 1969, 280). Unasked and therefore unstudied is the question, What are the effects— moral, political, economic, and ecological—of these choices?

The reason for this blind spot, I believe, is that Lazarsfeld and his collaborators were interested in determining the inputs, if you will, of choice making, the forces and processes that led people to make particular decisions about fashion, taste, and public affairs. Lazarsfeld believed it was essential to diagram the "structure of the act of purchasing." He noted that this was a complex process and that "the action of a purchase is markedly articulated and that different phrases and elements can be distinguished in it." Among the elements he singled out are time of deliberation, anticipated features of purchase, relation to previous purchases, and the psychological coordinates of a purchase (Lazarsfeld 1969, 280). The output, or what happens after the choice was made, was outside his purview.

What is interesting here is that the question about output was exactly the one that consumer activists were asking. Students of influence and consumer activists were considering two sides of the same coin, hence their shared interests in the relationship between people and markets. Both posited that, notwithstanding the forces of markets, consumer choice was a form of power in modern society. But they understood the meaning and exercise of that power in different ways. Consumer activists have not only questioned the significance of the different choices available to us as consumer and citizens, they have also called attention to the moral and social *aftermath* of choice. Their focus was not so much on why people made a particular choice, although they were interested in this to the extent that false advertising and an insufficiently critical media may have played a role. Instead, they explored the causal impact of consumption. Like the scholars of influence, they described consumption and communication as fundamentally social acts, envisioned a similar networked world, and had similar ideas about webs of influence. However, consumer activists believed that the act of consumption set off an irrevocable causal chain. Indeed, the raison d'etre of consumer activism was to announce that personal influence need not only be interpersonal. Consumption decisions affected far more than one's peer group or one's neighbors. In a market society, consumers exercised enormous influence every time they purchased a good, even if they were generally unaware of this power. "Did your stockings kill babies?" asked a pamphlet for a Boston organization promoting a boycott of Japanese-made goods in the late 1930s. The answer for these boycotters was "yes" (Glickman 2005). For consumer activists, the effects of consumption were far reaching and therefore needed to be harnessed for socially useful causes. For these activists, face-to-face contact was one part of a much broader picture that considered the effects of shopping on people we could never see.

Both motivation research and consumer activism took consumption to be a fundamentally social activity. But the two approaches understood the social in different ways. For example, *Personal Influence* discusses fashion as socially oriented largely by focusing on the crucial role of peer group approval (p. 249). Consumer activists tended to emphasize the social costs or benefits of fashion: Was an article of clothing made by sweatshop labor? Was it produced in a fascist country? Did the production of it degrade the environment? One approach focuses on the process of how decisions are made, the other on the consequences of those decisions. For the former, personal influence could be understood as a mediating force; for the latter, personal influence was, once exercised, fundamentally impersonal in the sense that the outcome was determined at the act of purchase. The consummation of a purchase was, in effect, the ratification of the social conditions of production that gave rise to the good purchased. Neither the intentions of the purchaser nor the shopper's interpersonal position as an "influencer" or "influencee" mattered anymore since the outcome was determined by the act of purchase, not the motivations of the purchaser. In both cases, interpersonal relations were crucial, but in the former case, these relations were face to face and local; in the latter, they were anonymous and far reaching.

II

Personal Influence makes what it calls "everyday matters" a topic of social research. And it does so, on the model of *Middletown*, by taking residents of a typical city to stand in for Americans more generally. The specific choices of

Decatur's women at a specific and momentous time are adduced as evidence supporting the theory of influence. The "part played by people" in the title refers not only to the specific people of Decatur but to the role of any comparable congeries of persons in a nationwide (and perhaps even global, at least in "modern" societies) process, "the two-step flow of mass communications."

To the extent that the authors recognized that not all academics accepted the legitimacy of the study of the everyday—or at least the aspects of the everyday relating to consumption and politics that they analyzed—they felt the need to defend this choice. As they noted, many scholars at the time made a "distinction between dignified and undignified topics of research" and "the study of the effect of advertising on purchases is frowned upon" in some circles (pp. 6-7). Yet the authors argued that "the empirical study of human action could hardly find better material than this to develop systematic knowledge" (p. 7). Throughout the book, what struck me was the confident tone that they were discussing something important and had found a way to advance knowledge about how choices were made.

This confidence owes to their conviction that the local and specific information they collected contributed to what they call "systematic," as opposed to particularistic, knowledge. If *Personal Influence* was a case study, it was one that its authors took to have broad implications. In reading the book—published by a trade press, well written, unabashedly concerned with everyday matters—I was reminded of Lionel Trilling's comment that sociology in the 1950s did what the novel had done previously: provided a picture of American society as a whole (Peters and Simonson 2004, 293). Indeed, what they provide is a highly specific portrait of a town and its people, a portrait whose coordinates are not the political leaders of Decatur or momentous historical events but its ordinary residents describing everyday conversations and decisions.

At the same time, *Personal Influence* steps back from this specific town at a moment in time. What makes Decatur as a specific place most useful is its typicality; similarly, the decision making of its citizens are seen as examples of generalizable processes—indeed, before we meet the residents of Decatur in part II, we are given in part I an exhaustive literature review that establishes the validation in many studies of the "two-step flow of communications." As Todd Gitlin (1978, 221) has noted, "Katz and Lazarsfeld did not intend simply to make assertions about the relations between more and less media-exposed women in Decatur, Illinois in 1945; they intended general statements, valid across the boundaries of time." Accordingly, the book highlights not only citizens and consumers of Decatur but what I have called in the title of this article "the citizen" and "the consumer."

And this relates, I think, to a third intriguing element of *Personal Influence*: the things that go unmentioned. For all of the exhaustive explanation of methods, the development of the "two-step" model and the justifications of the city choice and survey questions, two aspects of the study are insufficiently explained. One is the decision to interview women only, and the other is the relative lack of discussion of the fact that the Decatur study occurred in 1945 when America was still fighting the war with Japan. Early in part II, the authors noted that "we began by interviewing a cross-sectional sample of some 800 women in Decatur, Illinois" (p. 138). Were they mirroring the adage of the advertising trade journal *Printers' Ink* that "the proper study of mankind is man . . . but the proper study of markets is women"?[1] Similarly, the book does not sufficiently discuss how the wartime atmosphere of rationing and shortages might have affected consumption decisions in the summer of 1945. If the war years were a time of what historian Daniel Horowitz (2004, chap. 1) called "chastened consumption"—a chastening that was both voluntary and forced—what impact might this have had on individual consumption decisions? Moreover, how might this have affected how women would talk with researchers about their consumption choices?

Some of these silences may be explained by the fact that the Decatur study was completed ten years before the book was written and because, as I understand it, the people who carried out the study were not involved in the writing of the book. These decisions seem to be part of the universalizing tendencies of midcentury sociology. And here I wonder whether we might apply David Hollinger's (1975) writings on the cosmopolitan vision of mid-twentieth-century Jewish intellectuals and social scientists to Lazarsfeld. Lazarsfeld had experienced anti-Semitism of the political kind as a young man in Vienna but also of the academic kind in the United States. In his memoir, he quotes from a letter responding to Robert Lynd's recommendation of him, which, demurring from Lynd's view, asserted that "Lazarsfeld clearly shows the marks of his race." Lazarsfeld claimed that he was not "seriously hampered, because it never occurred to me to aspire to a major University job" (Lazarsfeld 1969, 300-301). Whatever the motivation, Lazarsfeld sought in his work to recognize individual difference within a framework of generalizable social principles. To be sure, Katz and Lazarsfeld emphasized difference in the book, particularly class difference. Indeed, "opinion leaders" only made sense in the context of having a special sphere of influence. Katz and Lazarsfeld also noted degrees of influence of women with large families and that "highly gregarious women . . . are more likely to be opinion leaders."

By saying little about the decision to interview only women and the timing of the study, the authors also seem to be implying a certain kind of universalism. Their study is not so much of specific people in a specific time and place (to the extent that Decatur is a specific place, it was chosen, as a lengthy appendix painstakingly explains, precisely because of its typicality) as of a *process* common in midcentury America. In this sense, the book participates in the process that critic Leslie Fiedler described as "dreaming aloud the dreams of the whole American people" and that Fieldler attributed to Jewish-American writers of midcentury but that we could equally attribute to midcentury social research of the sort spearheaded by Lazarsfeld (Hollinger 1975, 66-67). That is perhaps why they do not dwell on the details of who they interviewed or the times and places of the interviews.

Personal Influence is an extraordinary achievement of mid-twentieth-century American social science, which repays our attention in the early twenty-first century. The book was a timely work of social science and moral inquiry whose historical context my remarks have aimed to elucidate. In this work, Katz and Lazarsfeld offered intriguing reasons to analogize consumption and citizenship. If their approach paid too little attention to the aftermath of consumption decisions, it offered scholars important reasons to understand consumption as a multidimensional political activity.

Note

1. *Printer's Ink* 7 (November 1929): 113.

References

Cohen, Lizabeth. 2004. *A consumers' republic: The politics of mass consumption in postwar America*. New York: Knopf.

Czitrom, Daniel J. 1982. *Media and the American mind: From Morse to McLuhan*. Chapel Hill: University of North Carolina Press.

Easton, John. 2001. Consuming interests. *University of Chicago Magazine* 93 (August). http://magazine .uchicago.edu/0108/features/index.htm#Top.

Gitlin, Todd. 1978. Media sociology: The dominant paradigm. *Theory and Society* 6:205-53.

Glickman, Lawrence B. 1999. Born to shop: Consumer history and American history. In *Consumer society in American history*, ed. Lawrence B. Glickman, 1-14. Ithaca, NY: Cornell University Press.

———. 2004. Consommer pour rééformer le capitalisme américain: Le citoyen et le consommateur au début du XXe siècle. *Sciences de la Société* 62:17-43.

———. 2005. "Make lisle the style": The politics of fashion in the Japanese silk boycott, 1937-1940. *Journal of Social History* 38:573-608.

Hollinger, David. 1975. Ethnic diversity, cosmopolitanism, and the emergence of the American liberal intelligentsia. In *The American province: Studies in the history and historiography of ideas*, 56-73. Bloomington: Indiana University Press.

Horowitz, Daniel. 2004. *The anxieties of affluence: Critiques of American consumer culture, 1939-1979*. Amherst: University of Massachusetts Press.

Katz, Elihu, and Paul F. Lazarsfeld. 1955. *Personal influence: The part played by people in the flow of mass communications*. New York: Free Press.

Lazarsfeld, Paul. 1969. An episode in the history of social research: A memoir. In *The intellectual migration: Europe and America, 1930-1960*, ed. Donald Fleming and Bernard Bailyn, 270-337. Cambridge, MA: Harvard University Press.

Peters, John Durham, and Peter Simonson. 2004. *Mass communication and American social thought: Key texts, 1919-1968*. Lanham, MD: Rowman & Littlefield.

This analysis explores the transformation of public communication in the United States from a two-step flow of messages passing from mass media through a social mediation process, to a one-step flow involving the refined targeting of messages directly to individuals. This one-step flow reflects both a transformation in communication technologies and fundamental changes in the relations between individuals and society. Opinion leaders who played a pivotal role in the two-step paradigm are increasingly less likely to "lead" because they are more likely to reinforce latent opinions than to reframe them. And because the mass media in the one-step flow are increasingly fragmented and differentiated, they contribute to the individualizing process through shrinking audiences, demographically driven programming, and transmitting targeted political advertising and news spin.

The One-Step Flow of Communication

By
W. LANCE BENNETT
and
JAROL B. MANHEIM

Keywords: one-step flow; two-step flow; strategic communication; campaign; social networks; targeting; narrowcasting; data mining; persuasion; public information

Fifty years ago, the Free Press published Elihu Katz and Paul F. Lazarsfeld's (1955) soon-to-be-classic study, *Personal Influence: The Part Played by People in the Flow of Mass Communications*. Though the concept had earlier roots (Berelson, Lazarsfeld, and McPhee 1954, especially chap. 6; Lazarsfeld, Berelson, and Gaudet 1944), it is to this volume that contemporary scholars turn for the classic statement of the "two-step flow of communication" hypothesis. In the first step, messages are issued by the mass media to what is, to all outward appearances, a more or less homogeneous mass audience. In the second, innumerable small group interactions powered by horizontal opinion leaders interpret and contextualize these mediated messages for their participants, who then internalize the resulting content. The end result is a more or less differentiated understanding of the message across various social boundaries. This was a nontrivial finding.

For society at large, one implication was that there were limits to the potential influence of

DOI: 10.1177/0002716206292266

mediated communication—limits set by each individual's knowledge networks and social interactions, some of which might be systematic in character, others products of chance. Yet at the same time, mediated communication was potentially so integral to interpersonal communication—providing it with both stimuli and information—that the two might no longer be distinguishable. This meant that mass society could never be entirely homogeneous but also that individual social locations could never be entirely isolated from mass influence. Even in his recent work, Katz (Kim, Wyatt, and Katz 1999) has continued to argue the central importance of personal conversation—even the most casual of talk—in the democratic process. Indeed, he and his coauthors viewed such discourse as the very definition of democracy (Kim, Wyatt, and Katz 1999, 361).

For political communication professionals—a class of operatives that was only beginning to develop at the time, but was destined to grow into a determinative force in American politics—the implications were similarly consequential. For they suggested that effective political communication—by which we mean influence— required not merely the management and control of mediated messages but also understanding and controlling how these messages would be processed through social interaction before their effects would become manifest. In other words, it became apparent that the so-called "water cooler effect"—by which mass mediated messages reach audience members who were not directly exposed to them through secondary interactions with friends and colleagues—was not merely a means of expanding the audience for a given message but was a potentially success-critical mechanism for assigning it meaning. Perhaps more than any other single research finding, this realization led communicators to incorporate the study of opinion dynamics with that of message effects in developing their art. The heavy reliance we see today on integrated programs of focus group research and public opinion polling in any effort at mass political persuasion is a direct outgrowth of that realization.

But that was then; this is now. Our thesis is that society, communication technologies, and individual communication habits have changed fundamentally in ways that affect how individuals receive and process information. These social and technological changes directly challenge the underlying assumptions of the two-step flow hypothesis because they have isolated increasing numbers (though surely not all) of today's citizens from the very groups that traditionally provided vital cues

W. Lance Bennett is a professor of political science and Ruddick C. Lawrence Professor of Communication at the University of Washington, where he also directs the Center for Communication and Civic Engagement (www.engagedcitizen.org). The general focus of his work is with how communication processes affect citizen engagement with politics. Publications include Mediated Politics: Communication in the Future of Democracy *(Cambridge) and* News: The Politics of Illusion *(Longman). He has received the Ithiel de Sola Pool distinguished career award and lectureship and the Murray Edelman Career Achievement Award in Political Communication, both from the American Political Science Association.*

Jarol B. Manheim (PhD, Northwestern, 1971) is a professor of media and public affairs, and of political science, at George Washington University, where he was the founding director of the School of Media and Public Affairs. His research interests are in the area of strategic political communication. His work has appeared in the leading journals of political science, journalism, and mass communication.

for interpreting information. The combination of social isolation, communication channel fragmentation, and message targeting technologies have produced a very different information *recipient* than the audience members of the Eisenhower era.

Even as individuals have become less likely to participate in groups, they have gained greater command of their own information environments, often participating in multiple, fluid social networks oriented to self-expression, generally organized around lifestyles (Giddens 1991; Bennett 1998). These networked individuals are hard to reach in large numbers with effective messages, as evidenced by the spiraling costs of marketing campaigns in both politics and consumer arenas. At the same time, these networks are often worth the expense of targeting as evidenced by the efforts to reach so-called "soccer moms" in the 2000 elections and "Nascar dads" in 2004. Given the decline of group identifications and loyalties, individuals, even when reached, are hard to hold, whether in terms of attention or adoption of message content. Witness the rise of so-called permanent campaigns aimed at branding individuals to products, ideas, candidates, leaders, and policies.

[C]ommunicators . . . will . . . have substituted their own audience selection and targeting skills for the role formerly assigned to peer group interaction. This is the one-step flow of communication

---

In these and other respects, today, the communication process is aimed at the individual or at the direct messaging of assembled networks of like demographics. The mass context is still important, but more as an affirming echo chamber than as a social cueing system. The technologies of focus grouping and polling are still relevant, but they are increasingly augmented or supplanted by massive databases aimed at identifying and characterizing individual members of the mass audience and at delivering messages directly to these individuals through the most efficient and narrowest possible channel. Whether that channel is direct mail, targeted telemarketing, receiver-sensitive Web sites, specialized e-mail lists, or some other means, the objective is the same—to fit the boundaries and framing of the message to the needs, wants, expectations, beliefs, preferences, and interests of the audience member. In the aggregate, such messages may form a global statement of position or action, but for the individual audience members only the most relevant and potentially persuasive portions of that global entity are visible. To the extent that communicators are effective in achieving this objective, they will, for all practical purposes, have substituted their own audience selection and targeting skills for the role formerly assigned to peer group interaction. The availability and content of each message will have been shaped upon transmission to anticipate and replace the social interaction component of the two-step flow. This is the *one-step flow of communication*.

The key phrase here, of course, is "to the extent that communicators are effective." Clearly, the effectiveness of even the most sophisticated one-step communication efforts is limited, and there are, to be sure, residual pockets of two-step communication scattered throughout contemporary society. Some of these pockets are sustained by highly localized social networks and by the identification of individuals with them. As Huckfeldt and his colleagues (1995) suggested, some of these "social cells" remain closed to outside influence, while others are better integrated with external information networks. Even relatively coherent local "social cells" are under pressure from the continued development and growing efficiencies of targeted information and communication technologies that deliver strategically personalized communication (Turow 1997). Indeed, self-initiated technological applications such as viral marketing may be redefining personal networks themselves in ways that open them to increased outside penetration (see, for example, Subramani and Rajagopalan 2003). Looking at society more broadly, it is also clear that older demographics are more likely than younger ones to belong to membership organizations that serve as transmission belts in the two-step flow (Putnam 2000). Our overall argument is about trends that point to the decline of a social membership society and the rise of a lifestyle network society in which information is less likely to be cued by proximate authoritative opinion leaders.

The achievement of a one-step flow among large-scale publics is typically neither simple nor inexpensive. It requires, at the very least, a marriage of basic communication skills with the availability of vast and highly differentiated data on members of the prospective audience, the ability to manipulate and organize the data in ways that permit the linkage of specific cases with specific attributes, the capability to identify the physical or electronic location of the specific individuals (or resident locations of like demographics) in the database, and access to some suitable form of narrowcasting technology. That list of prerequisites may appear to be insurmountable, and in the era of the two-step flow, it was. But today, half a century later, each of these elements is readily available to those able to afford them. Both the hardware and software now exist to reach large numbers of individuals (generally targeted as demographic clusters) directly with messages that appeal to their personal emotions and their very identity (Turow 1997). Their use produces an interaction, not *among* members of peer groups, but *between* the technology and the individual audience member.

This means that the Republican voter opening her door or agreeing to talk on the phone with a partisan canvasser may receive a different political message than her similarly Republican neighbor, based on their known differences in issue interests, political donation histories, religious or sexual preferences, or consumer purchasing patterns. Moreover, her responses or donation levels may be entered in a wireless data transmission device after the contact has ended and uploaded into the party's district or national database. As the database is fueled by other interactions, it is programmed to change incrementally in real time, adjusting the configurations of target populations, message impact evaluations, and next approach strategies. At least that is the scenario for canvassing of the near future being offered by both parties. Another slice of that scenario has each party claiming a database of upwards of 150 million individuals, with anywhere from several to several hundred pieces of information on each person. These information bits may include education; employment; sexual preference; dona-tion histories; organization memberships; purchasing patterns; and other private traces left behind through credit purchases, marketing survey responses, or Internet surfing behavior, to name but three potential sources. These data are mined by companies that resell them to communication clients such as governments, interest organizations, political consultants, parties, and corporations. Howard (2006) suggested that a less transparent, less public political culture may result from these developments.

We believe that the underlying relations between individuals, society, sources, and messages are, indeed, changing in ways that suggest the need to formulate a new communication paradigm. But we also wish to hold open the question of whether the communication technologies that serve this paradigm must neces-sarily be developed and deployed in ways that isolate individuals and fragment society. Our concerns in this article are twofold: how better to understand the two-step paradigm in relationship to its changing social and historical contexts and whether the emerging one-step process can be theorized and researched in ways that offer insights about more and less positive developments in social and democratic communication processes.

Social Reality and Communication Paradigms

Communication models are rooted in assumptions about the social structures inhabited by the individuals and groups being studied. Researchers may fail to for-mally theorize these deeper social structures, but they rely on assumptions about them in designing research and interpreting results. For example, as elaborated below, the two-step flow rests on assumptions about a pluralist social order that both invite intuitive acceptance of the model and guide its empirical applications. Those assumptions may have been reasonable in 1950, but they seem less reason-able today. We suggest that the model seems most appropriate to understanding communication flows in American society from roughly the early decades of the twentieth century until the 1980s, a period that various scholars have associated with the rise and fall of a civil society defined by federations of social groups from national service organizations to bowling leagues (Putnam 2000).

We see the upward arc of the two-step flow (long before it had been identified formally) in the dawn of modern public relations, when Edward L. Bernays and others on the Committee on Public Information during World War I realized that the mass propaganda messages aimed at mobilizing support for the war were best delivered by a legion of "four minute men," those respected members of local communities who stood up in theaters and other town meeting places to deliver scripts from on high as their own (Ewen 1996).

The downward arc of the paradigm coincides with the rising tide of studies indicating that the social cues people needed to interpret messages from mass media sources were often embedded in the media context itself. Indeed, the later decades of the two-step flow paradigm (roughly from the 1980s through the mid-1990s) saw a notable decline in research findings that supported earlier wisdom about the minimal effects of mass communication (Klapper 1960), and a rise in findings that mass media content produced substantial direct effects without notable secondary social processing (Iyengar and Kinder 1987; Iyengar 1991; Mutz 1998). In this twilight period of the two-step flow, the group-based society declined, yet the mass media continued to reach large audiences through relatively few channels. Under these circumstances, journalists and other content developers such as entertainment producers became practicing sociometricians, writing social and political cues into the demographically targeted narratives we call news and entertainment. In the public information sphere, social cues were coded in terms of recognized news sources (organization leaders, public officials) or ideological labels (Zaller 1992).

Both media and society have continued to change since the wave of studies showing direct mass media effects such as agenda setting, framing, and priming, among others. One change is that conventional mass media reach smaller audiences, while niche media attract increasing numbers, making it harder to send effective generalized messages but easier to target specialized appeals. Another change is that individuals in fragmented late modern societies have assumed more responsibility for managing their own emotional and cognitive realities, often apart from group influence processes (Giddens 1991; Bennett 1998; Mutz 1998). This implies less reliance on interpersonal influence particularly in the area of politics and public affairs, a factor that may be associated with both the declining importance of politics for many people, and the tendency to avoid political talk in many social relationships (Mutz 1998; Eliasoph 1998).

All of this suggests that we are at an important moment in communications history for thinking carefully about (1) how we define the models that may become the next paradigm and (2) what we would like those knowledge structures to do. Accumulated experience with the old paradigm offers some guidance. While we believe that there were, indeed, some broad correspondences between the two-step flow and the observable social structure of the United States, we also think that there are some important cautionary tales to be told.

One of the leading critics of the two-step flow paradigm, Todd Gitlin (1978), argued that the two-step model was more the product of broad conceptions of social pluralism shared by social scientists in the early 1950s than it was ever empirically supported by strong or consistent findings. Gitlin argued that pluralism and related behavioral research orientations were congenial to funding agencies and communications industry support for the early Lazarsfeld studies. In Gitlin's critique, the two-step flow was the perfect antidote for unsettling critical-theory-based notions of a mass society in which media were strong, intrusive forces, akin to hypodermic injections.

Gitlin's (1978) reading of the Katz and Lazarsfeld (1955) studies suggests several anomalies that might have challenged their conclusions about the two-step process. For one thing, the interpersonal influence findings were based on data gathered largely before the rise of broadly available television programming, which has become the sine qua non of mass media influence. Perhaps more curious is the fact that Katz and Lazarsfeld brushed aside their own acknowledged finding that in the area of public affairs, fully 58 percent of opinion changes were made without remembered personal contact, meaning that the main effect was presumably from the mass media. Consistent with this anomalous finding, a bare 38 percent of reputed influentials and influencees in the area of public affairs confirmed that they had in fact made an attempt to influence someone or been influenced (Gitlin 1978, 219).

Since four areas of information flow were studied by Katz and Lazarsfeld (1955) (fashion, marketing, movies, and public affairs), the major discrepancy in the area of public affairs was apparently easier to ignore in declaring general empirical support for the model. Yet subsequent decades of research by other scholars addressing a variety of information flows, in an array of settings, and published in leading journals, also failed to produce consistent support for the model, resulting in any number of proposed amendments and revisions (examples include Burt 1999; Harik 1971; Weiman 1982). The most careful studies tended to discover multiple flow patterns, from the preferred horizontal flow of the two-step model, to, in some cases, a half dozen different flow directions, including direct media effects (Robinson 1976). Yet none of these perturbations in the paradigm shook the standing of the simple and compelling two-step flow idea. They were brushed aside in a manner typical of the normal science process operating in paradigms as described by Kuhn (1962). Gitlin (1978, 205) argued that it was hard to challenge this "dominant paradigm" of media sociology when the likes of Daniel Bell talked about the "received knowledge" of "personal influence" and pronounced *Personal Influence* "the standard work" (see Bell 1975, 218).

In the ensuing decades after the publication of *Personal Influence*, research into political sociology, social psychology, and communication accelerated, producing a rich trove of knowledge about human behavior in general and human behavior in politics in particular. We—the social scientific community—knew much less in 1955 than we know today, and we were far less sophisticated in our thinking. And that, in turn, makes the lasting influence of *Personal Influence* all the more remarkable. Consider, for example, the study of attitudes and attitude change. It was after the two-step flow was promulgated that social psychologists developed such theories as Festinger's (1957) cognitive dissonance, Katz's (1960) functional analysis, belief-based models of attitude change such as Fishbein's (1967a, 1967b) summative model, Sherif and Sherif's (1967) social-judgment-involvement approach, or Petty and Cacioppo's (1986) elaboration likelihood model, to name but a few of the more prominent subsequent conceptual advances. Similarly, the study of public opinion benefited only later from Kelman's (1961) work on compliance, identification, and internalization of meaning; Converse's (1964) analysis of belief systems; McCombs and Shaw's (1972) breakthrough study of agenda setting; or even such essential building-block notions as indexing (for example, Tannenbaum 1955) or framing (developed earlier but perhaps best characterized in Entman [1993]). In political sociology, Robert Lane had yet to write *Political Life* (1959); and C. Wright Mills, who played an early role in Katz and Lazarsfeld's project and actually served as a field-worker on the Decatur study, was only then at work on his best-known book, *The Power Elite* (1956). Berger and Luckman's (1966) reality was still a social construct away. Even though some of this work, including some of the early work, directly challenged the dominant paradigm, most of it continued to motor alongside for some time, causing little disturbance.

The two-step paradigm was further supported by the failure of early election studies to find substantial campaign media effects, and so, political science came under the influence of the communication variable-averse Survey Research Center at the University of Michigan, which we know today as the Inter-University Consortium for Political and Social Research (ICPSR), the early work of which was typified by Campbell et al. (1960). To this day, political science has been slow to develop a robust agenda of work on media and politics at the core of the field. Meanwhile, mass communication research would soon reinforce the dominant paradigm under Joseph Klapper's statement of the minimal effects hypothesis in his *The Effects of Mass Communication* (1960), a view that was still prevalent twenty years later, prompting James Lemert to pose the rhetorical question in his own book title, *Does Mass Communication Change Public Opinion After All?* (1981).

Broad scholarly belief in a pluralist American social structure also surely helped general acceptance of the model and discouraged its modification or ongoing critical specification. We are not suggesting here that the group dynamics underlying pluralistic theories were unimportant in the mass communication process of earlier years. Indeed, they almost certainly continue to operate even today for those who hold strong social memberships. Our point is that the strength of the underlying social science consensus surrounding pluralism and behavioral research may have led to an overly simplified notion of mass communication based on discounting the many anomalous findings that challenged the paradigm. Those anomalies, if examined more carefully, might have challenged communication theory to accommodate other social processes and more direct media effects that may have existed all along. Indeed, there may have been more continuous evolution of theory from a two-step dominant model to a one-step flow as both society and media continued to change. Herein lies a cautionary lesson for thinking about the next paradigm: if we are at a point where both social structure and media technologies are changing rapidly once again, we will be well served by more careful specifications of the underlying social and technological factors involved.

The One-Step Flow:
Society, Technology, and the Audience

Observers such as Joseph Turow (1997) have credited the rise of refined, highly personalized marketing technologies themselves with the breakup of society. While Turow has drawn useful attention to the transformation of various modes of communication into marketing exercises, it seems to us unlikely that communication, alone, can account for changes as fundamental as the decline of social group membership or the isolation of individuals from each other. The individuation of social experience and the decline of broad social memberships, even at the all-embracing levels of class and church that we see in European societies, are changes that are sweeping most postindustrial democracies (Inglehart 1997; Bennett 2005). Indeed, social theorists such as Giddens (1991; see also Bennett 1998) have linked the impact of global economic change to social structure, resulting in the increasing isolation of individuals and the rise of new emotional and identity processes around self-expression and lifestyle. It cannot be surprising that, as these lifestyles become central, the media habits that are at the core of so much of them also begin to proliferate and fragment around personal realities.

[T]he emergence of new technologies and targeting models for reaching people seems as much an effect of a fragmenting social order as a cause.

Given these developments, the emergence of new technologies and targeting models for reaching people seems as much an effect of a fragmenting social order as a cause. The ongoing interaction between technology and social receptivity is notable in the development of media and audience relationships that point to increasing individuation in the delivery and reception of information. Silicon-based computing, digitalization, miniaturization—these and other core technological developments have changed not only the nature and use of our machines but the relationship between machines and human society. That is as true of politics and democratic practice as it is of any other human endeavor. Indeed, the changes have been so extensive and of such a type that they must, necessarily, call into question even so venerable a theory as the two-step flow. Consider the following:

1. Evolving media formats. In 1955, television was primarily a black-and-white version of radio, with visual renditions of such radio dramas as the Lone Ranger, and with former newspaper reporters reading (literally) the events of the day to a camera. Telephones were hardwired, and long-distance communication often required the intervention of an operator. Cell towers were elements of prison architecture, computers—the few that existed—filled entire floors of buildings, and the World Wide Web was not even a glimmer in the eyes of scientists working for the Advanced Research Projects Agency (ARPA), the Defense Department agency that spurred development of the Internet, which itself was not established until 1958 as part of the reaction to the Soviet Union's launch of *Sputnik*. This matters because different communications media have different attributes, different patterns of human interaction, and different implications for political life. Compare the appointment-based society that gathered around network broadcast news with the emergence of the podcast society increasingly driven by personalized, on-demand news aggregators.

2. Evolving individual media use habits. Herbert Krugman (1965, 1966, 1971; Krugman and Hartley 1970), in a series of experimental studies in the 1960s and 1970s, demonstrated that people processed information from television differently from the way they consumed from print media. Differences were evident in such biometrics as galvanic skin response and brain wave patterns, which consistently showed that television viewing was a relatively passive activity, less psychologically involving than reading. The prevailing form and effect of human interaction with the Internet and related *new* technologies is still to be determined, though there is early evidence that Internet use enhances participation, information seeking, and social interaction rather selectively (Shah, Kwak, and Holbert 2001; Tewksbury 2003; Hardy and Scheufele 2005). The mobility of the cellular culture, which has seen actual declines of 3 to 4 percent per year in the number of residential telephone subscribers in recent years, has rendered the direct-dial area code, a twentieth-century technological wonder in its own right, a pseudo-geographic anachronism in the twenty-first. More to the point, cell phones have rendered individuals reachable virtually anywhere, anytime, and not just with personal calls but with content ranging from music to political information. Such technologies have enabled citizens to send and receive information instantly in organizing demonstrations and protests, enabling them to make news and integrate information and action in real time. As the movement expression coined by Indymedia goes in the one-step era, people can *"be the media"* (Rheingold 2002). And though the Web had existed only since 1995, and then in a nascent form, by 2000 more than half of all Americans under the age of fifty-five were entering the online world at least once a week (U.S. Census Bureau 2000). Today, individuals not only are receivers of information, but also producers and distributors it in shifting and often faceless knowledge networks such as blogs, lists, and action alerts forged through social technology rather than personal influence.

3. Evolving social distribution of media. Just as there have been micro-level differences in the ways people interact with and process information from various media, there are macro-level differences in the roles that such media play in society. As new media become available, the potential develops for substantial changes in the relative influence of more traditional forms. We saw this occur in the 1960s, when television emerged as the primary source of news about politics. In 1952, for example, 32 percent of Americans reported that they relied on television as their primary source of campaign news while 28 percent relied on radio. Just a dozen years later, in 1964, television was the medium of choice for 58 percent of the public, and radio for less than 4 percent. Newspapers remained in the low-to-mid 20s throughout the period. (Nimmo 1970, 116). By the 1990s, Americans were spending far more time interacting with their television sets than with newspapers—roughly seven times as much annually (U.S. Census Bureau 1999). Now, it appears that dramatic shifts *away* from broadcast television, along with other media formerly known as "mass," are under way. Between 1993 and 2004, for example, regular consumption of newspapers reported in national surveys dropped from 58 to 42 percent, radio from 47 to 40 percent, local television news from 77 to 59 percent, and television network newscasts from 60 to 34 percent. In contrast, between 1994 and 2004, regular consumption of news from the Internet rose from 0 (1994 was the last pre-Web year) to 29 percent (Pew Research Center for the People and the Press 2004). Not only are the media for information consumption becoming more personalized, but the information formats are also shifting. These shifts away from mass media experiences may account for the broad questioning of the objectivity of the press and the filtering of facts according to personal values and incipient political interests.

There is reason to believe that these and similar trends matter. For example, we know from the post–*Personal Influence* literature on attitude change and persuasion that certain kinds of learning are facilitated by low levels of psychological involvement. If, as Krugman (1965, 1966, 1971) suggested, television viewing is a more passive experience than reading, it follows that the shift to television as the primary source of political information would have facilitated certain kinds of persuasive efforts and impeded others. In an era dominated by print, for example, media consumption *required* and rewarded attentive participation in the communication process. In an era dominated by television, *in*attentive participation was presumed and was quite possibly satisfying in and of itself. In the first instance, the political persuader employing the dominant medium would employ cues designed to stimulate understanding in social context, and perhaps even self-actuated information seeking, elements of the two-step world. But in the second, she would employ cues designed to bypass the critical faculties of the audience member and to preselect and link the message with some desired set of perceptions or values that had been targeted in advance and that not only required no social interpretation but effectively discouraged seeking one. That was the first step into a one-step world in which, in a sense, there is no sociology.

Differences in the means of exchange between audience members and their media aggregate into systemic differences in the means of exchange between the

FIGURE 1
HOMOGENIZATION OF THE FOX NEWS AUDIENCE

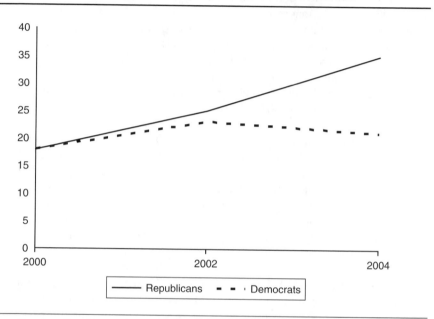

Source: Based on Pew Research Center for the People and the Press (2004).

polity and its citizens. Manheim (1976), Kubey and Csikszentmihalyi (1990), Putnam (2000), Bennett and Manheim (2001), and others have offered a variety of arguments over the implications that such ongoing reconfiguration may have for the nature of power, the conduct of politics, and the character of daily civic life. Similarly, though we have less evidence in hand as to the psychological dynamics of virtual interaction with the news, such scholars as Davis (1999), Norris (2001), and Bimber (2003) have suggested that the most recent shift in media preferences, incorporating the Internet and related technologies, may have equally significant implications for civil society and for the place of individual citizens in it.

Under this scenario of changing social relationships and media patterns, even "old media" provide new opportunities for effective one-step communication. Consider, for example, the homogenization of the audience for Fox News, widely regarded as appealing primarily to conservative viewers. As illustrated in Figure 1, as recently as 2000 18 percent of both Republicans and Democrats, respectively, reported that they watched the cable network regularly. By 2004, however, a clear and expanding gap had emerged, with Republicans doubling their own reported viewership and nearly doubling that of their Democratic counterparts. The result is an increasingly homogeneous audience and one that offers persuaders a venue for narrowcasting their messages—distributing them to large numbers of like-minded recipients. In the world of professional persuaders, messages that are distributed through such specialized channels can be nuanced in ways designed to (de)mobilize one audience segment—in this case Republicans—while minimizing the risk of such collateral effects as (de)mobilizing their opponents—here, Democrats—or having inconsistent messages reach diverse audience segments. From the perspective of the audience member, this narrowcasting reduces the diversity of information that is on offer and does so in ways that align directly with his or her *presumed* needs, wants, and expectations. This mapping of content into mind-set looks much less like a Texas two-step than it does dancing in front of the mirror.

In the case of *new* media, the opportunities for personalizing messages are immensely greater, and their exploitation can be immensely more sophisticated. Consider, for example, the marketing practices of online retailer Amazon.com, as summarized in part by Waller (2003). When a customer selects a product for viewing, a Web page appears with information about that product. That information includes, among other elements, a list of other products purchased by other customers who also purchased the item in question. We can think of these as "affinity" purchases. This information is derived from the merchant's database of sales information and can be generated for any book or other product that Amazon sells. Underlying the selection is a potentially vast pool of data that capture clusters or networks of interrelated products. The process is called data mining, and it can be used in a variety of ways. The same data, for example, can support construction of a list of all purchasers of any given book or any combination of affinity products. These lists can be drawn on the basis of demographic, economic, psychographic, sociographic, or other information that is included in the database.

[T]here is considerable potential for . . . direct personal messaging to be rendered coherent and connected through technologies . . . that enable people to explore and evaluate linked topics and meet others "face to face" to form online and offline communities.

Extending this example one more step will make the larger point. Regular customers of Amazon.com also know that whenever they log on to their accounts, they are greeted by suggested purchases, the selection of which is based on their own recent purchasing or browsing behavior. More than that, customers have the option of receiving regular e-mails from the company advising them of new products that are judged likely to appeal to them. And they *also* have the option of voluntarily adding to the information the company stores about them by responding to marketing surveys, thereby enriching Amazon's data mining capabilities. This combination of data mining, audience differentiation, and communication outreach creates a unique, specialized, affinity-based, but highly individualized and personalized shopping experience for each Amazon customer. Add the ease with which the databases of one organization can be exchanged with those held by others, and the potential to exploit personalized information for purposes of persuasion is magnified many times (Howard 2006).

The very same technologies, when applied in a political rather than a commercial context, and by electoral, programmatic, ideological, or other kinds of inherently political actors rather than by merchants, have the potential to deliver information to individuals across a society in such a way that each person receives it through channels and embedded in cues that make clear its relevance for her or him individually. Where implemented, this process can be designed to replace in whole or in part the sociological dynamic of the two-step flow. And, precisely because it is based on interest, preference, and need data provided by the targeted individual himself or herself, it may also be more effective than peer group exchanges in anticipating and responding to the personalized concerns of each audience member. Though definitive data are not yet available on this last point, Zarsky (2006) has made much the same argument with respect to the advertising in particular. As he put it,

> For a successful . . . campaign that will have an optimal effect on a consumer's perception, attention and comprehension, advertisers require *knowledge* about their target consumers, and the ability to *target* them directly. In the offline world . . . these attempts to collect and tailor information are inferior to the online dynamic. . . . Since the dynamics of online advertising offers advantages both in collection and in tailoring, it will prove more effective in meeting advertisers' objectives—achieving influence by crossing the crucial barriers of perception, attention and comprehension (every one of which requires a specific dataset that the online environment makes available). Meeting these objectives will also be made possible by applying . . . data mining technology . . . , which will assist content providers in identifying the preferences, traits and other personal attributes of every user. (p. 218)

Many fear that these communication modes, from automated recommendation systems to the burgeoning blogosphere, mainly produce self-centered churn with little coherent social impact. Yet there is considerable potential for such direct personal messaging to be rendered coherent and connected through technologies such as Really Simple Syndication (RSS) feeds, action lists, and meet-up sites that enable people to explore and evaluate linked topics and meet others "face to face" to form online and offline communities.

The push technologies pioneered by online retailers and adapted by commercial and political marketers can be either stealthy or transparent, depending on the privacy standards, norms, and agreements prevailing between technology developers and their audiences. Thus, individuals may be given the choice to opt in or out of databases, and they may be given choices about which of their response behaviors in credit purchases or in online environments are shared with data miners and their known or unknown clients. Or they may not.

Communication Technologies and Political Choice

The evolving communication technologies and applications that support the one-step flow are not entirely deterministic in terms of whether they must isolate individuals or short-circuit potentially useful social interaction such as deliberation and critical exchanges of ideas by the public. There are *choices* being made daily about how the one-step process becomes routinized. We would do well to recognize and assess those choices.

The factor that most favors the predominance of isolating and divisive communication technologies in the one-step era is the rise of professional communication strategists advising parties, candidates, leaders, interest organizations, and their issue campaigns (Blumler and Kavanaugh 1999). The resulting culture of communication favors a top-down, war room, strategic control relationship between client and target audience (Howard 2006). Insofar as shaping audience responses by pushing emotional buttons is thought to favor client success more than, say, initiating open dialogues between candidates and voters, client interests will trump democratic values. As one of the founders of modern consulting, Joseph Napolitan, remarked when one of the authors challenged an audience of political consultants to consider the democratic consequences of some of their practices, Why should consultants be obligated to worry about democracy when their primary obligation is to advance the immediate goals of their clients? (remarks made at the annual meeting of the International Association of Political Consultants, Malta, November 9-12, 2001). A notable result of this mentality is the rise of what Bennett (1989) has called a "managerial democracy" in which citizens are symbolically moved in and out of the political picture as strategic elements of communication campaigns.

[T]he most important point about information transmission in the one-step era is not that campaigns are permanent or ubiquitous. The real point is that campaigns are definitive.

The managerial polity and its communication regime have developed not of necessity, but through the gradual accretion of choices born of a culture of opinion management. The result leaves politicians hard-pressed to ask citizens for sacrifice or commitment because such things are not born of communication manipulations alone. Consider in this light Patterson's (2002) observations about the political landscape facing the citizen in post-9/11 America:

The organizations they might have joined fifty years ago are now run by professional managers, who solicit dues but do not invite active participants. The war in Afghanistan was fought by professional soldiers, the bioterrorism threat was relegated to professional scientists, homeland security was entrusted to professional law enforcement and intelligence officers. Even the appeal to sacrifice was missing. Americans were urged to keep spending, lest the economy sink. . . . The modern campaign, too, is a thoroughly professional operation. Voters have no expectation that they will be asked to do anything more than send a check and vote on election day. (p. 186)

Another consequence of the chosen forms of one-step communication flow is what many scholars and pundits have noted as the unboundedness of campaign-related communication. The so-called "permanent campaign" is a characterization that is most commonly, but not exclusively, applied to electoral campaigns. Even issue advocates and activists become caught up in permanent campaigns, largely because the entry of numerous groups and individuals in many issue networks decentralizes the control of campaigns and makes them harder to turn on and off (Bennett 2003).

But the most important point about information transmission in the one-step era is not that campaigns are permanent or ubiquitous. The real point is that campaigns are definitive. The campaign *style* of communication—its intellectual bases, assumptions, practices, effects, and consequences—literally *defines* political communication (and, in important ways, political organization) in the current era. And this is true in venues far removed from contests for public office. Bimber (2003, 104-7) referred to the current communication and information age as "post bureaucratic," indicating that social networks and the information that flows over them are increasingly hard to distinguish in organizational terms, particularly in contrast to an earlier era in which information was largely managed by bureaucratic organizations that channeled its social flow.

Conclusion: Normative Implications of a New Paradigm

The evolution of an ethos of managed or engineered consent that connects the two-step and one-step eras helps highlight an important distinction between the empirical and normative aspects of communication paradigms. Critiques such as Gitlin's (1978) argue that many of the choices about specifying the two-step flow model were not just weakly supported empirically, but they were strongly normative, meaning they conveyed a sense of inevitable objective reality when other possibly valid models of communication in society were available. There is a similar danger in the way we think about the one-step flow. Many practitioners today argue that there are few alternatives to the increasingly costly and privacy-invading methods used to reach individuals in fragmenting societies. The stark alternative is seen as chaos and lack of cohesiveness in the important process of engineering consent.

But there are, in fact, fairly clear alternative ways in which we could think about how the one-step flow could operate in democracies. There are practical choices to be made about technologies that render messages more or less engaging, transparent, public, exclusive, divisive, or cohesive. These choices are not just technological; they are also political. They affect whether citizens become further isolated through communication processes that emphasize unidirectional and highly manipulative information flows or whether citizens share known social networks through the transparent interactive capabilities that are available through the same technologies. Just as there is little reason to ascribe patterns of social fragmentation to communication processes alone, there is equally little reason to think that fragmented societies require communication processes that further compound the fragmentation. For example, it is just as possible to employ deliberative models of polling (see Fishkin 1991) that bring individuals together to explore ideas in public as it is to implement stealthy communication practices that feed messages to individuals based on known emotional preferences aimed at short-circuiting such deliberation. Similarly, it is just as possible to write software that enables recipients of messages to share their reactions and meet online or offline to discuss them, as it is to send individual messages soliciting or triggering individual responses.

This suggests another implication of how we think about the paradigm shift in the message-audience-response relationships of the contemporary era. The ways in which communicators choose among the technological alternatives for reaching fragmenting audiences may, in turn, have profound interactive effects on those audiences and their subsequent social and political relationships. It is important to emphasize here that technologies exist that have the potential to create mutual understanding and peer-to-peer communication across various issue and demographic divides (Price and Capella 2002; Iyengar, Luskin, and Fishkin 2004). Indeed, many social-movement networks have employed transparent social networking technologies with the aim of creating sustainable social bonds through the communication process (Bennett 2003).

In the current transition between two historic public communication eras, it appears that the chosen emphasis is more toward the stealthy technologies that isolate individuals than toward transparent networking technologies that may unite citizens in common cause (Bennett 2004). The likely explanation for this, as noted earlier, is that many of the communication consultants who steer much of the democratic process today do not work for social or democratic values but for the political success of partisan clients (Blumler and Kavanaugh 1999). But let us recall that the professionalization of politics is itself a product of particular perspectives and knowledge developed within the two-step paradigm. Recognizing the transition of that paradigm into a fundamentally different *one-step* flow of communication will lead scholars and practitioners to generate alternative perspectives and knowledge that will similarly shape the future. The choices of professionals, if left to their own devices and driven by their current motives, will shape the polity in less salutary ways for the next half century. Our choices as scholars should guide them.

References

Bell, Daniel. 1975. The end of American exceptionalism. *The Public Interest* 41:193-224.

Bennett, W. Lance. 1989. Marginalizing the majority: Conditioning public opinion to accept managerial democracy. In *Manipulating public opinion*, ed. Michael Margolis and Gary Mauser, 321-61. Pacific Grove, CA: Brooks/Cole.

———. 1998. The uncivic culture: Communication, identity, and the rise of lifestyle politics. *PS: Political Science & Politics* 31:741-61.

———. 2003. Communicating global activism: Strengths and vulnerabilities of networked politics. *Information, Communication & Society* 6 (2): 143-68.

———. 2004. Political communication and democratic governance: From mass society to personal information networks. Paper presented at the conference on Democracy in the Twenty-First century: Prospects and Problems, University of Illinois, Urbana, October 24-26.

———. 2005. Civic learning in changing democracies: Challenges for citizenship and civic education. Paper presented at the annual meeting of the American Political Science Association, Washington, DC, September 1-4.

Bennett, W. Lance, and Jarol B. Manheim. 2001. The big spin: Strategic communication and the transformation of pluralist democracy. In *Mediated politics: Communication in the future of democracy*, ed. W. Lance Bennett and Robert M. Entman, 279-98. New York: Cambridge University Press.

Berelson, Bernard R., Paul F. Lazarsfeld, and William N. McPhee. 1954. *Voting: A study of opinion formation in a presidential campaign*. Chicago: University of Chicago Press.

Berger, Peter L., and Thomas Luckman. 1966. *The social construction of reality: A treatise in the sociology of knowledge*. Garden City, NY: Doubleday.

Bimber, Bruce. 2003. *Information and American democracy: Technology in the evolution of political power*. New York: Cambridge University Press.

Blumler, Jay G., and Dennis Kavanaugh. 1999. The third age of political communication: Influences and features. *Political Communication* 16 (3): 209-31.

Burt, Ronald S. 1999. The social capital of opinion leaders. *Annals of the American Academy of Political and Social Science* 566:37-54.

Campbell, Angus, Philip E. Converse, Warren E. Miller, and Donald E. Stokes. 1960. *The American voter*. New York: John Wiley.

Converse, Philip E. 1964. The nature of belief systems in mass publics. In *Ideology and discontent*, ed. David Apter. New York: Free Press.

Davis, Richard. 1999. *The web of politics: The Internet's impact on the American political system*. New York: Oxford University Press.

Eliasoph, Nina. 1998. *Avoiding politics: How Americans produce apathy in everyday life*. New York: Cambridge University Press.

Entman, Robert M. 1993. Framing: Toward clarification of a fractured paradigm. *Journal of Communication* 43:51-58.

Ewen, Stuart. 1996. *PR! A social history of spin*. New York: Basic Books.

Festinger, Leon. 1957. *A theory of cognitive dissonance*. Stanford, CA: Stanford University Press.

Fishbein, Martin. 1967a. A behavior theory approach to the relations between beliefs about an object and the attitude toward the object. In *Readings in attitude theory and measurement*, ed. Martin Fishbein, 389-400. New York: John Wiley.

———. 1967b. A consideration of beliefs and their role in attitude measurement. In *Readings in attitude theory and measurement*, ed. Martin Fishbein, 257-66. New York: John Wiley.

Fishkin, James. 1991. *Democracy and deliberation: New directions for democratic reform*. New Haven, CT: Yale University Press.

Giddens, Anthony. 1991. *Modernity and self-identity: Self and society in late modern society*. Stanford, CA: Stanford University Press.

Gitlin, Todd. 1978. Media sociology: The dominant paradigm. *Theory and Society* 6:205-53.

Hardy, Bruce W., and Dietram A. Scheufele. 2005. Examining differential gains from Internet use: Comparing the moderating role of talk and online interactions. *Journal of Communication* 55:71-84.

Harik, Ilia F. 1971. Opinion leaders in the mass media in rural Egypt: A reconsideration of the two-step flow of communication hypothesis. *American Political Science Review* 65:731-40.

Howard, Philip. 2006. *New media campaigns and the managed citizen.* New York: Cambridge University Press.

Huckfeldt, Robert, Paul Allen Beck, Russell J. Dalton, and Jeffrey Levine. 1995. Political environments, cohesive social groups, and the communication of public opinion. *American Journal of Political Science* 39:1025-54.

Inglehart, Ronald. 1997. *Modernization and postmodernization: Cultural, economic, and political change in 43 societies.* Princeton, NJ: Princeton University Press.

Iyengar, Shanto. 1991. *Is anyone responsible?* Chicago: University of Chicago Press.

Iyengar, Shanto, and Donald Kinder. 1987. *News that matters: Television and American opinion.* Chicago: University of Chicago Press.

Iyengar, Shanto, Robert Luskin, and James Fishkin. 2004. Deliberative public opinion in presidential primaries: Evidence from an online deliberative poll. Paper presented at the conference Voice and Citizenship, University of Washington, Seattle, April 23-24.

Katz, Daniel. 1960. The functional approach to the study of attitudes. *Public Opinion Quarterly* 24:163-204.

Katz, Elihu, and Paul F. Lazarsfeld. 1955. *Personal influence: The part played by people in the flow of mass communications.* New York: Free Press.

Kelman, Herbert C. 1961. Processes of opinion change. *Public Opinion Quarterly* 25:57-78.

Kim, Joohan, Robert O. Wyatt, and Elihu Katz. 1999. News, talk, opinion, participation: The part played by conversation, in deliberative democracy. *Political Communication* 16:361-86.

Klapper, Joseph T. 1960. *The effects of mass communication.* New York: Free Press.

Krugman, Herbert E. 1965. The impact of television advertising: Learning without involvement. *Public Opinion Quarterly* 29:349-56.

———. 1966. The measurement of advertising involvement. *Public Opinion Quarterly* 30:583-96.

———. 1971. Brain wave measures of media involvement. *Journal of Advertising Research* 11:3-10.

Krugman, Herbert E., and Eugene L. Hartley. 1970. Passive learning from television. *Public Opinion Quarterly* 34:184-90.

Kubey, Robert, and Mihaly Csikszentmihalyi. 1990. *Television and the quality of life: How viewing shapes everyday experience.* Hillsdale, NJ: Lawrence Erlbaum.

Kuhn, Thomas. 1962. *The structure of scientific revolutions.* Chicago: University of Chicago Press.

Lane, Robert E. 1959. *Political life.* New York: Free Press.

Lazarsfeld, Paul F., Bernard Berelson, and Hazel Gaudet. 1944. *The people's choice.* New York: Columbia University Press.

Lemert, James B. 1981. *Does mass communication change public opinion after all? A new approach to effects analysis.* Chicago: Nelson-Hall.

Manheim, Jarol B. 1976. Can democracy survive television? *Journal of Communication* 26:84-90.

McCombs, Maxwell D., and Donald E. Shaw. 1972. The agenda-setting function of mass media. *Public Opinion Quarterly* 36:176-87.

Mills, C. Wright. 1956. *The power elite.* New York: Oxford University Press.

Mutz, Diana. 1998. *Impersonal influence: How perceptions of mass collectives affect political attitudes.* New York: Cambridge University Press.

Nimmo, Dan. 1970. *The political persuaders: The techniques of modern election campaigns.* Englewood Cliffs, NJ: Prentice Hall.

Norris, Pippa. 2001. *Digital divide: Civic engagement, information poverty, and the Internet worldwide.* New York: Cambridge University Press.

Patterson, Thomas. 2002. *The vanishing voter: Public involvement in an age of uncertainty.* New York: Random House.

Petty, Richard E., and John T. Cacioppo. 1986. The elaboration likelihood model of persuasion. In *Advances in experimental social psychology,* vol. 19, ed. Leonard Berkowitz, 123-205. New York: Academic Press.

Pew Research Center for the People and the Press. 2004. *News audiences increasingly politicized.* http://people-press.org/reports/display.php3?ReportID=215.

Price, Vincent, and Joseph Capella. 2002. Online deliberation and its influence: The Electronic Dialogue Project in Election 2000. *IT & Society* 1:303-29.

Putnam, Robert D. 2000. *Bowling alone: The collapse and revival of American community.* New York: Simon & Schuster.

Rheingold, Howard. 2002. *Smart mobs: The next social revolution.* Cambridge, MA: Perseus.

Robinson, John P. 1976. Interpersonal influence in election campaigns: Two-step flow hypothesis. *Public Opinion Quarterly* 40:304-19.

Shah, Dhavan V., Nojin Kwak, and R. Lance Holbert. 2001. "Connecting" and "disconnecting" with civic life: Patterns of Internet use and the production of social capital. *Political Communication* 18:141-62.

Sherif, Carolyn W., and Muzafer Sherif. 1967. The social judgment-involvement approach to attitude and attitude change. In *Social interaction*, ed. Muzafer Sherif, 342-52. Chicago: Aldine.

Subramani, Mani R., and Balaji Rajagopalan. 2003. Knowledge-sharing and influence in online social networks via viral marketing. *Communications of the Association for Computing Machinery* 46:300-307.

Tannenbaum, Percy H. 1955. The indexing process in communication. *Public Opinion Quarterly* 19:292-302.

Tewksbury, David. 2003. What do Americans really want to know? Tracking the behavior of news readers on the Internet. *Journal of Communication* 53:694-710.

Turow, Joseph. 1997. *Breaking up America: Advertisers and the new media world.* Chicago: University of Chicago Press.

U.S. Census Bureau. 1999. Media usage by consumers, 1992-1999. *Statistical abstract of the United States.* Figure 18.1. Washington, DC: U.S. Census Bureau.

———. 2000. Multi-media audiences—Summary 2000. *Statistical abstract of the United States.* Table 911. Washington, DC: U.S. Census Bureau.

Waller, Angie. 2003. *Data mining the Amazon.* N.P.

Weiman, Gabriel. 1982. On the importance of marginality: One more step into the two-step flow of communication. *American Sociological Review* 47:764-73.

Zaller, John R. 1992. *Nature and origins of mass opinion.* New York: Cambridge University Press.

Zarsky, Tal Z. 2006. Online privacy, tailoring, and persuasion. In *Privacy and technologies of identity—A cross-disciplinary conversation*, ed. Katherine Strandburg and Daniela Stan Raicu, 209-24. Berlin: Springer.

The Influence of *Personal Influence* on the Study of Audiences

SONIA LIVINGSTONE

This article looks back at the publication of *Personal Influence* (Katz and Lazarsfeld 1955) to bring into focus the multistranded history of discussion and debate over the mass media audience during the twentieth century. In contrast with the heroic narrative, constructed retrospectively, that prioritizes cultural studies' approaches to audiences, the author suggests that this rich and interdisciplinary history offers many fruitful ways forward as the agenda shifts from mass media to new media audiences. Although audience research has long been characterized by struggles between critical and administrative schools of communication, and between opposed perspectives on the relation of the individual to society, Katz and Lazarsfeld's work, and subsequent work by Katz and his collaborators, suggests possibilities for convergence, or at least productive dialogue, across hitherto polarized perspectives as researchers collectively seek to understand how, in their everyday lives, people can, and could, engage with media to further democratic participation in the public sphere.

Keywords: *Personal Influence*; Elihu Katz; audience research; audiences and publics; new media users; individual and society

W hen audience research took center stage in media and communication theory in the 1980s, with the development of audience reception studies, two ways of constructing the

Sonia Livingstone is a professor in the Department of Media and Communications at the London School of Economics and Political Science. She has published widely on the subject of media audiences and, more recently, on children, young people, and the Internet. Her books include Making Sense of Television *(Routledge, 1998, 2nd ed.),* Talk on Television *(with Peter Lunt, Routledge, 1994),* Young People and New Media *(Sage, 2002),* Audiences and Publics *(edited, Intellect, 2005), and* The Handbook of New Media *(edited, with Leah Lievrouw, Sage, 2006).*

NOTE: I thank Jay Blumler, Rob Farr, Michael Gurevitch, Elihu Katz, Tamar Liebes, Rodney Livingstone, Peter Lunt, David Morrison, and Peter Simonson for constructive discussions during the writing of both this article and my earlier, more detailed, account of Katz's career on which the present article draws (Livingstone, 1997).

DOI: 10.1177/0002716206292325

ANNALS, *AAPSS*, 608, November 2006
233

back story emerged. One located the origins in British cultural studies and tells a story of gradual recognition of the critical distance, even resistance, of a heterogeneous public to the ideological power of a hegemonic or culturally imperialist mass media (Morley 1992, 208; Nightingale 1996). The other tells of the gradual convergence of several theoretical traditions, critical and administrative, in a productive exploration of the diverse ways in which people respond actively, even creatively, to the mass media (Jensen and Rosengren 1990; Lindlof 1991; Livingstone 1998c). Although the latter account encompasses the former, it is the former that has become canonical, telling a linear, heroic narrative of intellectual progress in freeing the audience from the tyranny of mass ideology and so relocating audiences, plural, in relation to the social and cultural contexts where meanings are, instead, primarily reproduced in daily life. As an account, it is effective, providing a rallying call for the study of audiences, a call whose energy is only now beginning to dissipate. But it is limited in crucial ways.

First, as a history it is misleading, for it writes out of the picture the other valuable strands of argument and empirical research that have, over the decades, illuminated our understanding of people as audiences. Particularly, as I shall argue here, it repolarizes a debate that significant attempts have been made to transcend, that between critical and administrative approaches to the study of communication (Levy and Gurevitch 1994). Second, it no longer works, for as we move from an era dominated by mass media, and hence a mass audience, to a newly diversified, individualized, and globalized media and information environment, many other traditions of audience research prove more creative, constructive, and, indeed, critical, in rethinking people's relation to media. The cultural studies approach is struggling to find the path ahead, and many are leaving the domain of audience analysis (Livingstone 2003).

Far from unique, this end-of-the-century struggle over how to conceptualize and study the extent to which people's relation to the media is primarily one of hegemonic influence has strong echoes with an earlier struggle in the middle of the past century, one that was formative in framing the study of the television audience thereafter. By going back to the publication of *Personal Influence* (Katz and Lazarsfeld 1955) and even earlier, we can reconstruct a longer history of debate, discussion, and disagreement between diverse approaches to the study of media and communication than is retold in the heroic narrative of cultural studies approaches to audiences, in which any attempt to look earlier than the Birmingham Centre of Cultural Studies tends to return simply to Frankfurt and the emergence of critical theory. Important as these bodies of work are, undoubtedly, they represent only one side of the debate over, broadly, liberal versus critical accounts of the autonomy of the individual (or, conversely, over the power of social institutions in influencing behavior). To progress the debate, both sides must be represented, and represented fairly. To see the study of audiences as simply pulled between cultural studies versus uses and gratifications, or media imperialism versus autonomous viewers, or even active versus passive viewers, is a simplification that, while it may do rhetorical work for some in establishing intellectual narratives of progress, writes out much of the richness, the complexity, and the insights of diverse audience researchers working over many decades in many countries around the world.

With the benefit of hindsight, I will look back to the publication of *Personal Influence* to draw out these debates—some of which proved strongly influential in shaping the subsequent study of audiences—to show that, far from being a marginal subfield, the study of audiences represents a crucial site in which to analyze critically how political and economic power is played out in people's everyday lives. As Martin Allor (1988, 217) observed, "The concept of audience is . . . the underpinning prop for the analysis of the social impact of mass communication in general." For *Personal Influence* was not just about "the part played by people in the flow of mass communications" but was also, more significantly, about the part played by people—acting as individuals, in peer or community groups, and through institutions—in the construction and reconstruction of meanings in society. This should raise critical questions about power, interest, and inequalities, potentially integrating and so transcending rather than repolarizing the many conceptual oppositions—theoretical versus empirical or critical versus administrative or cultural versus economic—that have, sometimes unhelpfully, framed the study of media and communication.

[F]ar from being a marginal subfield,
the study of audiences represents a crucial
site in which to analyze critically how
political and economic power is played
out in people's everyday lives.

I shall take Elihu Katz's own career as my narrative device in this article, first because his career exactly spans the polarized story of audiences that I wish to trace here, with the publication of a series of influential books eloquently punctuating, and so marking, the twists and turns in audience research. And second because he has been a vocal commentator on these twists and turns, consistently calling for the productive convergence of multiple traditions of study[1] and so, often implicitly, a quiet critic of attempts to construct linear histories that write out intellectual diversity and debate (Katz et al. 2003).[2]

Personal Influence: Setting a Social and
Democratic Framework for the Study of Audiences[3]

In *Personal Influence: The Part Played by People in the Flow of Mass Communication*, Katz and Lazarsfeld (1955) significantly amended Harold Lasswell's (1948) classic question for mass communication research, "Who says what to whom with what content on what channel?" by demonstrating that the supposedly direct flow of mass media influence is mediated by preexisting patterns of interpersonal communication in local communities. The innovative concept of the two-step flow challenged the popularity of the direct effects model as well as the separate study of mass and interpersonal communication, and it undermined the image of the viewer and listener as part of a mindless, homogeneous mass. Since this was the heyday of the "minimal effects" approach, *Personal Influence* is often regarded, simplistically, as yet another nail in the coffin of the "hypodermic needle" model of media research (a model often referred to but rarely referenced because it was rarely advocated in so naïve a formulation; cf. Pooley 2006 [this volume]).

But the agenda for this book was broader and more subtle.[4] It showed that opinion leaders (see Lazarsfeld and Gaudet 1944) seek out mass media messages relevant to their expertise and disseminate these through vertical or horizontal flows in their local community, especially during periods of uncertainty, resulting in a selective transmission process (which resists or facilitates social change) mediated by interpersonal relations in primary groups (see also Katz 1957). Much of the book is concerned with these group processes as they operate in local contexts.[5] Hence, sidestepping the more usual production-text-audience framework of mass communication research, *Personal Influence*, like much of Katz's subsequent work, examines various permutations of the relations among three different domains: media (primarily institutional contexts, though also texts), public opinion (and its role in democratic processes), and conversation (as embedded in interpersonal or peer networks). So *Personal Influence* conceives of the active audience as firmly located in local groups and communities. In *The Uses of Mass Communications* (Blumler and Katz 1974), an active viewer is conceptualized primarily in terms of the individual needs that motivate selective exposure. The viewers in *The Export of Meaning* (Liebes and Katz 1990) are engaged in divergent reception according to their cultural backgrounds. And in *Media Events* (Dayan and Katz 1992), the viewer is participating in domestic conversation as part of the new global cultural sphere.

To develop this broader focus, integrating media audiences into the democratic project of the public sphere, Katz, like his teachers Merton and Lazarsfeld before him, has followed the social theorist, Tarde, who argued for the rationality of public opinion and who opposed the claimed mindlessness of the masses, as "the social theorist of diffusion *par excellence*" (Katz, Levin, and Hamilton 1963, 241). Seeing Gabriel Tarde as the originator of the active/passive voter/viewer debate, Katz identified similarities between Lazarsfeld's proposal of the two-step flow (Lazarsfeld and Gaudet 1944) and Tarde's social psychological essay of 1898, "La conversation" (Katz 1992). And he added, with an eye to the revisions of the two-step flow developed in response to Todd Gitlin's well-known critique (1978) of the theory's functionalist approach: "ironically, Tarde's hypothesis anticipates the *revision* that the two-step hypothesis has undergone (and is still undergoing), in its current emphasis on the flow of influence not the flow of information; on the group as a unit of analysis, not the individual; and on the mutuality of conversation, not the relay from leaders" (Katz 1992, 81).

Within this framework, everyday talk is central—people talk about the media, their talk is mediated, and they talk in ordinary, social contexts. Processes of influence are multiple and intersecting, and questions of effect are repositioned, so that effects do not occur at the tail end of a linear process of media influence, but they fan outwards from the individual to society and vice versa.[6] Instead of asking what effect do the media have on the people, Katz surely posed the counter question—what do the people do with the media—for rhetorical purposes. His real intention was to clear a space to ask, instead, what is the effect (on individuals, on society, on democracy, and on the media) of people sharing, or diverging from, a common conversation? And what does it matter if the terms or topics of the conversation come from the mediated or face-to-face experience, from local social groups or even other parts of the world?[7]

In *Media Events*, written with Daniel Dayan, Katz tried to show what a more contextualized notion of effects or media power would look like, using an anthropological perspective that emphasizes ceremony, ritual, and community, integrated with an account of the social and institutional arrangements that link media and audience. Dayan and Katz (1992) used the phenomenon of media events—the live broadcasting of "historic" events such as the Olympic Games, Kennedy's funeral, the British royal wedding—to demonstrate the inextricable interconnections between everyday conversations, media processes, and public opinion. Without requiring citizens to leave their homes (i.e., while "not being there"), the celebration of such "media events" allows for national or even global participation in a potentially transformative ritual whose form and meanings must be negotiated among institutions, broadcasters, public relations experts, technicians, fans, and ordinary readers and viewers at home.

Media Events also illustrates the potential for convergence across disciplines, itself a key concern of *Personal Influence*, by locating questions of active viewing in both global and local (as well as national) contexts. As the primary group is, increasingly, constituted through an imagined rather than a face-to-face community, and as the media become inextricably embedded in everyday life, this kind of multifaceted analysis may be a more sophisticated way, if not the only way, of addressing the question of influence or effects. For Dayan and Katz (1992), media events illuminate both the opportunities and dangers of a media-dominated democracy. They can create a national or even international sense of occasion, providing liminal moments in which a society may reflect upon, idealize, and at the same time, authenticate a vision of itself for itself. Yet if these liminal moments substitute for political participation and political change, then it is their potentially reactionary, manipulative, or narcotizing effects, rather than their potentially progressive, educational, or democratic effects, that should be at the forefront of our concern. Indeed, Dayan and Katz claimed, though perhaps did not always demonstrate, a wide range of effects for media events, far wider than anticipated in *Personal Influence*, including effects on participants and on institutions, at the time of the event and subsequently, including the ways in which live broadcasting confers legitimacy and charisma on the "celebrities" involved, the interruption of everyday routines that casts viewers into roles proposed by the script of the ceremony, effects on the climate of opinion by encouraging or inhibiting the expression of certain beliefs, changes to the organization of politics and political campaigning, and instances of direct political or social change resulting from a media event.[8]

Exerting Personal Influence Toward Convergence

These complexities that we grapple with today, as society becomes more globalized, and as the media become more diversified, have long roots in the history of the field. To figure out how today's debates over audiences can move forward, it is worth recognizing how they emerged and developed, so as to identify the key arguments that continue to underlie our understanding of mediated power in everyday life. Two debates are central, and both can be traced back to *Personal Influence* and the intellectual climate of that period. They concern, essentially, the politics of research and the politics of the researched; or, as they have more usually been characterized, the debate between administrative and critical schools of communication, and the debate over the relation between the individual and society.

The politics of research: Administrative and critical approaches to mass communication

Fifty years ago saw significant optimism about both social science and the mass media as two forces that, if used appropriately, could further the project of the enlightenment, educating the public as rational, informed citizens equipped to participate in a democratic society. For Paul Lazarsfeld, director of the Princeton Office of Radio Research (later the Columbia Bureau of Applied Social Research), the task was to develop the study of mass communications in this direction, using empirical methods to combine social psychology and sociology to understand what broadcasting means (and could mean) in the lives of its listeners and viewers. But determining how to further the project of the enlightenment was, and is, no easy matter.

Max Horkheimer's (1972) essay on traditional and critical theory, first published in 1937, set out the epistemological and political framework for the critical theory of the Frankfurt School. At the same time, Lazarsfeld (1941, 8) had specified the parameters of administrative (or positivist) research on mass communications as research that "is carried through in the service of some kind of administrative agency of public or private character."[9] He also attempted "to explain the 'critical approach' sympathetically to an American audience" (p. 325), arguing that critical research could contribute challenging problems, new concepts, useful interpretations, and new data and suggesting that it is the task of administrative research to translate these into empirical studies—a task in which he later saw himself as having failed (Jay 1973; Lazarsfeld 1969).

Interestingly, Theodor Adorno (1969) had also advocated a link between critical ideas and empirical research, noting "one of the most important justifications for empirical research—that virtually all findings can be explained theoretically once they are in hand, but not conversely" (p. 364). Yet he clearly found Lazarsfeld's approach frustrating: "I considered it to be my fitting and objectively proffered assignment to *interpret* phenomena—not to ascertain, sift, and classify facts and make them available as information" (p. 339), particularly as the Rockefeller Foundation had, as he saw it, ruled out the analysis of "the system itself, its cultural and sociological consequences and its social and economic presuppositions" (p.343) when funding the Princeton radio project.

Arguably, then, these early attempts at convergence were not successful (although see Simonson and Weimann 2003). Consequently, the same distinction was drawn and maintained in the study of audiences: critical researchers "construe audience members as embodying larger social and political structures . . . [while administrative researchers] embrace the liberal-pluralist ideal of democratic life . . . [which regards individuals as] potential sites of creativity, novelty, independence, and autonomy" (Swanson 1992, 322). Although Katz was briefly connected to the Frankfurt School tradition, having written his master's thesis in 1950 supervised by Leo Lowenthal[10] at the Columbia University Bureau of Applied Social Research, *Personal Influence* was the first in a series of broadly administrative books (for example, see Coleman, Katz, and Menzel 1966; Crain, Katz, and Rosenthal 1969). Yet he inherited Lazarsfeld's interest in the idea of integrating critical and administrative schools of mass communication.

Katz wrote his first bridge-building article in 1959 when mass communications was just being formed as a discipline, and its arguments for convergence between social science and the humanities read today with a strikingly modern feel (Katz 1959).[11] Later, in exploring the idea of the active audience as an opportunity for integrating contrasting approaches, Katz argued that "activity inheres in the creative translation of media messages by individuals in the process of perceiving and attributing meanings" (Katz 1979, 75). Blumler, Gurevitch, and Katz (1985) saw this creative process of meaning negotiation as a route "to build the bridge we have been hoping might arise between gratifications studies and cultural studies" (Katz 1979, 75). The attempt continued in *The Export of Meaning*, written with Tamar Liebes, for in studying audience reception of *Dallas* (Liebes and Katz 1990), Katz took uses and gratifications in the direction of literary and humanistic approaches to texts (though he was less successful in taking uses and gratifications theory with him; Elliott 1974).[12]

Although, as Hanno Hardt (1992, 236) noted skeptically, "there is no history of a systematic acknowledgement of Marxist scholarship by traditional communications research in the United States," Katz (1987, S30) added hopefully, "some of us are still trying." Some may argue that the separation of administrative and critical mass communications research has been to the advantage of both schools, for each developed its own strengths. However, recently many in audience research have declared this a stale, even a false, dichotomy, to be transcended rather than perpetuated (Levy and Gurevitch 1994; Schrøder et al. 2003). Moreover, it is not in practice an easy distinction to sustain. Katz (1987, S30) pointed out the contradiction in attacking "the 'administrative' orientation for providing powerful tools of persuasion to the marketers, politicians, etc. while arguing that the effects of such persuasive attempts are invisible in the short run." Kurt and Gladys Lang (1983, 131-32) added that administrative research contains "much that is critical of existing institutional arrangements and practices" and that "empirical research can be used by any group, including crusaders against the status quo" (p. 132)—the work of George Gerbner (Gerbner et al. 1986) and that of the Glasgow University Media Group (Eldridge 1993) come to mind here. Katz (1978, 135) noted further that contemporary critical media studies also "betrays an interest in affecting policy"; indeed, present political and economic conditions surely mean that policy-relevant research findings must be forthcoming from critical scholars.

The individual and society

The relation between the individual and society, a founding debate in social science, has been variously interpreted in the analysis of mass communication.[13] The Columbia School was always more sociological than its rival, the Yale School, which, following Lasswell's sender-message-receiver model, took a strongly psychological and experimental approach to analyzing media influence in terms of cognitive persuasion theory (Hovland, Janis, and Kelley 1953). Robert Merton's (1955, 510) description of the emerging field of the sociology of knowledge, when applied to media research, characterizes the Columbia School thus:

> Searching out such variations in effective audiences, exploring their distinctive criteria of significant and valid knowledge, relating these to their position within the society and examining the socio-psychological processes through which these operate to constrain certain modes of thought constitutes a procedure which promises to take research in the sociology of knowledge from the plane of general imputation to testable empirical inquiry.

Hence, Katz consistently locates cognitive and motivational accounts of audience activity in the context of the primary group and social networks (even in his uses and gratifications work; see Katz, Gurevitch, and Hass 1973), though he—as ever—seeks convergence between these traditions also (Katz 1960). His subsequent sociological diffusion research (Katz, Levin, and Hamilton 1963) can be contrasted with the more social psychological uses and gratifications approach (see Blumler and Katz 1974), in terms of their starting point (text/message versus audience need), context (social structure and culture versus individual habits), and effect (acceptance of intended message versus need gratifications). However, in both approaches, the mass media are seen as plural, as are audiences; moreover, the sociocognitive processes of media influence are foregrounded. Thus, throughout his work, Katz has argued against a view of mass society comprised of monolithic and homogeneous media and a mass audience of defenseless viewers (cf. Peters 2006 [this volume]).

[T]hroughout his work, Katz has argued against a view of mass society comprised of monolithic and homogeneous media and a mass audience of defenseless viewers.

In offering a formal analysis of the many possible relations between the individual and societal influence, Alexander and Giesen (1987, 14) outlined five major accounts of the micro and macro link as follows:

> (1) rational, purposeful individuals create society through contingent acts of freedom; (2) interpretive individuals create society through contingent acts of freedom; (3) socialized individuals re-create society as a collective force through contingent acts of freedom; (4) socialized individuals reproduce society by translating existing social environment into the microrealm; and (5) rational, purposeful individuals acquiesce to society because they are forced to by external, social control.

I have previously mapped diverse approaches to audiences onto this scheme, albeit with some hesitation (Livingstone 1998a). Option 1, I suggested, is adopted by those who conceptualize *the audience as a market* (or aggregate of individuals). In option 2, those who draw on interpretative or phenomenological sociology also assert the agency of individuals in developing an idea of *active and creative audiences*, though the focus is switched from the individual as "rational actor" to the individual as "symbolic interpreter." By contrast, option 5, *the audience as duped mass*, represents—or is often represented as—the pessimistic starting point from which critical theory, cultural studies, and feminist approaches have been seeking escape routes. Option 4, *the audience as generally conformist but just occasionally resistant*, recognizes some exceptions to option 5—as in Hall's (1980, 1994) analysis of the mismatch between processes of encoding and decoding.

But audience reception studies have been greatly exercised over the question of how far to extend this argument, taking option 4 further toward the social constructivist option 3, or even option 2. Empirical investigation seems to invite an ever more active audience, but then empirical investigation will always reveal diversity of response, depending on the specificities of context; hence, the interpretation of such diversity—how much diversity makes a difference?—remains contentious. Undoubtedly, as Larry Grossberg (1993, 89-90) has observed, cultural studies is committed to "the fact that reality is continually being made through human action," and this view has led many researchers to explore ways in which audiences "devise inventive ways of resisting, subverting, or otherwise re-making messages or technologies" (Lindlof 1987, 28). Yet when David Morley (1993, 17) argued that "local meanings are so often made within and against the symbolic resources provided by global media networks," it is evident that much hangs on the balance between "within" and "against." A similar uncertainty, between options 2 and 4, is evident when John Thompson (1994, 44) shifted from the claim that "the appropriation of this material by recipients is a process that always takes place in particular social-historical circumstances" to the claim that appropriation "is an active, creative and selective process in which individuals draw on the resources available to them in order to receive and make sense of the symbolic material transmitted by the media."

The synthetic middle option seems underexplored, though for Alexander and Giesen (1987) it is the most desirable, not least because it comes closest to *the audience as public*, recognizing that democracy rests on the informed consent of the thinking citizen who is in turn socialized within a liberal/pluralist framework (Couldry, Livingstone, and Markham forthcoming; Livingstone 2005). While often read, in polarized fashion, as asserting option 1 or 2 against some version of option 5, I suggest that *Personal Influence* represented the first of several steps by which Lazarsfeld and Katz, and later Katz and his colleagues, sought to explore the possibilities of option 3; hence the formative importance of Tarde's examination of the links between public opinion, everyday conversation, and the media institutions. Indeed, John Durham Peters (1989) has argued that a strongly democratic or pluralist political agenda underpins *Personal Influence*, claiming that "much of the history of American mass communication theory and research is an attempt to carry out a political project without being articulate about that project" (p. 199) and that discussion of media effects is really a discussion of "the perils and possibilities of democracy" (p. 200), of "how to conceive of the public sphere in an age of mass media" (p. 212).

The underlying debate, therefore, concerns mass society, a debate "which turns on the question of the viability of democracy in an age of media and bureaucracy" (Peters 1989, 216). Mendelsohn (1989) concurred: "this limited effects paradigm is deeply embedded in the theory of action that was first promulgated as a rationale for basing new 18th- and 19th-century democratic governance on public opinion and popular will" (p. 819; cf. Kadushin 2006 [this volume]).[14] Thus, Peters (1989, 215) argued that "the genius of *Personal Influence* was to rescue the public sphere from the media" and thereby to permit an alternative approach to participatory democracy even in a media age. Yet he, like others, was skeptical of the argument that the mass media, far from undermining the public sphere, are, instead, supporters of it through the medium of active debate within primary groups. Just as Herbert Schiller (1989), commenting on *The Export of Meaning*, questioned whether divergent and resistant interpretations among audiences have any actual effect on established power structures, Peters asked whether the interpersonal step of the two-step flow has any identifiable effect in shaping collective understandings or ordering social worlds, questions that the contributors to *Audiences and Publics* (Livingstone 2005) have recently taken up (see also Couldry and Markham 2006 [this volume]).

Although it argued for a shift from direct to indirect effects, thereby opening the way for a more complex analysis of mediations and contextualizations, *Personal Influence* represents an imperfect exemplar of how to converge multiple perspectives (particularly by comparison with *The Export of Meaning* and *Media Events*). It is often cited—fairly—by its critics for endorsing the problematic (though still commonplace) transmission model of the media (Carey 1989). Given the concurrent debates between Adorno and Lazarsfeld, its bibliography is striking for the absence of critical theory (indeed, of any European) works. And by prioritizing empirical social scientific methods over high theory, the effect was to lead mass communication research firmly in an administrative direction, divorcing it from the emerging school of critical mass communications (Lang and Lang 1983, 2006 [this volume]).[15] Gitlin (1978, 208) claimed that *"Personal Influence* can be read as the founding document of an entire field of inquiry" and criticized it precisely for its implicit attack on the analyses of power, influence, and ideology advocated by critical mass communication research. And it was this critique that led Stuart Hall (1980), two decades later, to launch his critical encoding/decoding approach to audiences (which analyzed mass communication as a circuit of linked practices of production, circulation, consumption, and reproduction[16]) through a direct attack on the work of James Halloran and the uses and gratifications approach.[17] Thus, the debate continued in the next generation.

Influences on Research in an Age of Media Convergence

However, for the generation following, we must again rethink. In mass communication theory, audiences represented one of three central components in the analytic framework, together with production and texts. Encoding and decoding, uses and gratifications, models of media effects—each has been conceived for the age of mass media, and mass society, and each is now being rethought as the media and communication environment becomes increasingly diversified, globalized, individualized, and privatized. The insight of *Personal Influence*, that processes of media influence are mediated by social contexts, including community and face-to-face interactions, is now a starting point rather than a discovery.

The evocative image that captured, and worried, the public imagination is no longer that of the immobile viewer sitting on the sofa silently staring at the screen. Rather, it is of multitasking in front of the computer, creating as well as receiving messages, networked online as well as embedded in a noisy world of interaction offline, distracted rather than focused, communicative rather than silent, perhaps even on the move rather than pinned to the domestic interior. Yet this figure too is the object of public anxieties, some familiar and some new.

Hence, as part of the development of new media theory, these three core components of mediation are being reconceived. Lievrouw and Livingstone (2006) offered a translation for the changing communication environment that seeks to avoid an overfocusing on technological change and that brackets assumptions about the "mass" (this is not to say the "mass" is obsolete; rather that it should not simply be presumed). We argue that research must analyze the *artifacts or devices* used to communicate or convey information (raising questions of design and development), the *activities and practices* in which people engage to communicate or share information (raising questions of cultural and social context), and the *social arrangements or organizational forms* that develop around those devices and practices (raising questions of institutional organization, power, and governance). Significantly, we do not specify the relations among these components a priori. Where mass communication research spent decades struggling with and, latterly, unpicking the assumption of linearity (that production produces texts that impact on audiences, following the sender-message-receiver model), new media research need make no such assumption.[18]

Through the activities and practices with which people engage with new forms of media, people are evidently diverse, motivated, resistant, literate, and so forth. Hence our dual stress on social shaping and social consequences in the *Handbook of New Media* (see Lievrouw and Livingstone 2006), for it is precisely the dynamic links and interdependencies among these component processes that should guide the analytic focus. However, since these dynamic interrelations are not infinitely flexible, we also stress that these artifacts, activities and social arrangements (and the relations among them) become routine, established, institutionalized, and so taken for granted, together constituting the communications infrastructure of everyday life. How should this be researched? Of the multiple trajectories that recently converged on the study of audience interpretation or reception, revitalizing this area of mass communication theory, most can trace a history back to the early days, and early debates, that characterized the establishment of the field in the early- to mid-twentieth century. And in sketching a way forward for the analysis of people's responses to, critical engagement with, and social positioning by new forms of media and communication, we would surely wish to retain an equally broad agenda (Press and Livingstone 2006).

Thus, in asking how people engage with new media, and how new media position and influence them, important questions can be drawn out of a cultural studies perspective about the institutional and cultural processes of encoding and decoding. However, equally valuable questions, from a critical communication perspective, will concern the power relations between producers, distributors, and consumers. Globalization theory adds a crucial perspective, for the new media are—in a manner little anticipated by the largely national (or, sometimes, universalistic) focus of traditional mass communication research—also global (or local) media (Tomlinson 1999). Poststructuralist theories of the textually inscribed role of the reader raise fascinating possibilities in relation to convergent, hypertextual multimedia (Burbules 1998). Such approaches interface with information science to reframe "user" research in relation to new literacies (Kress 2003) and the shifting politics of participation (Jensen 2005). Feminist theory must and will continue to ask about new (and old) forms of exclusion or discrimination, as well as about alternative or subcultural readings, in the new media environment (Van Zoonen 2002). Ethnographic studies of the consumption of new media similarly are extending lessons from the study of established media to pose new questions about mediated consumption and the diverse cultures of the everyday (Fornas et al. 2002; Miller and Slater 2000). Last, people's engagement with media—old and new—is part of their activities as publics, as citizens, for better or for worse, and so is not to be hived off as just a matter of the domestic or private sphere (Livingstone 2005).

These are all exciting developments, but the continuities are also important. Though the shift from mass communication theory to theorizing mediation in all its forms will occupy scholars for some time to come, the broader agenda that *Personal Influence* prioritized—the examination of the relations between mediation, conversation, and community to understand the potential, positive and negative, of the media in democratic society—remains paramount. If Katz and Lazarsfeld were to review the emerging field of new media research, they might be concerned at the balance between theory and empirical research—much is still sketchy, short on empirical support, tentative in its methodology. Still, for the study of people's engagement with the new media environment, that is, for the study of audiences as publics and of publics as mediated, this is still early days. It is to be hoped that, in developing these initial steps into a sustained research program, scholars will continue to draw on the multiple intellectual traditions, convergent epistemologies, and bold surmises that motivated earlier steps toward the same democratic project fifty years ago, as evidenced by *Personal Influence*.

Notes

1. Sills (1981) identified the three major features of Lazarsfeld's research style as being collaboration with others, creation of research institutes, and the search for a convergence between different intellectual traditions; all features that clearly influenced Katz's own approach to research. Indeed, the preface to his doctoral dissertation was headed "an essay in convergence," and in this he points to the influence of Merton also (Katz 1956).

2. Concerned with establishing a broad and multidisciplinary field of mass communications, Katz's emphasis on convergence reflects a conviction that ideas evolve best through responding to the challenge of alternative positions, that they become vulgar versions of themselves if they remain within hermetically sealed traditions (he has been critical of uses and gratifications research in this respect), and that ideas develop more productively if divergent tendencies and hostilities are countered.

3. A cautionary note—one of Katz's books was about the genre of soap opera, and so it is appropriate to begin this section by observing that the sequence of books discussed here is neither comprehensive nor

finished, that multiple strands are discernable as one looks across them, and that they can be read in different ways. Nonetheless, I shall offer a particular reading, my own interpretive context being as a social psychologist, an end-of-the-century audience researcher, and an advocate of convergent approaches to diversity in theory and method.

4. Yet misreadings persist: for Sproule (1989), *Personal Influence* played a key role in (re)writing research history to create "the magic bullet myth" of direct media effects to demonstrate the success of the Columbia School by putting media research on a scientific footing. Equally inappropriately, *Personal Influence* has been read as demonstrating null effects. It is important to recognize that Katz and Lazarsfeld felt themselves led by the *data* to emphasize the mediating, but not wholly undermining, role of the social and communicative context in processes of effect. And this in turn led Katz to argue against the kind of broad theorizing that results in what he sees as the untestable or at least typically untested theories of hegemony and ideology. Hence, Boudon (1991) regarded *Personal Influence* as an example of Merton's middle-range theory, where middle-range theories attempt to integrate relevant hypotheses (here, the idea of a two-step flow of influence) and empirical regularities but assume that "it is hopeless and quixotic to try to determine the overarching independent variable that would operate in all social processes" (p. 519).

5. Thus, the social psychology of the group is used to account for the diffusion of media effects, thereby linking interpersonal and mass communications in a manner often neglected in subsequent research (although see Hawkins, Wiemann, and Pingree 1988).

6. This is by contrast with the traditional model, which holds that the communication process is essentially linear, with the audience positioned as passive receiver at the end of an influential and unidirectional process of information transmission.

7. One cannot ask about influence without asking about effects and, at present, the reductive account of "media effects" advocated by extreme advocates of both critical and administrative traditions has all but eliminated a subtle and fruitful discussion of media influence and effects from theoretical discussion in media and communications (Livingstone 1996): we need to find a language with which to return to this important agenda.

8. Katz characterized each decade in the history of mass communications as an oscillation between conceptions of active and passive viewers, and hence between minimal effects and powerful media (1980); though, in a moment of disillusion, he concluded that "we teeter back and forth between paradigms, without getting very far. We need to perform some crucial experiments and to agree on appropriate research methods rather than just storing a treasury of contradictory bibliographical references in our memory banks" (1992, 85). This oscillation can itself be seen as stemming from the contradictions within the liberal-pluralist approach to media research, an approach that sees the audience both as public and as mass (Livingstone 2005). However, from the addition of interpersonal communication as a second step in the flow of media influence in the 1950s to the selective and motivated viewer of *The Uses of Mass Communications* in the 1970s (Blumler and Katz 1974); the interpretive, culturally grounded viewer countering cultural imperialism in *The Export of Meaning* in the late 1980s (Liebes and Katz 1990); and the locally embedded but symbolically connected viewer of *Media Events* in the early 1990s (Dayan and Katz 1992), he has consistently argued for a sociopsychological, selective viewer (not, however, a wholly autonomous or "sovereign" consumer). Hence, "the effects of the media are mitigated by the processes of selectivity in attention, perception, and recall, and . . . these, in turn, are a function of predispositional and situational variables such as age, family history, political affiliation, and so on" (Katz 1987, S26)—it is the task of research to map these processes of selectivity and their dependence on social context.

9. Katz (personal communication, 1996) has suggested that for Lazarsfeld, administrative research takes the client's problem as given while critical research asks whether the client may be part of the problem.

10. In his memoirs, Lowenthal, a founder member of the Frankfurt Institute of Social Research, discussed how he found it easier than Adorno "to combine the theoretical and historical outlook with the empirical requisites of sociological research" (Jay 1987, 140), although he also gave examples of how Lazarsfeld "failed to see the political and analytical meaning of my study [of biographies]" (Jay 1987, 132). He added, "finally I also learned—it wasn't particularly difficult—to assert my own individuality as a sociologist, while at the same time familiarizing myself with what seemed to be significant and important in American social research. Later I attempted to convey this synthesis to my students" (Jay 1987, 141)—of whom Katz was one.

11. In this article, Katz argued that, while the study of short-term media effects is "dead," research should now address not what the media do to people but what people do with the media (i.e., uses and

gratifications) and thereby aim for a more complex link to effects by building a bridge to the humanist tradition of studying popular culture.

12. Symptomatic of contemporary uses and gratifications, the typology of the active viewer proposed by Levy and Windahl (1985) misunderstands the hermeneutic nature of meaning creation, seeing it as gaining "a more or less clear understanding of the structure of the message" (p. 115); other contributors to that volume also regard the text as a source of given and obvious messages (Livingstone 1998b).

13. The roots of the disputes in media theory over social psychology—that is, about the autonomy and rationality of individuals subject to media influence—can be traced back to the 1920s and 1930s. Adorno's (1969) understanding of social psychology drew more on psychoanalysis, influenced by Fromm's work at the (Frankfurt) Institute of Social Research, than on the embryonic tradition of positivist social psychology. For researchers at the institute before the Second World War, it was their explicit aim to develop a critical social psychology "to explain the processes through which individual consciousness was adjusted to the functional requirements of the system, in which a monopolistic economy and an authoritarian state had coalesced" (Habermas 1989, 293). This approach contrasts with the largely individualistic social psychology that developed in America, though Smith (1983) identified Katz as part of this latter tradition, thus neglecting his more sociological concerns.

14. Katz's subsequent work typifies this broadly normative tradition, examining issues of media effects, bureaucracy, voters, public opinion, and so forth, to emphasize (and protect) the self-determining potential of the individual against the power of the mass media and to promote a professional-client model of producer-audience relations. Yet Katz rarely presented an explicitly political agenda beyond expressing his broad interest in the relation between media, public opinion, citizenship, and conversation.

15. Yet ironically, Lazarsfeld and others were originally motivated to conduct propaganda research because, as members of the Socialist Student Movement, they were concerned that their propaganda was unsuccessful in the face of that of the growing nationalist movement of Vienna in the 1920s. Indeed, when discussing the influential Marienthal study in Vienna, which linked social stratification and social psychology, Lazarsfeld (1969, 278) claimed that his work "had a visible Marxist tinge" and he recalled the almost accidental way in which he happened upon market research methods (and funding) when empirical research techniques were otherwise lacking to pursue these ends.

16. Hall drew directly on Marx's political economy, which emphasizes cycles of production/consumption, but he emphasizes that the media operate through symbolic exchange. Thus, relations between the practices linked by this circuit are understood discursively as "articulation" by analogy with exchange in the economic sphere (Pillai 1992).

17. See also the opening pages of Morley's *Nationwide Audience* (1980) and Hall's later reflections on the debate (1994).

18. Indeed, the challenge for research is, in many ways, the opposite, for we have yet to identify the ways in which people are also normative, unoriginal, mindless, influenced through new media. There is a terminological switch in the foregoing sentences that marks the shift from old to new media well. The term *audience* works poorly in this changed environment, and *users* does not work either, being a term that has little to do with information and communication (people are also users of pens, batteries, washing powder) and that lacks reference to any collective status: precisely unlike the mass audience of mass society, users are an aggregate of individuals with no collective status or power. In subtitling *Personal Influence, The Part Played by People . . .*, Katz and Lazarsfeld offered a fair alternative—*people* encompasses a focus on both individuality and collectivity, it permits investigation of both common knowledge and differentiated experience and, unlike *audience* or *user*, makes no misleading assumptions about the relations between media and the public sphere (Livingstone 2004).

References

Adorno, T. 1969. Scientific experiences of a European scholar in America. In *The intellectual migration: Europe and America, 1930-1960*, ed. D. Fleming and B. Bailyn. Cambridge: Cambridge University Press.

Alexander, J. C., and Giesen, B. 1987. From reduction to linkage: The long view of the micro-macro debate. In *The micro-macro link*, ed. J. C. Alexander, B. Giesen, R. Munch, and N. J. Smelser. Berkeley: University of California Press.

Allor, M. 1988. Relocating the site of the audience. *Critical Studies in Mass Communication* 5:217-33.

Blumler, J. G., M. Gurevitch, and E. Katz. 1985. REACHING OUT: A future for gratifications research. In *Media gratifications research: Current perspectives*, ed. K. E. Rosengren, L. A. Wenner, and P. Palmgreen. Beverly Hills, CA: Sage.

Blumler, J. G., and E. Katz, eds. 1974. *The uses of mass communications: Current perspectives on gratification research*. Beverly Hills, CA: Sage.

Boudon, R. 1991. What middle-range theories are. *Contemporary Social Psychology* 20 (4): 519-24.

Burbules, N. C. 1998. Rhetorics on the Web: Hyperreading and critical literacy. In *Page to screen: Taking literacy into the electronic era*, ed. I. Snyder, 102-22. New York: Routledge.

Carey, J. W. 1989. *Communication as culture: Essays on media and society*. New York: Routledge.

Coleman, J. S., E. Katz, and H. Menzel. 1966. *Medical innovation: A diffusion study*. Indianapolis, IN: Bobbs-Merrill.

Couldry, N., S. Livingstone, and T. Markham. Forthcoming. *Media consumption and public engagement: Beyond the presumption of attention*. Houndmills, UK: Palgrave.

Couldry, Nick, and Tim Markham. 2006. Public connection through media consumption: Between over-socialization and de-socialization. *Annals of the American Academy of Political and Social Science* 608:251-69.

Crain, R. L., E. Katz, and D. Rosenthal. 1969. *The politics of community conflict: The fluoridation decision*. Indianapolis, IN: Bobbs-Merrill.

Dayan, D., and E. Katz. 1992. *Media events: The live broadcasting of history*. Cambridge, MA: Harvard University Press.

Eldridge, J., ed. 1993. *Getting the message: News, truth and power*. London: Routledge.

Elliott, P. 1974. Uses and gratifications research: A critique and a sociological alternative. In *The uses of mass communications: Current perspectives on gratifications research*, ed. J. G. Blumler and E. Katz. Beverly Hills, CA: Sage.

Fornas, J., K. Klein, M. Ladendorf, J. Sunden, and M. Svenigsson, eds. 2002. *Digital borderlands: Cultural studies of identity and interactivity on the Internet*. New York: Peter Lang.

Gerbner, G., L. Gross, M. Morgan, and N. Signorielli. 1986. Living with television: The dynamics of the cultivation process. In *Perspectives on media effects*, ed. J. Bryant and D. Zillman. Hillsdale, NJ: Lawrence Erlbaum.

Gitlin, T. 1978. Media sociology: The dominant paradigm. *Theory and Society* 6:205-53.

Grossberg, L. 1993. Can cultural studies find true happiness in communication? *Journal of Communication* 43 (4): 89-97.

Habermas, J. 1989. The tasks of a critical theory of society. In *Critical theory and society: A reader*, ed. S. E. Bronner and D. M. Kellner, 292-312. New York: Routledge.

Hall, S. 1980. Encoding/decoding. In *Culture, media, language*, ed. S. Hall, D. Hobson, A. Lowe, and P. Willis. London: Hutchinson.

———. 1994. Reflections on the encoding/decoding model. In *Viewing, reading, listening: Audiences and cultural reception*, ed. J. Cruz and J. Lewis. Boulder, CO: Westview.

Hardt, H. 1992. *Critical communication studies: Communication, history and theory in America*. London: Routledge.

Hawkins, R. P., J. Wiemann, and S. Pingree, eds. 1988. *Advancing communication science: Merging mass and interpersonal processes*. Newbury Park, CA: Sage.

Horkheimer, M. 1972. Traditional and critical theory. In *Critical theory: Selected essays*, ed. M. Horkheimer. New York: Seabury Press.

Hovland, C., I. Janis, and H. H. Kelley. 1953. *Communication and persuasion*. New Haven, CT: Yale University Press.

Jay, M. 1973. *The dialectical imagination: A history of the Frankfurt school and the Institute of Social Research, 1923-1950*. London: Heinemann Educational Books.

———, ed. 1987. *An unmastered past: The autobiographical reflections of Leo Lowenthal*. Berkeley: University of California Press.

Jensen, K. B., ed. 2005. *Interface://Culture: The World Wide Web as political resources and aesthetic form*. Frederiksberg, Denmark: Samfundslitteratur Press/Nordicom.

Jensen, K. B., and K. E. Rosengren. 1990. Five traditions in search of the audience. *European Journal of Communication* 5 (2-3): 207-38.

Kadushin, Charles. 2006. *Personal influence:* A radical theory of action. *Annals of the American Academy of Political and Social Science* 608:270-81.

Katz, E. 1956. Interpersonal relations and mass communications: Studies in the flow of influence. PhD diss., Columbia University, New York.

———. 1957. The two-step flow of communication: An up-to-date report on an hypothesis. *Public Opinion Quarterly* 21:61-78.

———. 1959. Mass communications research and the study of popular culture: An editorial note on a possible future for this journal. *Studies in Public Communication* 2:1-6.

———. 1960. Communication research and the image of society: Convergence of two traditions. *American Journal of Sociology* 65 (5): 435-40.

———. 1978. Of mutual interest. *Journal of Communication* 28 (2): 133-41.

———. 1979. The uses of Becker, Blumler and Swanson. *Communication Research* 6 (1): 74-83.

———. 1980. On conceptualising media effects. *Studies in Communication* 1:119-41.

———. 1987. Communications research since Lazarsfeld. *Public Opinion Quarterly* 51:S25-S45.

———. 1992. On parenting a paradigm: Gabriel Tarde's agenda for opinion and communication research. *International Journal of Public Opinion Research* 4 (1): 80-86.

Katz, E., M. Gurevitch, and H. Hass. 1973. On the use of the mass media for important things. *American Sociological Review* 38 (2): 164-81.

Katz, E., and P. F. Lazarsfeld. 1955. *Personal influence: The part played by people in the flow of mass communication*. Glencoe, IL: Free Press.

Katz, E., M. L. Levin, and H. Hamilton. 1963. Traditions of research on the diffusion of innovation. *American Sociological Review* 28:237-52.

Katz, E., J. D. Peters, T. Liebes, and A. Orloff. 2003. Editors' introduction. In *Canonic texts in media research*, ed. E. Katz, J. D. Peters, T. Liebes, and A. Orluff, 1-8. Cambridge, UK: Polity.

Kress, G. 2003. *Literacy in the new media age*. London: Routledge.

Lang, K., and G. E. Lang. 1983. The "new" rhetoric of mass communication research: A longer view. *Journal of Communication* 33 (3): 128-40.

———. 2006. *Personal influence* and the new paradigm: Some inadvertent consequences. *Annals of the American Academy of Political and Social Science* 608:157-78.

Lasswell, H. D. 1948. The structure and function of communication in society. In *The communication of ideas*, ed. L. Bryson. New York: Harper and Brothers.

Lazarsfeld, P. F. 1941. Remarks on administrative and critical communications research. *Studies in Philosophy and Science* 9:3-16.

———. 1969. An episode in the history of social research: A memoir. In D. Fleming and B. Bailyn (Eds.), *The intellectual migration: Europe and America, 1930-1960*. Cambridge: Cambridge University Press.

Lazarsfeld, P. F., and H. Gaudet. 1944. *The people's choice*. New York: Duell, Sloan and Pearce.

Levy, M. R., and M. Gurevitch, eds. 1994. *Defining media studies: Reflections on the future of the field*. New York: Oxford University Press.

Levy, M. R., and S. Windahl. 1985. The concept of audience activity. In *Media gratifications research*, ed. K. E. Rosengren, L. A. Wenner, and P. Palmgreen. Beverly Hills, CA: Sage.

Liebes, T., and E. Katz. 1990. *The export of meaning: Cross-cultural readings of Dallas*. New York: Oxford University Press.

Lievrouw, L., and S. Livingstone. 2006. Introduction. In *Handbook of new media: Social shaping and social consequences*, ed. L. Lievrouw and S. Livingstone, updated student edition ed., 1-14. London: Sage.

Lindlof, T., ed. 1987. *Natural audiences: Qualitative research on media uses and effects*. Norwood, NJ: Ablex.

———. 1991. The qualitative study of media audiences. *Journal of Broadcasting and Electronic Media* 35 (1): 23-42.

Livingstone, S. 1996. On the continuing problems of media effects research. In *Mass media and society*, ed. J. Curran and M. Gurevitch, 2nd ed., 305-24. London: Edward Arnold.

———. 1997. The work of Elihu Katz: Conceptualizing media effects in context. In *International handbook of media research: A critical survey*, ed. J. Corner, P. Schlesinger, and R. Silverstone, 18-47. London: Routledge.

———. 1998a. Audience research at the crossroads: The "implied audience" in media theory. *European Journal of Cultural Studies* 1 (2): 193-217.

————. 1998b. *Making sense of television: The psychology of audience interpretation*. 2nd ed. London: Routledge.

————. 1998c. Relationships between media and audiences: Prospects for future research. In *Media, culture, identity: Essays in honour of Elihu Katz*, ed. T. Liebes and J. Curran. London: Routledge.

————. 2003. The changing nature of audiences: From the mass audience to the interactive media user. In *The Blackwell companion to media research*, ed. A. Valdivia, 337-59. Oxford: Blackwell.

————. 2004. The challenge of changing audiences: Or, what is the audience researcher to do in the Internet age? *European Journal of Communication* 19 (1): 75-86.

————, ed. 2005. *Audiences and publics: When cultural engagement matters for the public sphere*. Bristol, UK: Intellect Press.

Mendelsohn, H. 1989. Socio-psychological construction and the mass communication effects dialectic. *Communication Research* 16 (6): 813-23.

Merton, R. K. 1955. A paradigm for the study of the sociology of knowledge. In *The language of social research: A reader in the methodology of social research*, ed. P. F. Lazarsfeld and M. Rosenberg, 498-510. New York: Free Press.

Miller, D., and D. Slater. 2000. *The Internet: An ethnographic approach*. London: Berg.

Morley, D. 1980. *The nationwide audience: Structure and decoding*. London: British Film Institute.

————. 1992. *Television, audiences and cultural studies*. London: Routledge.

————. 1993. Active audience theory: Pendulums and pitfalls. *Journal of Communication* 43 (4): 13-19.

Nightingale, V. 1996. *Studying audiences: The shock of the real*. London: Routledge.

Peters, J. D. 1989. Democracy and American mass communication theory: Dewey, Lippman, Lazarsfeld. *Communication* 11:199-220.

————. 2006. The part played by gentiles in the flow of mass communication: On the ethnic utopia of *Personal influence*. *Annals of the American Academy of Political and Social Science* 608:97-114.

Pillai, P. 1992. Rereading Stuart Hall's encoding/decoding model. *Communication Theory* 2 (3): 221-33.

Pooley, Jefferson. 2006. Fifteen pages that shook the field: *Personal influence*, Edward Shils, and the remembered history of mass communication research. *Annals of the American Academy of Political and Social Science* 608:130-56.

Press, A., and S. Livingstone. 2006. Taking audience research into the age of new media: Old problems and new challenges. In *The question of method in cultural studies*, ed. M. White and J. Schwoch. Oxford: Blackwell.

Schiller, H. I. 1989. *Culture Inc.: The corporate takeover of public expression*. New York: Oxford University Press.

Schrøder, K., K. Drotner, S. Kline, and C. Murray. 2003. *Researching audiences*. London: Arnold.

Sills, D. L. 1981. Surrogates, institutes, and the search for convergences: The research style of Paul F. Lazarsfeld. *Contemporary Sociology* 10:351-61.

Simonson, P., and G. Weimann. 2003. Critical research at Columbia: Lazarsfeld's and Merton's "Mass communication, popular taste, and organized social action." In *Canonic texts in media research*, ed. E. Katz, J. D. Peters, T. Liebes, and A. Orluff, 12-38. Cambridge, UK: Polity.

Smith, M. B. 1983. The shaping of American social psychology: A personal perspective from the periphery. *Personality and Social Psychology Bulletin* 9 (2): 165-80.

Sproule, J. M. 1989. Progressive propaganda critics and the magic bullet myth. *Critical Studies in Mass Communication* 6 (3): 225-46.

Swanson, D. L. 1992. Understanding audiences: Continuing contributions of gratifications research. *Poetics* 21 (4): 305-28.

Thompson, J. B. 1994. Social theory and the media. In *Communication theory today*, ed. D. Crowley and D. Mitchell. Cambridge, UK: Polity.

Tomlinson, J. 1999. *Globalization and culture*. Chicago: University of Chicago Press.

Van Zoonen, L. 2002. Gendering the Internet: Claims, controversies and cultures. *European Journal of Communication* 17 (1): 5-23.

This article reviews the ongoing contribution of *Personal Influence* to our understanding of media's social consequences from the perspective of recent research (the London School of Economics "Public Connection" project, 2003-2006, conducted by the authors and Sonia Livingstone) into the extent to which shared habits of media consumption help sustain, or not, U.K. citizens' orientation to a public world. As well as reviewing specific findings of the Public Connection project that intersect with themes of *Personal Influence* (particularly on citizens' networks of social interaction and the available discursive contexts in which they can put their mediated knowledge of the public world to use), the article reviews the methodological similarities and differences between this recent project and that of Katz and Lazarsfeld. The result, the authors conclude, is to confirm the continued salience of the questions about the social embeddedness of media influences that Katz and Lazarsfeld posed.

Keywords: media consumption; public connection; talk; diary methodology

Public Connection through Media Consumption: Between Oversocialization and De-Socialization?

By
NICK COULDRY
and
TIM MARKHAM

We are suggesting . . . that the response of an individual . . . cannot be accounted for without reference to his social environment and to the character of his interpersonal relations.
—Katz and Lazarsfeld (1955, 25)

Part of us is immersed in world culture, but, because there is no longer a public space where social norms could be formed and applied, another part of us retreats into hedonism or looks for a sense of belonging that is more immediate . . . both individuals and groups are therefore less and less defined by the social relations which until now defined the field of sociology, whose goal was to explain behaviour in terms of the social relations in which actors were involved.
—Touraine (2000, 5-6)

Katz and Lazarsfeld's *Personal Influence* (1955) was a major step forward in our understanding of "media" as complex processes of

DOI: 10.1177/0002716206292342

THE ANNALS OF THE AMERICAN ACADEMY

mediation. By asking about the contribution of "person-to-person communication" to the circulation of media-sourced information and opinion (p. 1), Katz and Lazarsfeld marked a shift away from a research paradigm dominated by a concern with media's rhetorical power over "masses"[1] toward a more fine-grained account of how media messages filter through the intricate networks of social life. From this perspective, the fact that the influences they chose to track specifically were largely banal and short-term (choice of a fashion or a movie, an opinion about a current news story) rather than major and long term (the adoption of values, or political allegiances) was potentially an advantage, since it prioritized the question of how media have social consequences in the ordinary run of things. This emphasis remains important. It is reflected in recent theorizations of mediation's social consequences over the longer term (Silverstone 2005).[2] More than that, Katz and Lazarsfeld's famous two-step flow thesis, by ruling out of court the old paradigm of "a radio listener shut up in his room with a self-sufficient supply of the world outside" (p. 40) (what we might call the "plugged-in monad" model; Couldry 2004) remains a useful ally as and when that model gets revived in new circumstances.[3] If, more broadly, the battle continues against mediacentric accounts[4] that frame media's social consequences upon terms set principally by an examination of media's own outputs (considered to the exclusion of the vast range of other inputs into contemporary life), then we must remember that battle was begun with *Personal Influence*.

The wider significance of the book, however, extends beyond communications research. Nicholas Garnham (2000) recently has argued that communications' contribution to the feasibility of large-scale democracies is a question at the heart of Enlightenment debates, and Katz and Lazarsfeld claimed almost as long a lineage when they started their book with an epigraph from John Stuart Mill:

> And what is a still greater novelty, the mass do not now take their opinions from dignitaries in church or State, from ostensible leaders, or from books. Their thinking is done for them by men much like themselves, addressing them or speaking in their name, on the spur of the moment. (Mill, *On Liberty*, quoted in Katz and Lazarsfeld 1955, x)

In so doing, Katz and Lazarsfeld framed their account of how the mechanism of mass media influences daily life within a longer history of liberal inquiry into how democratic citizens come to feel part of a wider polity.[5] In the context of democratic theory (not only liberal but also republican), everyday talk and discussion is

Nick Couldry is a professor of media and communications at Goldsmiths College, University of London, and was previously a reader in media, communications, and culture at the London School of Economics. He is the author or editor of six books including Media Rituals: A Critical Approach *(Routledge, 2003) and* Listening beyond the Echoes: Media, Ethics and Agency *(Paradigm Books, 2006).*

Tim Markham is a lecturer in journalism at Birkbeck College, University of London, and was a research officer on the Economic and Social Research Council-funded project Media Consumption and the Future of Public Connection at the London School of Economics from 2003 to 2006. He is completing his DPhil on Bourdieu and journalism at Oxford University.

a central, not an incidental, focus for those concerned with the possibility of effective democracy. And that interest in the political and civic significance of talk is a thread through the later work of Elihu Katz and those who have worked with him (Eliasoph 1998; Wyatt, Katz, and Kim 2000).

While Katz and Lazarsfeld's contribution to the history of mediation research is assured and unproblematic, things are less straightforward when we consider *Personal Influence*'s place in the history of democratic theory and political science. For, as the opening quote illustrates, Katz and Lazarsfeld's rightful emphasis (in the context of communications research) on the social contexts in which media messages are received can appear within that second perspective to rest on an assumption—in 1955 probably fully justified, but now open to question— about the *fit* between the worlds we learn of through media (once, perhaps, they have been further mediated by local opinion formers) and the spaces in which we regularly act. Yet it is exactly this fit, or certainly its naturalness, that the French sociologist Alain Touraine (2000) challenges in his account of what might be wrong in the contemporary polity. In Touraine's account (so different from that of Gabriel Tarde who had inspired Katz), any local mediation of media messages is absent, and the resulting dislocation threatens any sense of belonging to a democratic society.

While by no means every commentator would agree with Touraine's (2000) pessimism (Schudson 1998), there is certainly a theoretical head of steam behind it, especially given the background of wider fears about declining voter turnout and declining trust in political institutions in "advanced" democracies. For Zygmunt Bauman (1999), it is the "bridges" between private and public worlds that are missing, undermining the very possibility of democratic politics in an excessively "individualized" society (Bauman 2001). While Putnam's (2000) detailed concerns are with the decline of interpersonal trust and network resources rather than with how people interpret the world directly or indirectly through media, the *Bowling Alone* thesis certainly laments the absence of the taken-for-granted informal exchanges that Katz and Lazarsfeld themselves saw expanding, not diminishing.[6] More broadly, the idea that the worlds of knowledge and experience made available through mass media might be *in conflict with*, not harmonized with, the everyday lifeworld was foreshadowed by Robert Merton's (1938) classic study of *anomie* before World War II,[7] but has found many echoes since in accounts both of media and of the scale of social life in general (Meyrowitz 1985; Beck 2000; Urry 2000).[8]

All this gives a continued, if controversial, relevance to Katz and Lazarfeld's wide-angled view of how mass media messages are themselves mediated by the structures and flows of local opinion.

Introducing the Public Connection Project

Against this background, we want to discuss some material generated by what, on the face of it, is a very different empirical project from Katz and Lazarfeld's, in spite of certain similarities. Like *Personal Influence*, the U.K. Public Connection project[9] (in which we have been involved with our colleague Sonia Livingstone since October 2003) was started against a background of doubts about media's contribution to the very basis of democratic engagement. We also shared with Katz and Lazarsfeld the sense that the only way forward was to study what people do and think on a daily basis in specific contexts that are *only partly* shaped by media themselves. But our project differed in focus, method, and context.

The comparison with Personal Influence

Our focus was on the broad question of whether, and under what conditions, people across both genders, all classes, and all ages are orientated, if at all, toward a public world beyond the private, and, if so, to what extent their media consumption helps sustain that orientation.

As to method, our primary data-gathering device was the self-produced diary produced in the context of an ongoing many-month relationship between the project and diarist, whereas Katz and Lazarsfeld's was a highly structured survey questionnaire (see below for a more detailed reflection on our methodological choices). Since we researched right across England, and since the diary process was extremely labor intensive on the part of our research team, only a relatively small number of diarists (thirty-seven) was feasible, although we balanced this at the end of our project with a nationwide survey (one thousand respondents). By contrast, Katz and Lazarsfeld's initial survey was administered to a large (eight hundred) but spatially very concentrated population. Our project, however, shared with Katz and Lazarsfeld's the issue of "confirmation": just as Katz and Lazarsfeld did not rely on people's statements (in their initial survey) of who influenced them, but sought to corroborate these with a follow-up survey of those alleged to influence, so we never intended to rely on the diaries as primary data in isolation. Our plan was always to follow up the diary with a reflexive semi-structured interview with the diarist (which was also able to pick up the threads of our initial interview before the diary had started).

As to context, the world of Decatur, Illinois, in 1945 described by Katz and Lazarsfeld, where people seemed happy to leave the flow of national media to be mediated by local opinion "leaders" before it reached them (p. 314), seems a world away from early-twenty-first-century Britain with its universally available campaigning national press, still prominent national terrestrial television and radio channels, and general sense of "media saturation." How far the different outcomes of the two projects are attributable to intercountry difference or common historical shifts in media density is something we will have a chance to assess when results are available from the parallel U.S. study, based at the Institute of Communication Research, University of Illinois at Urbana-Champaign, and directed by Bruce Williams and Andrea Press.[10] At fifty years' distance, we cannot expect the framing of our results to do more than partially overlap with Katz and Lazarsfeld's inquiry. To the extent that they do so, however, we hope to demonstrate the continued salience of their path-breaking questions.

Our research question

Our research question in the Public Connection project is best explained in terms of two connected and widely made assumptions about democratic politics that we have been trying to "test." First, in a "mature" democracy such as Britain, most people share an orientation to a public world where matters of common concern are, or at least should be, addressed (we call this orientation "public connection"). Second, this public connection is focused principally on mediated versions of that public world (so that "public connection" is principally sustained by a convergence in what media people consume, in other words, by shared or overlapping shared media consumption).

These assumptions are detachable from each other. Some believe the first without the second because they argue public connection is unlikely to be served by people's use of media. (Robert Putnam's [2000] well-known *Bowling Alone* thesis takes that position in relation to television.) Generally, however, it seems to us that many writers assume both, even if only tacitly—or at least that is our contention. Consequently, our concern is with the empirical question: can we find evidence for those assumptions in U.K. citizens' practice?

[T]here is an underlying assumption . . .
that most people are broadly oriented
in the direction of public matters so that, at
certain times, they are in a position to
pay specific attention either to traditional
electoral politics or to broader public issues
that have become contentious.

The first assumption is important because it underlies most models of democracy. Informed consent to political authority requires that people's attention to the public world can be assumed, or at least one can assume an *orientation* to the public world that from time to time results in actual attention. To be clear, no one believes that more than a small elite is continuously attentive to the world of politics, or indeed should be. But there is an underlying assumption—as we see it, political science's "bottom line"—that most people are broadly oriented in the direction of public matters so that, at certain times, they are in a position to pay specific attention either to traditional electoral politics or to broader public issues that have become contentious.[11] Put crudely, if this is not the case and people are facing *the other way*, then no amount of skilled political communication will reach them!

More specifically, when in this project we talk of *"public"* connection, we mean "things or issues which are regarded as being of shared concern, rather than of purely private concern," matters that in principle citizens need to discuss in a world of limited shared resources.[12]

We have been careful not to assume that a decline in attention to "politics" in the traditional sense means lack of attention to "politics" in general, let alone apathy. People's understanding of what constitutes politics may be changing (Bennett 1998; Axford 2001). The *media* landscape that may enable public connection is also changing. The multiplication and intense interlinking of media and media formats through digital convergence may lead to an intensification of public connection, as people become more skillful at adapting their media consumption to suit their everyday habits and pressures. Or it may lead to the fragmentation of the public sphere into a mass of specialist "sphericules" (Gitlin 1998) that can no longer connect sufficiently to form a shared public world. In this context, the question of where and how, and for what purpose, talk oriented to a public world occurs (including talk that might fit within the theoretical model of a public sphere) becomes crucial.

Our working assumption, then, is that the public/private boundary remains meaningful in spite of many other levels of disagreement over the content and definition of politics. But our understanding of the public/private boundary is not prescriptive. The point of our research has been to ask people: What makes up *their* public world? How are they connected to that world? And how are media involved, or not, in sustaining that connection to a public world (as they understand it)?

Methodological reflection

These are the questions we aimed to explore: first, by asking a small group of thirty-seven people to produce a diary for three months during 2004 that reflected on those questions; second, by interviewing those diarists, both before and after their diary production, individually and in some cases also in focus groups; and finally, by broadening out the themes from this necessarily small group to a nationwide survey (targeted at a sample of one thousand respondents) conducted in June 2005. The survey provided data on media consumption, attitudes to media and politics, and public actions, and also the contexts in which all of these occur.

Our thirty-seven diarists were evenly split across gender and three age categories (between eighteen and sixty-nine). We aimed indirectly for a wide socioeconomic range through two strategies: first, by recruiting in six contrasting regions (poor inner-city London, mid-income suburban London, poor inner-city South of England, prosperous suburbs of two Northern England cities, and a mixed-income rural area in the Midlands); and second, through recruiting people with varying levels of media access in each region. As a result, we achieved a broad span from single mothers living on limited incomes in London public housing to retired financial services executives. Men aged between thirty and fifty were difficult to recruit as were both genders in class D (unskilled manual labor), but we achieved a good range of home media access (broadly tracking then current U.K. national averages). There were nine nonwhite diarists, an over-representation demographically but important to ensure a range of views in relation to Britain's overwhelmingly white political culture.

The diaries were produced weekly for up to three months. We encouraged open reflection and avoided specific signals as to what people were to comment on. The diary data are particularly complex, our intention always being that the diary material would be "triangulated" by interview data. For ease of exposition, we will draw mainly from the interview data in this chapter. Crucial to our method was combining self-produced data—tracing respondents' own reflections as they developed under the pressures of everyday life and alongside changing public events—and semistructured interviews, conducted not just in advance of the diaries but after their completion, when the diarists could be invited to reflect on the accuracy and meaning of their reflections. Our idea, against the grain of so much political science that is exclusively dominated by survey methodology, was that we needed to listen to respondents' own voices produced and recorded in their own time, if we were to get a sense of what it "feels like" to be a citizen in contemporary Britain.[13]

It is however, worth reflecting here a little more on our method, as Katz and Lazarsfeld did with their own methodological reflections in *Personal Influence*. Our choice of the diary method as a key component in our multimethod study inevitably has a context and brings with it certain constraints. As a choice, it was informed most generally by an awareness of the concern with individual reflexivity in some strands of cultural studies research (compare Couldry 2000, chaps. 3 and 7) and also by the broad precedent of the U.K.'s Mass Observation study, started in the 1930s and still continuing to this date. Indeed, in our pilot research, we used alongside semistructured interviews the setting of questions to the current panel of Mass Observation diarists (Couldry and Langer 2005).[14] We were well aware, however, of the potential for self-delusion in this attempt to "get close" to respondents' own voices, and our approach was from the outset informed by Pierre Bourdieu's (1998) critique of scholastic authority, and its tendency to forget the institutional privileges built into the very possibility of academics' view of the social world as an object of research.[15] We knew that our data would be shaped by the power relationships between respondents and us (as representatives of a well-known academic institution) that had shaped its very production. For that reason, we looked for traces of those power relations in the diary and interview data. But we realized that, in the end, such influences cannot be avoided; indeed, Bourdieu argued it is one of the key delusions of academic research to think that they can! Instead, our aim was to look at diarists' accounts of their lives from more than one angle (including the retrospective interview) in the hope that certain distortions could be noted and, as far as possible, factored out. To this extent, there was some similarity between our methodological concerns and those of *Personal Influence* even if our specific methods were rather different.

Politics and public affairs as a special case

In pursuing any comparison between our project and *Personal Influence*, one further important limiting factor must be borne in mind. This is the distinctiveness, within the wider field of personal influence, of politics and public affairs. This for us was part of our primary focus, but it was only one of four areas in Katz and Lazarsfeld's study, which covered (p. 4) "daily household marketing," "fashion," "attendance at movies," and as well as "formation of opinion on *local* public affairs" (note the restriction).

More interestingly, Katz and Lazarsfeld make very clear that the area of "local public affairs" was the "outlier" in their argument. "Public affairs," they report, is the only area where social status (as opposed to life cycle) dominates your chances of being an opinion leader (pp. 273, 323-24). In addition, although public affairs are in principle an area whose context affects both genders in their capacity as voting citizens, influence over opinions was, they found, heavily gendered: indeed this was the only area where, it seemed, men's opinions heavily influenced (or at least were reported by women to influence) women's opinions (p. 276). While the relevance of Katz and Lazarsfeld's study is limited by the fact it was only women whom they researched, their conclusion is an important one: "better educated, wealthier women—that is, women of higher status, no matter what their life-cycle position—seem to move in a climate which promotes greater participation in public affairs [than women of lower status]" (p. 295).

The Public Connection Survey

There is no space here to discuss in detail the results of our nationwide survey administered on our behalf across the United Kingdom during the weekend of June 3 to 5, 2005, by ICM Research. Here, we will concentrate on two essential points: stratification and the discursive context for following the world of news.

Although in our survey and throughout our project, we deliberately used the term "public" in a broad way (covering not just traditional politics or "public affairs" but the much wider space of "issue" politics), we found broadly the same stratification of political and news engagement as Katz and Lazarsfeld, with the additional factor of age stratification suggesting that the levels of engagement found in 1945 Decatur are also historically quite distinct from those of the contemporary period.[16]

Our respondents overwhelmingly report that watching the news is important and a regular practice for them, while also agreeing that there is often too much media and that politics is too complicated. However, age makes a difference: a feeling of duty to follow the news increases with age, as do practices of regular news consumption and understanding of issues. As to class, those from what in the United Kingdom are called C2DE households[17] exhibit a distinctly higher tendency to agree that there is no point in following the news, that politics is too complicated, and that they have no influence over political decisions. Men are more likely to say they have a good understanding of issues and actively compared news sources, while more women than men agree that politics is too complicated to understand. People from ABC1 households (see note 15) tend overall to find media relevant and agree that different sources of news give different accounts of events, while those from C2DE households are more likely to agree that media are irrelevant to their lives. Respondents older than fifty-five and from ABC1 households are far more likely to agree that they know where they could find the information they needed about issues important to them. Gender and class therefore intersect to stratify the practice of following public matters, with signs that a specific, and disadvantaged, group has switched off more decisively. Looking from the other side of the equation, those who are disengaged from politics, as measured by their response to the prompt "Politics has little connection with your life" are more likely to be of lower socioeconomic status and to have left full-time education at an earlier age than those who disagree with the same prompt. Significantly, those who are disengaged from politics are very likely also to agree that the media cover issues that have little to do with their lives and exhibit lower media literacy, measured by their likelihood to compare different sources of information.

[A]ge makes a difference: a feeling of duty to follow the news increases with age, as do practices of regular news consumption and understanding of issues.

What about talk in our survey? We asked respondents to indicate whom they spoke to both about issues in general and about a particular issue that they named as currently the most important to them. Levels of discussion are high: 85 percent of respondents say they regularly talk to friends and 72 percent to family about issues. If we exclude those unemployed or past retirement age, gender is a predictor with men considerably more likely than women to report talking to colleagues about issues. Taking this same group and looking at their talk with family and friends, we found that an interest in traditional politics or issues is associated with reporting discussion about issues with friends.

This broad evidence of a discursive context for thinking about public issues is supported by other data. Respondents were asked if they thought their friends or colleagues would *expect* them to keep up with the main issues of the day. With a correlation of $r = .157$, age is the strongest demographic predictor of social expectation, but newspaper readership and using the Internet as a news source are also significantly correlated. Perhaps more important, people who cite social expectation are more likely to follow traditional politics ($r = .479$) and social issues ($r = .388$) rather than celebrity ($r = -.052$); they are also likely to have higher levels of media literacy, and, interestingly, are significantly more likely to vote ($r = .210$). This demonstrates clearly that the availability of *some form of discursive context* in which issues are discussed (and in which a level of proficiency is expected) is an important determining factor, if not for public action as such (beyond the minimal action of voting), then certainly for engagement with the public world. Most people report having at least one context in which they discuss issues: overall, 85 percent talk to friends, 73 percent to family, and 55 percent to colleagues at work[18] about the issues that interest them. Women are more likely ($r = .088$) to talk to family members, and men are more likely ($r = .117$) to talk to people at work about these issues.

The Public Connection Diary Data

Although the main questions of our project were with media consumption and people's overall orientation to a public world, we were interested also from the outset in the context for such orientation provided (or not) by everyday talk.[19]

Scale of social interactions

First, however, we want to introduce one further, demographically inflected factor that, given the local focus of Katz and Lazarsfeld's study, is not prioritized there, although it is implied in their very distinction between opinion leaders (who have wider links to the world) and others. This is the variation between people in scale of social interactions in which they are regularly involved.

Although inevitably the distinctions that can be made here are to some degree intuitive, we considered how our diarists differed in the scale of social interactions regularly described in their diaries and interviews: ranging from *local neighborhood* (local streets/village, small area of London), to *local area* (nearby villages, town, broad area of London), to *national* (including the metropolis of London as a whole), to *international*. The results were interesting. Seven diarists' social interactions seemed from their own account to be largely limited to their local neighborhood and nineteen to their local area, nine had regular social interactions on a national scale, and only two could be said to have regular social interactions on an international scale.

Clearly, there is potentially a link between one's scale of social interactions and the way one's opinions are influenced, and perhaps if *Personal Influence* were being repeated today—in an age of considerable, although still highly uneven levels of travel in everyday life—this would be investigated. Since we did not ask directly about opinion formation, we cannot resolve that point, but one implication of people's scale of social interactions is striking.

In our wider analysis (for detailed background, see Couldry, Livingstone, and Markham forthcoming, chap. 4), we found an important distinction between diarists we call "public world connectors" and those we call "media world connectors." For the former, the public world emerges principally out of their media consumption, whereas the latter's orientation to a public world is something which they *bring to* media and which further orients their use of media (that is, they have an involvement with a public world independent of their media consumption). We make no value judgment of course about which is the "better" type of "mediated public connection" (in our term), and many people fall somewhere between these two possibilities (we call them "multiple connectors"). In addition, other people whom we call "weak connectors" had no strong orientation either to a media world or a public world. But the distribution of public world connectors, media world connectors, multiple connectors, and weak connectors bears an interesting relationship to variations in people's scale of social interactions.

Those diarists whose social interactions are largely at a neighborhood level are unlikely to be public world connectors and likely instead to be either weakly connected or bidirectional. By contrast, those two diarists whose social interactions were regularly on an international scale were both public world connectors, and those whose social interactions were on a national scale were more likely to be public world connectors than anything else. (Those linked to their broader locality showed no particular pattern.) In a tentative way, therefore, this supports the link Katz and Lazarsfeld imply between "gregariousness" (defined in part by the scale of your social interactions beyond immediate neighbors; p. 227) and the way in which you orient yourself to the world through media ("opinion leadership" in public affairs being linked both to gregariousness and to a great breadth of media consumption).[20]

Talk about public issues

Most of our diarists reported to us in various ways on how they discussed with others public issues (in the broadest sense, that is, the type of issues they mentioned in their own diary): only four diarists appeared to have no discursive context sustaining their media consumption and possibly public orientation. To this extent, our data suggest some continuity with Katz and Lazarsfeld's emphasis on talk within social networks, rather than support for Touraine's (2000) more drastic "desocialisation" thesis.

We found, disappointingly often, evidence of a gendered authority structure in how people formed their opinions on public matters, similar to that Katz and Lazarsfeld found. Most often, this was in couples (with the male partner bringing home the daily paper for the female partner), but sometimes (among our younger respondents), it was produced across generations by the traditional "paterfamilias" figure:

> He sort of explains it all to me and still it makes no sense, waste of time. (Kylie, twenty-four, unemployed, urban London Southeast)

> No, I mean as soon as I sit down to read the paper, like I say, my partner reads it at work and he'll come in flipping pages and say, look at that story and drive you mad cause I just sat down to try and read it myself and he'll say look at that. (Andrea, twenty-five, nurse, Midlands rural)

> Well, dad's very willing to explain the stuff, it's just, I don't know, he, he's very very willing to explain but then he kind of puts stuff in when you know he just goes off on one. (Mary, eighteen, medical student, Northern suburb)

In one case, a diarist tells of talking to her son in a manner that reproduces the gendering but reverses the direction of generational influence:

> My son studied Media at school and college so I spent some time discussing advertising with him today. He made me realise that I don't think enough about information. (Jane, fifty-two, supermarket assistant, urban South)

As to where people talked, most people talked across the same range of contexts as was evidenced in the survey: twenty-four mention talking to their friends specifically about issues, twenty to their families, and fifteen to people at work. Work contexts are particularly subtle in their variety, ranging from (1) casual chat to colleagues in a work break (often with some form of media stimulus, whether Web surfing or newspapers) to (2) broader discussion about "issues" (what one diarist called "putting the world to rights") in a break from the workplace or on the journey home to (3) cases where talk was inherent to the work process itself (as with three of our diarists who respectively ran a beauty salon, managed a busy gasoline station, or ran a newsagents).

The last type of case takes us closest to the sort of informal social setting that Katz and Lazarsfeld envisaged (p. 10):

> [My newsagents' shop is] like a small village shop, plus . . . it's in the city, you know? So, I've got no competition; mine is only shop on the road. So they all come and talk to me. They all what happened in their house and where they went and what they did and which cinema they been to or what theatre or what show they been, they always ask me—and how you are and how was your day. So it was like a—in a small community, small town shop. (Pavarti, fifty-one, newsagent, suburban West London)

It is worth noting, however, that, by her own account, this diarist tended not to offer her own opinion, so cannot qualify in Katz and Lazarsfeld's terms as an opinion former.

Do such settings imply an element of regular group influence mediating the inputs from media themselves, as in Katz and Lazarsfeld's study? That is ambiguous perhaps, particularly in work settings where part of the point of media-stimulated talk is simply to fill the time between work phases in a socially neutral way:

> I mean we'll have conversations and it is always based on the newspaper. [The guys in the rostering department] . . . will come in and the main conversation is about the sport and you just talk about headline news and it'll be like "What do you think?" or "What did I think?" Or perhaps I'll bring in my *Heat* magazine and one of the lads will pick it up and be like "Whoah that's Kylie Minogue" and it will branch off into "Oh look she's getting married." (Janet, twenty-nine, airport administrator, Northern suburb)

Beyond the workplace, there were a range of accounts of the influence of social context on diarists' opinions. Some took it as natural that their friends or family would be in agreement with them:

> That kept us going. . . . I was discussing it with my friend as well, she was discussing with her friends, and you know everybody had the same opinion. (Pavarti)

> I was kind of meeting people that would agree with me and I suppose that cements your, once you know that other people feel the same way that you, I suppose it cements your opinion. (noncompleting diarist, male, twenty-nine, administrator)

Others, more rarely, made a point of demonstrating the independence of their views.

An important factor in our study, raised vividly in Nina Eliasoph's (1998) study of U.S. everyday talk about politics, was constraints on raising public issues. Sometimes, this takes the form of a general exclusion of any "serious" talk, for example when friends are on a night out:

> I think all my friends, we've all got children now, so when we, we don't see each other as much as we used to, still see each other quite a bit. So when we do go out, it's more for the laugh and the social rather, whereas when we used to see each other a lot more, you'd probably get all spectrums of a conversation coming in. Whereas now, it's all a bit more light hearted because we think, well I don't see you that often, you don't particularly want to be sitting there talking about doom and gloom that's going on in the world. (Marie, thirty-four, part-time accounts clerk, Midlands rural)

More important to any potential process of opinion formation are cases where even in a discussion about "issues," people avoid certain issues, particularly "politics." A number of our diarists mentioned this as normal, and some had naturalized it: "I don't really want to be the sort of arrogant sort of having heated debates on it" (Kylie). Or, looked at from the point of view of someone wanting *others* not to give her their opinions,

> My cynical friend would say that you know everybody should be obligated to know about politics and everybody should use their vote responsibly because he's really into that. . . . Whereas me, . . . I don't know where my line would be because I know I look at a lot of celebrity news but that's not important and I wouldn't say people were obliged to know about that at all. (Beccy, twenty-seven, marketing executive, Northern suburb)

But if it is "arrogant" to express a sharply differing opinion, or seen as "cynical" by others to insist on being engaged and critical on public matters, then it is clear that the space of everyday discourse about pubic matters is significantly reduced. And this was exactly how some diarists who *were* consistently engaged in a world of public issues felt:

> They just don't care. This is what I find quite astonishing really that most people I know really just don't care about what's going on. They're focused on their own thing and as long as they know that David Beckham's had a new hair cut and that they can go and get it done at the salon just like this, and they just carry on with stuff. (Josh, twenty-three, architecture student, Northern suburb)

> I talk about Iraq with my partner, with my mum, sometimes, you know—but—you know, a lot of people around me are very materialistic and that's just not on their minds. . . . [I] like to concentrate on reality—things—but a lot of people around me are more into their own lives than others that they never knew and are now getting killed 500,000 miles away. A lot of that, they don't care about the war, but they just don't make it a part of their lives. (Crystal, twenty-two unemployed, urban London Southeast)

The space of everyday talk about public issues, while significant, is clearly fractured in various ways that significantly qualify Katz and Lazarsfeld's original thesis.

Everyday debate

Such evidence of constraints on opinion formation—that is, constraints on the opportunities for people to influence each other on matters of public importance—must be set alongside plenty of evidence from our diarists that they had debates, and sometimes disagreements, and enjoyed them as part of everyday social interaction.

[T]here are hints that while family debates are open to everyone, opportunities for debates in more public settings (such as work or discussions with friends) are more open to those of higher social status.

While the volume of our data on this is too small to claim any broader significance for such a conclusion, there are hints that while family debates are open to everyone, opportunities for debates in more public settings (such as work or discussions with friends) are more open to those of higher social status:

Yeah, um, I'm lucky in as much as that my wife, my wife's sister and her husband very much politically minded. So we have a lot of good debates [laughs] on various, yeah, you know, various topics . . . it's not just what my opinion, it's just you know, you're sort of sharing with people, like-minded people. (Patrick, fifty-two, warehouseman, urban South)

I enjoy conversation and vigorous debate [with friends], um, being aware of the topical issues and having people to discuss them with, having sounding boards if you like. (Bill, sixty-one, retired managing director, Midlands rural)

I've discussed a lot at the magistrates . . . everyone has a cup of coffee and you have a chat and . . . inevitably you lunch and generally talk to the people you've been sitting with. But you get a good cross section of views there 'cause there's all sorts of people magistrates. And it's very interesting to hear people's views. (Edwards, sixty-four, retired financial services chief executive, Northern suburb)

In addition, we found, as expected, evidence of media stimulating debate that otherwise would not feature in local experience at all (for example, talk about a rare disease shown on television or the debate opportunity afforded by an online discussion group):

Lots of people watched it [a human-interest television programme titled *The Boy Whose Skin Fell Off*], my friend, mum and me rang each other during the break. Some of us talked about it for the next few days. (Sherryl, thirty, deputy play-leader, urban London southeast)

I take part in a number of Internet discussion forums [on religion], where people from any part of the world can meet in what some call "cyberspace" to discuss matters of mutual interest. This has the benefit of meeting people from all kinds of countries and backgrounds very easily. . . . A great way to learn from other people (Eric, forty-seven, computer analyst and lay preacher, urban London Southeast)

In this last example, we get a glimpse of opinion formation occurring well outside the parameters of any social group, from unknown and unseen discussants. This is an obvious area where the model of *Personal Influence* needs to be extended. We must emphasize, however, that it was the *only* example of its sort in all our data, where online discussion was surprisingly absent overall—indeed, this seems likely to prove a significant difference between our project and the parallel U.S. project run by Bruce Williams and Andrea Press.

Summary

We have found some evidence therefore of the older forms of authority structure (particularly between male and female partners) persisting in what, as Katz and Lazarsfeld pointed out, is the highly gendered area of public issues. However, any assessment of opinion formation overall in this area is constrained by evidence of the *gaps* in, and constraints upon, discussion and exchange of opinions on public matters, and particularly traditional politics. Unlike perhaps in the areas of fashion and cultural taste, the field of public discussion is limited as to who can regularly participate within it, and when and where. It is not an open space of discussion, still less of open opinion formation and deliberation.

This last point is reinforced by another finding that moves us beyond Katz and Lazarsfeld's concern with opinion formation on specific issues. This is the question of action. Although we regularly asked diarists not only how they talked about the issues they mentioned but also what public actions, if any, they took or had taken, *we found only one report in all our data of a discussion leading to public action.* The case in point was perhaps our most locally engaged diarist who told us she got to talking about trash recycling at a party and then decided with her friends to lobby the local council to revise how they collected domestic trash. Our point, however, is that this link between talk and action was rare. This raises the wider question of how *consequential* opinion formation on public issues is for wider democratic participation, even if it is greatly mediated by the opinions of those around us. Without a link between talk *and action*, surely, Katz and Lazarsfeld's implicit link back to the liberalism of John Stuart Mill is potentially broken.

Conclusion

In concluding, we want to build on this last point, while noting the continuities with Katz and Lazarsfeld's model that our research still registers. In this article, we have used the findings of the London School of Economics Public Connection project to explore the extent to which Katz and Lazarsfeld's account of opinion formation through "personal influence" in mid-twentieth-century America remains pertinent, particularly in the area of public affairs.

Certainly, looking back, their emphasis on the priority of local social groups, from this distance, might suggest they had what Dennis Wrong (1961) called an oversocialized conception of the citizen's everyday life, that is, an account of the social world[21] that exaggerates the degree to which individuals operate within a coherent and complete framework of social norms and values. Media are of course now a source of opinion and reference that is pervasive to a degree that could not have been fully anticipated in the 1940s and 1950s, and in that radically changed environment some argue (Bennett and Manheim 2006 [this volume]) that the individualizing tendency of particularly narrowcast media fosters precisely the de-socialized context for information transmission that Touraine (2000) diagnosed. Our findings are, in some respects, rather different. Both talk and social expectations remain, according to our survey, importantly linked with engagement in a public world through media, and Katz and Lazarsfeld's finding that there is a relation between the scale of people's social interactions and their degree of attention to public affairs has also been backed tentatively by the evidence of our diarist sample.

All this points to the continued salience of Katz and Lazarsfeld's questions to warn us off the more drastic prognoses of the de-socialization of contemporary life. Instead our concerns about the contemporary salience of *Personal Influence*'s argument—the argument that, by identifying the social networks through which mass transmissions are interpersonally mediated, we have identified a mechanism that effectively embeds media in the processes that sustain liberal democracy—lie elsewhere. For, as our diary data suggest, the problem may be not the absence of a discursive context for our tracking of a public world through media; for that discursive context probably exists for most people. The problem, in Britain at least, is rather the lack of any link between that discursive context and any opportunities for *doing anything* effective about the issues we learn about through media. In that sense, the problem with contemporary democracy is larger than any study about the social mediation of media consumption can address. Does that mean that Katz and Lazarsfeld's whole study is condemned to irrelevance? Quite the contrary—for it sustains our attention to one key term (talk) of a wider disarticulation that neither policy makers nor academics who care about the future of democracy can afford to ignore.

Notes

1. Contrast, for example, Cantril (1940).

2. As explained by Roger Silverstone (2005, 189), "Mediation . . . requires us to understand how processes of communication change the social and cultural environments that support them as well as the relationships that participants, both individual and institutional, have to that environment and to each other."

3. Sunstein's (2001) well-known critique of the Internet's consequences for democracy can be interpreted in these terms.

4. See Martin-Barbero (1993), Couldry (2006, chap. 2).

5. For a useful review of the broader background associated with this position, see Simonson (1986).

6. See their comment (Katz and Lazarsfeld 1955, 10) on the rise of the "beauty parlor."

7. Compare the more directly media-related argument of Lazarsfeld and Merton (1969).

8. Compare Castells's (1996, 477) comment that "the network society increasingly appears to most people as a meta-social disorder."

9. We gratefully acknowledge support under the ESRC/AHRB Cultures of Consumption Programme (project number RES-143-25-0011): for fuller discussion of the project, see Couldry, Livingstone, and Markham (forthcoming) and www.publicconnection.org.

10. Funded by the National Science Foundation. We appreciate the support and stimulation that Bruce Williams and Andrea Press have provided us during the course of our project.

11. In this sense, from the perspective of the United Kingdom at least, we are skeptical of the claim of Lance Bennett and Jarol Manheim (2006 [this volume]) that in a TV age "inattentive participation [is] presumed," unless we are discussing thoroughgoing elite models of democracy masquerading as participative. However, as noted in the main text, neither have we investigated assumptions of continuous attention, but rather the assumption of something in between continuous attention and inattention.

12. The word "public" is, of course, notoriously difficult, since it has a range of conflicting meanings (Weintraub and Kumar 1997), but there is no space to debate this, or defend our particular usage here: for more details, see Couldry, Livingstone, and Markham (forthcoming); and compare Geuss (2001) and Elshtain (1997).

13. For a call for political research to be opened out in this way, see LeBlanc (1999); and for a defense of the contribution of self-produced data in media research, see Bird (2003).

14. There is also a precedent for diaries in Herbert Blumer's early study of film audiences (cf. more broadly Blumer 1969, 41). Thanks to Pete Simonson for reminding us of this precedent.

15. For much more detailed discussion see Couldry, Livingstone, and Markham (forthcoming).

16. For interesting material on the Internet's contribution to debates about whether the disengagement of "youth" is principally a life stage or a more profound generational shift, see Pew Foundation (2000).

17. Although there are unresolved debates about how precisely class can be measured, public debate in the United Kingdom has for a long time drawn, and still does draw, on the distinction between ABC1 social categories (broadly, managerial, professional, and administrative classes) and C2DE social categories (skilled manual workers, unskilled manual workers, and unemployed).

18. After excluding those past retirement or without employment.

19. For an implicit link between our thinking on the project and a consideration of Katz and Lazarsfeld's questions, see Couldry (2004, 22).

20. See, respectively, Katz and Lazarsfeld (1955, 324 and 314).

21. Wrong's (1961) particular target was Parsonian structural functionalism.

References

Axford, Barry. 2001. The transformation of politics or anti-politics? In *New media and politics*, ed. Barry Axford and Richard Huggins, 1-30. London: Sage.

Bauman, Zygmunt. 1999. *In search of politics*. Cambridge, UK: Polity.

———. 2001. *The individualized society*. Cambridge, UK: Polity.

Beck, Ulrich. 2000. The cosmopolitan perspective: Sociology of the second age of modernity. *British Journal of Sociology* 51 (1): 79-106.

Bennett, Lance. 1998. The uncivic culture: Communication, identity, and the rise of lifestyle politics. *PS: Political Science and Politics* 31 (4): 740-61.

Bennett, W. Lance, and Jarol B. Manheim. 2006. The one-step flow of communication. *Annals of the American Academy of Political and Social Science* 608:213-32.

Bird, Elizabeth. 2003. *The audience in everyday life: Living in a media world*. London: Routledge.

Blumer, Herbert. 1969. *Symbolic interactionism*. Englewood Cliffs, NJ: Prentice Hall.

Bourdieu, Pierre. 1998. *Pascalian meditations*. Stanford, CA: Stanford University Press.

Cantril, Hadley. 1940. *The invasion from Mars: A study in the psychology of panic*. Princeton, NJ: Princeton University Press.

Castells, Manuel. 1996. *The rise of the network society*. Oxford: Blackwell.

Couldry, Nick. 2000. *Inside culture*. London: Sage.

———. 2004. The productive "consumer" and the dispersed "citizen." *International Journal of Cultural Studies* 7 (1): 21-32.

———. 2006. *Listening beyond the echoes: Media, ethics and agency in an uncertain world*. Boulder, CO: Paradigm.

Couldry, Nick, and Ana Langer. 2005. Media consumption and public connection: Towards a typology of the dispersed citizen. *Communication Review* 8:237-57.

Couldry, Nick, Sonia Livingstone, and Tim Markham. Forthcoming. *Media consumption and public engagement: Beyond the presumption of attention*. Basingstoke, UK: Palgrave.

Eliasoph, Nina. 1998. *Avoiding politics*. Cambridge: Cambridge University Press.

Elshtain, Jean. 1997. The displacement of politics. In *Public and private in thought and practice*, ed. Jeff Weintraub and Krishan Kumar, 103-32. Chicago: University of Chicago Press.

Garnham, Nick. 2000. *Emancipation, the media and modernity*. Oxford: Oxford University Press.

Geuss, Raymond. 2001. *Public goods, private goods*. Princeton, NJ: Princeton University Press.

Gitlin, Todd. 1998. Public sphere or public sphericules? In *Media ritual and identity*, ed. T. Liebes and J. Curran, 153-62. London: Routledge.

Katz, Elihu, and Paul Lazarsfeld. 1955. *Personal influence: The part played by people in the flow of mass communications*. Glencoe, IL: Free Press.

Lazarsfeld, Paul, and Robert Merton. 1969. Mass communication, popular taste and organised social action. In *Mass communications*, ed. T. Liebes and J. Curran. Urbana: University of Illinois Press.

LeBlanc, Robin. 1999. *Bicycle citizens: The political world of the Japanese housewife*. Berkeley: University of California Press.

Martin-Barbero, Jesus. 1993. *Communication, culture and hegemony: From the media to mediations.* London: Sage.

Merton, Robert. 1938. Social structure and anomie. *American Sociological Review* 3:672-82.

Meyrowitz, Joshua. 1985. *No sense of place: The impact of electronic media on social behavior.* New York: Oxford University Press.

Pew Foundation. 2000. *The Youth Engagement Initiative.* Washington, DC: Pew Charitable Trusts.

Putnam, Robert. 2000. *Bowling alone.* New York: Simon & Schuster.

Schudson, Michael. 1998. *The good citizen.* Cambridge, MA: Harvard University Press.

Silverstone, Roger. 2005. Mediation. In *The SAGE handbook of sociology*, ed. Craig Calhoun, Chris Rojek, and Bryan Turner, 188-207. London: Sage.

Simonson, Peter. 1986. Dreams of democratic togetherness: Communication hope from Cooley to Katz. *Critical Studies in Mass Communication* 13:324-42.

Sunstein, Cass. 2001. *Republic.com.* Princeton, NJ: Princeton University Press.

Touraine, Alain. 2000. *Can we live together?* Cambridge, UK: Polity.

Urry, John. 2000. *Sociology beyond societies.* London: Routledge.

Weintraub, Jeff, and Krishan Kumar, eds. 1997. *Public and private in thought and practice.* Chicago: University of Chicago Press.

Wrong, Dennis. 1961. The oversocialized conception of man. *American Sociological Review* 26 (2): 183-93.

Wyatt, Robert, Elihu Katz, and Joohan Kim. 2000. Bridging the spheres: Political and personal conversation in public and private spaces. *Journal of Communication* 51 (1): 71-92.

Personal Influence: A Radical Theory of Action

Katz and Lazarsfeld's *Personal Influence* presents a "theory of action" that privileges interpersonal influence. In contrast, classic theories of action from Hobbes, Kant, Freud, and Parsons ignored the impact of personal influence in their theories of human action. Once scholars recognized the importance of adding interpersonal influence to the action scheme, they saw that influences naturally radiated from the immediate interpersonal environment to the larger social network. Both the interpersonal environment and further social network connections have been loosely termed "social capital." Long before the term "social capital" entered the social science lexicon, *Personal Influence* explored the consequences of a network of advice-giving others. Ahead of its time, the book lacked some currently available technical and conceptual resources to fully meet its ambitious goal of locating the relative impact of personal influence on individual decision making. Nonetheless, current students of social capital and decision making have more to learn from this book than they may realize.

Keywords: theory of action; social networks; social capital; *Personal Influence*

By
CHARLES KADUSHIN

This article is about how the theoretical melded to the practical, a hallmark of the Lazarsfeld school that Elihu Katz so much exemplifies, took advantage of a revolution in the theory of action to study the impact of personal influence on individual decision making.

Charles Kadushin is a distinguished scholar, Cohen Center for Modern Jewish Studies; and a visiting research professor of sociology at Brandeis University. He has taught at Columbia University in the Sociology and Social Psychology Departments, at Yale University in the School of Management and in Graduate Sociology, and at the Graduate Center of the City University. One of the founders of the social network field, and an expert on survey research, he is the author of five books including The American Intellectual Elite *(Boston: Little, Brown, 1974), which has been republished with a new introduction by Transaction Press in 2005, as well as many journal articles.*

NOTE: I have benefited from the comments of Peter Simonson, Bethamie Horowitz, and Ghislaine Boulanger.

DOI: 10.1177/0002716206292575

First, I will show that the Katz-Lazarsfeld practical "accounting scheme" for action is nothing less than a "theory of action" in the tradition of Hobbes, Kant, Freud, Parsons, and others. The revolution that accounting schemes created has been largely unrecognized because it is so sensible and down to earth. Unlike any of the prior theories of action, "accounting schemes" were anchored in twentieth-century interpersonal theory and the prosaic realities of marketing and voting studies (Kadushin 1968). This anchoring inevitably led to the notion of what must seem obvious and commonplace to us today: other people are an important aspect of an individual's life and strong influences on an individual's actions. As I will show, oddly enough, this was not part of previous theories of action. Second, once one searched for the impact on individuals of their "interpersonal environment" (Rossi 1966), I will show that it was a natural reach to ask about the impact of other people on those in the focal person's interpersonal environment. In short, *Personal Influence* (Katz and Lazarsfeld 1955) directly led to the study of social networks beyond what social network people now call the first-order zone.

Personal Influence paid the price for being ahead of its time: the accounting scheme was not clearly applied as a theory of action so that for some decisions crucial information was omitted.

The interpersonal environment, the network that stretches beyond this immediate environment, the relative impact of different members of this environment, as well as the search for others who might help to provide information or opinions are all called in present terminology "social capital," thus confusing rather than clarifying the skein of influence and diffusion. If it is all "social capital," then we are hard pressed to make analytic distinctions between culture, network, and influentials. *Personal Influence* was much clearer about these distinctions. Third, it will be admitted that *Personal Influence* paid the price for being ahead of its time: the accounting scheme was not clearly applied as a theory of action so that for some decisions crucial information was omitted. And the technology of network studies, particularly studies of ego networks, had not been sufficiently developed in 1945 when the study went into the field so that both conceptualizing and tracing these networks proved very difficult. To be sure, we are still struggling with working some of these problems out.

I have been throwing about some fancy terms: theory of action, social capital, and interpersonal influence. To set the stage for investigating these abstract ideas, I quote from *Through the Looking Glass*, a treatise written by a famous mathematician and logician, Charles Lutwidge Dodgson—aka Lewis Carroll:

"I don't know what you mean by 'glory,' " Alice said. Humpty Dumpty smiled contemptuously. "Of course you don't—till I tell you. I meant 'there's a nice knock-down argument for you!' " "But 'glory' doesn't mean 'a nice knock-down argument,' " Alice objected. "When *I* use a word," Humpty Dumpty said in rather a scornful tone, "it means just what I choose it to mean—neither more nor less." (Dodgson 1871, chap. 6)

The genius of Katz and Lazarsfeld was taking the concepts of action theory, social capital, and influence—even though only influence was directly named by them—and making them concrete and useful. By tying abstract concepts to such mundane acts such as buying groceries and then inquiring about them through survey research, it became clear what they "choose it to mean." As will be seen, they added to classic theories of action that were often quite abstract an explicit outline of how individuals went about specific commonplace actions. Every action included an actor and his or her characteristics, values, and goals, as well as the actor's connections to the surrounding social system. Overtly or covertly, every actor was influenced in one way or another by persons in his or her environment—hence the title *Personal Influence*.

Classic Theories of Action

Let me begin with "theory of action," an idea with a long history but most often associated in sociologists' minds with Talcott Parsons, a contemporary of Paul Lazarseld's. Theories of action were a device of social theorists—then known as philosophers—to develop a theory of basic human character, not to study concrete actions, but rather to describe and classify human societies, often through the device of imagining an implicit "social contract" that took place some time in the past. This effort continued right through the eighteenth, nineteenth, and twentieth centuries. Parsons seized on these theories to develop his own understanding of social systems. Since the Enlightenment and later philosophies have an explicit or implicit dialogue with Hobbes, it seems reasonable to begin with his formulation:

There be in animals two sorts of motions peculiar to them: One called vital, begun in generation, and continued without interruption through their whole life; such as are the course of the blood, the pulse, the breathing, the concoction, nutrition, excretion, etc.; to which motions there needs no help of imagination: the other is animal motion, otherwise called voluntary motion; as to go, to speak, to move any of our limbs, in such manner as is first fancied in our minds. (Hobbes 1651/1957, chap. 6, para. 1)[1]

Hobbes develops a version of what might be called Freudian "drive theory." People are motivated to act through some combination of biological drives and some overlay of learned needs. Since satisfying one person's drives inevitably impinges on the satisfaction of another, Hobbes (1651/1957) comes to his famous formulation of the "war of every man against every man" (chap. 8, para. 13) in which, in the natural state without further regulation, "[T]he life of man [is], solitary, poor, nasty, brutish, and short" (chap. 8, para. 9). "Drive theory" is present in the anti-Hobbsian Kant, as well. "[F]or Kant, *all* action of finite rational agents involves being *impelled* [*angetrieben*] to action by drives [*Triebfedern*], that is, by the sensible influence of feeling on the faculty of desire" (Grenberg 2001).

Almost all theory of action for more than one hundred years included some forms of drive theory. Parsons's (1937/1949) famous original formulation in *The Structure of Social Action* included four major components of action:

1. An actor.
2. An end—a future state of affairs to which the action is oriented.
3. A situation:
   a. Part of which the actor has no control over—the conditions.
   b. Part of which the actor does have control over—the means.
4. A normative orientation that governs which means are related to which ends.

Oddly, drives were not directly included in the scheme but entered in the characteristics of the actor and the end that was sought. Influenced by classic Freudian psychoanalytic theory (true interpersonal influence since Parsons was psychoanalyzed between the writing of *The Structure of Social Action* and the writing of *The Social System*) Parsons corrected this omission in *The Social System* (1951), in which it was explained that "actor" includes "need-dispositions," in other words, drives as a special case of motivations. The general scheme of the "second edition" of the theory of action was stated in several ways by Parsons, but this somewhat opaque summary seems to capture the essence of it:

> The most elementary components of any action scheme …may be reduced to the actor and his situation. With regard to the actor our interest is organized around the cognitive, cathectic and evaluative modes of his orientation; with regard to the situation, to its differentiation into objects and classes of them. (p. 7)

The situation has been redefined.[2] The ends and the norms become part of the situation and reappear as an appraisal of the situation (cognitions), an emotional valence replacing the more simple "ends" (cathexis), the more general notion of evaluation replaces norms, and actors have been given drives. Very importantly, actors and ego's expectations of them become part of the situation, for other actors are a key class of "objects." The interaction components as well as the motivational one are key additions. We note, however, that both the egos and alters in this interaction scheme consist of abstractions: role relations between statuses. The purpose of the scheme, however, is not to describe concrete actions but, in keeping with the grand tradition of the enlightenment and subsequent philosophy, to describe and classify social systems. In fact, Parsons rarely described any concrete actions in his entire oeuvre. One of the few is an action relegated to a footnote in an attempt to clarify the original means, ends, and norms scheme. The act is transporting oneself from Cambridge to New York. The automobile is the means. The actor has a degree of control over where and when the automobile shall go. The end is getting to New York (Parsons 1937/1949, 44, n. 2). No norms governing the use of the automobile are described; nor are we told why anyone would want to go from Cambridge to New York.

Parsons argues that at the level of abstraction with which he is working, the scheme is logically complete. But is it? A striking feature of all action theory until the first part of the twentieth century—when social scientists began analyzing interaction mechanisms rather than general sociability—is that drives are paramount, and the direct influence of other actors is ignored unless that influence is role or norm based or generally a component of society and sociability. Personal influence per se does not exist. In contrast, modern psychoanalytic theory, for example, rejects drive-based theories of action in favor of relational-based theories. Character and motivation are formed not only on the basis of biological "need dispositions" but as a result of interaction with others, a point Cooley (1909) made in the beginning of the twentieth century but which in American psychoanalysis has been most associated with Harry Stack Sullivan (1953) and in British object relations theory with Fairbairn (1952/1966).[3] I quote from Stephen Mitchell (1986), an influential exponent of relational analysis:

> For Freud, the object of study in psychopathology is the individual mind. His "intrapsychic" model traces neurotic symptoms back to processes and structures arising within the mind of the patient. Sullivan felt that Freud had incorrectly framed the phenomena in question. Psychopathology is best approached, Sullivan believed, not in terms of one person, but in the context of actual interactions among persons, in terms of what he called the "interpersonal field." Personality and psychopathology do not exist in germinal form within the child, simply unfolding as a bud into a blossom; personality and psychopathology derive from, are composed of, interactions between the child and significant others. To understand the person in a meaningful way, you have to view the person in the context of the field from which he or she emerged and operates. (p. 458)

Katz and Lazarsfeld are in this tradition but come to it through a very different path.[4] The story begins with Paul Lazarsfeld as a student in Berlin in the 1920s where he was exposed to the now-famous series of studies by the Russian social psychologist, Bluma Zeigarnik (1927/1967), who was interested in the conditions under which people remembered tasks that had been interrupted. Lazarsfeld became interested in studying *completed* tasks, that is, the empirical study of action itself. Rather than being purely experimental, a key method, though not the only one, was the retrospective questioning of subjects who had completed an act to ascertain their views of the reasons for their acts. It was necessary to study relatively simple acts such as going to the movies because it was easier directly to ask people how they went about such actions, though Lazarsfeld was also interested in long-term sequenced acts such as career choices. Trivial acts such as most buying behavior and, for that matter, voting are trivial only from the point of view of the actor in that long contemplation and change in one's feelings over time as one is contemplating the action are not likely to take place. But the individual acts do have very important aggregated consequences for social systems. Just as important in the era before NIH and NSF, social systems affected by such trivial acts of buying soap were willing to invest money in finding out why people bought the soap.

Accounting Schemes as a Theory of Action

As Katz and Lazarsfeld pointed out in *Personal Influence*, and as Lazarsfeld and colleagues have written elsewhere (as early as 1934) (Lazarsfeld 1934), merely asking "Why?" about an action is an invitation to logical disaster since people can answer on any number of incomparable dimensions (Kadushin 1968).

> For instance, in reply to "Why did you make this change?" a woman might tell us at great length about the advantages of her new brand of coffee; but she might never tell us that she had learned it from a household column in a magazine. (Katz and Lazarsfeld 1955, 168)

Hence, the inquiry must be guided by what they called an "accounting scheme." But an accounting scheme is nothing other than a theory of action, though it was not called anything so grand. Since it was regarded as common sense, which indeed it was, Katz and Lazarsfeld did not directly contest prevailing theories of action. Had they taken themselves seriously as social philosophers, some of the problems of *Personal Influence* might have been avoided since the accounting scheme might have been better specified in the data gathering.

Since Lazarsfeld's school of "Reason Why" did not regard itself as promulgating an abstract theory of action, the schemes were only as elaborate as the needs of a particular investigation. Kornhauser and Lazarsfeld as early as 1935 (Kornhauser and Lazarsfeld 1935/1955) reviewed a number of early studies of buying and proposed that the elements of those actions could be partitioned into the individual—including his or her motivations and other characteristics of the *individual* such as the state of his or her knowledge at the time; and the *situation*—consisting of the characteristics of the product, the way it was sold, as well as various influences on the individual. Not very different from Parson's formulation in 1937 (Parsons 1937/1949)—except for the important fact that influence, personal and otherwise, is an *explicit* part of the situation. Adding the idea of influence of the other, though we might take that idea for granted, turned out to have revolutionary consequences. While the time it takes for the act to unfold is an essential part of accounting schemes and is explicitly mentioned in *The Structure of Social Action*, since as Parsons explains, the very notion of an "end" implies an effort over time to get there, for example, driving from Cambridge to New York, the time dimension seems largely to have been dropped from *The Social System*'s (Parsons 1951) theory of action. Time is an "obvious" factor if one is studying concrete actions because time may divide an action into phases of essentially different acts, complicating the investigation. For example, going to the movies logically involves at least two decisions: first, to go to the movies; and second, to see a particular film. There is a feedback process, of course, between the phases: a particularly attractive film may affect the decision to go to a movie in the first place. But the factors that affect the decision to go to the movies in general are likely to differ from those that affect the decision as to which movie to see. As it turns out, one must make an additional decision in going to the movies: whom to go with. For in this particular act, the "situation" is complicated by the social system in which moviegoing is embedded: people generally go to movies with at least one other person, so that the wishes and desires of the other are automatically part of the moviegoing decision making, which is not necessarily the case in shopping for groceries. The choice of whom to go with may affect the choice of the movie in a feedback system, and the choice of movie may also affect whom to go with. I mention the social aspect of moviegoing because "obvious" as this might seem, the script for the interview guide did not sufficiently take this into account in the decision-making process, though it did inquire into the extent to which moviegoing was a social occasion.

This example reinforces the idea that an accounting scheme needs to be taken seriously as a complete theory of action and a failure to do the preliminary research and theory development can cause much trouble later on. *Personal Influence* clearly suffered from this, and reading the clever attempts to get around this problem, acknowledged in the text, sometimes makes for painful reading. That said, the survey context and its limitations in available time for the survey (these days when we use the telephone for survey research, we are usually limited to twenty minutes) and in the talent of the interviewers pose serious challenges for realizing a full theory of action inquiry; and the more complex the decision, the greater the challenge. Still, the question in one form or another, "Why did you do it?" is as problematic in surveys as it is in crime investigations. Current survey research often has "why" questions that may be summed up to 100 percent when in fact, logically, each category applies to every action or decisions the survey inquires about.

Once we have all the components of a theory of action, we need to assess the "cause" of the action. We are back to Hobbes, who, as you may remember, gave up on "causes" altogether. There is simply not enough time here to review general schemes for weighting or ranking the various components of an action—even if we agree to privilege personal influence. The book struggles with this, but is hampered by the incomplete accounting schemes. It specifically asks "why," but then the data are often not available on crucial details, a matter the authors ruefully acknowledge. For example,

> Now it turns out—at least when movies are the subject of study—that our scheme should have distinguished between two types of interpersonal influence; "Inner ones pertaining to the primary group which attended the movie jointly, and "outer" ones pertaining to all the other people. (Katz and Lazarsfeld 1955, 202)

Given an accounting scheme in which personal influence is a factor, the investigator has to come up with research into actual and potential influencers, the immediate ones and the larger social surround, and to try to assess their relative influence as compared with other factors in the accounting scheme ranging from sources of information in the mass media to the attractive aspects of the object being bought. The second key component of *Personal Influence* therefore involves tracing the networks of influencers in what we now call the sociometry of ego networks. The first part of the book is devoted to a theory of influence in small groups. It still reads like a primer of propositions network theorists ought to take into account. An inventory of elementary propositions about social networks' impacts on individuals is still missing in the literature, as anyone who has tried to develop a social networks course can testify. Although written fifty years ago, *Personal Influence* might be a good start. Of course, the survey was designed in 1945, years before Katz's survey of the small group literature on interpersonal impact and so again, most of its propositions were not directly built into the survey design for testing.

Social Capital

If *Personal Influence* was ahead of its time in terms of the investigation of action, it was light years ahead of its time in terms of investigating the effect of various forms of ego and community networks on decision making. In many ways, its goals are yet to be realized, and because the empirical study of large-scale networks was in its infancy, *Personal Influence* had a great deal of difficulty in realizing its aims. But we need to backtrack a bit and discuss "social capital."

As typically used, "social capital" can refer to the general availability of useful others, and/or the availability of specific useful others, and/or the ability or talent of an individual to select persons in his or her interpersonal environment who might be able to solve a particular problem. The social capital literature often confuses latency with the active enlistment of useful others and/or the often causal impact of others on an action or a goal (Kadushin 2004). All of these have been called social capital. (Parenthetically, ability, talent, or motivation are very important components of this search; recall the often ignored fact that in the famous Milgram [1967] "Small World" experiments, most chains were not completed.) *Personal Influence* separates these components and shows, for example, that the general availability of knowledgeable others—often a characteristic of social class, or life cycle—may not be as effective and certainly is not the same as the active participation of others in helping a person come to a decision. The "gregariousness" variable shows the effects of a general social circle of active others who are interested in the same things as the respondent and contrasts this with class and life cycle. The analysis goes beyond demonstrating the importance of social capital generally and attempts to show the relative effect of relevant others in contrast with other influences in the "situation." The details in "two-step flows"—that is, the education of others about the subject matter of the decision and then the importance of various others and their social location—vary according to the decision or the action being studied. Furthermore, and something few studies of social capital have undertaken, *Personal Influence* locates persons who lend their social capital to others and studies their characteristics. If you will, it is a study of social capitalists.

Personal Influence *locates persons who lend their social capital to others and studies their characteristics. If you will, it is a study of social capitalists.*

This brings us to the metaphor of social capital, its utility and limitations, and its applicability to personal influence. If we take the metaphor seriously, then this leads us to an investigation of "what's in it" for the influentials. Capitalists earn interest on the money they lend. Influentials and other "brokers" such as the apocryphal "godfather" do make a profit, but not necessarily directly in monetary terms. Banking favors to be redeemed at a later date is the godfather method and one common in less extreme ways among machine politicians and even in benign social circles—and dare we say, academic circles. The prestige or deference gained is a reward for being an influential. But note the limitation of the metaphor: if I lend you money, then I do not have the use of it, and that is why interest is charged. On the other hand, if I suggest to you that we both go to see a particular "good" movie, not only do I not lose this information, but also in addition to my having gained "points" by this recommendation, I have the pleasure of seeing the movie. So what is the equivalent of monetary interest here? Though our fascination with influentials has been whetted over the fifty years since *Personal Influence* was published, we still do not have adequate systematic investigations of network brokers and influentials—their motivations, how they make their "profits," the degree to which they themselves search for information and wisdom that they can pass on to the circle of their friends, and the extent to which they themselves rely on other people or on various media. One of the more fertile grounds for understanding the profits of social brokers and influence peddlers is the study of corruption. Aside from congressional investigations and court cases, we have made some progress since Lincoln Steffens (1948), but clearly this remains fertile ground.[5] This is leading us further away from our topic, however, and it is not clear that corruption broker findings can be generalized to influence over shopping decisions, though critics of our consumer economy may argue this point.

In accessing financial capital, borrowers typically exert some effort to find the best interest rates and the terms most suited to their needs. Again, the social capital metaphor is a major stretch. Money is fungible, but the information and advice gained in the *Personal Influence* examples are difficult to compare and weigh. Whatever the case, in the consumption decisions studied in *Personal Influence*, the decision makers are generally passive. They are "accidental consumers." Respondents do not search for the best products, the best buys, or the best movies. Information comes to them in an almost accidental fashion as a result of environmental influences, including, of course, personal influence. As I noted, an important aspect of the theory of social capital that is often ignored is the difference between potentially available networked resources and those that a focal person has directly activated. *Personal Influence* does not directly inquire into the efforts respondents may have made to acquire consumer product information, though it does inquire into the latent network of potential experts, for example, "Do you know anyone around here who usually knows something about the movies and can tell what's a good picture to see?" If the answer was yes, the instrument inquired further into the age, sex, occupation, and name as well as address of the person named. It would be nice to know the difference between the characteristics of members of the latent network as compared with those of the effective network. Because of various difficulties in tracing these persons, however, we do not have a good catalogue of potential versus actual influentials. Some work, however, was done in trying to pin down the sequence of information sources in an attempt to assess the impact of different kinds of sources. Position in the sequence is used as an indicator of "shopping" for information. Those for whom a key source of information occurred after several other sources is said to have "shopped" for information. So once again, *Personal Influence*, has the idea right, has its heart in the right place, but neither the theory nor the technology was available then to adequately sort out the relative impact of networked resources.

Conclusion

The hallmark of the Columbia School was the melding of empirical with theoretical studies. In a complex interaction, each informed the other. We have seen how until the twentieth century action theory overlooked the influence of others on an action, something that seems obvious to us today. Katz and Lazarsfeld by systematically studying personal influence in such mundane acts as going to the movies and buying clothes, not only brought the term into general use and advanced the study of the diffusion of information but made major contributions to the theory of action and to the study of social networks. Self-conscious as *Personal Influence* was about its nascent network theory, it may not have been as self-conscious as it might have been about its theory of action. For both social network theory and for action theory, in many ways we have yet to reap the full benefits of this pioneering work.

Notes

1. This is not the place to get into the complex history of social contract theories, and we are ignoring Rousseau, but it is important to social science that there was a countermovement in the Scottish common

sense philosophers of the Enlightenment (Broadie 2002) who insisted on man as inherently social by nature and by the very hardwiring of his brain, to use a modern term (Bryson 1945). In this view, sociability did not arise as a result of some mythic "social contract" but was itself a basic drive. A precursor of Cooley's (1909) "looking glass self" and Mead's "taking the role of the other" (Mead and Morris 1962) was found in Adam Smith's concept of sympathy for the other as a basic human trait (Weinstein 2001). That said, these views did not seem to have been taken into account or recognized by Parsons or by Weber in their versions of action theory. Scottish commonsense philosophers did have some eventual traction in social psychology and in theories of interaction, but seem not to have been explicitly credited.

2. Compare with classical Freudian drive theory. Drives have four components: the *source* (Parsons's actor)—which is biological, together with the somatic process whose stimulus is represented in mental life by the drive; *pressure* (Parsons's need)—the amount of the force with which the drive is experienced; *aim* (Parsons's ends or goal)—satisfaction or discharge. The goal is to discharge the uncomfortable excitation and return to homeostasis to reduce the tension; the *object* (Parsons's situation or role relation) (originally the mother's breast) enables the drive to be discharged. The object is attached to a mental representation by energy. The amount of energy or libido is called *cathexis*. But the object is secondary to the drive for the most important aspect of action is to be satiated and to return to homeostasis. Objects can be quite variable (Brenner 1955). No wonder that social theorists complain that there is no theory of change in Parsons since the goal is always homeostasis. From our point of view, note also that the objects—interpersonal or otherwise—are not basic to the theory.

3. Both books are collections of papers written years earlier.

4. Paul Lazarsfeld's mother, Sophie Lazarsfeld, was a famous Adlerian psychoanalyst, a system her son did not hold in high regard. It is "no accident" that psychoanalytic theory was not high on his personal set of influences.

5. Court records can be analyzed in network terms. See Baker and Falkner (1993).

References

Baker, Wayne E., and Robert R. Falkner. 1993. The social organization of conspiracy: Illegal networks in the heavy electrical equipment industry. *American Journal of Sociology* 58:837-60.

Brenner, Charles. 1955. *An elementary textbook of psychoanalysis*. New York: International Universities Press.

Broadie, Alexander. 2002. *The Cambridge companion to the Scottish Enlightenment, Cambridge companions to philosophy*. New York: Cambridge University Press.

Bryson, Gladys. 1945. *Man and society: The Scottish inquiry of the eighteenth century*. Princeton, NJ: Princeton University Press.

Cooley, Charles Horton. 1909. *Social organization*. New York: Charles Scribner's Sons.

Dodgson, Charles Lutwidge [Lewis Carroll]. 1871. *Through the looking-glass, and what Alice found there*. London: Macmillan and Co.

Fairbairn, W. Ronald D. 1952/1966. *Psychoanalytic studies of the personality*. London: Tavistock.

Grenberg, Jeanine M. 2001. Feeling, desire and interest in Kant's theory of action. *Philosophy/Philosophie* 93 (2): 153-79.

Hobbes, Thomas. 1651/1957. Leviathan; or, the matter, forme and power of a commonwealth, ecclesiasticall and civil. Oxford: Basil Blackwell.

Kadushin, Charles. 1968. Reason analysis. In *International encyclopedia of the social sciences*, ed. D. L. Sills. New York: Macmillan/Free Press.

———. 2004. Too much investment in social capital? *Social Networks* 26:75-90.

Katz, Elihu, and Paul F. Lazarsfeld. 1955. *Personal influence*. New York: Free Press.

Kornhauser, Arthur, and Paul F. Lazarsfeld. 1935/1955. The analysis of consumer actions. In *The language of social research*, ed. P. F. Lazarsfeld and M. Rosenberg. Glencoe, IL: Free Press.

Lazarsfeld, Paul F. 1934. The art of asking why: Three principles underlying the formulation of questionnaires. *National Marketing Review*.

Mead, George Herbert, and Charles William Morris. 1962. *Mind, self, and society from the standpoint of a social behaviorist*. Chicago: University of Chicago Press.

Milgram, Stanley. 1967. The small-world problem. *Psychology Today* 1 (1): 62-67.

Mitchell, Stephen A. 1986. Roots and status. *Contemporary Psychoanalysis* 22 (3): 458-66.

Parsons, Talcott. 1937/1949. *The structure of social action*. Glencoe, IL: Free Press.

———. 1951. *The social system*. Glencoe, IL: Free Press.

Rossi, Peter W. 1966. Research strategies in measuring peer group influences. In *College peer groups*, ed. T. M. Newcomb and E. K. Wilson. Chicago: Aldine.

Steffens, Lincoln. 1948. *The shame of the cities*. New York: P Smith.

Sullivan, Harry Stack. 1953. *The interpersonal theory of psychiatry*. New York: Norton.

Weinstein, Jack Russell. 2001. *On Adam Smith, Wadsworth philosophers series*. Belmont, CA: Thompson Learning/Wadsworth.

Zeigarnik, Bluma. 1927/1967. On finished and unfinished tasks. In *A sourcebook of gestalt psychology*, ed. W. D. Ellis. New York: Humanities Press.

Personal Influence and the Effects of the National Youth Anti-Drug Media Campaign

By
ROBERT HORNIK

Personal Influence (Katz and Lazarsfeld 1955/2006) put forward and tested a variety of hypotheses about how social contexts constrain media effects. Five such hypotheses are described: three about interactions of media exposure with social context (Stability, Conformity, and Instrumental) and two about two-step flow effects (Relay and Message Interpretation). Each is tested here with data from the evaluation of the National Youth Anti-Drug Media Campaign. The evaluation of the campaign has suggested boomerang outcomes—more exposure to the campaign led to more interest in marijuana use. This article examined whether those effects were magnified through interactions with siblings. In general, no evidence showed that older siblings' beliefs or behavior interacted with younger siblings' exposure to campaign messages in producing effects. However, evidence showed that the two-step flow did operate: older siblings were themselves affected by their own exposure to the campaign and, in turn, affected the beliefs and behaviors of their younger brothers and sisters.

Keywords: mass media; personal influence; drug use; two-step flow; sibling; antidrug campaign

Personal *Influence* (Katz and Lazarsfeld 1955/2006) outlines a set of hypotheses about how it is that the social context of an individual will affect the persuasive impact of mass media exposure. The first sections of that book describe the various and distinct mechanisms through which the social context might work. This article takes that list of mechanisms and

Robert Hornik is Wilbur Schramm Professor of Communication and Health Policy at the Annenberg School for Communication, University of Pennsylvania. He has evaluated more than twenty-five large-scale public health communication programs including the National Youth Anti-Drug Media Campaign, and directs the Center of Excellence in Cancer Communication Research at Penn. He is author of Development Communication *and editor of* Public Health Communication: Evidence for Behavior Change.

NOTE: I am grateful to Susana Ramirez and Shawnika Hull for help in preparing this article.

DOI: 10.1177/0002716206291972

ANNALS, *AAPSS*, 608, November 2006

applies it explicitly to data collected for the evaluation of the National Youth Anti-Drug Media Campaign. That evaluation (Hornik et al. 2003) concluded that the campaign, which cost the U.S. government more than $1 billion, appeared to produce a boomerang effect; the more young people were exposed to the campaign advertisements, the more likely they were to report promarijuana cognitions and also to initiate marijuana use. This chapter begins with that result. It then elaborates the result following the hypothesized mechanisms of *Personal Influence*.

Personal Influence argues that the social context matters for media effects in a variety of distinct ways. It is useful to divide these hypotheses into two broad categories: hypotheses that suggest that the effects of individual exposure to messages will be contingent on their social context and hypotheses that suggest a two-step flow more directly: the campaign will affect the social influencers who will directly focus the individuals.

Social context moderates the effects of individual campaign exposure:

1. The stability hypothesis: The social network around an individual can be more or less consistent with regard to a particular issue or it can be more or less stable in general; insofar as the network is inconsistent or unstable, media effects from individual exposure to messages should be larger.
2. The conformity hypothesis: The social network around an individual provides its own persuasive influence; insofar as the persuasive ideas in media messages are accepted by the social network, those messages will be more persuasive; insofar as they contradict that network's opinions, they will be less persuasive. (Conformity may not be the best term for this influence; it is not the only mechanism through which social network opinions constrain media influence. For example, there may also be greater credibility associated with personally communicated messages.)
3. The instrumental support hypothesis: The social network provides more or less instrumental support for behavior; insofar as it provides material support for behaviors advocated in media messages, those messages will produce more behavior change.

Campaigns affect social influencers who, in turn, affect individuals:

4. The message interpretation hypothesis: Social networks provide meaning as people make sense of media messages. An individual's interpretation of media messages (and thus, presumably, their effects) will be affected by the way that social networks interpret those messages.
5. The relay hypothesis: Social influencers may be directly exposed to media messages. Network members may be persuaded by their own exposure and in turn persuade others in the network. This relay function of social networks is closest to the term most often associated with the argument of *Personal Influence*—the two-step flow.

In addition to these specific hypotheses about direct social network effects, the volume addresses the structure of the social networks themselves: their size; the strength of affiliation; the relationships between the members; the operational style—for example, democratic versus authoritarian—the likelihood of overlapping memberships, which can create cross pressures. Differently structured networks would be expected to produce varying effects on media persuasiveness.

However, these important arguments are, in most cases, not so easily tested with the drug campaign data, so they are not further discussed.

These ideas are elegantly elaborated in the original volume. They were a counterweight to the prevailing assumption that the influence of media is individual and direct. They recognized that individuals were embedded in social networks, which both influenced individuals directly and moderated and mediated the influences of the media on individuals. That focus was consistent with the other studies coming from Columbia (cf. Wright 1989) and independently from the rural sociologists concerned with diffusion of innovation (cf. Rogers 2003; Ryan and Gross 1943) although these diffusionists only later dealt with the intersection of media and interpersonal networks. They opened a powerful theoretical tradition and one that continues to compete with and complement more individual psychological perspectives. However, as intriguing as the ideas were, the actual empirical work explicitly testing these hypotheses about the intersection of media and interpersonal networks has been rare. The original volume depended mostly on claims by interviewees of contact with their social networks and use of media, but not as much on direct evidence of influence, establishing the flow from mass media to putative influencers and then to influencees. There are mountains of research about the operations of social networks; there are mountains of research about the effects of media and about the influence of social context and social networks on the interpretation of media content. But even now there is much less research documenting either the mediating or moderating role of social networks in the flow of *specific* mass communication influence. Indeed, in the specific area of examination of this study, the idea that siblings affect the effects of media exposure, not a single parallel study was unearthed.

[T]he actual empirical work explicitly testing [Personal Influence's] hypotheses about the intersection of media and interpersonal networks has been rare.

Literature

There are many studies that address and some that establish the likely influence of social networks on individual behaviors of all sorts (e.g., Allen et al. 2003). Some of the results to be reported below support such claims of social network influence on youth marijuana cognitions and use. However, they are not relevant for this study unless they address media persuasion effects as well. The personal influence hypotheses deal with media effects in the context of social networks. The relevant studies must include measures of at least three constructs: exposure to mass mediated persuasive messages, cognitions or behaviors of the target audience, and information about the social context in which possible media effects might occur. The analyses will focus on marijuana use by young people and will be limited to the social context defined by siblings; the search for relevant studies focuses in similar domains. It turns out that the relevant literature, despite fifty years of *Personal Influence* sitting on our shelves, is not so large.

A first search in the literature could find no studies that focused on siblings and media message effects. Most of the somewhat on-topic studies deal with parental mediation of television effects. By and large, they focus on alternative ways that parents interact with their children concerning television content, and sometimes they try to extend that to understand how the different forms of mediation affect substance use or aggression or other behaviors. They do show that parent or peer interaction with a youth around media can be associated with some outcomes (cf. Austin, Pinkleton, and Fujioka 2000; Austin and Yin 2003; Ennett et al. 2001; Nathanson 1999, 2001). None directly consider evidence for the argument that the effects of exposure to specific messages from a campaign or on a specific topic are mediated through a social context.

These data, in contrast, lend themselves particularly well to examining the social network effects of parents and of siblings. The current article deals only with sibling influence. The data set permits systematic examination of older siblings (and parent influences, although they are not examined here) because it includes data gathered directly from them as well as from the younger siblings.

Ideally, one would want also to examine the influence of other adults, of other institutions with which youth affiliate, and particularly of friends and peers. In fact, there is also a good deal of information about friends and peers of target youth in the data set. However, that material relies on self-reports by youth of their perceptions of others around them. As indirect reports, they have strength because they may represent what the youth may perceive and thus may represent what is affecting them; as indirect reports, however, they also have a weakness: they do not permit separation of the actual beliefs and behavior of others from what a youth projects as the opinion or behavior of others given his or her own beliefs. Because of that uncertainty, and because of an interest in focusing this article, the analyses below are limited to tests of the personal influence hypotheses related to siblings.

The Data

The data collected for the evaluation are from a representative national sample of around eight thousand youth aged nine to eighteen who were followed for up to three years and four rounds of interviews or until they were age nineteen. Each household could contribute up to two youth respondents—hence the availability of sibling data. Each of those youth interviewees had a corresponding parent (typically the same individual) also interviewed four times over three years. There were about six thousand parents interviewed. Given that the evaluation had found evidence for a persuasive effect (albeit an undesirable one) in this data and direct measures of the youth and a sibling and a parent, this evaluation promises an unusual opportunity to examine social context effects. While the Decatur study did include some independently collected data from putative influencers as well as influencees, that data made up a small part of the study. Most claims in the Decatur study depended on self-reports of influence by the primary interviewees.

The sample for the current article was selected from the broader sample. It includes only youth drawn from households where two youth were interviewed. Each sibling pair was included if there were data from at least two rounds of interviews for the younger sibling and data from the first round from the older sibling. There were 1,769 sibling pairs with at least one set of such two-round data. Each two-round set of interviews is considered one lagged case. Thus, individual sibling pairs can contribute up to three cases to this sample—if a youth was interviewed for four rounds of data and his or her sibling was interviewed for the first three rounds, the youth would contribute three lagged cases. In fact, the average sibling pair contributed 2.33 cases to the sample, with a total N of 4,130.

The overall sample for the evaluation was developed from a multistage cluster sample. In the overall evaluation, appropriate weights were developed to match the U.S. population, and analyses took direct account of the complex sample design in correcting standard errors. However, for this article such weights are not employed and standard error corrections are not introduced. Those were appropriately used for the full evaluation. However, given that the primary purpose of this analysis is to test theory rather than make claims about the national population, there is a justification for fully exploiting the available sample. Thus, the analyses that follow use the observed ns in statistical tests rather than the smaller effective sample size that would have been available after weighting and complex sample corrections. A separate sampling concern is raised by the inclusion of up to three cases per youth in each sample. There is some risk that claims of significance are exaggerated because the observed standard errors are smaller than the true standard errors. This bias may be present because some cases appear more than once in the data set, if a particular sibling pair is included at multiple ages. The statistical adjustments for nonindependence are not made formally here. However, the actual design effect associated with this repetition of cases for the four major outcome variables ranges from 1.16 to 1.39. Thus, the underestimation of standard errors is small, and it is unlikely that there are substantial effects on claims of significance. Still, this might mean that some claims of significant effects would be less strong if all appropriate corrections were included.

The ns in the different analyses vary sharply. In particular, the analyses using past year marijuana use and the nonintention to use marijuana tend to include much of the sample, while the analyses that focus on marijuana social norms and attitudes-beliefs have smaller eligible samples. This is a reflection of the fact that the instruments used for youth younger than twelve were different from those used for older youth, and the "younger" instrument did not have identical measures of norms and attitudes to the "older" instrument. Many of the sibling pairs eligible for these analyses include youth who were younger than twelve when first measured, or even when measured for the first two rounds; they were not eligible for analyses requiring the social norm and attitude-belief baseline measures. This means that there were different ns for the four outcome variables with two implications: the power to find effects is less with the norm and attitude-belief outcomes; and that those analyses tended to include samples that were, on average, older than those in the past year or intentions analyses.

Measures. The primary outcome measures are past year marijuana use, intentions to not use marijuana in the next year, an index of normative beliefs about marijuana use, and an index of beliefs and attitudes about marijuana use assessed at the lagged round. The predictor variables include the same variables assessed at the prior round for the younger sibling and for the older sibling. In addition, there is a measure of exposure to the campaign, based on frequency of youth recall of specific television ads shown to them on laptop computers and recently broadcast by the campaign. Also, youth were asked to evaluate a subset of ads on three dimensions, and their average across all ads shown was considered the mean ad evaluation. One analysis makes use of a measure of perceived family togetherness reported by both siblings. Major control variables included parents' reported level of education; youth age; gender; round of interview; and a risk of marijuana use score derived from a set of other variables shown to predict marijuana use, including youth prior tobacco and alcohol use; sensation seeking; urban residence; parent marijuana, tobacco, and alcohol use; religiosity; and whether the household included one versus two parents. (Measures are fully described in Hornik et al. 2003.)

Analysis. The boomerang effects have been previously established for the population of youth who were nonusers at the prior round of interviewing only. This was a focus of the evaluation on the grounds that prevention of initiation of use was a distinct goal for the national campaign. However, in the analyses presented here, we seek to exploit the full sample of youth. Rather than limiting the analysis to nonusing youth, we incorporate statistical controls for prior use in all appropriate analyses. However, the narrative begins with establishing that the previously reported boomerang effects continue to hold regardless of prior use status. However, this difference in approach, along with the less conservative statistical approach taken, leads to one important caveat: this analysis does not provide a substitute or replication of the formal campaign evaluation. It should not be used to make overall claims about the effects of the campaign on U.S. youth.

As already noted, most analyses address four outcome variables: marijuana use in the past year, definite nonintention to use marijuana in the next year, a scale derived from multiple measures of antimarijuana beliefs and attitudes, and a scale derived from multiple measures of perceived social norms supporting nonuse of marijuana. Analyses with the first two measures use logistic regression, while those with the second two use ordinary least squares (OLS) regression. If there are promarijuana effects of media exposure, analysis will show a positive coefficient for the marijuana use measures but a negative coefficient for the other three outcomes.

Almost all analyses involve the use of the measure of exposure to specific television ads. This is a four-category ordered variable based on a continuous measure of exposure. However, we establish that the four-category measure has essentially a linear relationship with each of the outcomes, and so it is treated like an interval variable without transformation for all analyses.

Many of the analyses involve a test of the interaction between the exposure measure and some characteristic of the social context in their joint effects on an outcome variable. Simple multiplicative interaction terms are employed for this purpose, with statistical significance estimated on the basis of the additional variance accounted for by the interaction term.

The major threats to causal claims from observational studies are two: that an observed association is merely the result of the effects of some third variable on the two observed variables, or that the observed association is the result of reverse causation (not exposure causing marijuana use, but marijuana use causing recall of exposure). We address the first by implementing substantial statistical controls. Obviously, there may be other unmeasured variables that may still threaten claims of effects. We address the causal direction issue by focusing most analyses on lagged effects; the independent, control, and social context variables are assessed at the prior round and the outcome variables at the follow-up round. Most analyses exploit the two round nature of the data set.

All of the analyses focus on the influence of the older sibling on the younger sibling. It is, of course, possible that the influence flows the other way or is mutual. Also, given that there are sometimes more than two siblings in a household, but only two are included in the study, it is quite possible that a more complex dynamic in the family is lost. Nonetheless, to allow the analyses to proceed in a fairly straightforward manner, and because of the sensible idea that older siblings are influences on younger siblings, it was worth proceeding with this assumption. This leaves the opportunity for investigating more complex hypotheses to other investigators. The analyses are performed with SPSS.

Analyses

The basic relationship of ad exposure and initiation of marijuana use

Specific ad exposure at the prior round positively predicts use of marijuana by the subsequent measurement round. The effect is largely monotonic across the four categories of exposure and is statistically significant. A parallel relationship (negative because of how the measures are ordered) is found when nonintention to use, and attitudes and beliefs, or social norms opposing marijuana use are the lagged outcome variables. The relationships are reduced when a variety of potential confounders are controlled, including parental education, youth age and gender, an overall estimate of risk for marijuana use, and round of baseline measurement. Table 1 presents the percentage using in past year, the proportion not declaring a firm nonintention to use, and the mean levels of antimarijuana beliefs and norms as a function of exposure category. The relative odds or unstandardized regression coefficient capturing the simple association and the associations after controls are also presented in the table. The apparent boomerang effects remain for marijuana use and social norms, are marginal for intentions (p = .054), and are no longer significant for the attitude-belief index (p = .214).

This analysis provides the foundation for the explicit tests of the social context hypotheses: is it the case that if we know something about the social context of these youth, we can establish the conditions under which these apparent effects have taken place, or, alternately, can we show that the effects reappear for the intention and attitude-belief measure under some social contingencies? The analysis begins with the hypotheses that suggest that the effects of exposure to the campaign are contingent on the social context.

The stability hypothesis

The social network around an individual can be more or less stable or consistent; insofar as the network is unstable, media effects from individual exposure to messages should be larger. The network may be inconsistent because of disagreement about the specific issues at hand (marijuana use) or it may be unstable in a more general way—a family that is not "together."

This hypothesis is tested with two approaches to measuring stability/inconsistency. The first focuses on evidence of discrepancy in cognitions about marijuana use between the target youth and his or her sibling. The degree to which they are different is assumed to represent greater inconsistency in the attitude environment. The absolute value of the discrepancy at the prior wave of measurement is used as the estimator of instability. Parallel inconsistency estimates are developed based on all four measures. The second approach relies on a direct measure of family stability—youth are asked to indicate their agreement with the statement, "There was a feeling of togetherness in our family." We assume that youth who report lower levels of togetherness are indicating some family instability.

> *Hypothesis 1a:* To the extent there is a discrepancy between youth and sibling in reported marijuana use, intentions, attitude-belief, and social norms, there will be a larger effect of campaign exposure on the lagged measure of the respective outcome.

The scores of the youth were subtracted from the scores of their siblings, and the absolute value was calculated on the observed difference. The test for the social context effect was whether there was additional variance accounted for in

TABLE 1
MARIJUANA OUTCOMES AT FOLLOW-UP ROUND AS A FUNCTION OF SPECIFIC AD EXPOSURE AT PRIOR ROUND, WITH AND WITHOUT CONFOUNDER CONTROLS

Specific Ad Exposures Recalled per Month at Prior Round	Outcome Measures at Follow-Up Round			
	Percentage Using Marijuana in Past Year	Percentage Other Than "Definitely Not" on Intention to Use Marijuana	Mean Score on Antimarijuana Attitude-Belief Scale	Mean Score on Antimarijuana Social Norms Scale
Less than one time	3.4	89.6	109.1	119.6
One to three times	6.2	84.5	92.4	93.6
Four to eleven times	8.2	78.2	86.2	86.0
More than eleven times	9.1	78.7	88.1	84.5
Exposure effects				
Relative odds: per category (confidence interval [CI])	**1.46** **(1.26, 1.69)**	**0.74** **(0.68, 0.81)**		
Relative odds: with confounders controlled (CI)	**1.21** **(1.19, 1.65)**	**0.89** **(0.79, 1.00)**		
Unstandardized regression coefficient (CI)	—		**−6.9** **(−11.3, −2.5)**	**−12.0** **(−16.4, −7.7)**
Regression coefficient with confounders controlled (CI)	—		−2.7 (−6.8, 1.5)	**−6.3** **(−10.4, −2.2)**
n for bivariate analysis	4,077	3,972	3,262	3,262
n for controlled analysis	3,529	2,915	2,819	2,819

NOTE: Controls include prior year marijuana use, age, risk score (and gender, parent education, race-ethnicity; measurement round). The last three were not significant and were removed from the final models. Significant results appear in bold.

TABLE 2
FOLLOW-UP ROUND ANTIMARIJUANA ATTITUDE-BELIEF INDEX
AS A FUNCTION OF PRIOR ROUND CONTROLS, EXPOSURE,
SIBLING-YOUTH DISCREPANCY ON THE ATTITUDE-BELIEF INDEX,
AND THEIR INTERACTION ($n = 1{,}969$)

	Constant	Age	Risk Score	Past Year Use	Attitude Discrepancy	Exposure	Exposure × Discrepancy
Mean		13.1	.04	.05	112.9	1.60	183.7
SD		0.97	0.07	.21	90.3	0.91	198.8
B. coefficient	**192.0**	**–5.7**	**–302.7**	**–92.0**	**–0.216**	**–11.0**	**0.103**
Confidence interval	122, 261	–11.0, –0.4	–375, –230	–116, –68	–0.33, –0.10	–19.5, –2.6	0.04, 0.16
p value	<.001	.034	<.001	<.001	<.001	.011	.001

NOTE: Significant results appear in bold.

the respective regression equation when the interaction of exposure and the discrepancy was added to an equation including control variables and main effects for exposure and the discrepancy.

In three of the four analyses (data not shown), there was no evidence for an interaction between the discrepancy score and the exposure measure in their joint effects on the respective outcome. In only one case was there an interaction, and it was somewhat difficult to interpret. In Table 1, it was noted that there was no significant association of exposure and the belief-attitude index when the control variables were introduced. However, when the discrepancy of the sibling and the youth was incorporated and the interaction calculated, both the main effect of exposure and the interaction become significant, as shown in Table 2.

The interaction is positive, suggesting that when the youth and sibling are more discrepant, the effects of exposure on the attitude-belief index are less negative. Specifically, among those with the least discrepant views, there is a significant bivariate negative relationship between exposure and antidrug beliefs/attitudes. Among the group with the highest discrepancy, this effect disappears and even turns significantly positive. This is not consistent with the social context hypothesis, which suggested that the smallest media exposure effects would be found among those with the smallest discrepancy.

Hypothesis 1b: Youth who come from a family perceived as feeling less together will show stronger media persuasive effects.

The second analysis done under the stability hypothesis uses the perception of the family as being together. This measure is scored 0 or 1 for both youth and sibling, with 1 given to youth who said that this was often or always true for their families (about 50 percent of youth said this). The average of the youth's and sibling's scores are used to characterize the family. Again, prediction of the four outcomes was considered. None of the analyses with this measure showed a significant interaction of togetherness and exposure (data not shown).

Overall, of eight tests of the stability hypothesis (four with the discrepancy score and four with the togetherness score), only one showed evidence for an interaction with exposure, and that was in the wrong direction, with the youth with more consistency with siblings showing more effects of exposure.

The conformity hypothesis

The social network around an individual provides its own persuasive influence; insofar as the persuasive ideas in media messages are accepted by the social network, they will be more persuasive; insofar as they contradict that network's opinions, they will be less persuasive.

The test of this hypothesis follows the same analytic approach as the stability analyses. It asks whether the effects of exposure are contingent on the cognitions or behavior of the sibling. Will a youth whose sibling expresses promarijuana views be more vulnerable to the promarijuana effects of the campaign than a youth whose sibling is less supportive of marijuana use?[1]

> Hypothesis 2: The effect of direct exposure to persuasive messages is contingent on the nature of the siblings' attitudes—if they are supportive of the idea in the persuasive message, mass media messages will have a larger effect.

This hypothesis is tested by predicting each lagged youth outcome from prior round measures of controls, youth exposure and the older sibling scores on matched outcomes, as well as from the prior round interaction of youth exposure and sibling outcome measures. These analyses appear in Table 3.

None of the interaction terms in these four analyses were significant. There is no evidence consistent with the hypothesis that youth exposure effects are contingent on the siblings' prior round position on the outcome variables.

The instrumental support hypothesis

Effects of the campaign on behavior may be contingent on opportunities to take action. If the social network provides an opportunity for action, mass media effects will be larger. An older sibling many not only provide supportive or nonsupportive cognitive context for the younger sibling who is exposed to ad; he or she may provide concrete assistance to the younger sibling, making it easier to take an action consistent with a message.

> Hypothesis 3: If a younger sibling has an older sibling who offers him or her marijuana, the promarijuana effects of the campaign on use will be larger.

This hypothesis turned out to be untestable with the sibling data.

Among the questions asked respondents was whether anyone had offered him or her marijuana and, if so, who made the offer. One of the options was a brother

TABLE 3
COEFFICIENTS FOR PREDICTION OF FOUR LAGGED YOUTH OUTCOMES FROM PRIOR WAVE MEASURES OF EXPOSURE, SIBLING OUTCOME, AND THEIR INTERACTION, ALONG WITH CONTROLS; ODDS RATIOS (MARIJUANA USE AND INTENTIONS) OR UNSTANDARDIZED COEFFICIENTS (ATTITUDE-BELIEF AND SOCIAL NORMS) ARE REPORTED

	Constant	Age	Risk Score	Youth Past Year Use	Youth Prior Round Outcome	Sibling Prior Round Outcome	Exposure	Exposure × Sibling Prior Round Outcome
Marijuana use (relative odds)	**0.00**	**1.47**	**156.6**	**12.24**		**2.47**	1.13	1.13
Marijuana nonintention (relative odds)	**30.01**	**0.76**	0.037	0.258	**1.94**	0.247	**0.789**	1.25
Antimarijuana attitude-belief (unstandardized coefficient)	**45.1**	**−1.37**	**−179.9**	**−24.6**	**0.47**	**0.12**	2.42	0.002
Antimarijuana social norm (unstandardized coefficient)	**136.3**	**−8.3**	**−140.6**	**−24.1**	0.46	0.14	−1.22	0.001

NOTE: Significant results appear in bold. ns for the respective equations: use: 3,517; intentions: 2,907; attitude-belief: 1,969; social norms: 1,969. The ns are small for the attitude-belief and social norms analysis because many youth are missing for those variables on the prior round. These measures were only assessed for youth aged twelve to eighteen, and many of the younger siblings were younger than twelve the first time they were measured. A parallel analysis, eliminating the prior outcome measures for the youth for those two equations, moves the sample ns to about 2,800. The essential results, nonsignificant coefficients for the interaction terms, are replicated.

293

or sister. If there were enough siblings reported as offering marijuana, it would have been possible to test the interaction of sibling offers and campaign exposure. However only 1.3 percent of the respondents (53) claimed that a sibling offered marijuana. This was an insufficient number to permit testing whether the campaign had larger promarijuana effects if the sibling had offered marijuana. When youth reported that they had been offered marijuana, they almost always pointed to other youth, not family members, as the source.

The next two hypotheses turn from contingent effects of the social context to two-step flow effects: whether the campaign influenced the older sibling, who in turn influenced the younger sibling.

The relay (or two-step flow) hypothesis

The relay hypothesis can be seen as a variant of the conformity hypothesis. Rather than focusing on whether the older siblings cognitions and behavior provide a context in which the younger siblings respond to the campaign, it asks whether the influence of the campaign on the older siblings is retransmitted to the younger siblings.

> *Hypothesis 4:* The campaign affects the older siblings' marijuana cognitions and behavior, and the older siblings' cognitions and behaviors affect their younger brothers' or sisters' cognitions and behaviors.

The analysis for these effects require two stages: showing that the older siblings show the same effects as the target youth, as displayed in Table 1; and showing that the target youth lagged outcomes are affected by the older siblings' outcomes measured at the prior wave, controlling for the target youth outcomes at the prior wave (as well as the standard control variables).

The siblings analysis shows campaign effects substantially parallel to the target youth analysis in Table 1 (unsurprisingly). There are significant effects shown on lagged marijuana use (odds ratio [OR] = 1.17, $p < .05$, $n = 3,658$), on nonintentions (OR = 0.902, $p < .05$, $n = 3,644$), and on the social norms scale (coefficient = -4.7, $p < .01$, $n = 3,620$), but not on the attitude-belief scale (coefficient = -1.3, $p = .44$, $n = 3,620$), once control variables (age, risk score, prior round score on outcome variable, gender, and parent education) are entered. This satisfies stage 1 for testing this hypothesis.

Stage 2 requires showing an effect of prior round sibling scores on these cognitive and behavioral variables on lagged round scores of the target youth on parallel measures. To simplify this analysis, we examined whether the set of prior round sibling measures predicted each of the four outcomes, over and above the effects of control variables and the prior round measure of the target youth outcome.

There is evidence that older siblings' beliefs and behavior at the prior round are predictors for all four lagged youth outcomes. Table 4 displays results from each of the four equations. In the table, the individual significant coefficients are displayed, along with the information about the magnitude and significance of

TABLE 4
PREDICTION OF LAGGED YOUTH OUTCOMES FROM SIBLING
PRIOR ROUND OUTCOMES, CONTROLS, AND PRIOR
ROUND YOUTH OUTCOME

Predictor	Lagged Youth Outcomes			
	Past Year Use (Relative Odds)	Nonintention (Relative Odds)	Antimarijuana Attitude-Belief (Unst. Coeff.)	Antimarijuana Social Norms (Unst. Coeff.)
Youth variables				
Age	1.461	0.765	−1.22	−8.18
Risk score	209.7	0.029	−183.6	−141.2
Prior year use	12.38	0.237	−22.6	−20.5
Prior round score on outcome	—	6.61	0.471	0.457
Sibling prior round				
Use	1.882	—	—	−13.2
Nonintention	—	—	—	—
Antimarijuana attitude-belief	0.996	1.002	0.083	—
Antimarijuana social norms	—	1.002	0.067	0.122
R-squared or Nagelkerke R-squared— youth variables	30.0 chi-square = 47.57, $p < .001$	28.7 chi-square = 418, $p < .001$	28.5 $F = 194.2$, $p < .001$	27.0 $F = 180.1$, $p < .001$
Incremental R-squared or Nagelkerke R-squared— sibling variables	3.9 chi-square = 9.82, $p = .002$	2.3 chi-square = 8.42, $p = .004$	2.0 $F = 13.7$, $p < .001$	2.0 $F = 14.3$, $p < .001$
n	3,492	2,886	1,955	1,955

NOTE: Only significant results included.

the block of four older sibling predictors. The claim that the siblings' cognitions and behavior matter is based on the overall effect of all of the sibling measures from the prior round, captured in the incremental effects row in the table. The use of the overall effect reflects a judgment that the hypothesis of sibling influence on any one outcome is not limited to the sibling score on that outcome on the prior round; it is just as reasonable to argue that older sibling beliefs and attitudes affect the younger sibling's perceived social norms as that they influence the younger sibling's own belief-attitude score.

This version of the two-step flow hypothesis is then supported; we have evidence both that the campaign affected older siblings' behavior and cognitions and that older sibling behavior and cognitions have an effect on their younger siblings' behaviors and cognitions. The effects are not large; they add about 2 to 4 percent in predictive power.

It is worth noting that while there is evidence for the two-step process outlined here, there is inadequate evidence for a direct effect of older sibling exposure on younger sibling lagged outcomes. There is a simple significant association of older sibling exposure and younger sibling lagged outcome. However, for each of the four lagged outcomes, when the control variables representing the youth's own characteristics (age, risk score, prior year use) are entered, any association of sibling exposure with youth lagged outcome is no longer significant. The product of the two effects (campaign on sibling outcomes; sibling outcomes on youth lagged outcomes) is not large enough to be detectable as a direct effect.

> *[W]e have evidence both that the [National Youth Anti-Drug Media Campaign] affected older siblings' behavior and cognitions and that older sibling behavior and cognitions have an effect on their younger siblings' behaviors and cognitions.*

The message interpretation hypothesis

Social networks provide meanings for situations that do not explain themselves, including media messages. Those meanings influence how those messages are understood and thus what effects they are likely to have.

> *Hypothesis 5:* Older siblings' interpretations of the ads affect their younger siblings' interpretations.

One of the ways that older siblings may affect younger siblings is by the way they interpret the advertisements broadcast by the campaign. The ads themselves are intended to convey various antidrug messages. However, given the evidence that they produce prodrug outcomes, it seems likely that the interpretation given to the ads is not the intended one. This raises the issue of where the counterinterpretation might come from. One possibility, consistent with the *Personal Influence* argument, is that it comes from the social context. In this case, this would mean that a youth's interpretation of the ads is influenced by the interpretations offered by his or her older siblings. Since these data offer evidence about the evaluations of the ads offered by both members of sibling pairs, it is possible to test this hypothesis directly.

For as many as two ads that they had seen, youth were asked how they evaluated them on three criteria (there was a fourth, but it is not used for these analyses): whether they agreed or disagreed that this "ad got my attention," "ad was convincing," and "ad said something important to me." The evaluation scores could vary from −2 to +2, with +2 equaling *strong agreement*, −2 equaling *strong disagreement* and 0 equaling *neutrality* as to the value of an ad. The mean evaluation score among the younger siblings was 0.93, while among older siblings it was a less positive 0.78.

The test examined the association of the youths' own lagged evaluation and their older siblings' prior evaluation of the ads. The correlation was positive (r = .161) and the beta remained positive (.094) when the youth's own prior year ad evaluation, age, risk score, and past year's marijuana use were controlled. The unstandardized coefficient from the OLS multiple regression equation was .095—if the older sibling was one point higher on the evaluation scale, the younger sibling was about one-tenth of a point higher in the follow-up round. Interestingly, the lagged association was actually higher than the cross-sectional correlation between sibling and youth evaluations (r = .102). This test of the social influence hypothesis is supported.

However, it is probably worth noting that the implied assumption of this analysis—that the effects of youth exposure are contingent on the ad evaluation—is not consistent with most of the evidence. The youth's evaluation at the prior round does predict the outcomes at the lagged round even when the usual variables are controlled. However, the interaction of youth evaluation and exposure does not predict the lagged youth outcomes. Thus, while we can show that sibling evaluations affect youth evaluations, we cannot show that youth evaluations condition the effects of youth exposure on the outcomes. A possible explanation for that failure is presented in the discussion below.

Discussion

The article presented two types of analysis to test the social context hypotheses described in *Personal Influence:* the first asked whether the social context affected individual exposure effects; the second asked whether the influence of the campaign on older siblings was passed through to younger siblings. In general, the evidence drawn from the first set of analyses was not supportive; most tellingly, whatever the sibling's beliefs and behavior were concerning marijuana, the apparent effects of the campaign did not vary significantly. The evidence drawn from the second set of hypotheses was supportive. Most clearly, older siblings appeared to both be affected by the campaign and in turn seemed to affect the behaviors and cognitions of their younger brothers and sisters. Also, their evaluations of the campaign ads appeared to affect the younger siblings ad evaluations. However, these pass-through or two-step flow effects were not so strong that they provided a significant correlation between older sibling exposure and younger sibling outcomes, once control variables were included.

How are these results to be interpreted? First, why is it that the social context did not seem to condition the response to the campaign? There are three competing explanations: the first is that the hypothesis was wrong for sibling effects. In other words, the younger sibling interpreted the campaign independently of the elder's beliefs and behaviors. The second explanation is that the measures of sibling cognitions and behavior, which were used as surrogates for the actual context in which the youth received the campaign, did not capture that context. That is, what older siblings reported as their cognitions about marijuana use did not define the context that they provided their younger siblings as they received the campaign. The sibling context, for example, contained more complex messages—even if the older sibling was positive about marijuana use, he or she may have tried to hide that from the younger sibling. Or similarly, it might be that there were sibling effects but they require further digging down— seeing whether siblings who are particularly close in age or of the same gender, or those who talk a lot with one another, show these interactions, while others do not. These analyses do not separate these subgroups of siblings. They are possible with this data set, but have not yet been undertaken. The third explanation is that the statistical analysis was insufficiently sensitive to capture interactions. Although these analyses included relatively large samples, interactions are always hard to detect. In most cases, the observed interaction coefficients were in the predicted direction, but they were not sufficiently far from zero to be significant. This limitation would also constrain optimism about finding statistically significant interactions among subgroups of siblings, even if theory would argue for digging down further.

However, if the interactions did not show evidence consistent with the social context hypotheses, the two-step flow analyses did show such effects. These are statistically easier analyses and depend on finding main effects rather than interactions, and thus they have greater power to find effects, Also, because they separate the analyses into two stages—showing campaign effects on older siblings and then showing cross-sibling effects on cognitions and behavior—they have a simpler task. Hence, we are willing to claim a two-step flow on the basis that there was evidence for an effect at each stage even though we could not show a direct effect of older sibling exposure on younger sibling outcomes. The greater power to detect main effects and the simpler criterion for success may explain why the effects appear more readily.

Clearly, these analyses and the claims made here do have some limitations. The statistics were not conservative insofar as they do not account for the complex sample design and the nonindependence of the cases; also, while the control variables were important ones, it is certainly possible that there are other, not included variables that might explain the apparent effects. As tests of the theory of *Personal Influence*, they are only a start, even for these data: analyses with parents, and with the information about peers, would enrich the relevance of this as a test. It would seem quite likely that the effects of campaign exposure would be different depending on what parents and peers were saying about it.

One more result, not detailed here, bears on this idea. The evaluation report, in finding the apparent boomerang effect, considered a variety of possible mechanisms. The most persuasive of them was that the ads contained a meta-message. While the individual ads all had an explicit antidrug argument, the exposure to a large number of such ads might have contained an opposite message—that drugs were a big problem and that everyone was using them. Thus, the meta-message might have led youth to believe that many of their peers were using marijuana and that this, in turn, led them to consider drug use as an option for themselves. There was evidence consistent with this path of effect: the more exposure to the ads, the more youth believed that other kids were using marijuana; the more they believed that other kids were using marijuana, the more likely they were to initiate use themselves. This is partly directly linked to the hypotheses of personal influence. But it is also a different version of the social influence hypothesis: social influence may not only be conditioned on the actual social context but also on the virtual social context captured through mediated experience.

Note

1. Whereas for the stability analyses we focused on the absolute value of the discrepancy, ignoring the direction of the difference, for this analysis we use the actual sibling score at the prior wave on each of the four outcome variables. Given that older siblings on average tend to be more promarijuana than younger ones, the level of absolute discrepancy tends to correlate with having siblings with relative promarijuana cognitions and behavior. Thus, the tests with the absolute values of discrepancy and those with the observed value of the sibling's score are not independent in practice, even if they are independent in underlying logic.

References

Allen, Mike, William A. Donohue, Amy Griffin, Dan Ryan, and Monique Mitchell Turner. 2003. Comparing the influence of parents and peers on the choice to use drugs. *Criminal Justice & Behavior*, 30 (2): 163-86.

Austin, Erica W., Bruce E. Pinkleton, and Yuki Fujioka. 2000. The role of interpretation processes and parental discussion in the media's effects on adolescents' use of alcohol. *Pediatrics* 105:343-49.

Austin, Erica W., and J. Yin. 2003. The relationship of parental reinforcement of media messages to college students' alcohol-related behaviors. *Journal of Health Communication* 8:157-69.

Ennett, Susan T., Karl E. Baumann, Vangie E. Foshee, Michael Pemberton, and Katherine A. Hicks. 2001. Parent-child communication about adolescent tobacco and alcohol use: What do parents say and does it affect youth behavior? *Journal of Marriage and Family* 63:48-62.

Hornik, Robert, David Maklan, Diane Cadell, Carlin Barmada, Lela Jacobsohn, Vani Henderson, Anca Romantan, Jeffrey Niederdeppe, Robert Orwin, Sanjeev Sridharan, Robert Baskin, Adam Chu, Carol Morin, Kristie Taylor, and Diane Steele. 2003. *Evaluation of the National Youth Anti-Drug Media Campaign: 2003 report of findings*. Washington, DC: Westat.

Katz, Elihu, and Paul Lazarsfeld. 1955/2006. *Personal influence: The part played by people in the flow of mass communication*. 2nd ed. New Brunswick, NJ: Transaction Publishers.

Nathanson, Amy I. 1999. Identifying and explaining the relationship between parental mediation and children's aggression. *Communication Research* 26 (2): 124-43.

———. 2001. Parents vs. peers: Exploring the significance of peer mediation of antisocial television. *Communication Research* 28 (3): 215-74.

Rogers, Everett. 2003. *Diffusion of innovations*. 5th ed. New York: Free Press.

Ryan, Bryce, and Neal C. Gross. 1943. The diffusion of hybrid seed corn in two Iowa communities. *Rural Sociology* 8 (1): 15-24.

Wright, Charles R. 1989. *Mass communication: A sociological perspective*. 3rd ed. New York: Random House.

True Stories

By
ELIHU KATZ

If *Personal Influence* (Katz and Lazarsfeld 1955) has survived, it is thanks to Paul Lazarsfeld. Having stumbled on the idea of the "two-step flow of communication" in his study (Lazarsfeld, Berelson, and Gaudet 1944/1948, chap. xvi) of how voters made up their minds in the 1940 presidential election, it was typical of him, as empiricist and entrepreneur, to take the next step toward confirming the hypothesis that messages from the media are intercepted by "opinion leaders" who filter them, selectively, to their peers. Fieldwork for what was called the Decatur Study was begun toward the end of World War II, and its aim was to trace the flow of influence in the making of everyday decisions. I had no share in the design or fieldwork for the study, nor in most of the subsequent analysis. At the time, I was just beginning in Columbia College and, a year later, in the U.S. Army.

This was also the moment when the Bureau of Applied Social Research was being established at Columbia University, and Paul Lazarsfeld's lifelong partnership with Robert Merton was being launched. The study enlisted Bernard Berelson as advance man, C. Wright Mills as field director, and a large posse of interviewers. Like *The People's Choice* (Lazarsfeld, Berelson, and Gaudet 1944/1948), its predecessor, the Decatur Study was designed to zoom in on decisions in the making, employing (1) a panel method of repeated interviews with the same sample of respondents, (2) a method for weighting the

Elihu Katz is a trustee professor of communication at the Annenberg School of the University of Pennsylvania and professor emeritus of sociology and communication at the Hebrew University of Jerusalem. His most recent books include The Export of Meaning: Cross Cultural Readings of "Dallas" *(with Tamar Liebes) and* Media Events: The Live Broadcasting of History *(with Daniel Dayan). He studied with Paul Lazarsfeld at Columbia University and began his career at the University of Chicago. He holds honorary degrees from the Universities of Ghent, Montreal, Paris, and Haifa.*

DOI: 10.1177/0002716206293441

relative impact of the several media in decision making, and (3) a method for determining whether interpersonal influence played a part in the process. Peter Rossi, David Gleicher, and Leo Srole each made major contributions to the analysis and interpretation of the data. And it took eight more years, until about 1953, for Lazarsfeld to invite me to undertake additional analysis, to put a theoretical wrapping on the findings, and to weave the whole together as a book. Using somewhat different methods, Robert Merton (1949) had long since completed his study of "Cosmopolitan and Local Influentials"—a 1943 study of interpersonal influence in the realm of public affairs in a town in New Jersey.

I am asked to look back to the creation of *Personal Influence* and to contemplate its career—past, present, and possible future. I began to do so in my new Introduction to the fiftieth anniversary edition (Katz 2005) and in the Lazarsfeld Lecture at Columbia University (Katz 1987). But inasmuch as our editor has asked a dozen or so distinguished colleagues to do the same, I find that my memory is no match for theirs. Historians, sociologists, political scientists—newcomers and old-timers—have reread the book. They dig deep into the sometimes shadowy past of the Decatur Study; contextualize it in time and space; and reconsider its standing in the sociologies of mass communications and small groups and its implications for the applied fields of marketing, advertising, and media. Their "true stories"—based not alone on memory, but on research—are sometimes different from mine. They tell me things that I don't remember—or never knew. They reconstruct a past of which I was sometimes unaware, or hadn't noticed, or for which I deserve no credit (or blame) at all. Often, though, our stories coincide. I take all the stories to be "true," even my own. Rashomon rides again. What I propose, then, is to consider these true stories, side by side with mine.

I will proceed under four headings: The first is called "Authorship, or the Cast of Characters," especially in view of the complex logistics of fieldwork and analysis, as well as the elapsed time between the conception of the field study in 1944 and publication of the book in 1955. The second set of comments is called "Contexts, or Sociology and History," in which I will explore the allegation that the study ignores its own place and time—the town of Decatur, Illinois, in 1945—preferring to "universalize." The third section will deal with issues of "Theory, Ideology, and Their Consequences," addressing allegations that the Decatur Study undermined the potential of communication research by understating the true power of the media, by lumping voters and consumers together, and by subservience to the media industry. The fourth section, "Some Things that Went Right," will consider some of the things being said about the positive directions to which *Personal Influence* has pointed.

Authorship, or the Cast of Characters

Let me begin with a parable, a blasphemous one. Allow me to recall the day when God summoned Moses to Mt Sinai. When he arrived, God is supposed to have explained that He had the outline of a Book in mind, written with the help of some favorite angels, but wanted one of the nations to adopt it, to live by its precepts, and for one of its sons to prepare it for publication. God revealed that He had been turned down by several nations, and by several potential collaborators. So Moses said OK, and his tribe said "we accept," and he proceeded to transcribe the Book at God's dictation, incorporating parts of the drafts prepared for Him by senior angels. When the Book was completed, and its abstract etched in stone, God was pleased. He invited Moses to add a section of his own and to bind it together with the rest. To his surprise, God then turned to Moses and said, "Moses, You be first author." This was God's way of rewarding Moses, but it is also true, in view of the Matthew effect (soon to be proclaimed),[1] that He had little to lose. And perhaps this was also His way of showing the angels who's boss. Moses did more than his share in marketing the Book and in debating it, mostly with his own people. He even followed the example from which he had benefited, and bestowed first authorship on some of his own disciples. Moses never claimed first authorship; indeed, he spent a lot of energy explaining how it happened; but as time went by, God seemed firmly entrenched in second place. It wasn't fair, but neither was it easy to fix—each time, over again. In the end, though, a lot of scholarship caught up with Moses, and he agreed that it would only be right if he were to be punished. Therefore, in addition to the honors that had been showered on him, he agreed to being buried in an unmarked grave in an unknown place.[2]

Paul Lazarsfeld was not God—even to his graduate students—and I am not Moses—but that's what came to mind when I seated myself to write. As I proceed, I will try to relate my own story to the other stories recorded in these pages, weaving their arguments "in" and "out" as best I can. True stories all. Let's now return to the question of authorship, which sounds straightforward, but isn't. In fact, I will now propose four different kinds of authors.

Even those who believe that there are no authors, and that only cultures write books, cannot deny that the Decatur Study and its methodologies are the brainchild of Paul Lazarsfeld. But on a more abstract level, it can also be argued that the final product may be attributed to a collective new look at postwar culture. One can point to the "rediscovery of the primary group" in the 1950s and the consequent decline of mass society theory. Scannell reads Riesman's (1950) "other directedness" as harbinger of this change. It is in this sense that Zeitgeist may be dubbed the author of *Personal Influence*, with its latent message of the "communal," or "conversational," or "deliberative" that Peters sees diffusing from New York's "Mercurians" (Slezkine 2004) to the Midwest.

And if we take a step down the ladder of abstraction, it can be said that the Bureau of Applied Social Research is the collective author. Like in a Broadway play, an infrastructure is at work in survey research "without whom" large-scale projects cannot be tackled. Behind the scenes, then, stood the Bureau of Applied Social Research, whose Golden Age of creativity in the 1950s and 1960s produced scholars, books, and papers that have been hailed by some as canonic. All of the contributing authors were junior members of the Bureau at the time, and the Acknowledgments to *Personal Influence* name seven or eight more professionals—not all academics—who made important contributions. As Morrison reminds us, the Bureau is the fruition of Paul Lazarsfeld's dream of establishing an institute for applied social research that, financed by clients and other funding agencies, would address practical problems of politics, culture, and business and address academic issues as well. Before leaving Vienna, he had made a start in this direction, together with Hans Zeisel, Marie Jahoda, Hertz Herzog, and others. With support from the Rockefeller Foundation and prominent broadcasting barons, he turned attention to the new medium of radio, and leapfrogged his institute from Princeton to Newark to Columbia, which, soon after, formally appointed Lazarsfeld as well as Merton. In spite of the much-remarked differences between the two men, they became fast friends and lifelong partners. When Lazarsfeld completed his classic study of how voters make up their minds, the partners—now directors of the new Bureau—decided to mount a further study that would expand on the same theme in the everyday areas of marketing, fashions, moviegoing, and local politics. The book was completed in 1955, when my Part One, relating interpersonal and mass communication, situated the Decatur Study in the context of (what today might be called) social networks, very different from the image of mass society and mass manipulation that underlay early thinking on the mass media. In addition to the star-studded cadre of doctoral students who were charged with analyzing the data, it could not have been accomplished without the infrastructure of the Bureau. From the contract with Macfadden Publications, to the design of the sample, to the posse of interviewers who descended on Decatur, through the decade of stick-to-itiveness that kept the study alive, it could not have been accomplished without an organizational structure. And what an organizational structure (Morrison 1976; Barton 2001)!

Still at the institutional level, it is worth recording the contribution of the GI Bill, which accounts for more than a few of our careers, and Jeremiah Kaplan's Free Press of Glencoe, pioneer publisher of social science. But the organization that got more than it dreamed of is Macfadden Publications. In 1945, Macfadden invested a reputed $20,000 in the Decatur Study, hoping that it would confirm that "opinion leaders" were to be found among readers of *True Story*, the kind that would advise their working-class peers about what to buy and how to vote. *Time* magazine, *Life*, and other media moguls made similar investments in other Bureau studies, and for much the same reasons. The preliminary findings presumably pleased Macfadden and its advertisers, even if the full report would take years to produce. In fact, more than ten years passed before the publication of *Personal Influence* in 1955, whose Part Two publicly unveiled the Decatur findings.[3] The book evoked wide interest as well as angry response from those who were convinced that it understated the power of the media. Fifty years later, the name Macfadden lives on in *Personal Influence*, even if the company is much less visible. Not bad for $20,000.

At a more concrete level, even if Lazarsfeld and the Bureau are inseparable, real people did the work. The aforementioned doctoral students, not sufficiently acknowledged in *Personal Influence*, did good and hard work on the sections of the study to which they were assigned. My job was to put the whole together while composing a Part One that would identify those aspects of small groups that might have bearing on mass communication and vice versa, unlikely as that sounded at the time. All I know—perhaps I should know more—is that Lazarsfeld had a falling out with Mills over the conception of the study (whether interpersonal influence moved vertically or horizontally through the class structure?); over commercial sponsorship of the study; over the conduct of the analysis; and even earlier, says Summers, over the administration of the fieldwork. Subsequently, Peter Rossi, Robert Gleicher, and Leo Srole were commissioned to analyze and report on (1) the relative impact of the several media and interpersonal influence in the making of decisions (Rossi, Part Two, Section Two of *Personal Influence*) and (2) the matrices of who influences whom (Gleicher and Srole, Part Two, Section Three). After substantial sections of the report had been prepared, and even more time had elapsed, Lazarsfeld—still apparently unsatisfied as to how to paste the pieces together—turned to me, his newest doctoral student, to complete the work, perform additional analysis—and to propose a qualitative introduction to the study as a whole. Even at this point, all is not clear. Small-group research and group dynamics research had a prominent place in the sociology and social psychology of the 1950s. Lazarsfeld's discovery of the mediating role of interpersonal influence in the flow of mass communications suggested to me that it would be interesting to review the flourishing literature on small groups for its possible bearing on the dynamics of consuming media. I recall that I proposed this project to Lazarsfeld, but Pooley tells a different story. His claim is that Edward Shils (1951) was there first, and that Lazarsfeld found in Shils's studies of the primary group a possible theoretical wrapping for his repeated findings that the power of the media to influence everyday decisions might be contingent on the intervention of interpersonal influence, an idea that I then developed.

[F]rom the very first, [Personal Influence's] collaborators themselves divided over interpretation of the data.

At the bottom of the ladder stand the readers, to whom theorists of reception would attribute authorship. Indeed, from the very first, the collaborators themselves divided over interpretation of the data. More cogent examples are closer at hand. For example, several contributors to this volume read *Personal Influence* as a study of postwar community, or as a study of the everyday life of Midwestern women—leading us directly into the second theme of this Afterword.

Contexts, or Sociology and History

A critical chorus echoes through the commentaries ingathered here to the effect that *Personal Influence* takes pains to disguise itself for what it isn't and to conceal what it really is. Why do they conceal the fact that the respondents are women, ask Douglas and Glickman? Why do they obscure the survey respondents' femaleness by referring to "people" (in the subtitle of the book) or, worse, why do they speak of "he" (Part One)? Why don't the authors tell us that these women have just returned from wartime jobs to their roles as housewives and consumers? Why don't they tell us more about the lives of these women—and their other roles? Why don't they tell us more about the town in which the study was conducted—especially after taking such pains to establish its (statistical) representativeness? Why don't they tell us about the cultural turn to other-directedness that dates to the postwar period (Scannell)? Why don't they remind us that their conclusions about mass communication are based on radio broadcasting and that television might soon change all that? And if they're so smart, why didn't they predict—as Bennett and Mannheim now do—that opinion leaders would be put out of work by the custom-tailored messages of the new personalized media?

In a word, *Personal Influence* is criticized for its universalizing pretensions, that is, for overgeneralizing its findings as if they were applicable anywhere and anytime. While some of these "complaints" are regrets over research opportunities forgone, they are not postmodern calls for "local" narrative. These are not simple arguments that small is beautiful or that sociology has forgotten history, or pious calls for taking account of the specificities of time and place and technologies. Rather, I read them as expressions of concern over the situational limits of social science. They have to do with the perennial problem of accounting for those contextual aspects of research—whether in the laboratory or in the field— that are likely to limit its generalizability. I believe them to be asking whether there may be something about postwar Decatur (the resurgence of consumerism?), or the prospect of television, or, indeed, about female respondents that should give pause to those who would generalize from the Decatur Study to the proposition that people everywhere and always will consult other people prior to forming opinions. Of course, such warnings should indeed limit conceit, but, equally important, they may lead to the legendary (but not often implemented) kind of further research that will confirm or disconfirm the proposition and specify whether and how it varies under conditions specified by the objections. Consider how tempting it was to dismiss Sherif's (1952) classic experiment on the workings of interpersonal influence because it was based on the optical illusion that a pinpoint of light in a darkened room will appear to move. The beauty of the Bureau of Applied Social Research is that it took such thinking seriously, moving from study to study in the search to confirm or disconfirm, as does Robert Hornik in this volume.

So it was with Decatur. Lazarsfeld had little interest in a "community study." His aim was not to revisit Middletown but to revisit a hypothesis that arose in the course of his earlier study of voting decisions to see whether it would be confirmed in other domains. It is a fair guess that he had no special interest in the site of the study, even if his near-ritualistic concern with representativeness led him there; it is certain, in any case, that a larger study or a national sample would have been organizationally and financially unmanageable. On the other hand, he was, indeed, concerned about context, not for its own sake but because the culture of the town might have bearing on the findings, as he himself points out (Lazarsfeld, Berelson, and Gaudet 1944/1948, xxvii). It is also true that major Bureau studies were almost all community based, as Simonson points out.

[W]omen were referred to as "people" in the subtitle of the study . . . because they were, indeed, making decisions in their presumed areas of specialization.

It seems doubtful that he had any special interest in female respondents except insofar that they were more likely than men to be decision makers in the realms of everyday shopping and fashion, and perhaps in deciding which movie to see. (And, of course, he was interested in women because Macfadden was.)

That's why women were referred to as "people" in the subtitle of the study. Not to disguise the possibility that they limited the study's generalizability, but because they were, indeed, making decisions in their presumed areas of specialization. It follows that there is room for the objection that women and men are not interchangeable. *The People's Choice* finds that husbands influenced the voting decisions of wives (maybe still do), and it is probably correct to guess that men's fashion decisions are more influenced by women than vice versa. Such questions are at the very heart of the Decatur Study, which asks who influences whom in which domain, and the findings certainly imply that women cannot "stand in" for men in certain respects, just as older women—influential in marketing decisions—cannot stand in for younger women. In this sense at least, the objection is sustained. Women, like men, are special kinds of people, and it is the circulation of influence—the flow—among these differences that were of interest in the Study.

Nor is there reason to believe that Lazarsfeld took account of the changing roles of women at the end of World War II, even if one may assume—with the critics—that these changes affected their interests and activities. Might the findings of the study have been different during the war or prior to it? Probably. But Lazarsfeld was not so much interested in these probabilities. He had no interest in producing an index of consumer behavior.

Pooley gives us reason to believe that Lazarsfeld had taken notice of the American sociology of the "primary group" as refracted in the writings of Edward Shils (1951) and of the variety of ties that bind, from primordial to civil. If true, it might have suggested to him that the character and extent of interpersonal influence might vary by time and place. Gabriel Tarde, the French social psychologist, suggested as much in his essay on "Conversation" and the public sphere (in Clark 1969). However reasonable, no evidence suggests that he was concerned that what he found in Decatur might not hold true in New York; nor did he give thought, as Peters does, to the nature of the exchange between the two. For the purposes of the study, it is unlikely that he (or I) gave much thought to the image of Decatur as a smallish town occupied with local gossip, in comparison to the cosmopolitan concerns of New York, as Tarde might have done.

What surely did occupy him was the different effects of the several media. He had early studied "radio vs. the printed page" (Lazarsfeld 1940) and differentiated between the two in the voting study. In the Decatur Study, the media were differentiated according to their relevance to each domain (fashion, public affairs). Researchers took an important step to determine the characteristic constellation of media, and their relative position in the sequence that led to the making of a decision. Lazarsfeld named this mapping procedure "an accounting scheme" (*Personal Influence*, pp. 189-91).

If Lazarsfeld had been asked to predict how his main findings might change in the era of television, I believe that he would have stood his ground. Would he have been proven wrong? Have women discontinued their consultations with peers because fashion and household goods are represented so much more vividly on television than they were on radio and magazines? Now that television has brought politics into the living room, has the flow of political influence between men and women become more symmetrical? Will the new media of personal tailoring finally annihilate the second of the two steps? Bennett thinks yes, and one infers that Mutz (1998), too, thinks that television might be having more direct influence than its predecessor. I doubt it. But let's not hold all this against Lazarsfeld, sixty years later, even if they're right.

Theory, Ideology, and Their Consequences

More troubling than the critiques of the universalistic pretensions of *Personal Influence* are the allegations that the book had crippling consequences for the then-developing field of media studies. These critiques assert (1) that the focus on effects of the media in the short run and on everyday decisions distracted scholarly attention from the study of media impingement on bigger things, (2) that the focus on interpersonal influence and limited effects shields (intentionally?) the captains of the culture industry from the blame they deserve, (3) that the theory of mass society and its presumption of powerful media was introduced as a straw man to set the stage for the "discovery" of interpersonal influence and limited effects, and (4) that the lumping together of decision making in the domains of voting and shopping is reprehensible.

> *Fortunately or unfortunately,* [Personal
> Influence's *focus on the short run of media
> influence*] *probably did give currency to the
> conclusion that the ostensibly omnipotent
> media have only* "limited effects."

To these critiques, one can immediately concede that media studies at the Bureau of Applied Social Research, *Personal Influence* among them, did indeed focus on the short run of media influence on opinions, attitudes, and actions. This relates to the interest in the dynamics of decision making, to the accessibility of such research—methodologically speaking—as well as to the (perhaps naive) question of whether the mass society can be easily manipulated by the elites of business and politics. Fortunately or unfortunately, this emphasis probably did give currency to the conclusion that the ostensibly omnipotent media have only "limited effects." This conclusion still holds for well-designed evaluations of "campaigns" as evidenced in Hornik's careful study of an expensive antidrug campaign. Indeed, academic research has no evidence of massive media effects in the short run, even in advertising. But that conclusion should not be applied to domains in which media power may be (or may not be) much greater. Did not media rally public opinion for the current war in Iraq (packaging Saddam Hussein and al-Qaeda)? Did not the media make impeachment "thinkable" during the Watergate affair (Lang and Lang 1983)? Did not the media hasten the retreat from Vietnam, or the much-delayed U.S. intervention in Kosovo? Answers to these questions are less than clear-cut, research-wise (see Hallin 1986), but the questions are of a different sort, obviously, than those that were asked at the Bureau in the 1950s. Lang and Lang are right in "blaming" the Bureau for defining media-effect studies so narrowly—or, indeed, for failing to call more explicit attention to the typology of other kinds of effects that Lazarsfeld had early published (in Lazarsfeld 1948; also see Katz 2001), even if his actual research was more narrowly focused. Too bad.[4]

The Langs' objection may have had more than theoretical consequences. It differs, however, from the more ideological approach that characterizes Gitlin's (1978) famous attack. Gitlin (correctly) sees *Personal Influence* as part of the

Bureau's reapportioning of power between media and mass, and declares this a travesty. Opinion leaders, argues Gitlin, are mere conduits for the messages of the media and are, therefore, unwitting collaborators in the hegemonic process.[5] Attributing independence to interpersonal influence obscures its reinforcing role, says Gitlin, thus deflecting criticism from the media as powerful agencies of social control (to which, ironically, Noelle-Neumann [1984] would agree). Powerful institutions, Gitlin implies, are only too pleased to find their power understated. Moreover, the decisions studied by Lazarsfeld are mere decoys, he says, because they conceal genuine alternatives. Rather than an exercise in democracy, the study of consumer choices between the two major colas or voters' choices between the two major parties is, yet again, a collusion with the economic and political establishments, which are only too happy to suppress "third parties." Lazarsfeld's (1940) brilliant defense of "administrative" research—helping responsible institutions to diagnose and confront the problems they face—takes explicit account of such biases, while acknowledging the complementary role played by "critical" research in making the "client" (of administrative research) a part of the problem.

To the allegation that the Bureau dismissed the theory of mass society too quickly, there are at least two sides. One side says that the term *mass* does not characterize any society and that the concept itself is hardly useful (Williams 1958/1989). This side also might say that early theorists of mass communication did not have direct, powerful effects in mind, and hence the "discovery" of interpersonal influence and limited effects is only a kind of grandstanding. Others disagree. The term *mass* is certainly applicable to the first half of the twentieth century says Scannell, and David Riesman (1950) is the herald of its demise. Theorists and researchers of propaganda in the early days of radio expected powerful effects, and retreated only much later.

True, the "theory of mass society" was discredited by Shils and others who saw the primary group as underpinning large institutional structures. This is the theme that I pursued in Part One of *Personal Influence*, abetted by Shils, Homans, Lewin, Bales, Festinger, and the social psychology of small-group research. The question of whether Shils influenced Lazarsfeld who influenced me to move in this direction, or whether the routing proceeded differently, is addressed above. But that is a small question compared with the big one of whether the retreat from mass society and powerful effects was a capitulation to the powers (and clients) that be.

Finally, consider Gitlin's (1978) objection that it is frivolous to treat consumers and voters in the same breath, as if decision making in the two domains were commensurable. Yet what is one to do if they are roughly comparable behaviorally—even if they "ought" to be different, as Schudson says? In fact, there *is* some difference, as the critics—and the authors—point out in that the extent of direct media influence *is* greater in the domain of public affairs than in the other domains; but that only exacerbates the problem.[6] Schudson confesses to being plagued by this problem, and together with Glickman, proposes that there is a (partial) way out. They argue, each in his own way, that certain consumer decisions are political (as was the Boston Tea Party, for an ancient example) and that certain political decisions are about consumerism (whether to dig for oil in Alaska, for example).

Some Things that Went Right

It's been mostly argument so far, pro and con. Let's now try for a happier end by turning to a few nominees for praiseworthy outcomes of the Decatur Study and of *Personal Influence*.

A series of three Bureau studies may be described methodologically, as attempts to introduce sociometry into survey research. It began in *The People's Choice* when voters verbally described the persons who had influenced them, continued in *Personal Influence* where influencee and influential were paired and interviewed, and culminated in the so-called Drug Study (Coleman, Katz, and Menzel 1966), where the social and professional relationships of communities of physicians could be sociometrically mapped. This progression led from the study of dyads to the study of networks and from the study of decision making to the study of diffusion.

In this sense, *Personal Influence* deserves kudos for being among the forerunners of the current interest in network theory and the revived interest in tracing the epidemiology of ideas and practices—and diseases! Hornik is well aware of how the social embeddedness of individuals contextualizes media effects. Some of the foremost sociologists of social networks (Burt 1992, for example) are carrying the torch.

Livingstone goes on to propose that the tempering of media power implicit in the networks of *Personal Influence* jibes with the redistribution of power to audiences implicit in the gratifications theory of the Bureau (Blumler and Katz 1974) and the resistance theory of the Birmingham School (Hall 1992). These ideas, she says, belong to the history of audiences, acknowledging that research on audiences long preceded the upstart claims of cultural studies, as Curran (1990) has long maintained. The "active audience" has had its ups and downs both in theater and in journalism, as Livingstone shows in recent work, and it would be no surprise to Gabriel Tarde, for one, that "press-conversation-opinion-action" (Clark 1969; Katz 2006) might still (or again) help to describe the public sphere.

It seems fair to say that the uphill efforts to resurrect participatory democracy and community—in the struggle against the increased alienation noted by Putnam (2000), Eliasoph (1998), and others and against the prophets of the new media and their fragmentation of society—find support, even today, in the everyday fraternity of *Personal Influence*, its predecessors, and successors. The Bureau itself continued along these lines, mounting the Berelson, Lazarsfeld, and McPhee (1954) study of voting and Wright and Cantor's (1967) study of opinion leadership, and culminating in the study of physicians' decisions to adopt new drugs (Coleman, Katz, and Menzel 1966). Thus, the idea of opinion leadership—which implied interception and negotiation of media messages—helped to restore the spotlight to "conversation," and from conversation to deliberation and debate—of the kind that is supposed to nourish the public sphere, even if Schudson (1997) doubts it.

This is a good time to recall, with Kadushin, that Lazarsfeld's guiding interest was in the psychology of decision making, or to switch frames slightly, in the dynamics of choosing. Kadushin invokes a larger frame still, alluding to Lazarsfeld's well-known sorting of the various types of influence ("the art of asking why"; Lazarsfeld 1935), in his striving for "a theory of action." These labels allude to the comforting messages of *Personal Influence* that (1) democracy is about choice, not about imposition; and (2) choices are made in the informal deliberations of small groups of family and friends, not by a tyrannical majority or by hegemonic duplicity. One does not have to be a critical theorist nowadays to suspect that these small comforts may be manipulative, or to be a neocon to applaud them. There is a lot of room in between—then, and maybe even now. Half a century ago, they were a relief from the threat of mass society (Kornhauser 1959), real or imagined. Lazarsfeld seems to have found pleasure in these thoughts. Livingstone agrees with Peters that " 'the genius of *Personal Influence* was to rescue the public sphere from the media' [Peters 1989, 215] and thereby to permit an alternative approach to participatory democracy even in a media age."

◦ ◦ ◦

Elsewhere, I have elaborated on the extensions of certain of these ideas and methodologies (Katz 2006, 1987). But here and now, these thoughts have been greatly enriched by the privilege of reading the essays contributed to this volume and to the honor of networking with their authors, both virtually and in person. Our greatest debt on this occasion—if I may be allowed to speak for both authors—is to Peter Simonson, editor and convener of the symposium; to Peter Bearman of Columbia University, director of the Institute that succeeded the Bureau; and to Michael Delli Carpini, dean of the Annenberg School, for their sponsorship and encouragement. It seems fitting, ceremonially speaking, to add that these reflections are being written at the Center for Advanced Study in the Behavioral Sciences, in Stanford, California, where Paul was in residence when *Personal Influence* was, at last, put to bed.

Notes

1. "For unto every one that hath shall be given, and he shall have abundance," quipped Robert Merton, citing the Apostle Matthew, "but from him that hath not shall be taken away even that which he hath" (Merton 1968/1973, 445).

2. In this parable, only the angels are not consonant with tradition. In his introduction to *The Influentials*, Gabriel Weimann (1994) also invokes Moses. But he assigns him the role of "opinion leader."

3. Elmo Roper, the pioneer pollster, was closely associated with Lazarsfeld and the Bureau and wrote a Foreword to *Personal Influence*. Interestingly, his heirs have recently published a book on the power of interpersonal influence (Keller and Berry 2003).

4. Ironically, Dayan and Katz's (1992) *Media Events* is accused of ascribing too *much* power to television by Couldry (2003). Parenthetically, it might be noted that these events may also be classified as "short run."

5. Gitlin's (1978) allegation that opinion leaders simply forward what they see and hear in the media was nourished, admittedly, by the sometimes misleading formulations in *Personal Influence* and elsewhere. The thrust of the concept is otherwise, however, at least in later years. For an evenhanded analysis of this ostensible contradiction, see Pooley (2006, 291).

6. The area of public affairs was very poorly operationalized in *Personal Influence*, whereas the other three domains dealt with very specific decisions to change. This is a very likely explanation for some of the differences observed in the area of changing opinions about public affairs.

References

Note: Articles in this volume are not further referenced below.

Barton, Allen. 2001. Paul Lazarsfeld as institutional inventor. *International Journal of Public Opinion Research* 13 (3): 245-69.

Berelson, B., Paul F. Lazarsfeld, and William N. McPhee. 1954. *Voting*. Chicago: University of Chicago Press.

Blumler, Jay G., and Elihu Katz, eds. 1974. *The uses of mass communication*. Beverly Hills, CA: Sage.

Burt, Ronald S. 1992. *Structural holes: The social structure of competition*. Cambridge, MA: Harvard University Press.

Clark, Terry N. 1969. *Gabriel Tarde on communication and social influence*. Chicago: University of Chicago Press.

Coleman, James S., Elihu Katz, and Herbert Menzel. 1966. *Medical innovation: A diffusion study*. Indianapolis, IN: Bobbs-Merrill.

Couldry, Nick. 2003. *Media rituals: A critical approach*. London: Routledge.

Curran, James. 1990. The "new revisionism" in mass communications research. *European Journal of Communication* 5:2-3.

Dayan, Daniel, and Elihu Katz. 1992. *Media events*. Cambridge, MA: Harvard University Press.

Eliasoph, Nina. 1998. *Avoiding politics: How Americans produce apathy in everyday life*. Cambridge, MA: Cambridge University Press.

Gitlin, Todd. 1978. Media sociology: The dominant paradigm. *Theory and Society* 6:205-53.

Hall, Stuart. 1992. Cultural studies and its theoretical legacies. In *Cultural studies*, ed. L. Grossberg et al. New York: Routledge.

Hallin, Daniel. 1986. *The "uncensored" war*. New York: Oxford University Press.

Katz, Elihu. 1987. Communications research since Lazarsfeld. *Public Opinion Quarterly* 51:S25-S45.

———. 2001. Lazarsfeld's map of media effects. *International Journal of Public Opinion Research* 13 (3): 270-79.

———. 2005. Introduction to second edition. In Elihu Katz and Paul F. Lazarsfeld, *Personal influence: The part played by people in the flow of mass communications*. New Brunswick, NJ: Transaction Publishers.

———. 2006. Rediscovering Gabriel Tarde. *Political Communication* 23:1-8.

Katz, Elihu, and Paul F. Lazarsfeld. 1955. *Personal influence: The part played by people in the flow of mass communications*. Glencoe, IL: Free Press.

Keller, E. B., and J. Berry. 2003. *The influentials: One American in ten tells the other nine how to vote, where to eat, what to buy*. New York: Simon & Schuster.

Kornhauser, William. 1959. *The politics of mass society*. Glencoe, IL: Free Press.

Lang, Gladys E., and Kurt Lang. 1983. *The battle for public opinion*. New York: Columbia University Press.

Lazarsfeld, Paul F. 1935. The art of asking why in marketing research. *National Marketing Review* 1:32-43.

———. 1940. Remarks on administrative and critical communication research. *Studies in Philosophy and Social Science* 9:2-16.

———. 1948. Communication research and the social psychologist. In *Current trends in social psychology*, ed. Wayne Dennis, 218-73. Pittsburgh, PA: University of Pittsburgh Press.

Lazarsfeld, Paul F., Bernard Berelson, and Hazel Gaudet. 1944/1948. *The people's choice*. New York: Columbia University Press.

Merton, Robert K. 1949. Patterns of influence: A study of interpersonal influence and of communications behavior in a local community. In *Communications research 1948-49*, ed. P. F. Lazarsfeld and F. Stanton. New York: Harper.

———. 1968/1973. The Matthew Effect in science: The reward and communications systems of science are considered. *Science* 159 (3810): 56-63.

Morrison, David. 1976. *Paul Lazarsfeld: The biography of an institutional innovator*. Leicester, UK: University of Leicester Press.

Mutz, Diana C. 1998. *Impersonal influence*. Cambridge: Cambridge University Press.

Noelle-Neumann, Elisabeth. 1984. *The spiral of silence*. Chicago: University of Chicago Press.

Peters, John Durham. 1989. Democracy and American mass communication theory: Dewey, Lippman, Lazarsfeld. *Communication* 11:199-220.

Pooley, Jefferson D. 2006. *An accident of memory*. PhD diss., Columbia University, New York.

Putnam, Robert. 2000. *Bowling alone*. New York: Simon & Schuster.

Riesman, David. 1950. *The lonely crowd*. New Haven, CT: Yale University Press.

Schudson, Michael. 1997. Why conversation is not the soul of democracy. *Critical Studies in Mass Communication* 14:297-309.

Sherif, Muzafer. 1952. Social factors in perception. In *Readings in social psychology*, ed. D. Swanson, T. Newcomb, and E. Hartley. New York: Holt, Rinehart & Winston.

Shils, Edward A. 1951. The study of the primary group. In *The policy sciences: Recent developments in scope and method*, ed. D. Lerner and H. D Lasswell. Stanford, CA: Stanford University Press.

Slezkine, Yuri. 2004. *The Jewish century*. Princeton, NJ: Princeton University Press.

Weimann, Gabriel. 1994. *The influentials*. Albany: State University of New York Press.

Williams, Raymond. 1958/1989. *Culture and society 1780-1950*. New York: Harper.

Wright, Charles R., and Muriel Cantor. 1967. The opinion seeker and avoider: Steps beyond the opinion leader concept. *Pacific Sociological Review* 10:33-43.

QUICK READ SYNOPSIS

Q
R
S

Politics, Social Networks, and the History of Mass Communications Research: Rereading *Personal Influence*

Special Editor: PETER SIMONSON
University of Colorado

Volume 608, November 2006

Prepared by Herb Fayer, Jerry Lee Foundation

DOI: 10.1177/0002716206294313

Perpetual Revelations: C. Wright Mills and Paul Lazarsfeld

John H. Summers, Harvard University

Background   This article narrates the prehistory and post history of *Personal Influence* as an episode in the biographies of Paul Lazarsfeld and C. Wright Mills. It begins in 1945, when Lazarsfeld sent Mills to Decatur, Illinois, to undertake the fieldwork, and ends with Mills's death in 1962.

Decatur Study   In the Decatur study, everybody answered three questions.
- Has anybody recently solicited your opinion concerning international, national, or community affairs or news events?
- Have you changed your opinion recently about any such events?
- Do you know anybody who keeps up with the news, anybody you trust to help you decide your opinion?

Answers from the Study   The three questions asked, in the same sequence and with varying follow-up questions, covered not only public affairs but also fashions, movies, and brands. The intention was straightforward: who were the opinion leaders?
- Question 1 gave a list of people who claimed they had been consulted.
- Question 2 yielded people who had influenced the opinions of the women interviewed.
- Question 3 was a general list of esteemed people in Decatur.

Two-Step Flow Those voters who had changed their political opinion over the course of the election attributed the change to casual conversations among family and friends, to face-to-face interactions, rather than to formal media.

- Upon this insight, Lazarsfeld mounted his "two-step flow of information" hypothesis.
  - *Step 1:* Information came from the formal media.
  - *Step 2:* Informal groups or individuals mediated the information for other groups or individuals.

The Study To detect the "opinion leaders," the analysis of the data needed to yield clues to three main problems.

- Could the actual flow of interpersonal influence in Decatur be isolated? Could "opinion leaders" be isolated as a social type?
- Could the influence be isolated in relation to the class structure of a community?
- Did the influence flow vertically, up and down class lines, or horizontally, within classes?

NOTE: Did their testimony mean that the first person could be called an opinion leader, and the second an opinion follower? The actual answers seemed to require a third category, so that the "opinion leaders" could be said to have given advice, "opinion followers" could be said to have gotten advice, and a third, "opinion relayers," could be said to have given and gotten. But the design of the study had not anticipated the need for this third category.

Mill's Feud The profession, Mills charged, was in the grip of "grand theory" and
with Lazarsfeld "abstracted empiricism"; the first tendency he charged to Talcott Parsons, the second, to Lazarsfeld.

- Mills and Lazarsfeld criticized the integrity of each other's work.
- Mills died in 1962 of a heart attack, age forty-five. Lazarsfeld and Merton, the men who urged him to New York in 1945, declined an invitation to attend his campus memorial service.

Personal Influence and the
Bracketing of Women's History

Susan J. Douglas, University of Michigan

Background One of the central contradictions of the Decatur study is that it simultaneously disguises that it is women who are being studied here yet universalizes them as representative of the general population.

- The study represses what was distinctive to women's experiences in the 1940s; stereotypes them by focusing on their interest in fashion, marketing, and movies; and yet uses women as exemplars for everyone.

- Here we have a path-breaking study of women's reception of and relations to the mass media that underplays that very fact and, as a result, missed enormous opportunities.
- It is this tension and the contradictory attitudes toward women in this study that is explored in this article.
  - *Personal Influence* perpetuated the rather retrograde notion that women's experiences are somehow timeless.
  - This article reviews what *Personal Influence* revealed about the two-step flow within women's interpersonal networks and what it failed to capture that we so much wish we knew.

Opinion Leaders   One of the most telling and insightful categories the researchers developed to determine who were opinion leaders was that of "gregariousness":

- Status and gregariousness were linked, and both helped determine whether a woman was an opinion leader.
- The opinion leader women read more magazines, newspapers, and books and listened to the radio more often than did those they influenced, so the mass media remained an important resource as part of the nexus and diffusion of decision making.
- In public affairs, authority flowed top-down, with high-status, gregarious women being the most sought-out opinion leaders.
- Certain of these women were deemed "cosmopolitans": people concerned with news and trends outside of their own community who consumed national media that originated elsewhere.

Third-Person   What is difficult to determine from this study is the role of the third-person
Effect   effect in shaping some of the results.

- When asked about decisions to change from buying one product brand to another, personal contacts had the most influence, magazine and newspaper advertising the least, and of those exposed to radio advertising, only 7.5 percent reported it to have affected their choices.
- The fashion leaders, not surprisingly, admitted to being influenced by the media; after all, fashion magazines and movies set themselves up as the arbiters of glamour and the latest styles.

Women and   The study of women's often deeply contradictory relationship to the media,
the Media   including "down market" fare like soap operas and romance novels, gained new life in the wake of the women's movement.

- Indeed, it was, in part, feminist reaction against the limited effects model, as embodied in *Personal Influence*, that gave rise to new path-breaking work on gender and the media.
- Feminist scholars took up this work because they recognized the absolute centrality of the mass media to women's sense of self, their possibilities, and to sustaining prejudices that kept women as second-class citizens.
- By 1955, despite the fact that more women were working outside the home than ever before, the mass media hailed women as housewives, mothers, and consumers, not as producers or citizens.

Q
R
S

Conclusion

Despite the blind spots of *Personal Influence*, the Decatur study paid explicit attention to women's reception of media messages and to their influence on other women in areas where women traditionally made the major decisions—shopping, fashions, and movies—and an area where they did not: public affairs.

- Thus, *Personal Influence* pioneered the study of the flow of influence among women about products and information first laid before them in the mass media.
- One could claim that no comparable attention was again paid to women as audiences of the media until the early 1970s and the rise of feminist media studies.
- Thus, *Personal Influence* was a crucial reminder that women, despite being individual targets of much media fare, were also embedded in social networks through which they influenced other women and were, in turn, influenced by them.

NOTE: Rereading the book reminds one how much still needs to be done here by scholars about the interactions between individual girls and women, their social networks, and the mass media.

The Influences Influencing
Personal Influence: Scholarship
and Entrepreneurship

David E. Morrison, University of Leeds

Background

Lazarsfeld is seen as an innovator in higher education, having established in Vienna in 1925 the first social science research center of its kind in the world, and later the Bureau of Applied Social Research at Columbia University.

- This article examines the structural situation of the Bureau, showing how Lazarsfeld developed the role of entrepreneurial scholar to finance its operations.
- Lazarsfeld's psychological makeup made for ready cooperation with the world of business; the Bureau required commercial fund-raising.
- The final part of the article examines how the study was "sold" to *True Story* magazine.

*The Research
Bureau*

While *Personal Influence* has rightfully come to occupy one of the intellectual peaks of mass communications research, its facilitation was a dependent of a development of the research bureau.

- The development of research bureaus in the 1940s and 1950s represented a new organizational form of intellectual life more appropriate for large-scale empirical social research than the traditional structure of a teaching department.

- With the bureaus came the creation of an absolutely new intellectual role: that of the managerial or entrepreneurial scholar not just capable of managing a research organization, but also able to sell research.
- The bureau did indeed depend on support from the media industry.
  - Lazarsfeld's enmeshment with the media industry, at one point, made even those close to him question his commitment to academic life.

Student Labor   Given the commercial pressure to "perform," it is perhaps not surprising that most of the students' time was taken up with the mastery of routine research procedures, the most complex aspects being left to senior researchers.

- Some graduate students complained that they were not really being trained by learning through doing but were in fact exploited drudges.
- The least frequently learned or improved skills were those involved in analysis, design, and the final drafting of reports.
- Lazarsfeld's position was that if it was not for the money that his market research activity provided, many of the students would not be in a financial position to complete their studies.

Influencers   Below are some of the influencers on Lazarsfeld's methods.

- *The businessman:* Never would Lazarsfeld lose his awareness of, and appreciation for, commercial money as a source for funding research.
  - His style of work required substantial amounts of money, and the organization necessary for the conduct of his empirical work also required big money.
- *Exile and acceptance:* It was quite clear to Lazarsfeld that he would have to build his own world. He says, "I took it for granted that I would have to make some move similar to the creation of the Vienna Research Centre if I wanted to find a place for myself in the U.S."
  - He was described as a typical refugee, feeling he had to manipulate the people around him to secure his position.
- *Personality and approval:* Lazarsfeld was always very sensitive about his Jewishness, and one can also say that he was sensitive, perhaps excessively so, about his foreignness.

NOTE: At no point is one replacing structural explanations for Lazarsfeld's enmeshment with the world of commerce with psychological ones, merely showing how personality interacts with structure to assist process.

Conclusion   To understand fully the influences influencing *Personal Influence*, it is necessary to move beyond administrative research to a wider research setting that Lazarsfeld was instrumental in creating, namely, the development of the research bureau.

- For the production of knowledge, the Bureau of Applied Social Research had to depend on conducting applied work for a variety of "administrations."
  - In the case of *Personal Influence*, it was a magazine publisher.
- The scholastic position of *Personal Influence* is established, but that position, as shown, was created out of a much wider set of influences than those that immediately came to bear on the Midwest town of Decatur, not least Lazarsfeld's own personal path to establishment.

The Katz/Lowenthal Encounter:
An Episode in the Creation
of *Personal Influence*

Gertrude J. Robinson, McGill University

Background

In the 1930s, members of the Institute of Social Research from Frankfurt emigrated to New York to escape the Nazis. Among them were Horkheimer, Adorno, and Lowenthal.

- The Institute employed two general approaches in its analysis of Nazi authoritarianism.
  - One stressed the centrality of monopoly capitalism and changes in legal, political, and economic institutions, with only a passing glance at social psychology or mass culture.
  - The other saw Nazism as the extreme example of a general trend toward irrational domination in Western countries.
- Adorno introduced the concept of the "culture industry," and increasingly Institute members came to feel that the culture industry enslaved people in more effective and subtle ways than the crude methods of domination practiced in earlier years.

Lazarsfeld

While the Institute group settled in at Columbia the members were unaware that another émigré scholar was also trying to establish a footing in the city: Paul F. Lazarsfeld, a social psychologist, trained in empirical research.

- Lazarsfeld's idea to investigate radio effects fit in well with earlier U.S. empirical concerns of which Lazarsfeld was, however, unaware.
- Advertisers were interested in establishing national markets, while Roosevelt's and Goebbels's radio successes raised questions about radio's social and political implications.
- Harold Lasswell's propaganda work and Allport and Cantril's *Psychology of Radio* (1935) seemed to indicate that radio had stronger political impact than print.
- Lazarsfeld created a research center that eventually became Columbia's Office of Radio Research (1940-1944) with Robert Merton. Elihu Katz studied with them and helped with the production of *Personal Influence*, a portion of which was his PhD thesis.

Radio Studies

Personal Influence provided three important insights:
- The importance of "people" in mass communication processes.
- The development of sophisticated survey methods.
- And the "limited effects" of radio messages on individual audience members.

Lazarsfeld Studies

Lazarsfeld's more numerous Bureau contributions are brilliantly illustrated in two of his studies: *Mass Persuasion* (1946, 1973) and his "Patterns of Influence" (1949).

Lowenthal

Lowenthal's "The Triumph of Mass Idols" (1944) followed the idea that the culture industry was subtly enslaving and that literature needed to be used to identify the social and cultural structures that promoted such enslavement.

- Lowenthal concluded there was evidence that in the stage of corporate capitalism, the rise of the entrepreneur increasingly turned into pure fiction; and second, that America had transformed into a consumer society in which people were interested only in consumption.
- The challenging work opportunity came in 1949, when Lowenthal set up a research division for the "Voice of America," after having analyzed German armed forces radio programs at the end of the war.
  - These researchers as well as their radio producers pioneered work in developing new ways of analyzing media effects.
  - His colleagues were the pollsters Joseph Klapper and Ralph White and the social-psychologist Marjorie Fiske.

Q
R
S

Conclusion   In spite of their generational differences, the careers of Katz and Lowenthal have one great similarity: both are "border travelers," and they have consequently contributed to the geographical transfer of ideas.
- In Katz's case, the transfer is from the United States to the young state of Israel.
- For Lowenthal, the transfer was from Germany to the United States in the 1930s.
- As border travelers, Katz and Lowenthal also played key roles in setting up new research institutions, which would use their scholarly expertise.
- Finally, Katz's and Lowenthal's expansion of their theoretical horizons as a result of their cross-border engagement is well documented in their scholarly work.

NOTE: Through their outgoing personalities, integrity, and deep engagement with the world, they demonstrate that scholarly transfer "matters" in the globalized twenty-first century and that insightful scholarship from the past, including their own, provides bridges for the future.

The Part Played by Gentiles in the Flow of Mass Communication: On the Ethnic Utopia of *Personal Influence*

John Durham Peters, University of Iowa

Background   The author argues that *Personal Influence* is not only a landmark study within the sociological literature on networks, influence, and decision making. It is also an allegory of Jewish-ethnic identity in the mid-twentieth-century United States and a sideways commentary on modern Jewish involvement in communications.
- The book sees a utopian imagination of society in which Jews and Gentiles alike are centrally involved in the flow of communications.
- As well as managing communications institutions themselves, Jews have played an influential role in the intellectual interpretation of communications—as judges, activists, and media scholars and critics.

- Jews have arguably been the most successful communicators in history, providing a treasure trove of content to world culture.
- More than any other group in history, Jews have made enormous contributions to the channels, interpretation, and content of communication. *Personal Influence* is one chapter in this story.

Influence   *Personal Influence* moves from modern, anonymous society back to the honeycomb of face-to-face relationships, so it moves from the mass media to human communicators as the chief purveyors of influence.

- Behind the design of this study was the idea that persons, and especially opinion leaders, could be looked upon as another medium of mass communication, similar to magazines, newspapers, and radio.
- The whole book can be read two ways: as a social study advancing knowledge of the social psychology of influence and as a gambit in the drama of Jewish assimilation in mid-twentieth-century America.
- *Personal Influence* is a Jewish defense of the social self, connected and connecting to others amid the Gentile-genteel picture of the solitary and rational individual.

NOTE: Ostensibly, private opinions are often generated and reinforced in intimate groups of family, friends, or coworkers. Even an individual's seemingly personal opinions may be by-products of interpersonal relations.

Communicators   Just about everyone gets to be a communications trader in the world of *Personal Influence*, including, above all, "girls, wives, and matrons."

- Opinion leaders are obviously such, but the influencees are also understood as full participants in the flow of communication.
- Everyone gets to take part in the betwixt-and-between of exchange.
- Katz and Lazarsfeld conceive of interpersonal and group relations as networks of exchange instead of as closed bubbles.

NOTE: The book is not only a political defense of American democracy in an era of mass communication but also an ethnic-cultural defense of influence and networking as worthy activities, indeed the vital center of democratic life.

A Cross-   In conception and interpretation, *Personal Influence* is fruitfully read as a
Cultural Study cross-cultural study in which Jewish cosmopolitans laid out their go-between network theory onto the Protestant locals, and everyone came out a happy family of white communicating Americans.

- The text of *Personal Influence* has a certain gaiety or lightness, especially in its various "discoveries"—the small group, interpersonal relations, and above all, people.
- It is a delicious irony that mass communication researchers wrote a book announcing the discovery of interpersonal communication.
- The study was explicitly designed to take place in a kind of ethnic tabula rasa—the methodological choice goes together with a fantasy of a world in which people would no longer have particular markings.

Conclusion   *Personal Influence* achieves what structuralists call a "markedness reversal." Whether Katz and Lazarsfeld were conscious of the rich history of "people" as a term or not, the Jewish fascination with interpreting the puzzling ways of "the peoples" (the goyim) serves as a rich context for understanding the otherwise unmarked notion of "people" that social scientists study, or in the case of this book, "discover."

- *Personal Influence* might be read alongside *The Jazz Singer* as two distinct approaches to how Jews might lay claim to membership in liberal America.
- In plays and film, Jews were widely considered to be a distinct race and discrimination was still quite overt; Jews played the parts of groups more racially marked on the color spectrum to suspend or background their own marked status or, more pointedly, to demonstrate that identity categories are no more binding than theatrical roles—*The Jazz Singer* whitened Jews and *Personal Influence* Judaized whites.
- The notion that ethnic identity can be freely performed, loaned, and borrowed is, of course, the essence of liberal pluralism, and it is one of the great cultural creations of mid-twentieth-century American Jews and their Gentile partners.

NOTE: Katz and Lazarsfeld unite mobile purveyors of the text and sedentary channelers of word of mouth—and they are all discovered to be people. The two-step flow performs an impressive piece of cultural work: writing and orality, text and interpretation, mobile and sedentary, mass and interpersonal, Jew and Gentile all shake hands within it.

Personal Influence and the End of the Masses

Paddy Scannell, University of Michigan

Background

Personal Influence was a key text in the then new and exciting field of mass communication, itself embedded in the larger field of American sociology.

- Two key considerations in what exogenous history of this famous sociological text look like:
  - What in the first place called forth the question of the media as a concern for sociology, and how was it raised?
  - What set of circumstances produced the Decatur study, its results, and its conclusions?
- From this perspective, *Personal Influence* is not so much a sociological text that resonates within the field of sociology as a historical text that resonates within its own historical, changing time and place.
- The question of communication, when it arose, was an extension of sociology's basic question—hence a sociology of *mass* communication in which the emphasis falls on the first rather than the second term.

Mass Communication

The study of mass communication was driven not so much by fear of the revolutionary potential of the masses as anxiety about their well-being.

- What was the effect of powerful new communication technologies on the ordinary man?

- Was he not vulnerable to manipulation because he was ill informed through lack of education and psychologically suggestible through economic insecurity?
- Lazarsfeld's key study was *Radio and the Printed Page*, whose aim was to answer the question, What will radio do to society?"
- When we get to the other side of the forties and into the early fifties, the masses have faded away along with the power of the media.

Influences from "Others"

The Decatur study was to identify the influence of others on the individual's shopping purchases, fashion tastes, movie choices, and news-related opinions.

- It is a key argument in Riesman that the new character type is, by definition, more involved in relations with other people than the old self-possessed (self-absorbed) inner-directed type.
- The rise of *sociability* is the manifest sign of the new people-minded social type.
- The study of the two-step flow, which endogenously checks personal influence exogenously discloses the rise of sociability in postwar, postmodern society.
- In such newly recovered *personal* relationships (relations between people as persons in their own right), the values that pertain to such relationships—intimacy, trust, sincerity, and authenticity—take on new meaning and significance.

NOTE: In the 1950s in the United States and in Europe, everyday life begins to achieve visibility and recognition as something distinctive and meaningful in its own terms and for its own sake. It becomes a good in itself, an end in itself, and not merely the means whereby labor reproduces itself as the instrument of capital.

- The role of personal influence in the formation of tastes, attitudes, purchases, and media consumption is convincingly established: it is an "almost invisible, certainly inconspicuous, form of leadership at the person-to-person level of ordinary, informal, everyday contact."

Conclusion

Personal Influence resolves a riddle—read as a key historical text, it points to the fading of the politics of poverty and the question of the masses and the emergence of a politics of plenty and the question of everyday life.

- The social question no longer presents itself only in terms of economic and political concerns.
- The importance of everyday life shows up in all sorts of ways:
  - It is there in the theatre, novels, and films of the decade but nowhere more so than television, which now becomes the definitive new medium of everyday life.

  Significantly, it begins to show up as a new kind of politics, as the politics of the masses gives way to the politics of everyday life.

  Rosa Park's action on a bus in Alabama perfectly encapsulated the emerging politics of everyday life.

Final Note

It is the argument of this article that the full significance of *Personal Influence* cannot be grasped by a purely immanent sociological reading.

- The exogenous historical reading necessarily starts from the internal history of the text and its position (at the time and since) in sociology, both of which are crucial to its understanding.
- But moving outward from this, we must think of it as embedded in the economic, political, social, and cultural determinants of its own and present times as these impinged upon and shaped the concerns of sociological work in progress.
- What the book discloses both in its internal history *and* as a response to the historical process of its own time (its inner and outer dialectic, so to speak) is the passage from modernity to postmodernity.

Q
R
S

Fifteen Pages that Shook the Field: *Personal Influence*, Edward Shils, and the Remembered History of Mass Communication Research

Jefferson Pooley, Muhlenberg College

Background

Personal Influence's fifteen-page account of the development of mass communication research has had more influence on the field's historical self-understanding than anything published before or since.
- According to Elihu Katz and Paul Lazarsfeld's two-stage narrative, an undisciplined body of prewar thought had concluded naively that media are *powerful*—a myth punctured by the rigorous studies which showed time and again that media impact is in fact *limited.*
- This article traces the emergence of the *Personal Influence* synopsis, with special attention to
  - Lazarsfeld's audience-dependent framing of key media research findings, and
  - the surprisingly prominent role of Edward Shils in supplying key elements of the narrative.

*Media
Persuasion*

As early as 1942, Lazarsfeld and others started to note the difficulty of bringing about attitude change through media persuasion.
- This observation was not yet framed as a claim of minimal media impact, nor as a happy repudiation of precursor overreach.
- The discovery of the obstinate audience was discussed as a *technical* problem, as an obstacle in the design of effective propaganda.
- There was a concern, on one hand, for finding out how to make persuasion *work* and, on the other, an effort to draw sweeping conclusions about media impact—making it hard to formulate a clean, coherent statement of limited effect.

- The many social scientists who had mobilized for propaganda service came away from their wartime experience with a basic consensus:
  - Persuasion is not a simple affair.
  - It only works under certain conditions that should be heeded in future propaganda work.

Personal Influence *and* The People's Choice

Lazarsfeld, in his and Katz's *Personal Influence* narrative, characterized his own body of media research as the progressive unfolding of a counterintuitive insight: that the media have only minimal effects.

- In *The People's Choice* (1944), Lazarsfeld had stated that short-term media persuasion does not, on its own, change minds or behavior very easily.
- He noted that face-to-face influence works better than the mediated sort.
- He also surmised that the two kinds of persuasion may be complementary, or at least relatable in some way.

NOTE: In the first fifteen pages of *Personal Influence*, the finding that direct, broadcasted appeals only infrequently bring about observable change (on their own) was boldly redeployed to support a much farther-reaching assertion: that media have only limited effects.

- Some of Lazarsfeld's findings in *The People's Choice*, which had already been put to various use—the better performance of face-to-face over mediated persuasion in short-term campaigns, the hypothesis of a two-step flow—could be brought together in one coherent narrative.

Lazarsfeld and the Shils Effect

The quest for scientific *distinction*—for peer respect—was one of Lazarsfeld's fundamental academic stimuli.

- The other crucial aspect for understanding Lazarsfeld is the *field* in which he staked his claims to credit—the extremely peculiar and fast-evolving field of *public opinion research*.
- This cluster of public opinion research served as the institutional context in which he made his highly entrepreneurial career.
  - The study of mass media was the opinion cluster's most pronounced topical research area.
- *Personal Influence*, published after he had effectively left the field of media research, was in this sense a last-word reputational sealant—a chance to establish, retroactively, the novelty and relevance of his fifteen-year effort.
  - The powerful-to-limited-effects story line was deployed in just these terms, as a summative and retroactive claim to the novelty and coherence of his body of media research.
- Why was the story line that Edward Shils put forward, under his name, the framing that Lazarsfeld and Katz selected for *Personal Influence?* Shils's story was selected, but why?
  - Very little attention had been paid, before Shils and Morris Janowitz's key 1948 *Wehrmacht* article, to the importance of small-group ties as an ongoing buffer between persuaders and their targets.
  - The Shils small-group story, in this context, was an irresistible aid.

Personal Influence and the New Paradigm: Some Inadvertent Consequences

Kurt Lang and Gladys Engel Lang,
University of Washington

QRS

Background

This article argues that the "new" conventional wisdom of the 1950s and 1960s, pitting personal influence versus mass media influence, discouraged a generation of sociologists from researching the effects, particularly long-range effects, of mass communication.

- Now some fifty years later, we are reexamining and critiquing the conclusions that Katz and Lazarsfeld drew from their study and the reception of their findings.

Reception of the Book

Personal Influence was immediately tagged as a major work when published.

- The book continues to be widely cited.
- It was acknowledged at the time for its elaboration of an explicitly sociological perspective on the mass media audience, one that looked beyond demographics and put a new emphasis on the multiple social relationships through which the media content is filtered, reinterpreted, and/or reinforced.

Mass Media Influence

Conclusions about mass media influence were drawn from surveys asking respondents what they recalled about specific influence incidents. The authors used these data

- to examine how informal leaders exerted influence "horizontally," that is, within their immediate surroundings; and
- to give a firmer grounding to the "two-step flow" hypothesis, according to which mass media reach well-informed opinion leaders, who then act as transmitters of information and influence.

By changing the focus away from effects that occur en masse and over time toward the concrete responses of individuals, they concluded—incorrectly—that personal influence was more powerful than influences from the mass media. This downplay of mass media influence had some unintended consequences.

- It put into question the value of further inquiry by sociologists into the new worlds these media had opened and into the more subtle influences the media might have over time.
- Another casualty of this reorientation was the sociological, as opposed to the ideological, concept of mass.
  - The fact that the members of media audiences do not live their lives in total isolation from other people, that they do not constitute a mass of anonymous individuals without any local attachments or shared ideals and common ideas does not render the concept of mass as related to mass communication obsolete.
  - The utility of this concept depends on whether one looks at the media-created audience in its entirety or at the concrete local audiences, whose members sift, evaluate, discuss, and bring past experience to bear on the media content.

Q
R
S

The Limits of Interpersonal Influence

That people will seek advice from whomever they believe to know more than they do in deciding to try a new brand or to decide what movie to see seems pretty obvious. However,

- Consumer and media choices are less than fully autonomous but constrained by what is available, actively promoted, and/or in line with prevalent taste.
- An overly exclusive focus on how *individuals* choose has been at the expense of research on larger *aggregate* patterns of choice.
- Some influences of exposure may be too subtle for respondents to be aware of. Inability to name a specific item of information that has caused them to change their mind does not rule out the existence of media influences.
- Equally undeniable is that people do form pictures of the larger world beyond their direct experience and outside the orbits within which they move. An accumulation of impressions, each by itself of little consequence, can result in a significant movement of opinion.

Opinion Formation

Direct media influence differs fundamentally from everyday decision making and opinion formation on public issues.

- People hold political opinions but actually make decisions only when specifically called upon to cast a vote.
  - The ideas and imagery that go into a vote develop as part of an ongoing discourse, with both influential and influencee being oriented to what the media carry and/or have highlighted over the years.
  - Viewed from this macro-perspective, the longer-term influence of mass communication on public opinion looms as relatively more important than it does when examining specific influences on private consumption.
  - Certainly, the effect of demonstrations that make news cannot be measured most successfully in isolation. Any influence on a participant is apt to be communicated to others who may only have "seen it on TV" so that the significance imputed to the video event comes to overshadow the "true" picture of the event, namely, the impression of a participant who was actually there. What all too often has been lost in the shift to the "new" mass communication paradigm with its emphasis on the part played by people is the simple and obvious fact that without a first step as the initial impetus in the two-step flow there might never have been a second or further step.

The Debate Has Not Ended

Now to return to a question raised by Katz in his introduction to the anniversary edition of *Personal Influence*: Why has the struggle over the relative power of the individual, the media, and interpersonal influence lasted so long?

- Part of the answer lies in the promotional themes for the book, which overemphasized the superior power of personal influence.
  - Many questions about media monopolies and chummy relationships between journalists and the establishment have not been asked as often as they should have.
- Commitments made to sponsors of the study limited the leeway researchers had to add questions in which they were especially interested. Also, the sample in the study consisted solely of women.

- Things change—evidence shows that the average woman has become more sensitive to what the formal media convey.
- Finally, the long-term and society-wide consequences of any new medium are difficult to demonstrate by methods based on the individual as the unit of observation. Without minimizing the part played by people, there is much more yet to learn about the long-range and society-wide effects of the mass media.

Q
R
S

As Time Goes By . . .

Thelma McCormack, Institute for Social Research

Background
: *Personal Influence* is a study of political and consumer decisions in small primary groups—how ordinary people were both influenced and influencing.
- The Vietnam War challenged the paradigm as a new generation of scholars turned to larger units—state and society—and the power the media might have in reinforcing class structure.
- The conclusion raises questions about the future based on globalization and the decline of the nation-state.
- *Personal Influence* examined the process of influence among individuals, from person to person, and recognized two things:
  - All of us could be both influenced and influencing others.
  - The group was an actor, not just the tabula rasa that would passively record the attitudes, opinions, and ideas of others.

Personal Influence
: *Personal Influence* crossed several thresholds—from the study of journalism as a craft to a profession; from the study of individuals, acting and thinking alone to the study of small groups; from the study of affinity groups to the study of factions and differences within them; from the study of policies to the study of the formation of consensus.
- Most important of all was the move from the study of technology—and naive theories of technological determinism to the study of the social construction of meaning.
- Process, groups, divisions within groups, the formation of consensus, and interpretation are the key ideas that together constitute a matrix, a paradigm that opened a floodgate of new research.
- *Personal Influence* was both a beginning and an end. Its roots were in the early study of voting behavior and grassroots democracy; its future lies in political activism on one hand, aesthetics on the other—or what Walter Benjamin called "the aestheticization of politics."

Post Vietnam
: After Vietnam, the country was changing; there was a new focus on the media as texts that could, via bias, editing, and self-censorship, manipulate audiences.
- What was clear from studies was that the media and the study of communication fell between our understanding of the material base, the means of production, and superstructure as ideologies.

- Journalists were ideologues writing about ideologues claiming an arm's-length distance.
- Gitlin raised a point of what was the distinction between understanding of events by insiders and outsiders.

Polls

The public opinion poll was one of the extraordinary innovations.

- Critics regarded polls or any similar measuring device as part of a system of social control, one of the ways of "managing consensus," a strategy for manipulating the public and justifying the establishment.
- Polls could be part of a managerial function of the state but also part of a critical dialogue eventually transforming the state, making it more responsive and empowering citizens.
- Noelle-Neuman attributed a different function for opinion polls. They were, she said, a standard that voters consulted because they wanted to be certain they were in the mainstream.

Rational Choice Theory

James Coleman influenced by Max Weber and Talcott Parsons was one of the few sociologists urging us to think in terms of rational choice theory.

- Rational choice theory is a radical change from sociology based on community, neighborhoods, social interaction, and gradualism.
- Its starting point is elsewhere, in the board rooms of the corporate unit—it has given legitimatization to studies in formal organization.
- It is the theoretical shadow of a highly rationalized global economy—it is light years away from the humanism of *Personal Influence*, which was instrumental in the development of the nation-state and an economy moderated by compromise and social legislation.

Conclusion

Personal Influence turned a spotlight on the social psychology of small groups and their empowerment, looking at a frangible process that moved erratically toward a resolution.

- It showed us turning to friends, family, and neighbors for practical advice on how to vote, buy winter clothes, discipline children, where to vacation, how to give and receive medical advice.
- Although our economy has changed toward a more privatized and competitive one, a new economy that takes pride in its ability to move information at incredible speed, the earlier Keynesian economy of the 1950s remains part of our heritage.
- As long as we have an open society, we will have elections, and as long as we have elections we will have polls, but neither may be as important in the long run as the larger international power structure.
- We are moving toward the study of events—the wedding of Charles and Diana, the visit of Sadat to Israel, and other similar events that elicit the attention of the entire nation, if not the Western world.
  - They are events that engage the public's attention beyond the level of politics-as-usual, and eventually, they become part of a system of markers that are internalized to become part of our collective memory.

The Troubling Equivalence of Citizen and Consumer

Michael Schudson, University of California,
San Diego

Background   As Todd Gitlin observed in his 1978 critique of *Personal Influence*, the authors treated consumer choices and voting choices as equivalent. This article
- contends that consumer choices have often been political,
- argues that political choices can be and often have been consumer-like, and
- calls for a reconsideration of what the differences between the worlds of politics and consumption really are.

Gitlin's Critique Ironically, Gitlin's critique may be stronger than he intended: the passive sovereignty of most consumers most of the time is matched by the passive sovereignty of most voters most of the time.
- When the women the *Personal Influence* team studied looked for advice in daily living, they overwhelmingly turned to other women.
- When these same women turned to other people for advice on public affairs, they overwhelmingly turned to men.

Choices   Implicit in Gitlin's critique and in other critiques that object to treating political choices as consumer choices is a view that there are fundamental differences between political choices and consumer choices:
- Citizens vote, consumers demand.
- Citizens are public spirited and consumers are self-interested.
- Citizens inhabit cooperative communities and consumers live in isolated locales.

There are three reasons to complicate the consumer/citizen contrast:
- Sometimes consumer choice is political in even the most elevated understandings of the term.
- Sometimes political choices are complex matters of family, ethnic, and religious tradition; emotional links to one brand rather than another; based on limited information and limited experience; and expected by the individual to have limited personal impact, not unlike a great many consumer decisions.
- The elevation of politics to the realm of the highly intellectualized, highly instrumentalized, and highly public-regarding does not encourage political participation and may not even increase the quality of reasoning in voting or the intensity of political commitment and action of voters.

Consumer   The contrast between citizen and consumer stands not outside our civic life
versus Political but is a constitutive element of it.
Choices
- A consumer choice can be political, such as boycotting grapes to support farm workers or driving a hybrid car for ecological reasons.
- Political choices can be consumer-like based on a person's pocketbook benefits or how taxes will affect their budget.

- Making political choice less consumer-like is a task democracies undertake at their peril.
- The new voter should be motivated by ideas and ideals and information, not by social pressure or the social pleasure of a free drink and an extra dollar in the pocket.

Concerns   Below are some concerns expressed by the author of this article.
- Is there a way to take politics seriously without making political interest severe?
- Is there a way to identify the distinctive value of public affairs without dismissing or demeaning the ordinary experience of private life, including the life of consuming?
- Is there a way to recognize that the high political theory and publicly legitimated political knowledge used to draw in very narrowly the circle of the politically adept now confront a politics broadened and loosened in ways that are largely to the good?

Conclusions   The author finds the commensurability between consumer and political choices that Katz and Lazarsfeld posited is more of an enduring provocation than a fault in their study.
- We will not enhance the value of public affairs by positing the moral weakness of consuming.
- Better to find strategic opportunity in consuming to enlarge the points of entry to political life and to underline the political dimensions of our world with cases in point.
- There are ways for the consumer and the citizen in each of us to meet.
  - One should have to step *up* to the political stage and be a little better than oneself, whereas in consuming it is normally enough to be oneself and not step on the toes of others.
  - In consuming, the circle of people one thinks about tends to be small; in politics, the circle of people one *should* be thinking about should extend to the boundary of whatever polity one is acting in—if not further.
- Consuming feels good not only because it may provide material pleasures but also because it is enacted largely within a comfortable social circle—politics feels tense and dangerous, even under relatively peaceful circumstances because it is performed in the midst of and because of significant conflict with others.

The Consumer and the Citizen
in *Personal Influence*

Lawrence B. Glickman, University of South Carolina

Background   In *Personal Influence*, the advertiser, the radio executive, the propagandist, and the educator are all interested in the effect of their message.
- The book establishes a similarity in the interactions among the message, the media, and people in these and other realms.

- In *Personal Influence*, political topics and items of consumption are tantalizingly, sometimes jarringly, juxtaposed.
- The book also treats "campaigns" of all sorts—from rolling out new candidates to rolling out new products—as analogous processes.
- Such equivalences between electoral politics and daily consumption may seem at first glance to be flip and/or politically suspect, and critics have been wary of this linkage.
  - To say that politics and consumption are related or even similar processes, however, is not automatically to reduce the one to the other, or to demean the political.
  - To link consumption and politics is not necessarily to lament the degradation of politics as another site of passive, therapeutic meaninglessness.
  - Scholars and consumer activists have noticed similarities in the structure of the two, and activists have traded on the assumption of overlap between politics and consumption.

Networks

Lazarsfeld assumes that people make choices, not autonomously, but in the context of a variety of networks—communication and consumption networks, while distinct, operate in analogous ways.
- Katz and Lazarsfeld sought to show that individual agency was central to what they called the "flow of mass communications" and also to what we can call the flow of mass production and consumption.
- A key challenge posited by Katz and Lazarsfeld is to question the supposed relative powerlessness of shoppers in the web of consumption and of individuals in the web of communication.
- In both cases, "opinion leaders" serve as important nodes on these information and material circuits, not only passing on but interpreting and shaping the meaning of information and goods.

Consumer Choice

Notwithstanding the forces of markets, consumer choice is a form of power in modern society.
- In a market society, consumers exercise enormous influence every time they purchase a good, even if they are generally unaware of this power—their purchases influence business decisions worldwide.
- For consumer activists, the effects of consumption were far-reaching and therefore needed to be harnessed for socially useful causes.

Individual Differences

Lazarsfeld sought in his work to recognize individual difference within a framework of generalizable social principles.
- To be sure, Katz and Lazarsfeld emphasized difference in the book, particularly class difference.
- Katz and Lazarsfeld also note degrees of influence of women with large families and that "highly gregarious women . . . are more likely to be opinion leaders."

Conclusion

Personal Influence is an extraordinary achievement of mid-twentieth-century social science.
- The book was a timely work of social science and moral inquiry whose historical context the author has aimed to elucidate.

- In this work, Lazarsfeld and Katz offered intriguing reasons to analogize consumption and citizenship.
- If their approach paid too little attention to the aftermath of consumption decisions, it offered scholars important reasons to understand consumption as a multidimensional political activity.

Q
R
S

The One-Step Flow of Communication

W. Lance Bennett, University of Washington;
and Jarol B. Manheim, George Washington University

Background   It is to *Personal Influence* that contemporary scholars turn for the classic statement of the "two-step flow of communication" hypothesis.

- In the first step, messages are issued by the mass media to what is, to all outward appearances, a more or less homogeneous mass audience.
- In the second, innumerable small-group interactions powered by horizontal opinion leaders interpret and contextualize these mediated messages for their participants, who then internalize the content.

NOTE: The end result is a more or less differentiated understanding of the message across various social boundaries.

Media Influence   For society at large, one implication was that there were limits to the potential influence of mediated communication.

- Each individual's knowledge networks and social interactions set limits, some of which might be systematic in character, others products of chance.
- At the same time, mediated communication was potentially so integral to interpersonal communication—providing it with both stimuli and information—that the two might no longer be distinguishable.
- This meant that mass society could never be entirely homogeneous but also that individual social locations could never be entirely isolated from mass influence.
- One must note the central importance of personal conversation—even the most casual of talk—in the democratic process.
- Effective political communication (influence) required understanding and controlling how these messages would be processed through social interaction before their effects would become manifest.
  - The "water cooler effect"—by which mass-mediated messages reach audience members who were not directly exposed to them, through secondary interactions with friends and colleagues—was not merely a means of expanding the audience for a given message, but it was also a potentially success-critical mechanism for assigning it meaning.

Thesis   The authors' thesis is that society, communication technologies, and individual communication habits have changed fundamentally in ways that affect how individuals receive and process information.

- These social and technological changes directly challenge the underlying assumptions of the two-step flow hypothesis.
- The combination of social isolation, communication channel fragmentation, and message targeting technologies have produced a very different information *recipient* from those in the 1950s.
- Given the decline of group identifications and loyalties, individuals, even when reached, are hard to hold, whether in terms of attention or adoption of message content.
- The goal of the communicator is to identify the most effective specialized channels and to fit the boundaries and framing of messages to the needs, expectations, beliefs, preferences, and interests of the audience member.
- To the extent this is accomplished, the combination of social and physical technologies preempts the role previously played by social interaction within the audience, creating a *one-step* flow.

One-Step Flow   The achievement of a one-step flow among large scale publics is typically neither simple nor inexpensive. It requires, at the very least, a marriage of basic communication skills with the availability of vast and highly differentiated data on members of the prospective audience.

- We could think in alternative ways about how the one-step flow could operate in democracies.
- People make practical choices about technologies–both technological and political–that render messages more or less engaging, transparent, public, exclusive, divisive, or cohesive.
- The choices affect whether citizens become further isolated through communication processes that emphasize unidirectional and highly manipulative information flows, or whether citizens share known social networks through the transparent interactive capabilities that are available through the same technologies.

Conclusion   The ways in which communicators choose among technological alternatives for reaching fragmenting audiences may, in turn, have profound interactive effects on those audiences and their social and political relationships.

- It is important to emphasize here that technologies have the potential to create mutual understanding and peer to peer communication across various issue and demographic divides.
- Indeed, many social-movement networks have employed transparent social networking technologies with the aim of creating sustainable social bonds through the communication process.
- In the current transition between two historic public communication eras, it appears that the chosen emphasis is more toward the stealthy technologies that isolate individuals than toward transparent networking technologies that may unite citizens in common cause.
- Recognizing the transition of that paradigm into a fundamentally different one-step flow of communication will lead scholars and practitioners to generate alternative perspectives and knowledge that will similarly shape the future.

The Influence of *Personal Influence* on the Study of Audiences

Sonia Livingstone, London School of Economics
and Political Science

Q
R
S

Background

This article looks back at the book *Personal Influence* to bring into focus the debate over the mass media audience during the twentieth century.

- Katz and Lazarsfeld's work and subsequent work by Katz and his collaborators suggests possibilities for convergence, or at least productive dialogue, as researchers collectively seek to understand how, in their everyday lives, people can, and could, engage with media to further democratic participation in the public sphere.
- *Personal Influence* was not just about "the part played by people in the flow of mass communications" but was also, more significantly, about the part played by people—acting as individuals, in peer or community groups, and through institutions—in the construction and reconstruction of meanings in society.
- The above should raise critical questions about power, interest, and inequalities, potentially integrating and so transcending the many conceptual oppositions—theoretical versus empirical or critical versus administrative or cultural versus economic—that have, sometimes unhelpfully, framed the study of media and communication.

Communication Flow

In *Personal Influence*, the part played by people in the flow of mass communication demonstrates that the supposedly direct flow of mass media influence is mediated by preexisting patterns of interpersonal communication in local communities.

- The innovative concept of the two-step flow challenged the popularity of the direct effects model as well as the separate study of mass and interpersonal communication, and it undermined the image of the viewer and listener as part of a mindless, homogeneous mass.
- *Personal Influence* examines various permutations of the relations among three different domains:
  - media (institutional contexts, though also texts),
  - public opinion (and its role in democratic processes), and
  - conversation (as embedded in interpersonal or peer networks).
- Everyday talk is central. What does it matter if the terms or topics of the conversation come from the mediated or face-to-face experience, from local social groups, or even other parts of the world?

Media Events

In the book *Media Events*, Dayan and Katz say media events illuminate both the opportunities and dangers of a media-dominated democracy.

- They can create a national or even international sense of occasion, providing liminal moments in which a society may reflect upon, idealize, and at the same time authenticate a vision of itself for itself.
- Yet if these liminal moments substitute for political participation and political change, then it is their potentially reactionary, manipulative, or narcotizing effects, rather than their potentially progressive, educational, or democratic effects, that should be at the forefront of our concern.

Q
R
S

- Dayan and Katz look at the ways in which live broadcasting confers legitimacy and charisma on the "celebrities" involved, the interruption of everyday routines that casts viewers into roles proposed by the script of the ceremony, effects on the climate of opinion by encouraging or inhibiting the expression of certain beliefs, changes to the organization of politics and political campaigning, and instances of direct political or social change resulting from a media event.

Where Next?   The insight of *Personal Influence*, that processes of media influence are mediated by social contexts, including community and face-to-face interactions, is now a starting point rather than a discovery.

- The author argues that research must analyze the *artifacts or devices* used to communicate or convey information (raising questions of design and development), the *activities and practices* in which people engage to communicate or share information (raising questions of cultural and social context), and the *social arrangements or organizational forms* that develop around those devices and practices (raising questions of institutional organization, power, and governance).
- Where mass communication research spent decades struggling with the assumption of linearity (that production produces texts that impact on audiences, following the sender-message-receiver model), new media research need make no such assumption.

Conclusion   Though the shift from mass communication theory to theorizing mediation in all its forms will occupy scholars for some time, the broader agenda that *Personal Influence* prioritized—the examination of the relations between mediation, conversation, and community to understand the potential, positive and negative, of the media in democratic society—remains paramount.

- For the study of people's engagement with the new media environment, that is, for the study of audiences as publics and of publics as mediated, this is still early days.
- It is to be hoped that, in developing these initial steps into a sustained research program, scholars will continue to draw on the multiple intellectual traditions, convergent epistemologies, and bold surmises that motivated earlier steps toward the same democratic project fifty years ago, as evidenced by *Personal Influence*.

Public Connection through Media Consumption: Between Oversocialization and De-Socialization?

Nick Couldry and Tim Markham, University of London

Background   This article reviews the ongoing contribution of *Personal Influence* to our understanding of media's social consequences from the perspective of their recent research into the extent to which habits of media consumption help sustain, or not, U.K. citizens' orientation to a public world.

- The article reviews the methodological similarities and differences between this recent project and that of Katz and Lazarsfeld.
- The result, the authors conclude, is to confirm the continued salience of the questions about the social embeddedness of media influences that Katz and Lazarsfeld posed.

Media Complexity

Personal Influence was a major step forward in our understanding of media as complex processes of mediation.

- Using the contribution of "person-to-person communication" to the circulation of media-sourced information and opinion, Katz and Lazarsfeld marked a shift away from research dominated by a concern with media's rhetorical power over "masses" toward how media messages filter through the intricate networks of social life.
- It prioritized the question of how media have social consequences in the ordinary run of things.
- Katz and Lazarsfeld's famous two-step flow thesis, by ruling out of court the old paradigm of a radio listener shut up in his room with a self-sufficient supply of the world outside, remains a useful ally as, and when, that model gets revived in new circumstances.
- They framed their account of how the mechanism of mass media influences daily life within a longer history of liberal inquiry into how democratic citizens come to feel part of a wider polity.

Authors' Research Project

Like *Personal Influence,* the U.K. "Public Connection" project was started against a background of doubts about media's contribution to the very basis of democratic engagement.

- Like Katz and Lazarsfeld, this article's authors believed that it was crucial to study what people do and think on a daily basis in specific contexts that are only partly shaped by media themselves. However, the Public Connection project differed in focus, method, and context.
- Their focus was on the question of whether people across both genders, all classes and ages, are orientated, if at all, toward a public world beyond the private, and, if so, to what extent their media consumption sustains or works against that orientation.

Research Summary

We have found some evidence of the older forms of authority structure (particularly between male and female partners) persisting in what, as Katz and Lazarsfeld pointed out, is the highly gendered area of public issues.

- However, any assessment of opinion formation overall in this area is constrained by evidence of the *gaps* in, and constraints upon, discussion and exchange of opinions on public matters, and particularly traditional politics. The field of public discussion is limited as to who can regularly participate within it, and when and where.
- While a significant degree of both discussion and public action was found, there was very little evidence of discussion *leading* to action.

Conclusion

In this article, the authors have used the findings of the Public Connection project to explore the extent to which Katz and Lazarsfeld's account of opinion formation through "personal influence" in mid-twentieth-century America remains pertinent, particularly in the area of public affairs.

- Media are now a source of opinion and reference that is pervasive to a degree that could not have been fully anticipated in the 1940s and 1950s—the individualizing tendency of particularly narrowcast media fosters the de-socialized context for information transmission.
- The findings are, in some respects, rather different. Both talk and social expectations remain, according to the survey, importantly linked with engagement in a public world through media. Katz and Lazarsfeld's relation between the scale of people's social interactions and their degree of attention to public affairs has also been backed tentatively by the evidence of our sample.
- The authors' concerns about the contemporary salience of *Personal Influence*'s argument—the argument that, by identifying the social networks through which mass transmissions are interpersonally mediated, we have identified a mechanism that effectively embeds media in the processes that sustain liberal democracy—lie elsewhere.
- The problem may be not the absence of a discursive context for our tracking of a public world through media but rather the lack of any link between that discursive context and any opportunities for *doing anything* effective about the issues we learn about through media.

NOTE: In that sense, the problem with contemporary democracy is larger than any study about the social mediation of media consumption can address. Is Katz and Lazarsfeld's whole study condemned to irrelevance? Quite the contrary—for it sustains our attention to one key term (talk) of a wider disarticulation that neither policy makers nor academics who care about the future of democracy can afford to ignore.

Personal Influence: A Radical Theory of Action

Charles Kadushin, Brandeis University

Background   Once scholars recognized the importance of adding interpersonal influence to the action scheme, they saw that influences naturally radiated from the immediate interpersonal environment to the larger social network.

- Both the interpersonal environment and further social network connections have been loosely termed *social capital*.
- Long before the term *social capital* entered the social science lexicon, *Personal Influence* explored the consequences of a network of advice-giving others.
- The book lacked some currently available technical and conceptual resources to fully meet its ambitious goal of locating the relative impact of personal influence on individual decision making.
  - Nonetheless, current students of social capital and decision making have more to learn from this book than they may realize.
  - *Interpersonal Influence* directly led to the study of social networks beyond what social network people now call the first-order zone.

Q
R
S

The Personal   When personal influence is a factor, the investigator has to do research
Influence Factor   of actual and potential influencers, the immediate ones and the larger
                      social surround, and to try to assess their relative influence as compared
                      with other factors in the accounting scheme ranging from sources of infor-
                      mation in the mass media to the attractive aspects of the object being
                      bought.
                      • One key component of *Personal Influence* involves tracing the networks of
                        influencers in the sociometry of ego networks.

Studying   Although our fascination with influentials has been whetted over these fifty
Influentials   years, we still do not have adequate systematic investigations of network bro-
                      kers and influentials—their motivations, how they make their "profits," the
                      degree to which they themselves search for information and wisdom that
                      they can pass on to the circle of their friends, and the extent to which they
                      themselves rely on other people or on various media.
                      • In the consumption decisions studied in *Personal Influence*, decision mak-
                        ers are generally passive—they are "accidental consumers."
                      • Respondents do not search for the best products, the best buys, or the
                        best movies—information comes to them accidentally, as a result of envi-
                        ronmental influences, including, of course, personal influence.

                      NOTE: *Personal Influence* does not directly inquire into the efforts respon-
                      dents may have made to acquire consumer product information, although it
                      does inquire into the latent network of potential experts. It would be nice to
                      know the difference between the characteristics of members of the latent
                      network as compared with those of the effective network.

Conclusion   Katz and Lazarsfeld, by systematically studying personal influence in such
                      mundane acts as going to the movies and buying clothes, made major con-
                      tributions to the theory of action and to the study of social networks.
                      • Both for social network theory and for action theory, in many ways we
                        have yet to reap the full benefits of this pioneering work.

Personal Influence and the
Effects of the National Youth
Anti-Drug Media Campaign

Robert Hornik, University of Pennsylvania

Background   *Personal Influence* put forward and tested a variety of hypotheses about how
                      social contexts constrain media effects.
                      • Three hypotheses are about interactions of media exposure with social
                        context (Stability, Conformity, and Instrumental).
                      • Two hypotheses are about two-step flow effects (Relay and Message
                        Interpretation).
                      • Each is tested by the author with nationally representative panel data
                        from the evaluation of the National Youth Anti-Drug Media Campaign.

- The evaluation of the above campaign, surprisingly, has shown that more exposure to the campaign led to more interest in marijuana use.
  - This article examined whether those boomerang effects were magnified through interactions with siblings—in general, no evidence showed that siblings' beliefs or behavior interacted with individuals' exposure to campaign messages in producing effects.
  - However, older siblings were themselves affected by their own exposure to the campaign and, in turn, affected the beliefs and behaviors of their younger brothers and sisters, consistent with the two-step flow hypothesis.

Social Context   *Personal Influence* argues that the social context matters for media effects in a variety of distinct ways.

- *The stability hypothesis:* The social network around an individual can be more or less consistent with regard to a particular issue, or it can be more or less stable in general, with a more stable environment expected to reduce vulnerability to media influence.
- *The conformity hypothesis:* The social network around an individual provides its own persuasive influence: if that influence is in the same direction as media messages, those media effects will be larger; if the social network contradicts media messages, media influence will be less..
- *The instrumental support hypothesis:* The social network can provide more or less instrumental support for media-recommended behavior, with a corresponding enhancement or reduction in media influence.
- *The message interpretation hypothesis:* Social networks provide meaning as people make sense of media messages.
- *The relay hypothesis:* Social influencers may be directly exposed to media messages—network members may be persuaded by their own exposure and in turn persuade others in the network.

NOTE: All of the author's analyses focus on the influence of the older sibling on the younger sibling. It is possible that the influence flows the other way, or is mutual. Also, given sometimes more than two siblings are in a household, but only two are included in the study, it is quite possible that a more complex dynamic in the family is lost. Nonetheless, it was worth proceeding with this assumption, given that older youth are much more likely to initiate drug use before their siblings.

Discussion   The article presented two types of analysis to test the social context hypotheses described in *Personal Influence:*

- The first, whether the social context affected individual exposure effects.
  - In general, the evidence drawn from the first set of analyses was not supportive; most tellingly, whatever the sibling's beliefs and behavior were concerning marijuana, the apparent effects of the campaign did not vary significantly.
- The second, whether the influences of the campaign on older siblings was passed through to younger siblings.
  - Most clearly, older siblings appeared both to be affected by the campaign and to affect the behaviors and cognitions of their younger brothers and sisters; the second set of hypotheses was supported.

- Their evaluations of the campaign ads appeared to affect the younger siblings' ad evaluations also. These pass-through, or two-step flow effects, however, were not so strong that they provided a significant correlation between older sibling exposure and younger sibling outcomes, once control variables were included.
- Why is it that the social context did not seem to condition the response to the campaign? There are three competing explanations:
  - The first is that the hypothesis was wrong for sibling effects.
  - The second explanation is that the measures of sibling cognitions and behavior, which were used as surrogates for the actual context in which the youth received the campaign, did not capture that context.
  - The third explanation is that the statistical analysis was insufficiently sensitive to capture interactions.
- Clearly, these analyses and the claims made here do have some limitations. The statistics were not conservative insofar as they do not account for the complex sample design and the nonindependence of the cases; also while the control variables were important ones, it is certainly possible that other, not included variables might explain the apparent effects.

NOTE: The author is willing to claim a two step-flow; evidence for an effect appeared at each stage even though he could not show a direct effect of older sibling exposure on younger sibling outcomes. The greater power to detect main effects and the simpler criterion for success may explain why the effects appear more readily.

STATEMENT OF OWNERSHIP, MANAGEMENT, AND CIRCULATION
P.S. Form 3526 Facsimile

1. TITLE: THE ANNALS OF THE AMERICAN ACADEMY OF POLITICAL AND SOCIAL SCIENCE
2. USPS PUB. #: 026-060

3. DATE OF FILING: October 1, 2006

4. FREQUENCY OF ISSUE: Bi-Monthly
5. NO. OF ISSUES ANNUALLY: 6
6. ANNUAL SUBSCRIPTION PRICE: Paper-Bound Institution $ 554 Individual $ 84
   Cloth-Bound Institution $ 626 Individual $ 126

7. PUBLISHER ADDRESS: 2455 Teller Road, Thousand Oaks, CA 91320
   CONTACT PERSON: Mary Nugent, Circulation Manager
   TELEPHONE: (805) 499-0721

8. HEADQUARTERS ADDRESS: 2455 Teller Road, Thousand Oaks, CA 91320

9. PUBLISHER: Sage Publications Inc., 2455 Teller Road, Thousand Oaks, CA 91320
   EDITORS: Dr. Phyllis Kaniss, University of Pennsylvania, Fells Institute of Goverment
   3814 Walnut St., Philadelphia, PA 19104
   MANAGING EDITOR: Julie Odland

10. OWNER: The American Academy of Political and Social Science, 3814 Walnut St.
    Philadelphia, PA 19104-6197

11. KNOWN BONDHOLDERS, ETC.
    None

12. NONPROFIT PURPOSE, FUNCTION, STATUS:
    Has Not Changed During Preceding 12 Months

13. PUBLICATION NAME: THE ANNALS OF THE AMERICAN ACADEMY OF POLITICAL & SOCIAL SCIENCE

14. ISSUE FOR CIRCULATION DATA BELOW: SEPTEMBER 2006

15.	EXTENT & NATURE OF CIRCULATION:	AVG. NO. COPIES EACH ISSUE DURING PRECEDING 12 MONTHS	ACT. NO. COPIES OF SINGLE ISSUE PUB. NEAREST TO FILING DATE
A.	TOTAL NO. COPIES	3113	2945
B.	PAID CIRCULATION		
	1. PAID/REQUESTED OUTSIDE-CO, ETC	1506	1494
	2. PAID IN-COUNTY SUBSCRIPTIONS	0	0
	3. SALES THROUGH DEALERS, ETC	21	19
	4. OTHER CLASSES MAILED USPS	0	0
C.	TOTAL PAID CIRCULATION	1527	1513
D.	FREE DISTRIBUTION BY MAIL		
	1. OUTSIDE-COUNTY AS ON 3541	67	67
	2. IN-COUNTY AS STATED ON 3541	0	0
	3. OTHER CLASSES MAILED USPS	0	0
E.	FREE DISTRIBUTION OTHER	0	0
F.	TOTAL FREE DISTRIBUTION	67	67
G.	TOTAL DISTRIBUTION	1594	1580
H.	COPIES NOT DISTRIBUTED		
	1. OFFICE USE, ETC	1519	1365
	2. RETURN FROM NEWS AGENTS	0	0
I.	TOTAL	3113	2945
	PERCENT PAID CIRCULATION	96%	96%

16. NOT REQUIRED TO PUBLISH.

17. I CERTIFY THAT ALL INFORMATION FURNISHED ON THIS FORM IS TRUE AND COMPLETE.
    I UNDERSTAND THAT ANYONE WHO FURNISHES FALSE OR MISLEADING INFORMATION ON
    THIS FORM OR WHO OMITS MATERIAL OR INFORMATION REQUESTED ON THE FORM MAY
    BE SUBJECT TO CRIMINAL SANCTIONS (INCLUDING FINES AND IMPRISONMENT) AND/OR
    CIVIL SANCTIONS (INCLUDING MULTIPLE DAMAGES AND CIVIL PENALTIES).

Mary Nugent

                                        8/30/2006
Mary Nugent   Date
Circulation Manager
Sage Publications, Inc.

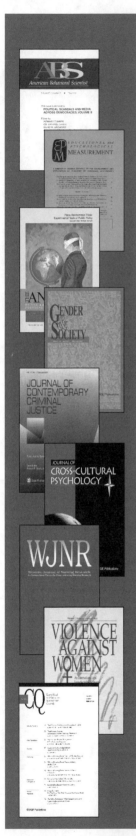